M000239375

CRIMINOLOGICAL
THEORIES

This book is dedicated to the cherished memory of
my parents, my sisters, and my brother

Lilly May Dornberger Moyer
June Henry Moyer
Nancy Elizabeth Moyer Newsome
Betty June Moyer Snell
Calvin Francis Moyer

CRIMINOLOGICAL THEORIES

Traditional and Nontraditional Voices and Themes

Imogene L. Moyer

Indiana University of Pennsylvania

Sage Publications
International Educational and Professional Publisher
Thousand Oaks ▪ London ▪ New Delhi

Copyright © 2001 by Sage Publications, Inc.

All rights reserved. No part of this book may be reproduced or utilized in any form or by any means, electronic or mechanical, including photocopying, recording, or by any information storage and retrieval system, without permission in writing from the publisher.

For information:

Sage Publications, Inc.
2455 Teller Road
Thousand Oaks, California 91320
E-mail: order@sagepub.com

Sage Publications Ltd.
6 Bonhill Street
London EC2A 4PU
United Kingdom

Sage Publications India Pvt. Ltd.
M-32 Market
Greater Kailash I
New Delhi 110 048 India

Printed in the United States of America

Library of Congress Cataloging-in-Publication Data

Moyer, Imogene L.
  Criminological theories: Traditional and nontraditional voices and
themes / Imogene L. Moyer.
        p. cm.
Includes bibliographical references and indexes.
  ISBN 0-8039-5850-1 (cloth: alk. paper)
  ISBN 0-8039-5851-X (pbk.: alk. paper)
  1. Criminology. 2. Criminology—History. 3. Feminist criminology.
I. Title.
  HV6025.M69 2001
  364—dc21   00-012750

    02 03 04 05 06 10 9 8 7 6 5 4 3 2

Acquiring Editor: Jerry Westby
Editorial Assistant: Vonessa Vondera
Production Editor: Denise Santoyo
Editorial Assistant: Candice Crosetti
Typesetter/Designer: Janelle LeMaster
Indexer: Kathy Paparchontis
Cover Designer: Ravi Balasuriya

Contents

Preface

Most previous criminological theory books have emphasized the traditional mainstream theorists to the exclusion of women and minorities and have emphasized a Positivist School approach. This book is an effort to provide a feminist expansion of the narrowly focused traditional theoretical perspective that has dominated criminological theory, research, and policy. Moyer (1996) used Cavan's continuum of behavior model to demonstrate the restricted nature of mainstream criminological theories and to illustrate the value of Cavan's conceptual scheme to convey the narrowness of theories of crime. The current expansion includes the extension of theory to comprise victimization and the interaction of race, class, and gender.

In addition to discussing more recent developments in theory such as feminist theory and the peacemaking perspective, this book diversifies the theorists, with the works of scholars such as Frances Kellor in Chapter 3; Ruth Shonle Cavan, E. Franklin Frazier, and Charles Henderson in Chapter 5; Frank Tannenbaum in Chapter 7; W. E. B. Du Bois in Chapter 8; and Vernetta Young, Sally Simpson, and Nanci Koser Wilson in Chapter 9. The works of these theorists have not been adequately recognized in past criminological theory texts. Although the chapters include both traditional mainstream theorists and nontraditional theorists, there is no claim here that all scholars and all perspectives that have made contributions to theory are covered. For example, the decision was made to provide only brief coverage of deterrence, routine activities, and biological theories as well as efforts to integrate theories. In these instances, the reader who wants to explore these theories further is provided with a few references to help get started.

Other features of this book include the exploration of Mills' (1959) conception of the sociological imagination, such as the impact of the historical setting and biography of the theorists on their works, and Williams' (1984) analysis of the demise of the criminological imagination. While the impact of the historical setting and the biography can be seen in the works of most of the theorists, it is especially obvious in the works of Durkheim and Merton. This book is also based primarily on the use of the theorists' original works. These writings add clarity to the understanding of their theories because the scholar is not relying on a secondary interpretation of the theory. This is particularly true when examining Beccaria's *On Crimes and Punishments*. It is hoped that theory students, particularly graduate students, will be encouraged to read some of the original works to gain a more accurate comprehension of the theory. Each chapter contains a section devoted to the theory perspective's assumptions about people and society.

The traditional definitions of theory have been applied to each theory/perspective to probe the extent to which each fits the social science definitions of theory. Most of the theories are unable to conform to these definitions. These definitions are efforts to fit the social sciences, in particular sociology and criminology, into the old paradigm as described by Kuhn (1970). The paradigm is considered "normal science" and calls for "the construction of elaborate equipment, the development of an esoteric vocabulary and skills, and a refinement of the concepts" (p. 64). Kuhn further notes that the paradigm governs the groups of researchers, and anomalies are discarded. However, he suggests a crisis occurs when new members of the paradigm (with a new world view) challenge the old paradigm, and a revolution begins. This revolution is a process. The 19th-century positivists introduced the social science paradigm which was continued through the functionalists into the 20th century until the interactionists began to challenge this paradigm. This challenge has continued through the conflict/Marxist theorists, the feminists, and the peacemaking theoretical perspectives. It should be interesting to see what new theories and paradigms emerge in the 21st century.

In the current criminal justice policy environment, it is critical that criminologists examine the interrelationship of theory, research, and policy. In this book, the classical school and the peacemaking perspective explicitly make policy recommendations and applications. Both theories recommend major changes in criminal justice policy. While much of today's policies, such as mandatory sentences and the death penalty, sound similar to Beccaria's proposals for certainty and severity of punishments, a reading of his original works reveals that he was opposed to many of the practices that exist in our criminal justice policies today. He advocated that, for deterrence to occur, punishments be just slightly greater than the pleasure gained by committing the crime. The peacemakers would replace punishment with compassion and love, which calls for a major change at individual, societal, and international levels.

Finally, it is essential for those who read this book to recognize that not all scholars will agree on the value of a specific theoretical perspective. Each scholar approaches theoretical criminology with different life experiences and world views but it is still important to read and understand each theory. Furthermore, it is not essential to agree with these theories but an intelligent explanation of the rejection is required. To provide this explanation, the opponent needs to read the original work in order to demonstrate in-depth and broad knowledge and understanding of a theory, perspective, or theorist's work. If this is done, a scholar should realize that most theories present at least some valuable viewpoints.

Acknowledgments

The seeds for this work on criminological theory were planted by two of my graduate professors: Joseph W. Rogers at Kansas State University and John F. Galliher at the University of Missouri–Columbia. I thank them for providing me with both the knowledge and the intellectual challenge to complete a quality product. Another scholar whose work and friendship have influenced my intellectual and professional growth is Ruth Shonle Cavan, whose works helped to direct me toward feminist criminology. She also was a great mentor for me at Northern Illinois University. The fourth major influence on my intellectual development in criminology is Gerald R. Garrett, whom I first met as a colleague and friend at the University of Maryland in Germany. He encouraged me to publish and to become active in professional organizations such as the Academy of Criminal Justice Sciences. I am grateful for his continued professional support.

Indiana University of Pennsylvania (IUP) has served as an important advocate for my intellectual growth in many ways. The graduate students in my criminological theory classes have challenged me to broaden my perspective and to be more inclusive. Whereas for years I have been including women theorists such as Cavan in my classes and scholarly work, students such as Vincent Miles and Shaun Gabbidon (Pennsylvania State University at Harrisburg) made me aware that W. E. B. Du Bois, E. Franklin Frazier, and other African American scholars also should be recognized for their important contributions to theories of crime. Marian Whitson (East Tennessee State University) assisted me in the selection of the African American women scholars to be included in the feminist criminology chapter. Although I take full responsibility for the inclusion of these scholars, I want to express my appreciation to these former students for their contributions. Several doctoral students also assisted me with the library research and the subject and author indexes. These graduate assistants include Shirley Miller, Judy Sturges, Youngyol Yim, Shaun Gabbidon, Cavit Cooley, and Ayn Embar-Seddon. I am grateful to all of these former students for their contributions to this book. I especially want to thank Gabbidon for writing the majority of the biographical insets, Cooley for writing the Interactionist School chapter and for doing such excellent research on Tannenbaum, and Embar-Seddon for writing the control theories chapter and for developing her perspective of the cultural and historical background for current control theory.

After I received a contract from Sage Publications for this book, IUP awarded me a semester sabbatical that enabled me to write four chapters during that time. I want to express my appreciation to my department, Brenda Carter (the dean), and the University Sabbatical Committee for recommending me for this sabbatical. Unfortunately, the completion of this work was delayed due to health problems that I encountered. I am greatly indebted to my colleagues and friends at IUP for their understanding of my situation. I am grateful to my friend, Kate Hanrahan, who has been a wonderful ally. She has been available when I needed medical assistance and has served as a consultant and sounding board for my teaching and for the process of writing this book. I want to especially thank Nanci Koser Wilson, Rosemary Gido, Jake Gibbs, Mark McNabb, Dennis Giever, Chris Zimmerman, Randy Martin, Barbara Hill Hudson, and Darlene Richardson for their encouragement and friendship that provided me with the strength and confidence to complete this book. Our faithful department secretary, Vicki Morganti, went beyond the call of duty by helping me with charts and tables for the book and by providing support for my teaching needs. Most important, I want to thank Elizabeth Kincade, whose professional counseling helped me to recuperate after surgery, to develop a vision of a more positive future, and to find the strength to complete this project. Many friends outside of IUP provided thoughtful comments on the manuscript and provided emotional support for the writing of the book. I especially want to thank Agnes Baro (Grand Valley State University) for her review of the original book proposal. Her comments were most helpful.

The editorial staff at Sage Publications has provided wonderful support and encouragement to me in the process of writing this book. I especially appreciate the thoughtful suggestions of Dale Grenfall (editorial assistant) during the early stages of writing the book and Jerry Westby (senior acquisitions editor). Although Jerry joined the project during the final stages of writing the manuscript, he made himself available with valuable suggestions for editorial changes and provided thoughtful answers to my many questions and concerns. I am very grateful for his contributions in preparing the manuscript for production. Special thanks go to Terry Hendrix (senior editor) for his excellent editorial guidance and his understanding and support when I missed contract deadlines. He continued to encourage me to complete the book and was my advocate to Sage to provide me with more time. Without his professional skills and friendship, I would not have finished the task. Many thanks also go to the anonymous reviewers. Many of their comments and suggestions have been considered or used in this book.

Finally, I want to thank my very large family for their continued love and concern for my well-being. They, too, encouraged me to complete the book. Although many members of my family helped in various ways, I am especially grateful to Tresha Belveal, Evelyn Hagmeier, Helga Moyer, and Justin Snell. Beth Clark has been my "little sister" for 12 years and has become like family to me. It has been a special pleasure to watch her grow from an 8-year-old girl to a mature young woman. I am grateful for the cheer she brings to my life. Oh, yes, and my cats—Alice, Cavan, and Trey—have brought joy into my life by just being there for me during difficult times.

CHAPTER 1

The Expansion of Criminological Theory

Approach to Criminological Theory

This book was envisioned while I was teaching criminological theory at the undergraduate and graduate levels. I was dissatisfied with the traditional texts available because of the unidimensional nature of theories of crime and criminals included in these texts—an emphasis on the poor, male, young, and urban as offenders. Most of these texts were written by white males and ignored theories by women and minorities. This theory book is much more inclusive and less unidimensional than traditional, mainstream criminological theory books. Questions are bound to be raised about my choices by some criminologists. The assumption is made that if one includes people such as Frances Kellor, Jane Addams, E. Franklin Frazier, and Ruth Shonle Cavan, then one is lowering the standards of scholarship or one is questioning the value of the contributions of scholars such as Émile Durkheim, Edwin Sutherland, Robert Merton, and Travis Hirschi.

The chapters that follow include the traditional scholars and the scholars who have been ignored or trivialized and are more multidimensional. By the inclusion of chapters on, for example, current feminist theory and peacemaking, the reader is able to gain a broader understanding of crime and criminal justice and to expand his or her knowledge of theoretical perspectives. Another difference between this book and many other theory texts is that this book is based heavily on the reading of the original works of theorists instead of the secondary sources used by most authors. This produces a more accurate account of theories and should encourage students, as well as the reader, to go to initially published documents to study the theory. This book also is intended to provide enough detailed explanation of each theory so that the traditional lecture can be minimized and supplemented with student participatory learning activities.

The Sociological/Criminological Imagination

An approach to theorists and theories with a sociological imagination (Mills, 1959) and/or a criminological imagination (Williams, 1984) is essential for an understanding of theories of crime, deviance, delinquency, and victimology. Mills (1959) argued that it is the sociological imagination that enables a scholar to understand the larger historical scene and to become involved in public issues. Mills stated that this imagination allows "the individual [to] understand his own experience and gauge his own fate only by locating himself within his period" (p. 5). Also, the individual may ask questions such as "What are the essential components of this society?" and "Where does this society stand in human history?" (p. 6). Mills further contended, "The sociological imagination enables us to grasp history and biography and the relations between the two within society" (p. 6). This book attempts to apply Mills's sociological imagination by providing a historical context for the times and by exploring the social and professional biography of major theorists. This also enables the scholar to grasp what societal issues and biographical troubles influenced the theorists' ideas (p. 5). Mills further posed

> social science as a set of bureaucratic techniques which inhibit by "methodological" pretensions, which congest such work by obscurantist conceptions, or which trivialize it by concern with minor problems, unconnected with publicly relevant issues. (p. 20)

Mills (1959) suggested that the sociological imagination is hindered by the grand theorists at one extreme and the abstract empiricists at the other. Grand theory, according to Mills, is a level of theory so general that it is impossible to get down from these higher generalities to observations and problems in their historical and structural contexts (p. 33). He also stated that "grand theory is drunk on syntax" (p. 34).

Like grand theory, abstracted empiricism seizes one juncture in the process of work and allows it to dominate. Considerations of method and theory are essential for the work of the sociologist, but in these two styles, they have become hindrances (Mills, 1959, p. 50). Mills (1959) claimed that the abstract empiricists are possessed by the methodological details that are not characterized by any substantive propositions or theories (p. 55). That is, methodology seems to determine the problems to be studied.

Williams (1984) argued that the demise of the criminological imagination, beginning during the 1970s, was the result of the increasing "empirical scientism" of the social sciences and the rise of criminal justice disciplines. Of special concern here is what Williams referred to as "empirical scientism," which he described as follows:

> There has been very little emphasis on the creation of theory; the general sentiment appears to be that the most appropriate theory construction involves highly specific, objective, and formatted statements about lower range phenomena. (p. 96) . . .
>
> We have followed the "hard" sciences into an alley where we are more concerned with measurement itself than with speculation about the substance being measured. . . . Statistical techniques were developed and augmented to draw more information

from data, and new computer programs made statistical analysis so easy that virtually every social scientist began to use them. Analysis, in fact, became statistical analysis. (p. 97)

In 1990, Bernard also suggested that the previous 20 years had seen an expansion of quantitative research in criminology (Bernard, 1990, p. 325). Before this, there were fewer journals, and they published articles including quantitative and qualitative research as well as theoretical and policy arguments. Now there are more journals, but they publish mostly quantitative research. Both Williams (1984, p. 103) and Bernard (1990, p. 331) argued that graduate programs in criminology focus heavily on research methodology and neglect criminological theory.[1] Bernard observed,

> Scientific theory and research are like the chicken and the egg—each comes from the other, but neither comes first. All research must be based on theory, and theory must be based on research. . . . Both theory and research are necessary for scientific progress to occur. (pp. 329-330)

Whereas the works of Mills (1959), Williams (1984), and Bernard (1990) discussed the interconnection between methodology and theory in the criminological imagination, Gilsinan (1991) added a third element in this scientific discourse—public policy. The empirical purists might object to policy as being too applied, but theory, research, and policy all are essential for the understanding of the discipline. That is, each one should inform and stimulate the other two. When a social scientist begins the process by going from the particular data to general theory, this often is referred to as grounded theory or a logical inductive system. It could be argued that Durkheim used the inductive method with his study of suicide. He began by gathering data on suicide and then developed a typology of suicide from these data. In his earlier work on the division of labor, Durkheim began with a general theory of the solidarity of society and later conducted research to test his theory—the logical deductive system. Sometimes policy emerges from research, and other times theory and/or research are stimulated by policy, as illustrated in Figure 1.1.

What Is Theory?

Some 40 years ago, Mills (1959) introduced the concept of the sociological imagination and the failure to develop what he called the "intellectual craftsmanship" (p. 211). Mills argued that this process involves the capacity to see a variety of perspectives at one time and to build up an adequate view of a total society and its components.[2] This section explores a variety of definitions of theory and how they apply to efforts to explain crime.

Theorists who demand a strict adherence to the social science definition of theory, such as Homans (1964) and Turner (1978), have tended to emphasize empirical research. That is, a theory is not valid if it is not empirically verifiable. Homans (1964) described the general characteristics of a theory (pp. 951-952; see also Table 1.1),

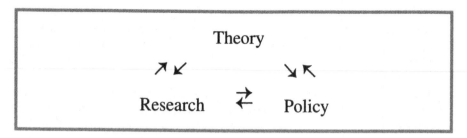

Figure 1.1. Theory, Research, and Policy Nexus

whereas Turner (1978) referred to the elements or building blocks of theory (p. 3). Both theorists stated that a theory begins with a set of concepts or a conceptual scheme. The first type of concept is descriptive (Homans, 1964, p. 952) or what Turner (1978) called nominal because it simply labels phenomena (p. 4). Homans (1964) illustrated the definition of descriptive concepts by using Durkheim's suicide study; religion is defined as Protestant, Catholic, or Jewish. According to Homans, operational definitions of concepts provide measurements of concepts such as suicide rates. Through these operational definitions, Turner (1978) asserted that variables are created that allow investigators to distinguish different events and situations (p. 5).

But these two scholars argue that a conceptual scheme alone is insufficient to constitute a theory. A theory also consists of a set of propositions (Homans, 1964, p. 952) or theoretical statements (Turner, 1978, p. 5). Each proposition or theoretical statement must state the relationship between two or more variables. Turner (1978) further declared,

> Relational statements represent a critical feature of theory, for only by stating the relationships between or among concepts is prediction, explanation, and understanding of events in the world possible. Relational statements bring together concepts, denoting variable properties of phenomena, and begin to pave the way for visualizing how one variable may be "caused" by another. (p. 5)

Homans (1964) also stated that the set of propositions must form a deductive system. When propositions are so derived, they are said to be explained. According to Homans, a theory is nothing if it is not an explanation. A deductive system also provides grounds for prediction. Finally, some of the propositions must be "contingent," that is, testable.

In reality, there are no theories of crime that fully meet this scientific test. Nearly all theories include concepts, but not all theories have definitions of these concepts. There are a few theories that contain a set of propositions or theoretical statements such as Sutherland's differential association theory (see Chapter 5) and Quinney's social reality of crime theory (see Chapter 8). Sutherland has been criticized for not operationally defining his concepts so that they are capable of being tested empirically. However, he stated,

TABLE 1.1   Homans' Classical Definition of Theory

1. Identifies a theory of a phenomenon with an explanation of it by means of a deductive system.
2. Presents the general characteristics of a theory as follows:
   A. A theory must consist of a set of concepts or conceptual scheme.
      Concepts may be *descriptive*, "serving to show what a theory is about."
      Other concepts are *operative*. These are variables, and "variables may be probabilities."
      "A conceptual scheme alone is insufficient to constitute a theory."
   B. A theory must consist of a set of *propositions*.
      Each proposition must state the relationship "such as varies directly with," between at least two of the variables.
      The propositions must form a *deductive system*.
      "A theory is nothing if it is not an explanation. . . . A deductive system also provides grounds for prediction."
   C. Some of the propositions of a scientific theory must be *contingent* and must be capable of being falsified or tested.

SOURCE: Homans, George Casper. (1964). Contemporary Theory in Sociology. In Robert E. Faris (Ed.), *Handbook of Modern Sociology* (pp. 951-956). Chicago: Rand McNally.

> Let me summarize my views this way: The value of such studies is likely to consist not in the attainment of a science of [criminology]. . . . I am opposed to an effort at this time to make [criminology] highly scientific . . . because I think we will be trying to define things about which we do not have enough information. (Sutherland, 1973, p. xxvi)

Quinney also has been attacked for his lack of scientific evidence to support his propositions. In Quinney's case, he used a historical approach by supporting his statements using historical records and governmental, educational, and other public documents.[3]

Merton (1968a) asserted that the conviction among some social scientists that we must achieve a grand theoretical system results from a misplaced comparison with the physical sciences (p. 48). Therefore, he introduced what he called "theories of the middle range" to bridge the gap between grand theorists and abstract empiricists. Merton suggested that theories of the middle range are

> theories that lie between the minor but necessary working hypotheses that evolve in abundance during day-to-day research and the all-inclusive systematic efforts to develop a unified theory that will explain all the observed uniformities of social behavior, social organization, and social change. Middle-range theory is principally used . . . to guide empirical inquiry. (p. 39)

Merton also referred to them as "stepping-stones in the middle distance." He further argued that our major task today is to develop special theories applicable to limited ranges such as his own anomie theory and Cavan's continuum of delinquent behavior (see Chapter 4). Merton claimed that if theory is to advance significantly, then it

> must proceed along . . . interconnected planes (1) by developing special theories from which to derive hypotheses that can be empirically investigated and (2) by evolving, not suddenly revealing, a progressively more general conceptual scheme that is adequate to consolidate groups of special theories. . . . [We] can look . . . toward progressively comprehensive sociological theory which, instead of proceeding from the head of one man, gradually consolidates theories of the middle range, so that these become special cases of more general formulations. (p. 51)

Merton provided a general definition of theory as "logically interconnected sets of propositions from which empirical uniformities can be derived" (p. 39). Although he presented a definition of theories (i.e., theories of the middle range) that applies to his conceptual scheme of anomie, his stated goal was for the development of theories that fit the scientific definitions of Homans (1964) and Turner (1978) discussed earlier.

Many criminological theories do not meet the criteria required by the definitions of Homans, Turner, or Merton. Some theorists are creating what Kuhn (1970) called new paradigms or scientific revolutions. Some of these theories may be viewed as interpretations of criminological findings, for example, Hirschi's (1969) bonding theory (see Chapter 6) and Sealock and Simpson's (1998) type-script theory (see Chapter 9). Another approach to theory may be called criminological orientations, for example, Becker's (1973) study of deviance (see Chapter 7); Mann's explorations of race, class, and crime (see Chapter 9); and Quinney's works on peacemaking (see Chapter 10). Each of the theories discussed in this book makes valuable contributions to our understanding of crime, deviance, delinquency, justice, and victimology. Although theorists who put an emphasis on the scientific stress the importance of an objective value system, all theorists make assumptions about people and society that influence their works.

Assumptions About People and Society

These basic assumptions can be used as a guide to the study of theory and as a perspective of how to approach theories. It is important to understand that all conceptual systems contain within themselves their antithesis and that most of these assumptions are not a dichotomy but rather a continuum. Thus, there should be no value judgments made about assumptions used. Although the assumptions need not be conscious, they do have an effect on the choice of subjects for investigation and also influence the framework of a theory. That is, assumptions determine the types of questions asked and the ways in which social scientists conduct research and analyze data.[4]

To develop an informed analysis of each theory, it is essential to approach each theory with the following questions. These questions provide a guide to the study of theory. They should be answered as one approaches a given theory.

1. Is the unit of study a macro level (i.e., society or large groups) or a micro level (i.e., individuals or small groups)? Most of the theories, such as Durkheim's division of labor and Becker's interactionist approach to deviance, have both levels. For example, Becker (1973) stated that "social groups create deviance" (p. 9), but on a more micro level, he claimed that "whether an *act* is deviant depends on how other people react to it" (p. 11).

2. Are social phenomena for analysis objective overt behavior or subjective covert behavior? This often is confusing to the young theorist because it does not involve the traditional understanding of subjective as biased and of objective as free of bias. Instead, the meaning intended here is that the objective overt is actual behavior such as walking and talking, whereas the subjective covert involves things such as perceptions, goals, values, and sentiments (Wallace, 1969, p. 48). This can be illustrated by Stanko's (1985) theory of "intimate intrusions." The objective overt behavior can be seen in male violence against women such as rape and battering. The sense of powerlessness, shame, humiliation, and self-blame that women feel when they experience male aggression would be subjective covert behavior (pp. 11, 17). This demonstrates how most theories define the social partly in terms of objective behavior and partly in terms of subjective behavior. What needs to be determined is how much stress the theory places on each.

3. Is society viewed as based on consensus and integration or as based on conflict, exploitation, and coercion? In this case, theories usually do not stress both consensus and conflict. Durkheim (1933), for example, emphasized consensus and integration in the division of labor when he stated, "There exists a social solidarity which comes from a certain number of states of conscience which are common to all the members of the same society" (p. 109). By contrast, Wilson (1993) claimed that in a patriarchal society, men seek to control and exploit women's sexuality in much the same way as a "masculinist science" dreams of conquering and exploiting the wilderness (p. 53).

4. Is society viewed as fluid or static? That is, are social phenomena of society viewed as becoming and emerging or as stable? It is clear that the 18th-century Classical School theorists, especially Cesare Beccaria, were advocating changes in the system of justice and in society. This suggests that they saw society as fluid. Those scholars who adhere to the peacemaking perspective of crime (e.g., Pepinsky, Quinney, Gibbs) also advocate change in the criminal justice system and in society. They would replace the emphasis on competition, oppression, and domination with a system based on compassion, love, peace, and a sense of community. Merton (1938), in his essay on "Social Structure and Anomie," aimed for stability but recognized that society is changing.

5. Is change or stability viewed as imposed on or generated by people and society? According to functionalists, stability was established during the 19th century through the collective conscience (Durkheim, 1933, pp. 80-81) and imposed by their definition of crime. The interactionist Goffman (1961) asserted that through the admission ceremonies, prison inmates are stripped of their old identities and given a

new "identity kit" (p. 20). Thus, change is imposed. Schur (1984) pointed out that devaluation and subordination have been imposed on women in our society (p. 41). Yet, he noted that women's individual and collective responses to being stigmatized are helping to achieve rapid changes in the status of women. Goffman (1961) and Schur (1984) both argued that stigmatization is imposed but that changes are generated by individuals.

6. Are people seen as active agents or as passive agents? This is tied closely to the previous question that asks whether change or stability is viewed as imposed or generated for people and society. If one sees phenomena as imposed on people, then it follows that people are seen as passive agents. If one sees phenomena as generated or created by people, then people are seen as active agents. Beccaria argued that people are free-willed active agents and that crime could be deterred by establishing a criminal code indicating the specific punishment for each crime defined in the code. By contrast, Cesare Lombroso, from the 19th-century Positivist School, suggested that criminals were biologically determined and, therefore, were passive agents. As with many of the other questions, it is common for theorists to include both active and passive in a particular theory. In *Stigma*, Goffman (1963) suggested that a biography or identity file may be imposed on a person, making that person a passive agent (p. 62). But he later asserted that individuals are active agents in their ability to control the disclosure, as well as its timing, of their stigma (p. 101).

Plan for the Book

The book takes a multidimensional approach by including "new" theorists, such as W. E. B. Du Bois, Pauline Tarnowsky, Frank Tannenbaum, Coramae Richey Mann, and Sally Simpson,[5] and by devoting chapters to recently developed perspectives, such as feminist theory and peacemaking, instead of making only brief mention of them. Each chapter also follows the sociological/criminological imagination (Mills, 1959; Williams, 1984) by including a discussion of the cultural and historical setting in which the theory was written and the biographies of specific theorists and their contributions to theory.[6] Many of these biographies were written by Shaun L. Gabbidon and are so designated. Where appropriate, the implications for research and policy are discussed. A few theories, such as the Classical School and peacemaking, contain suggestions for policy within the theories. I encourage the reader to explore the methodological and policy implications for theories that do not explicitly state this. Each chapter has a brief section analyzing the assumptions that the theorists make about people and society. Finally, I encourage the reader to use the various definitions of theory as a model to analyze which definition fits the particular theory and to explain why this theory fits the designated definition of theory. The chapters are organized in chronological order, beginning with the 18th-century Classical School and ending with the late 20th-century peacemaking perspective. This coverage is outlined in the Chronology of Criminological Theory chart (Table 1.2). The length of the chapters varies according to the number of the-

TABLE 1.2 Chronology of Criminological Theory

Macro/Micro Level Classical 18th Century	Micro Level Positivists 19th Century	Macro Level Functionalists 19th and 20th Centuries	Macro/Micro Level Chicago School 20th Century
Free will	Individual differences	Structure of society	Ecological
Rational	Scientific method	Equilibrium	Ethnographic
Hedonist	(logical, objective, and	Integration	Life histories
Contract theory	experimental)	Consensus	Conflict theory
Utilitarian	Deterministic		Process
		Durkheim	
Beccaria	Lombroso	Merton	Addams
Bentham	Ferri/Garofalo	Agnew	Park/Burgess
	Kellor	Cohen	Henderson
	Tarnowsky	Cloward/Ohlin	Thrasher
		Cavan	Reckless
			Cavan
			Frazier
			Shaw/McKay
			Sutherland (Cohen)

Macro/Micro Level Control 1960s	Micro Level Interactionists 1960s	Macro Level		Macro/Micro Level Peacemaking 1990s
		Conflict/Radical 1970s-1990s	Feminists 1980s-1990s	
Pragmatic	Societal reaction	Structure of society	Structure of society	Humanistic/Spiritual
Why do people	Arbitrary definition	Arbitrary definition	Arbitrary definition	Compassion/Caring
obey the rules?	Process of	Power differences	Power differences	Mutual community
	interaction	(class/race)	(class/race/gender)	Peace
Assumes neutral	Deviant careers	Vested interests	Vested interests	Feminist
human nature	Moral	Differential	Differential	Harmony
	entrepreneurs	enforcement	enforcement	Critical
Hirschi		Conflict/Coercion	Conflict/Coercion	Responsiveness
Sykes/Matza	Becker	Capitalist structure	Patriarchal structure	Inner corrections
Reckless/Dinitz	Lemert		Moulds	Gandhi
Gottfredson/Hirschi	Schur	Marx	Rafter/Natalizia	Addams
	Goffman	Bonger	Simpson	King
	Tannenbaum	Du Bois	Daly/Chesney-Lind	Pepinsky/Quinney
		Sutherland	Koser-Wilson	McDermott
		Quinney	Mann	Gibbs
		Chambliss	Young	Brock-Utne
		Reiman	Adler	Harris
			Simon	Lozoff and Braswell

orists and the amount of material available. For this reason, the early chapters are shorter than some of the later ones.

Chapter 2 covers the Classical School, which was the first systematic effort to explain crime and criminal behavior. The two major scholars in this perspective were

Cesare Beccaria and Jeremy Bentham. It is important to include their works because much of the current legal approach to crime is very similar to the theory that was emerging during the 18th century. Thus, the Classical School has important policy implications. There have been numerous efforts recently to develop and test deterrence theory as well as theories that build on the rational choice concept of the Classical School theorists, and these are explained briefly in an endnote to that chapter.

Chapter 3 examines the Positivist School. Cesare Lombroso usually is the major theorist associated with this school. In fact, Lombroso (1958) cited the findings of Tarnowsky in his book on the female offender. It appears that most current theorists either have not read this work or have decided not to recognize Tarnowsky's contributions. Frances Kellor was the first American and first woman to challenge Lombroso's research findings based on her research in American prisons. Yet, she is not included in most discussions of the Positivist School. Over the subsequent decades (1910s to 1990s), there have been efforts to develop biological explanations of crime and deviance, and these references are provided in an endnote to the chapter.

Chapter 4 is devoted to functionalist theory. This perspective begins with Durkheim during the late 19th century and continues through the 20th century. These scholars emphasized the scientific method that was begun by Lombroso and Kellor. Robert Merton built on Durkheim's works on anomie. The gang theorists (e.g., Cohen, Cloward and Ohlin) studied the juvenile delinquent subcultures. More recently, Robert Agnew tested strain theory. Ruth Shonle Cavan used a continuum of behavior conceptualization in an effort to broaden the definition of delinquency.

Chapter 5 contains the theoretical scholars within the Chicago School, which emerged during the late 19th century and reached its peak in scholarship during the 1920s and 1930s. As indicated in the chapter, there was much diversity in theory and methods, and many of our recent criminological theories are built on the theoretical framework established during the early years of the Chicago School. Most of the scholars in this school (e.g., Park and Burgess, Thrasher, Reckless, Shaw and McKay, Sutherland) have received broad and detailed coverage in most theory books. The theoretical contributions of Jane Addams, Ruth Shonle Cavan, E. Franklin Frazier, and Charles Henderson have been either ignored or minimized in most criminological theory books.

The theoretical perspectives contained in Chapters 6 and 7 emerged in criminology during the 1960s, although the interactionists could trace their theory to Max Weber, a 19th-century German sociologist. Ayn Embar-Seddon, the author of Chapter 6, argues that control theory has been influenced by early scholars such as the social psychologist Edward Ross, the psychologist Sigmund Freud, and the works of Émile Durkheim and George Herbert Mead. Recent scholars included in this chapter include Travis Hirschi, Gresham Sykes, David Matza, Walter Reckless, Simon Dinitz, and Michael Gottfredson.

Cavit Cooley, author of Chapter 7, suggests that the social disillusionment and changes that occurred during the 1960s had an impact on the development of interactionist theory. He further notes the influence of early pioneers (1900s to 1940s) such as Charles Cooley, George Herbert Mead, and Frank Tannenbaum. The chapter also includes the works of more contemporary theorists such as Edwin Lemert, Erving Goffman, Howard S. Becker, and Edwin Schur.

It can be argued that the seeds for the perspectives in the final three chapters—conflict theory, feminist theory, and peacemaking—were planted during the 19th century. Criminological conflict theory (Chapter 8) emerged during the 1970s and has its historical foundations in the works of Karl Marx, Willem Bonger, W. E. B. Du Bois, and Edwin Sutherland. It was the works of Richard Quinney and William Chambliss that helped to establish conflict/radical theory during the 1970s and 1980s. Jeffrey Reiman's *The Rich Get Richer and the Poor Get Prison* (Reiman, 1995), originally published in 1979, has received broad recognition as a text for undergraduate and graduate students and contains policy implications for the criminal justice system as well as for theory.

Feminist criminology (Chapter 9) has a historical and cultural heritage that begins during the 18th century with Abigail Adams and continues through the 19th century with scholars and activists such as Sojourner Truth, Ida Wells-Barnett, Elizabeth Cady Stanton, Susan B. Anthony, and Harriet Tubman. The chapter recognizes that feminists do not speak with one voice by including scholars such as Freda Adler, Clarice Feinman, and Darrell Steffensmeier among liberal feminists; Elizabeth Moulds, Nicole Rafter, and Elena Natalizia among Marxist feminists; Elizabeth Stanko and Nanci Koser Wilson among radical feminists; and Vernetta Young and Angela Davis among feminism and women of color. Two scholars, Coramae Richey Mann and Sally Simpson, are highlighted at the end of the chapter for their scholarship and many accomplishments that have helped to establish feminist criminology.

Chapter 10 explains the emergence of peacemaking in criminology. The historical and cultural setting for peacemaking includes Mahatma Gandhi, who led nonviolent protests in 19th-century India. It also includes Jane Addams, whose 19th-century accomplishments included the founding of the Hull House in Chicago; her participation in establishing child labor laws, mandatory education laws, and juvenile courts; and her advocacy of world peace during World War I. Martin Luther King, Jr., the American civil rights leader of the mid-20th century, had a major impact on peaceful change and was influential in the establishment of the peace movement. Current scholars included in that chapter are Richard Quinney, John Gibbs, J. Peter Cordella, Gregg Barak, Birgit Brock-Utne, M. Joan McDermott, M. Kay Harris, Fay Honey Knopp, Harold Pepinsky, Susan Caulfield, Peter Sanzen, Joseph Scimecca, Bo Lazoff and Michael Braswell, and John Fuller. Peacemaking began to develop in criminology during the 1990s and is in the process of developing a theoretical perspective.

Notes

1. In other words, instead of requiring doctoral students to take four or five methods and statistics courses and only one or two theory courses, we should balance the curriculum so that students understand the importance of statistical analysis and quantitative testing of theories as well as the importance of theory development, integration, and theoretical analysis.

2. If one were to apply Mills's concept of intellectual craftsmanship to crime, then it would require the ability to see the value of various theoretical perspectives of crime. There

is a tendency among criminologists to assume that a valid explanation of criminal behavior must have specific characteristics to be a theory or else it is not worthwhile.

3. Quinney, in particular, could be said to be challenging the paradigm established by mainstream criminologists that Kuhn (1970) referred to in *The Structure of Scientific Revolutions*. Kuhn argued that once a paradigm has been established by social scientists, "bringing a normal research problem to a conclusion is achieving the anticipated in a new way, and it requires the solution of all sorts of complex instrumental, conceptual, and mathematical puzzles" (p. 36). This ensures that scientists will not be lightly distracted by anomalies that might require some adjustments to the research. A crisis occurs when an anomaly is discovered and there are new members of the scientific paradigm with a different worldview. When this happens, a scientific revolution is begun. The theoretical perspectives discussed in Chapters 7 through 10 of this book illustrate challenges to the old paradigm and the beginning of a scientific revolution.

4. The inspiration for the development of the analytical questions that follow came from my doctoral theory classes at the University of Missouri. Some of the assumptions used here also came from the opening chapter of Wallace's (1969) *Sociological Theory*. Although the seeds were sown at the University of Missouri, I developed most of the assumptions during the years when I taught criminological theory, especially at the graduate level.

5. Some of these scholars (e.g., Tannenbaum, Simpson) have been mentioned in theory books, but their works have not been covered in depth. Furthermore, some other theorists (e.g., Du Bois) have received wide and in-depth coverage outside of criminology but basically have been ignored by crime theorists.

6. Some scholars might disagree with my choice of theorists to highlight, but it should be noted that some theoretical scholars declined to cooperate and clearly did not want their biographies included. I decided to honor their wishes.

The Classical School

Introduction and Historical Setting

The Classical School, which emerged during the 18th century, was the first systematic effort to explain crime and criminal behavior. Prior to the theories developed by the Classical School, criminal behavior was explained by supernatural powers and/or by the forces of nature.

Supernaturalists/Naturalists

Supernaturalists assumed that the good work that people performed was the result of God's power and that evil behavior was the devil's doing. Theologians stated that the original state of people was one of innocence and grace. According to church doctrine, this condition of innocence was lost in the Garden of Eden when Adam and Eve ate of the forbidden fruit. All of humankind, then, lives in agony and pain because the "first pair" chose to disobey the divine injunction (Vold, 1979, p. 20). Thus, early church theologians stressed the conflict between absolute good and absolute evil (Lilly, Cullen, and Ball, 1995, p. 12). When illnesses and natural disasters (e.g., tornadoes, earthquakes) occurred, they were explained as God's punishment for evil acts. Also, people who committed crimes were thought to be possessed by the devil. Religious groups today sometimes use these explanations (e.g., AIDS is God's punishment for homosexuality).

The naturalists rebelled against the authority of the church doctrine. These philosophers emphasized that there was an order to things in the world that was separate from religious influence. They stressed the importance of science in understanding the physical world. That is, they suggested that the human ability to reason, as well as observations and experiences, provided the tools for explaining much about the world.

Challenges to the Church and Aristocracy

The 18th century brought challenges to the rule of the church and the aristocracy. The beginnings of the industrial revolution and mercantilism gave rise to a new middle class that questioned many of the corrupt political practices. Citizens began to protest the vagaries and inconsistencies in the government and the management of public affairs. The church and the criminal justice system were exposed for their historical use of torture and secret inquisitions.

There also was an attack on the prevailing systems for administration of criminal justice. Judges were criticized for their capricious, arbitrary, and abusive practices. Punishments were uncertain and based on the purely personal justice of the various judges. Many judges were criticized for their tyrannical practices of barbaric punishments in some cases and leniency in other cases. Confessions were sought through many "trials by ordeal" and various means of torture.

Assumptions About People and Society

The Classical School of criminology rejected the spiritualists' emphasis on supernatural powers that control human behavior. Instead, Classical School theorists stressed that humans are rational and free to make their own decisions. As rational beings, people are active agents creating opportunities and making choices in their lives.

These theorists used both micro and macro units of analysis. Although Cesare Beccaria emphasized individuals' ability to control their own destinies (micro), he also was adamantly concerned with changes in the system of justice and in society (macro). Beccaria specifically urged the rulers to use their coercive power to crush the petty tyrannies and abuse of the privileged. This emphasis on the advantages of the powerful few and the misery of the poor suggests that the Classical School theorists saw society as based on conflict and coercion, not on consensus. The emphasis on change suggests that they saw society as fluid—in a state of flux. Whereas much of their theory stresses objective overt phenomena (e.g., criminal codes, punishments, judicial decisions), they also are concerned with subjective covert phenomena, as indicated by their view of people as free-willed rational agents seeking pleasure and trying to avoid pain/punishment.

Finally, these theorists advocated a contract system.[1] This suggests that people, as rational beings, would calculate the pleasure to be attained from certain behavior against the pain of punishment. If a criminal code specified the punishment with certainty, then this would deter crime. Cesare Beccaria and Jeremy Bentham both supported a utilitarian approach to crime.

Cesare Beccaria (1738-1794)

As indicated in the biographical inset on Cesare Beccaria (Inset 2.1), his interest in penology and crime was aroused by his friendship with two brothers, Pietro Verri (a distinguished Italian economist) and Alessandro Verri (a creative writer of note who held the office of protector of prisoners). Monachesi (1972, pp. 37-38) and Paolucci (Beccaria, 1963, pp. xii-xv) both credited the Verri brothers with providing the intellectual "prodding and assistance" necessary for Beccaria to write. Paolucci noted that the two brothers

> rallied the young Milanese intelligentsia around them and formed a society later known as the "academy of fists," dedicated to waging relentless war against economic disorder, bureaucratic petty tyranny, religious narrow-mindedness, and intellectual pedantry. (p. xii)

To propagate their ideas, they eventually established a periodical, *Il Caffe*. It is stated that Beccaria contributed to this publication.

Paolucci suggested that it was as a member of this avant-garde "academy of fists" that Beccaria first took up his pen on behalf of humanity (Beccaria, 1963). He indicated that it was the heated discussions at the Verri house, where the reformers met regularly, and the Verris' personal guidance that stimulated Beccaria to begin to read Montesquieu. Paolucci also noted that although Beccaria became an avid reader and attentive listener,

> he wrote only when his friends assigned a topic, elaborated the subject matter, and literally pieced his fragmentary utterances together for him. His first publication, a treatise "On Remedies for the Monetary Disorders of Milan in the Year 1762," was thus written at the suggestion and with the constant prodding of Pietro Verri, who had expert knowledge of the subject and who, when the work was attacked soon after publication, personally took up the burden of defending it. (p. xiii)

Beccaria's (1963) most important work, *On Crimes and Punishments,* was composed with similar prodding and assistance from Pietro Verri, whose influence was gratefully acknowledged by Beccaria. In the interests of humankind, Beccaria appealed (in that work) to the enlightened rulers of Europe to use all of their coercive power to crush the petty tyrannies of aristocratic privilege and bureaucratic abuse.

Essays on Crimes and Punishments

In *On Crimes and Punishments,* Beccaria (1963) stated a basic principle for society—"the *greatest happiness shared by the greatest number,*" which is the core of the concept of utilitarianism (p. 8). Beccaria began his treatise by declaring that people generally resist the force that tends to concentrate advantages, power, and happiness in the hands of a few while placing misery and weakness on the majority of citizens (p. 7). He further explained,

INSET 2.1

Cesare Beccaria (1738-1794)

Cesare Beccaria was born in Milan, Italy, on March 15, 1738. His family members were part of the aristocracy of Italy, and their lineage was well respected. Little is known about Beccaria's childhood. However, it is known that Beccaria spent 8 years of his life at the Jesuit College at Parma (Beccaria, 1963). Some inconsistencies arise when inquiring about Beccaria's success at Jesuit College. Vold (1958) indicated that Beccaria showed great ability in mathematics (p. 18), whereas others indicated that Beccaria left without distinguishing himself academically (Beccaria, 1963, p. xii; Martin, Mutchnick, and Austin, 1990, p. 3). After leaving Jesuit College, Beccaria went on to study law at the University of Pavia, graduating in 1758 (Martin et al., 1990, p. 3).

Soon after graduation, Beccaria returned to Milan and became interested in philosophy (Monachesi, 1972). This interest apparently was brought on by his exposure to the works of Montesquieu. His interest in penology and crime was initiated through his association with two brothers, Pietro and Alessandro Verri. Pietro was a distinguished Italian economist, and Alessandro was a noted creative writer. Together, they formed a study group that focused on literary and philosophical subjects. This group played an important role in the professional development of Beccaria. In 1762,

Beccaria published his first work, *Del disordine e de rimedi delle monete nello stato de milano nell anno 1762*. This publication focused on the need for reform of the monetary system in the state of Milan. Although not highly regarded at that time, it has been referred to as a quite original and provocative document (Monachesi, 1972, p. 37).

After Beccaria's first publication, Alessandro Verri, who held the position of protector of prisoners, asked him to conduct a study of the penal institutions. Although Beccaria had no previous knowledge of penology, Verri was able to provide him with the necessary guidance. Beccaria started the project in March 1763 and completed the document, *On Crimes and Punishments*, in 1764. The document initially was published anonymously because Beccaria feared that it would not be well received. The publication was well received, however, and Beccaria later was honored for producing it.

Although mostly noted for his second publication, Beccaria also was a university professor and government official. According to Vold (1958), "Beccaria's ability in mathematics led to a number of original and brilliant applications of quantitative methods in the fields of social and political study" (p. 18). Beccaria's posthumously published lectures, from when he was a professor of political economy in the Palatine School of Milan, remain the only other works by Beccaria in print (Monachesi, 1973, p. 49).

—Shaun L. Gabbidon
Pennsylvania State University at Harrisburg

SOURCE: Excerpted from the writings of Shaun L. Gabbidon with permission.

Very few persons have undertaken to abolish the accumulated errors of centuries by rising to general principles, curbing, at least, with the sole force that acknowledged truths possess, the unbounded course of ill-directed power which has continually produced a long and authorized example of the most cold-blooded barbarity. And yet the groans of the weak, sacrificed to cruel ignorance and to opulent indolence; the barbarous torments, multiplied with lavish and useless severity, for crimes either not proved or wholly imaginary; the filth and horrors of a prison, intensified by that cruellest tormentor of the miserable, uncertainty—all these ought to have roused that breed of magistrates who direct the opinions of men. (p. 9)

Beccaria then asked,

> But what are to be the proper punishments for such crimes? Is the death penalty really *useful* and *necessary* for the security and good order of society? Are torture and torments *just*, and do they attain the *end* for which laws are instituted? What is the best way to prevent crimes? Are the same punishments equally effective for all times? What influence have they on customary behavior? (p. 10)

After raising these questions, Beccaria proceeded to analyze the problems of crimes and punishments with "geometric precision."

Classification of Crimes

Although Beccaria was primarily concerned with punishment, he also developed a classification of crimes. He began this discussion by identifying three general categories of crimes. Beccaria (1963) stated that (a) some crimes directly destroy society or the person who represent it; (b) some crimes injure the private security of a citizen in his or her life, in the citizen's goods, or in the citizen's honor; and (c) some crimes are disruptive of the public peace and tranquillity. Then, he stated that "any action not included between the two extremes indicated above cannot be called a 'crime' or be punished as such" (p. 66). After that, he discussed specific offenses.

Crimes of lèse majesté. The first class of crimes, which Beccaria (1963) defined as the "gravest because [they are] most injurious," are those known as crimes of lèse majesté or high treason.

> Only tyranny and ignorance, confounding the clearest terms and ideas, can apply this name and consequently the gravest punishment. . . . Every crime, even of a private nature, injures society, but it is not every crime that aims at its immediate destruction. (p. 68)

Crimes against personal security. After these come the crimes against the security of individual citizens. Beccaria (1963) argued that "some crimes are attempts against the person, others against property" (p. 68). He advocated that the penalties for crimes against the person always should be corporal punishments because attempts against the security and liberty of citizens are among the greatest of crimes. Within this class are included not only the assassinations and thefts committed by persons of the lower class but also those committed by noblemen and magistrates. Beccaria elaborated on this point by suggesting the following:

> The great and rich should not have it in their power to set a price upon attempts made against the weak and the poor; otherwise riches, which are, under the laws, the reward of industry, become the nourishment of tyranny. There is no liberty whenever the laws permit that, in some circumstances, a man can cease to be a *person* and becomes a *thing*; then you will see all the industry of the powerful person applied to extract from the mass of social interrelations whatever the law allows in his favor. (p. 68)

With regard to thefts, Beccaria proposed the following policy for punishments:

> Thefts not involving violence should be punished by a fine. Whoever seeks to enrich himself at the expense of others should be deprived of his own. But since this is ordinarily the crime only of poverty and desperation, the crime of that unhappy portion of mankind to whom the right of property . . . has left but a bare existence, and since pecuniary punishments increase the number of criminals beyond that of the crimes . . . , the most suitable punishment will be . . . the temporary subjection of the labors and person of the criminal to the community as repayment. . . . But when the theft involves violence, punishment also should be a mixture of the corporeal and servile. (p. 74)

Beccaria also was concerned with personal injuries to honor. He argued that "personal injuries that detract from honor, that is, from the just portion of esteem which one citizen has the right to exact from others, should be punished with disgrace" (p. 71).

Crimes against public tranquillity. Lastly, among crimes of the third type, Beccaria (1963) included particularly those that disturb the public tranquility and quiet of citizens such as cries and upheavals in public streets and fanatical sermons that excite the easy passions of the curious multitude (p. 78). He further suggested that arbitrary laws—those not established by a code currently in the hands of all citizens—open the door to tyranny.

The Measure of Crimes

According to Beccaria (1963), the true measure of crime is the *harm done to society* (p. 64). He further argued,

> They were in error who believed that the true measure of crimes is to be found in the intention of the person who commits them. Intention depends on the impression objects actually make and on the precedent disposition of the mind; these vary in all men and in each man, according to the swift succession of ideas, of passions, and of circumstances. It would be necessary, therefore, to form not only a particular code for each citizen but [also] a new law for every crime. (p. 65)

Beccaria also objected to measuring a crime by the dignity of the injured person and the gravity of sinfulness of the crime.

The Origin of Punishments and the Right to Punish

Law as the origin of punishments. One of Beccaria's major contributions was his challenge to the rights of the sovereign to punish crimes. Building on the social contract philosophers, Beccaria (1963) explained the origin of laws as follows:

Laws are the conditions under which independent and isolated men united to form a society. Weary of living in a continual state of war and of enjoying a liberty rendered useless by the uncertainty of preserving it, they sacrificed a part so that they might enjoy the rest of it in peace and safety. . . . Some tangible motives had to be introduced, therefore, to prevent the despotic spirit, which is in every man, from plunging the laws of society into its original chaos. These tangible motives are the punishments established against infractors of the laws. (p. 11)

Beccaria concluded that punishments that exceed what is necessary for protection of public security are, by their nature, unjust.

Authority of judges. Beccaria also was concerned with the arbitrary punishments rendered by judges. Thus, he argued that only the laws can decree punishments for crimes. Authority for this can reside only with the legislator who represents the entire society united by social contract. Beccaria (1963) limited the power of the sovereign by insisting that the sovereign can only frame general laws binding all members. The sovereign cannot judge whether someone has violated the social contract. There must, therefore, be a third party to judge the truth of the fact, hence the need for a magistrate whose decisions, of which there can be no appeal, should consist of mere affirmations or denials of particular facts (p. 14).

Judges in criminal cases cannot have the authority to interpret laws because they are not legislators. Beccaria (1963) asserted,

For every crime that comes before him, a judge is required to complete a perfect syllogism in which the major premise must be the general law; the minor, the action that conforms or does not conform to the law; and the conclusion, acquittal, or punishment. (p. 15)

Beccaria also was opposed to judges' determinations of the "spirit" of the law. He further asserted that each judge had an individual viewpoint that might vary from one time to another.

The "spirit" of the law would be the product of a judge's good or bad logic, of his good or bad digestion; it would depend on the violence of his passions, on the weakness of the accused, on the judge's connections with him. . . . Thus, we see the same crimes differently punished at different times by the same court, for having consulted not the constant fixed voice of the law but the erring instability of interpretation. (p. 16)

Beccaria (1963) continued this line of reasoning by arguing that this fixed code of laws takes the arbitrary and controversial decisions out of the hands of judges. Therefore, the role of judges is reduced to simply determining the facts of the cases and determining whether or not the acts of citizens conform to the laws as written (p. 16). Beccaria also advocated that laws be stated clearly so that all can understand the criminal codes. He stated that "another evil evidently is the obscurity that makes interpretation necessary" (p. 17). He argued that an increase in the number of those who understand the code of laws would result in a decrease in the frequency of crimes because "undoubtedly ignorance and uncertainty of punishments add much to the eloquence of the passions" (p. 17).

Evidences and Forms of Judgments

Beccaria, then, advocated that the proofs of crimes must be determined by the law rather than by judges, whose decrees always are contrary to political liberty when they are not particular applications of a general maxim included in the public code. For Beccaria (1963), "The certainty required to prove a man guilty, therefore, is that which determines every man in the most important transactions of his life" (p. 21).

Proofs. Beccaria specified that the proofs of a crime can be distinguished as perfect (i.e., exclude the possibility of innocence) and imperfect (i.e., not exclude the possibility of innocence). Beccaria (1963) explained that one perfect proof suffices for condemnation of a crime but that an imperfect proof might require the convergence of as many as are necessary to establish that innocence is an impossibility (p. 21). Beccaria further considered the moral certainty of proof "more easily felt than exactly defined." That is why he urged the assignment of popular jurors, taken by lot, to assist the judge in determining proof of guilt or innocence. He also was concerned with the *credibility of witnesses.*

> The credibility of a witness, therefore, must diminish in proportion to the hatred, or friendship, or close connections between him and the accused. More than one witness is necessary, for so long as one affirms and the other denies, nothing is certain, and the right of every man to be presumed innocent prevails. The credibility of a witness becomes appreciably less, the greater the atrocity of the crime or the improbability of the circumstances. (p. 23)

Evidence acquired through abuses. Beccaria opposed the use of secret accusations, suggestive interrogations, and torture to obtain evidence. He contended that the customary use of secret accusations makes persons false and deceptive. This breeds suspicion and the masking of true feelings. With regard to suggestive interrogations, Beccaria (1963) indicated,

> Our laws forbid the use of leading or *suggestive* questions in a trial, questions, that is, which, as the learned say, explore what is *special* in the circumstances of a crime when they ought to be exploring what is *general*—those questions, in other words, which, because they have an immediate connection with the crime, *suggest* to the accused an immediate response. (p. 27)

Beccaria further suggested that when the guilt of the accused is beyond doubt, then interrogations are useless in the same way as a confession to the crime is useless when other proofs are enough to establish guilt. Beccaria also rejected the use of torture for acquiring evidence for the following reasons:

The first reason is surely applicable in the case of torture, for pain will *suggest* obstinate silence to a strong man, enabling him thereby to exchange a greater [punishment] for a lesser punishment, and to the weak it will *suggest* confession, so that he may free himself from present torment which is, for the moment at least, more efficacious than the fear of future pain. The second reason is also evidently relevant here, for if a *special* interrogation makes an accused person confess against his natural right, spasms of torture will do so the more easily. (p. 28)

Punishments

Beccaria (1963) proclaimed that the purpose of punishment is neither to torment and afflict a sensitive being nor to undo a crime already committed. Punishments and methods of inflicting them that are chosen, therefore, ought to make the strongest and most lasting impressions on the minds of men and inflict the least torment on the bodies of the criminals (p. 42).

Beccaria (1963) was an advocate of the pleasure-pain principle or *hedonism.*

For a punishment to attain its end, the evil which it inflicts has only to exceed the advantage derivable from the crime; in this excess of evil, one should include the certainty of punishment and the loss of the good which the crime might have produced. All beyond this is superfluous and for that reason tyrannical. (p. 43)

Beccaria further claimed that there must be a proper proportion between crimes and punishments. That is, the obstacles that deter persons from committing crimes should be stronger in proportion as the crimes are contrary to the common good and as the inducements to commit crimes are stronger (p. 62). Thus, Beccaria determined that pleasure and pain are the motives of sensible beings and that to deter crime, the pain of punishment must be greater than the pleasure received from the crime (p. 63).

Promptness, severity, and certainty of punishments. Beccaria declared that the purpose of punishment is deterrence. To be effective, punishment must be prompt and certain. In Beccaria's (1963) words,

The more promptly and the more closely punishment follows upon the commission of a crime, the more just and useful it will be. I say more just because the criminal is thereby spared the useless and cruel torments of uncertainty, which increase with the vigor of imagination and with the sense of personal weakness; more just, because deprivation of liberty, being itself a punishment, should not precede the sentence except when necessity requires. (pp. 55-56)

Beccaria considered it of the utmost importance that the crime and the punishment be linked together. He further argued that the punishment should be in as much conformity to the nature of the crime as possible. Thus, the promptness and certainty of the punishment was an essential element of deterrence for Beccaria. It might surprise many students of criminology to learn that Beccaria was not an advocate of severe punishment. Beccaria (1963) declared that a moderate certain punishment will make a stronger impression than will fear of a more severe one combined with the hope of impunity. Clemency and pardon become less necessary when punishments are more mild (p. 58). Beccaria concluded his argument by stating that "pardons and mercy are necessary to compensate for the absurdity of the laws and the severity of the sentences" (p. 59). Current advocates of deterrence theory, with its related policy of severity of sentences and its insistence on mandatory sentences, are not in accord with Beccaria's perspective on deterrence and policy.

The death penalty. In his writing, Beccaria (1963) challenged the usefulness of the death penalty (p. 45). He also raised the question, "What manner of right can men attribute to themselves to slaughter their fellow beings?" and concluded that the death penalty is justified only in cases where the security of the nation is endangered—when anarchy prevails—or where the person's death is "the only real way of restraining others from committing crimes" (p. 46). Beccaria continued,

> It is not the intensity of punishment that has the greatest effect on the human spirit but [rather] its duration, for our sensibility is more easily and more permanently affected by slight but repeated impressions than by a powerful but momentary action. . . . It is not the terrible yet momentary spectacle of the death of a wretch but [rather] the long and painful example of a man deprived of liberty who, having become a beast of burden, recompenses with his labors the society he has offended, which is the strongest curb against crimes. (pp. 46-47)

Beccaria concluded his treatise against the death penalty as follows:

> The death penalty cannot be useful because of the example of barbarity it gives men. . . . It seems to me absurd that the laws, which are an expression of the public will, which detest and punish homicide, should themselves commit it, and that to deter citizens from murder, they order a public one. (p. 50)

Critique of Beccaria

Paolucci suggested that Beccaria exaggerated the evils of the criminal procedures of his day (Beccaria, 1963, p. xxii). However, Beccaria's *On Crimes and Punishments,* in which he opposed the arbitrary and barbaric practices of the aristocracy and the criminal justice system of that time, has become a classic in modern criminology, and Beccaria has been credited as the founder of the Classical School of criminology.

Style and content. Although Beccaria's works were quite successful, he remained insecure, anxious, and withdrawn. When he was invited to Paris "so that due honor might be accorded the author of *On Crimes and Punishments,*" he at first refused to go because he was fearful of the impression that he would make. Paolucci reported, "On October 2, 1766, accompanied by Alessandro Verri, Beccaria took his departure, following his escort, it is said, not like a hero on his way to triumph but [rather] like a condemned prisoner on his way to the gallows" (Beccaria, 1963, p. xiv). Paolucci further stated that when Beccaria arrived in Paris, he was somber and anxious. Toward the end of his sojourn, he was so irritated that he closed himself in his room at the hotel. After having spent only 3 weeks in Paris, he went home alone, leaving us, as his pledge, the count Verri (p. xv). Beccaria's style of writing also has been criticized. It has been stated that many of his sentences are hopelessly involuted and that many of his clauses are strung together in a maze of complexity. Some critics have argued that Beccaria should not be considered the author of *On Crimes and Punishments*. Paolucci suggested that the style is that of "an impassioned plea"—a style suitable for a work pertaining to the practical and productive spheres of juridical discourse rather than to the theoretical (Beccaria, 1963, p. xvii).

Flawed logic. Beccaria argued that if there were a certain and prompt punishment prescribed in the legal code that was just greater than the pleasure or reward the person received from committing the crime, then that would deter crime. However, Beccaria made several assumptions that are false.

In stating that people are free-willed rational agents, he also assumed that crimes are planned and that criminals calculate the costs of their crimes before committing them. Although this might be true for most professional crimes, it is not true for many street crimes and certainly is not true for most murders. Researchers have noted that most murders occur between people who know one another and are unplanned. One of the most frequent types of murder occurs during domestic violence. Wolfgang (1958) suggested that these murders involve victim precipitation. That is, they are unplanned, spur-of-the-moment killings that occur during crisis situations. In fact, Wolfgang indicated that in many cases, it is simply a matter of chance as to who is the victim and who is the offender.

A second problem with Beccaria's logic is his assumption that people know and remember the prescribed punishment for each crime. This is especially problematic for the 18th century, when Beccaria proposed his theory, given that many people had limited access to education and books. Even today, it is a false assumption that citizens know and understand all of the crimes and punishments defined in our legal codes.

Finally, Beccaria seemed to assume that everyone experiences the pleasure of the crime and the punishment the same. Although he indicated that pain applied during torture would be experienced differently, he seemed to assume that the punishment prescribed in the legal codes would be uniformly experienced. This is not the case.

Beccaria's influence. In addition to the impact that Beccaria's works had on the 18th century, his works contain the seeds of some of today's theories. Although conflict theorists have not acknowledged their heritage from Beccaria, a careful reading of his works reveals his concern with inequities based on class. For example, in his discussion of crimes against personal security, Beccaria (1963) stated, "Within this class are included not only the assassinations and thefts committed by men of the lower class but also those committed by noblemen and magistrates" (pp. 68-69). He also was disturbed by the arbitrary and inequitable punishments given out by tyrannical judges.

Beccaria's ideas also can be found in the deterrence theories of the 1980s and 1990s. The current emphasis on mandatory sentences can be traced to Beccaria's emphasis on the certainty and promptness of punishments. However, the current trend toward the increased use of capital punishment contradicts Beccaria's position opposing the death penalty. Beccaria argued that the purpose of punishment is to deter crime. To accomplish this, the punishment needs to be just slightly greater than the advantage received from committing the crime. He also held that imprisonment is a greater deterrent than the death penalty. It should be noted that current criminal justice policies do not result in the uniformity, certainty, and celerity of punishments that Beccaria advocated.

Jeremy Bentham (1748-1832)

Jeremy Bentham, a contemporary of Beccaria, was a British jurist and philosopher (Lilly et al., 1995, p. 17). Although he shared many of the same ideas regarding crime and punishment as did Beccaria and was a much more prolific writer, most criminological theorists tend to give him minimal recognition.[2]

Bentham's Life and Times

Bentham was born on February 15, 1748, into a well-to-do middle class and Tory family of some standing in London (Bentham, 1948, p. ix). Jeremiah Bentham, his father, was the son of a lawyer, the grandson of a prosperous pawnbroker, and a lawyer himself. In the introduction to Bentham's work, Harrison stated that Jeremy was to practice law and enhance the family's property and standing but that his interests and abilities did not follow this path. At 20 years of age, Bentham had decided his vocation: He would provide a foundation for scientific jurisprudence and legislation (p. ix).

Geis (1972) stated that Bentham was "an eccentric personality, an incredibly prolific writer, a thinker who had the colossal temerity to attempt to catalogue and to label all varieties of behavior and the motivations giving rise to them" (p. 51).

Stark (1952), in the introduction to *Jeremy Bentham's Economic Writings,* stated,

> Bentham took up the study of political economy in 1786, when he was thirty-eight years of age; he abandoned it in 1804, when he had just turned fifty-six. Thus, it can be seen that he devoted eighteen years, perhaps the best years of his life, to the cultivation of a field with which his name has never so far been seriously associated. (pp. 12-13)

Stark also suggested that Bentham was influenced by the outstanding economist Nathaniel Forster, whom Bentham met at Oxford University in 1762. Bentham still was a boy at that time, but they met again 10 years later. Stark also stated that

Bentham was influenced by Adam Smith's *The Wealth of Nations,* originally published in 1776 (Smith, 1937).

Like Beccaria, Bentham was disturbed by the "incongruities, absurdities, contradictions, and barbarities" (Geis, 1972, p. 53) found in the criminal codes of his time. As a result, Geis (1972) indicated that Bentham "attempted to arrange affairs into a harmonious unity and brought to bear on illegal behavior a multiplicity of analytical concepts such as felicity calculus, greatest happiness, pain and pleasure, and utility" (p. 54). In fact, this utilitarian emphasis on the greatest happiness for the greatest number permeates much of Bentham's writing. We begin by examining his *Economic Writings* (edited by Stark, 1952).

Bentham's *Economic Writings*

Stark (1952) noted,

> The key to Bentham's philosophy of economics is, of course, the fact that he was a confirmed materialist. Now, the first and foremost consequence of a materialistic worldview is the conscious or unconscious desire to subordinate the social sciences to, and model them upon, the physical sciences. (p. 16)

Stark further indicated that Bentham believed that the goal of science should be to do good. Stark summarized Bentham's economic ideas by stating that Bentham believed that the greatest happiness of a nation could be achieved by establishing universal security, guaranteeing subsistence, maximizing abundance, and reducing inequity so far as possible. Bentham himself argued,

> The sole proper all-comprehensive end should be the greatest happiness of the whole community, governors and governed together—the *greatest happiness principle* should be the fundamental principle. (cited in Stark, 1952, p. 91) . . .
> Wealth produces more happiness when given to one who has little than to one who has much. The more one has, the less happiness wealth produces. (p. 113)

The remainder of this work contained an overview of various economic principles such as usury on loans, modes of operating government, taxation, and patents. In all of these areas, Bentham advocated economic equality. Thus, Bentham's works, as well as those of Beccaria, can be tied to early and current conflict theory.

Principles of Morals and Legislation

Bentham stated his "principle of utility" or "greatest happiness principle" in more detail in his 1789 publication of *Principles of Morals and Legislation,* edited by Harrison (Bentham, 1948). The key ideas contained in Bentham's principle are as follows:

> Nature has placed mankind under the governance of two sovereign masters, *pain* and *pleasure*. It is for them alone to point out what we ought to do as well as to determine what we shall do. (p. 125) . . .
>
> By the principle of utility is meant . . . that property in any object whereby it tends to produce benefit, advantage, pleasure, good, or happiness . . . [or] to prevent the happening of mischief, pain, evil, or unhappiness to the party whose interest is considered—if that party be the community in general, then the happiness of the community; if a particular individual, then the happiness of that individual. (p. 126)

In his chapter on sanctions or sources of pain and pleasure, Bentham (1948) declared that the legislator's sole standard and concern ought to be the happiness and security of the individuals of whom a community is composed (p. 147). Bentham then presented a detailed classification of pleasure and pain (pp. 147-163). This classification was followed by a treatise on penal law:

> The business of government is to promote the happiness of the society by punishing and rewarding. That part of its business which consists in punishing is more particularly the subject of penal law. In proportion as an act tends to disturb that happiness, in proportion as the tendency of it is pernicious, will be the demand it creates for punishment. What happiness consists of we have already seen: enjoyment of pleasures, security from pains. (p. 189)

Bentham used the term "national felicity" in discussing the legislature's responsibility to create law that maximizes "the greatest happiness of the greatest number" (Rosen and Burns, 1983, p. 45). Bentham (1948) included an extensive classification of offenses and of punishments in his *Principles of Morals and Legislation*. But he also proposed that there should be a "proportion between punishments and offences" (p. 289). Specifically, Bentham argued,

> The value of punishment must not be less in any case than what is sufficient to outweigh that of the profit of the offence. (p. 290) . . .
>
> The punishment should be adjusted in such manner to each particular offence, that for every part of the mischief there may be a motive to restrain the offender from giving birth to it. . . . The punishment ought in no case to be more than what is necessary to bring it into conformity with the rules here given. (pp. 292-293)

Critique of Bentham

Bentham shared many of the same concerns regarding governmental tyrannies and inconsistencies in England as did Beccaria in Italy. Whereas Beccaria introduced the concept of utilitarianism, it was Bentham who expounded on the principle of utility in several of his publications. Both Beccaria and Bentham argued that the purpose of punishment was deterrence. They proposed that for punishment to effectively prevent crime, it must be certain, prompt, and severe. They argued, however, that the pain of punishment should be just enough greater than the pleasure from the crime to deter the offender. Although the current penal code in the United States has many of the characteristics advocated by Beccaria and Bentham, both were opposed to capital punishment.

Although Bentham was much more of a prolific writer than Beccaria, his style of writing also was extremely complex, and his classifications of motives, offenses, and punishments make for very tedious reading. Beccaria has been credited as the founder of the 18th-century Classical School, whereas the contributions of Bentham have been ignored or minimized by most criminological theorists.[3]

The Neo-Classical School

The Neo-Classical School represented no major break with the basic premises of the Classical School. These theorists continued to state that people are rational creatures guided by reason who have free will. They also advocated the utilitarian principle that people are controlled by, and crime is deterred by, fear of punishment. Hence, the pain from punishment must exceed the pleasure obtained from the act.

The Neo-Classical School, however, did make some modifications in the administration of law based on the Classical School. These theorists modified the doctrine of free will by stating that the freedom to choose could be affected by incompetence of age or insanity. They also introduced the concept of premeditation and mitigating circumstances. However, the major rejection of the 18th-century Classical School was presented by the 19th-century Positivist School, to be discussed in Chapter 3.

Notes

1. The concept of a contract system used by the Classical School has as its foundation the 18th-century philosophers such as Thomas Hobbes, Jean-Jacques Rousseau, and François Marie Arouet de Voltaire. The social contract, according to these scholars, involved the natural human rights of citizens and the government. A citizen surrendered to the authority of the state the amount of freedom necessary to ensure protection of the rights of all citizens.

2. In reading Bentham's original works, some criminologists might be reminded of the efforts of the sociologist Talcott Parsons to develop a theory broad enough to explain all social behavior, organization, and change. Both Bentham and Parsons developed extensive categories of phenomena that make reading their works extremely tedious.

3. The contributions of Beccaria and Bentham have had an impact on more recent theories such as conflict theory (see Chapter 8) and deterrence theory. Many scholars have examined the validity of deterrence theory. Paternoster (1987), for example, conducted a review of deterrence literature for the 1972-1986 period to determine the impact of perceived certainty and severity of punishment on crime. Although he found some support in these studies, he stated, "However much we pride ourselves on being intelligent rational creatures, the truth may be that we are tempered somewhat with humanity. Let us hope so" (p. 215).

DISCUSSION QUESTIONS

1. If Beccaria were living today and continued to maintain the ideas contained in his *On Crimes and Punishments* (Beccaria, 1963), what would be his solution to the population explosion in our prisons today? Support your answer with details from this chapter.

2. Take a pro or con position on capital punishment and support your position using details from the works of Beccaria and/or Bentham.

3. What do you think were the societal conditions that served to motivate Beccaria's works?

4. Cite examples of how the Classical School has influenced the system of law in the United States. Why was the Classical School so influential?

5. Suppose that you are a feminist criminologist. What criticisms might you have of Beccaria and Bentham? Cite specific material from the two scholars.

CHAPTER 3

The Positivist School

Introduction and Historical Setting

Even though the Classical School (see Chapter 2) was modified by the Neo-Classical School, it continued to dominate the study of crime until the latter part of the 19th century. During this period, society was transformed from the agrarian-based aristocracies of 18th-century Europe and the rural farmlands of the United States into a complex industrialized society. The rational emphasis of the Classical School was replaced with a scientific approach to the study of multiple factors that explain the causes of crime.

The Search for Scientific Evidence

This new theory argued that crime was not a rationally reasoned behavior that could be deterred and controlled by punishment. Instead, the 19th-century Positivist School (or Modern School, as it was labeled by Cesare Lombroso) sought scientific proof that crime was caused by features within the individual. The early Italian Positivist School theorists, especially Lombroso, were influenced in their search for causes of crime by the evolutionary theories found in Darwin's (1859) *Origins of the Species* and Darwin's (1871) *The Descent of Man*. Frances Alice Kellor sought to determine the causes of crime among women during the early part of the 20th century. She was the first woman, and one of the first Americans, to attack Lombroso's biological interpretation of crime (Freedman, 1981, p. 113). Pauline Tarnowsky, a contemporary of Lombroso, conducted research on women offenders in Eastern Europe. The Positivist School emphasized a deterministic approach to the study of criminal behavior and the prevention of crime through the treatment and rehabilitation of offenders.

Assumptions About People and Society

The 19th-century Positivist School theorists were the first to claim the importance of looking at individual differences among criminals. Therefore, they used a predominantly micro level of analysis. Unlike the Classical School, which stated that people are active agents with free will, the Positivist School's emphasis on deterministic causes of crime suggests that people are passive and controlled. It further indicates that criminal behavior is imposed on people by biological (e.g., Lombroso, Kellor, Tarnowsky) and environmental (e.g., Lombroso, Ferri, Garofalo, Kellor) conditions. Lombroso and his students (e.g., Ferri, Garofalo), as well as Tarnowsky, were concerned primarily with objective overt phenomena of criminal behavior and innate physical characteristics of prisoners. Kellor's research in the United States studied both the objective overt (e.g., physical and environmental characteristics) and subjective covert (e.g., attitudes) phenomena.

Lombroso's original works were more unidimensional and stereotypical in that he defined criminals based exclusively on his study of male prisoners. His later works included a study of women in which he quoted extensively from Tarnowsky's study of women criminals. Kellor's study included more diversity because she did a comparative study of predominantly white women prisoners and college students in Ohio, Illinois, and New York and of black (Negro) women in southern prisons.

Cesare Lombroso (1836-1909)

Cesare Lombroso was identified by Wolfgang (1972) as the "father of the Italian School" of criminology (p. 241). As indicated in the biographical inset on Lombroso (Inset 3.1), he was born into a family of some wealth and influence. Therefore, Lombroso was able to attend the Gymnasium controlled by the Jesuits and to study medicine at major Italian universities. His family's position also afforded him the opportunity to serve as a physician in the military and in hospitals as well as to teach at the University of Turin. Lombroso used each of these positions as an opportunity to study the physical differences among soldiers, the insane, and criminals. Wolfgang indicated the sequence of Lombroso's interest and activity in criminology as follows:

> (1) the background behavior of the tattooed soldiers whom he observed while a physician in the Italian Army; (2) the application of physical measurements in his studies of the mentally alienated . . . ; (3) the extension of these physical and physiological techniques to the study of criminals, i.e., to the differentiation of criminals from lunatics; and (4) the direct analytical study of the criminal compared with normal individuals and the insane. (p. 237)

Contemporary Influences

Lombroso was influenced early in his life by the well-known philosopher and physician Paolo Marzolo. Under Marzolo's influence, as well as that of prior read-

INSET 3.1

Cesare Lombroso (1836-1909)

Cesare Lombroso was born November 6, 1836, in Venice, Italy. He was the second son of five children born to Aron and Zefira Levi Lombroso (Wolfgang, 1972). His family, on his father's side, can be traced back to North African Jews. By most accounts, it appears that his mother was from a wealthy family (Martin, Mutchnick, and Austin, 1990, p. 22). Early in his education, Lombroso took an interest in history. This was evidenced by two outstanding papers he wrote, at 15 years of age, titled "Essay on the History of the Roman Empire" and "Sketches of Ancient Agriculture in Italy" (Wolfgang, 1972, p. 233).

Lombroso, after writing a review of the first volume of Paolo Marzolo's *An Introduction to Historical Monuments Revealed by Analysis of Words*, was invited to meet Marzolo (Wolfgang, 1972, p. 233). This meeting led to a relationship that had an immense influence on Lombroso's life. Marzolo encouraged Lombroso to study medicine. Following Marzolo's advice, Lombroso enrolled at the University of Pavia and then at the University of Vienna. Lombroso received his degree in medicine from the University of Pavia in 1858 and his degree in surgery from the University of Genoa in 1859 (p. 233).

Lombroso, after graduating in 1859, volunteered for service in the Army Medical Service. It was during this period that he began to conduct observations and measurements of more than 3,000 soldiers to determine whether there were any physical differences between individuals throughout It-

aly. His findings indicated that those soldiers with obscene tatoos were the ones committing the greatest number of military infractions. Based on his findings, Lombroso subsequently identified tattooing as a criminal characteristic (Wolfgang, 1972, pp. 233-234).

After completing his research on soldiers, Lombroso received permission to clinically study the mental patients in the hospital of Saint Euphemia (Wolfgang, 1972, p. 235). In 1862, from this research, Lombroso presented several lectures that later were published. From 1863 to 1872, he headed various hospitals for the insane in Pavia, Pesao, and Reggio Emilia. During this period, Lombroso met and married his wife, Alexandria. Together, they had two children, Paola and Gina. Both children later would marry future colleagues of Lombroso (Martin et al., 1990, p. 22).

In 1876, Lombroso received his first appointment in legal medicine and public hygiene at the University of Turin. After 20 years, he was promoted to professor of psychiatry and clinical psychiatry. In 1906, he became a professor of criminal anthropology. In this last position, Lombroso received a French Legion of Honor Medal and founded the Museum of Criminal Anthropology. In these medical positions, he found the opportunity to study prisoners. Throughout his life, Lombroso published numerous books and essays on both female and male offenders and prisoners. His most notable publications include *The Criminal Man* (Lombroso, 1863) and *The Female Offender* (Lombroso, 1895) (Wolfgang, 1972, p. 235).

—*Shaun L. Gabbidon*
Pennsylvania State University at Harrisburg

SOURCE: Excerpted from the writings of Shaun L. Gabbidon with permission.

ings, Lombroso was led to begin the study of medicine at 18 years of age (Wolfgang, 1972, p. 233). Martin, Mutchnick, and Austin (1990) suggested, "So strong was the relationship between Lombroso and Marzolo that Lombroso named his first daughter Paola, in honor of his friend" (p. 24). Other early influences on Lombroso were the eminent specialist in internal medicine Skoda, the writings of the great pathologist Rokitanski, and the works of Darwin. It was Darwin who first used the term "atavistic man," a concept that Lombroso developed into a cause of crime (Martin et al., 1990, p. 27).

Lombroso both influenced and was influenced by younger students who studied with him at the University of Turin. The most prominent of these was Enrico Ferri (1856-1929), who at 24 years of age went to Turin in 1880 to study and eventually became Lombroso's son-in-law. It was Ferri who coined the term "born criminal" to refer to the atavistic type that Lombroso believed he had identified (Wolfgang, 1972, p. 239). Lombroso also was influenced by his student, Raffaele Garofalo (1852-1934), who had a distinguished career as a magistrate in the Italian courts and was concerned with reforms in criminal procedure (Vold, 1979, pp. 43-45).

Finally, Lombroso evidently was influenced by the French writings of Tarnowsky,[1] who had studied women criminals in Russia using techniques similar to those used by Lombroso. Although little is known about Tarnowsky, Lombroso and Ferrero (1958) cited her research extensively in *The Female Offender,* originally published in 1895.

Lombroso's Criminal Anthropology

The Positivist School of penal jurisprudence maintains that the antisocial tendencies of the criminal are the result of his or her physical and psychic organization, which differs essentially from that of normal individuals. It also aims at studying the morphology and various functional phenomena of the criminal with the object of curing, instead of punishing, him or her (Lombroso-Ferrero, 1972, p. 5). Thus, criminal anthropology employed by Lombroso looked at the organic and psychic constitution and the social life of the criminal.

Lombroso examined criminals and stated that they exhibit numerous anomalies in the face, skeleton, and various psychic and sensitive functions, so that they strongly resemble primitive races. It was these anomalies that first drew Lombroso's attention to "the close relationship between the criminal and the savage" and that made him "suspect that criminal tendencies are of atavistic origin" (Lombroso-Ferrero, 1972, p. 5).

Atavism. The born criminal, according to Lombroso, shows numerous specific characteristics that almost always are atavistic. Lombroso noted anomalies exhibited by criminals including

> the scanty beard as opposed to the general hairiness of the body, prehensile foot, diminished number of lines in the palm of the hand, cheek pouches, enormous development of the middle incisors and frequent absence of the lateral ones, flattened nose and angular or sugar-loaf form of the skull, common to criminals and apes; the excessive size of the orbits, which, combined with the hooked nose, so often imparts to criminals the aspect of birds of prey, the projection of the lower part of the face and jaws (prognathism found in negroes and animals), and supernumerary teeth (amounting in

some cases to a double row as in snakes) and cranial bones. . . . All these characteristics pointed to one conclusion, the atavistic origin of the criminal, who reproduces physical, psychic, and functional qualities of remote ancestors. (Lombroso-Ferrero, 1972, pp. 7-8)

Lombroso relied heavily on Tarnowsky's "study of 150 prostitutes and 100 female thieves" (Lombroso and Ferrero, 1958, p. 45) in discussing the anomalies of women. For example, Tarnowsky reported

the arm span of prostitutes and criminals to be less than the normal poor because they work. She also found that prostitutes had the shortest arms . . . [and] that Russian prostitutes have a longer hand than peasant women, but thieves have a shorter hand. (pp. 53-54)

Tarnowsky further claimed that normal women are more sensitive than prostitutes. She asserted that prostitutes have a severe deadness in the clitoris and that fewer criminals have a normal sense of taste, smell, hearing, and vision (pp. 138-141). Tarnowsky also reported that "almost all anomalies occur more frequently in prostitutes than in female offenders, and both classes have a larger number of the characteristics of degeneration than [do] normal women" (p. 85).

Lombroso and Ferrero (1958) suggested that women are less inclined to crime than are men because the female's cerebral cortex is less active than that of the male (pp. 110-111). The female criminal is only occasionally criminal because her degeneration is more apt to lead her to hysterical epilepsy or sexual anomalies—not crime. Lombroso summed up his findings on female criminals as follows:

While most female criminals are not completely degenerated, there are some who are more depraved than any male. . . . The female-born criminal is far crueller than the male-born criminal, often devising unusual methods of torture. . . . Women have many traits in common with children; their moral sense is deficient, [and] they are revengeful, jealous, [and] inclined to vengeance of a refined cruelty. In ordinary cases, these defects are neutralized by piety, maternity, want of passion, sexual coldness, . . . weakness, and an undeveloped intelligence. (Lombroso-Ferrero, 1972, pp. 147-152)

Epilepsy and hysteria. "The same phenomena which we observe in the case of born criminals appears again in the rare cases of moral insanity but may be studied minutely, and on a large scale, in epileptics, criminal or not" (Lombroso, 1968, p. 369; see also Lombroso-Ferrero, 1972, p. 58). Lombroso asserted that epilepsy can be manifested in various forms, one of which is characterized by fits of rage (Lombroso-Ferrero, 1972, p. 59). According to Lombroso,

Epileptics may have seizures accompanied by loss of memory and unconsciousness. . . . Sometimes, he is dazed, mute, and immovable; at others, he talks incessantly; at still others, he goes on with his ordinary occupations, traveling, reading, and writing. . . . Lombroso further claimed that epileptics may commit murder or crave blood, although not as often as born criminals. . . . During these seizures, epileptics are not responsible for their actions. (Lombroso-Ferrero, 1972, pp. 87-91)

Hysteria is a disease allied to epilepsy, of which it appears to be a milder form, and is much more common among women than among men. Physical characteristics are fewer in hysterics than in epileptics. The most common peculiarities are "small, obliquely placed eyes of timid glance, pale elongated face, crowded or loosened teeth, nervous movements of the face and hands, facial asymmetry, and black hair" (Lombroso-Ferrero, 1972, p. 93). Lombroso identified psychological characteristics of hysteria as women with a fair amount of intelligence but with little power of concentration, profoundly egotistical, impressionable, susceptible to suggestion, enjoy slandering others, revengeful, and prone to mood swings and to lying. Hysterics often will be guilty of multiple crimes including stealing and murder (pp. 94-95; see also Lombroso and Ferrero, 1895, pp. 223-232).

Criminaloids. In addition to the epileptic, hysterical, and inebriate lunatics and those insane from alcoholism, there remain a number of criminals (amounting to a full half) in whom the virus is, so to speak, attenuated—who, although they are epileptics, suffer from a milder form of the disease (Lombroso-Ferrero, 1972, pp. 100-101). Lombroso (1968) identified the criminaloids as

having a smaller number of anomalies in touch, sensibility to pain, psychometry, and especially less early baldness and grayness, and less tattooing. . . . The criminaloid is more precocious and relapses oftener—at least this is the case with pickpockets and simple thieves. . . . Criminaloids, then, differ from born criminals in degree, not in kind. This is so true that the greater number of them, having become habitual criminals thanks to a long sojourn in prison, can no longer be distinguished from born criminals except by the slighter character of their physical marks of criminality. (p. 374)

Without some adequate cause, then, criminality is not manifested in these persons. "A healthy environment, careful training, habits of industry, [and] the inculcation of moral and humane sentiments may prevent these individuals from yielding to dishonest impulses, provided always that no special temptation to sin comes in their path" (Lombroso-Ferrero, 1972, p. 101).

Insane criminals. Lombroso (1968) stated that even among the true insane criminals,

those forms predominate which we may call the hypertrophy of crime, the exaggeration of the born criminal, not only in bodily and functional characteristics but also in the manner of committing the crime and in conduct afterward. These serve to explain to us the extent of the impulsive, obscene, and cruel tendencies of the criminal[ly] insane, who are almost always obscure epileptics or born criminals upon whom melancholia and monomania have grafted themselves, according to the natural tendency of different forms of psychic disorders to take root together upon the corrupted soil of degeneracy. (p. 375)

Criminals by passion. Criminals of this class represent the antithesis of the common offender or born criminal. Whereas the born criminal's evil acts are the outcome of his or her ferocious and egotistical impulses, criminals from passion have "harmonious lines of the body, beauty of the soul, and great nervous and emotional sensitiveness" (Lombroso, 1968, p. 376). The criminals by passion have motives for violation of the law that stem from a pure spirit of altruism that is noble and powerful such as love or politics (p. 376; see also Lombroso-Ferrero, 1972, pp. 118-119).

Occasional criminals. Occasional criminals, or pseudo-criminals, have less depravity and display fewer physical anomalies. They do not seek the occasion for the crime but rather are almost drawn into it or fall into the meshes of the code for very insignificant reasons (Lombroso and Ferrero, 1958, p. 192; Lombroso, 1968, p. 376).

The female occasional criminals often show near normal maternal instincts and "near normal need of and dependence on men" (Lombroso and Ferrero, 1958, pp. 194- 195). Lombroso and Ferrero (1958) further stated,

> Occasional criminals are consequently capable of the spiritualized love which is especially womanly; but in the born criminal, there is only sensuality and lust. . . . Occasional female criminals do not sin on their own; this is how they differ from the others. . . . Friendship is a form of suggestion . . . , and in certain cases it results in the total absorption of the weaker personality in the stronger one. . . . Oftentimes, [a woman is] led into crime by the suggestion of another, usually her lover. (pp. 196-204)

Causes of Crime

Lombroso (1968) was concerned with the multiplicity of causes of crime. He stressed the importance of investigating each cause singly but indicated that "one can almost never assign a single cause unrelated to others" (p. 1). This section examines some of the more important factors considered by Lombroso as possible causes of crime.

Race and crime. Lombroso suggested that race is an important factor in crime in view of the atavistic origin of crime (Lombroso-Ferrero, 1972, p. 139). He stated that more primitive races or tribes are given to crime and that the predominance of crime in certain countries certainly is due to race (p. 139; see also Lombroso, 1968, p. 23). He argued that the effect of race clearly can be seen in certain localities whose inhabitants differ ethnically from the surrounding population and where the relative frequency or infrequency of crime coincides with the racial difference (Lombroso, 1968, p. 28).

Lombroso (1968) stated that the influence of race on criminality becomes plainly evident when we study the Jews and the gypsies, although the influence is manifested very differently in the two races (pp. 36-37). He asserted,

In the gypsies, we have an entire race of criminals with all the passions and vices common to delinquent types: idleness, ignorance, impetuous fury, vanity, love of orgies, and ferocity. Murder is often committed for some trifling gain. The women are skilled thieves and train their children in dishonest practices. On the contrary, the percentage of crimes among Jews is always lower than that of the surrounding population; although there is a prevalence of certain specific forms of offences, often hereditary, such as fraud, forgery, libel, and chief of all, traffic in prostitution, murder is extremely rare. (Lombroso-Ferrero, 1972, p. 140)

After arguing that racial differences explain crime, Lombroso took up some of the social causes of crime such as density of population, alcoholism, education, and wealth.

Density of population and crime. The influence of civilization in reference to crime may be seen better by examining its different factors one by one, especially density, for history teaches us that crime occurs only when a certain density of population has been reached. Prostitution, assaults, and thefts can be seen only rarely in primitive societies (Lombroso, 1968, p. 59). However, the agglomeration of persons in a large town provides a certain incentive for crimes against property. Robbery, frauds, and criminal associations increase, whereas there is a decrease in crimes against persons, especially homicides, due to the restraints imposed by mutual supervision (pp. 59-60; see also Lombroso-Ferrero, 1972, p. 146).

Lombroso (1968) noted that immigrants show a high degree of criminality and that the agglomeration of population produced by immigration is a strong incentive for crime (p. 65). This is partially due to the instability of immigrant groups (Lombroso-Ferrero, 1972, pp. 147-148).

Alcoholism and crime. "There is one disease that without other causes—either inherited degeneracy or vices resulting from a bad education and environment—is capable of transforming a healthy individual into a vicious, hopelessly evil being. That disease is alcoholism" (Lombroso-Ferrero, 1972, pp. 140-141). Lombroso believed that alcoholism is an important factor of criminality. In fact, he stated that alcoholism is the only disease capable in itself of causing criminality. Temporary drunkenness alone will give rise to crime because it inflames the passions, obscures the mental and moral faculties, and destroys all senses of decency.

Education and crime. Lombroso (1968) began his discussion of the relevance of education to crime by stating, "The absolute parallelism between education and crime, which many maintained several years ago, is today rightly regarded as an error" (p. 105). He then examined crime statistics in various European countries and the United States regarding education. Based on this analysis, he claimed that education favors crime only up to a certain point (pp. 107-108). After this point, the influence of education is reversed. Where education is diffused, the number of educated criminals increases, but the number of illiterate criminals increases even more. From this Lombroso concluded that the criminality of the moderately educated is decreasing. He did note, however, that most criminals can read and write.

Lombroso (1968) continued by stating, "Education has an indisputable influence upon crime in changing its character and making it less savage" (p. 111). He provided the following account of the relationship between education and types of crime committed:

> (1) Among illiterates, the crimes which lead are infanticide, abortion, theft, formation of criminal bands, robbery, and arson; (2) among those who can read and write imperfectly, extortion, threatening letters, blackmail, robbery, injury to property, and assaults predominate; (3) among those who have received a moderate education, bribery, forgery, and threatening letters prevail; (4) among the well educated, the predominant crimes are forgeries of commercial papers, official crimes, forgery and abstraction of public documents, and political crimes. . . . The minimum of forgeries and the maximum of infanticides are found among the illiterate. With the convicts of a higher education, the prevailing crime is forgery of public documents, breach of trust, and swindling. Infanticides and violent crimes are lacking.
>
> Accordingly, there is a type of crime for the illiterate, namely the savage type, and one for the educated, the milder but more cunning type. (p. 112)

Lombroso (1968) was opposed to education of prison inmates unless it was accompanied by special training to correct the passions and instincts instead of to develop the intellect (p. 114). For the ordinary criminal, elementary education is harmful because it places in his or her hands an additional weapon for committing crimes. Lombroso further stated that schools in prison bring bad individuals in contact with each other, develops their intelligence and power, and causes a greater number of educated recidivists. Lombroso's analysis of crime suggests that the relationship of education to crime is quite complex and that simplistic decisions based on his data are inappropriate.

Wealth and crime. Lombroso found it even more difficult to determine the effect of wealth on crime. One reason for this that he noted was the difficulty in determining a person's wealth. He did suggest that great wealth and great poverty correlate with crime. He claimed that poverty causes theft and that laziness and extravagance create the need for a great deal of money (Lombroso, 1968, p. 124; Lombroso-Ferrero, 1972, p. 150). He noted that wealth and poverty result in different types of crimes. The poor may steal to satisfy their own needs, and poverty may cause degeneration produced by scurvy, scrofula, anemia, and alcoholism in parents that often transforms into epilepsy and moral insanity. Lombroso (1968) further stated that poverty could drive criminals to commit brutal eliminations of individuals and may indirectly cause sexual crimes (pp. 133-134). Wealth also may be a source of degeneration from other causes such as syphilis and exhaustion. Crimes of the wealthy are committed because of vanity and to surpass the wealth of others. Ambition is one of the greatest causes of crimes against property, according to Lombroso.

In his discussion of education and wealth, Lombroso (1968) introduced some elements found later in conflict theory. For example, he suggested the following:

Where wealth is absolutely the greatest, it is always accumulated in the hands of a few, so that at the same time there is always great poverty, more keenly felt because of the contrast. This favors the tendency toward crime, on the one hand, and on the other furnishes better opportunities for it. . . .

If it is true, on the other hand, that urgent need drives the poor to wrongdoing, it is only to a very limited number of crimes, although these are the more violent ones, while the artificial wants of the rich, although less urgent, are more numerous, and the kinds of crime among them are infinitely more numerous also, as well as the means of escaping punishment, encouraged by the example of persons high in politics. (p. 134)

Crime Prevention and Policy

Lombroso stated that the punishments of the past, such as flogging, hard labor, imprisonment, and exile, should be replaced with efforts to cure the criminal. He suggested that the Positivist School has demonstrated the uselessness and injuriousness of prison but that it has no desire to leave society suddenly unprotected and the criminal at large (Lombroso-Ferrero, 1972, p. 154). We must try to prevent crime. Lombroso (1968) proposed that we must use what Ferri called "penal substitutes" (p. 244). The idea is that the legislator, recognizing and studying the causes of crime, seeks to neutralize them, or at least to decrease their effect, through preventive means.

For example, in the economic sphere, freedom of exchange prevents local scarcity and, hence, removes a fertile cause of theft and riot. The lowering of customs duties, or their abolition, prevents smuggling. A more equitable distribution of taxation prevents fraud against the state, and so forth. Lombroso's suggestions for the prevention of sex crimes include the diffusion of prostitution in the agricultural districts and especially in localities where there are a large number of sailors, soldiers, and laborers. This would make sexual intercourse accessible to all dissolute-minded young men (Lombroso, 1968, p. 259).

Preventive measures against the influence of poverty and wealth suggested by Lombroso (1968) involve the redistribution of wealth to ensure greater equality (p. 275). Thus, there would be greater equity in return for labor, and work would be accessible for every able-bodied person. This would be achieved through

limitation of the hours of labor according to the age of the worker and the nature of the work, especially in mines and in unhealthful trades, and the exclusion of women, also, from work at night, thus protecting their virtue and health and at the same time bringing larger returns to a greater number of workers. (p. 275)

Lombroso also proposed counteracting the excess of wealth among a few by making the rich share their profits with the laborers and by establishing progressive taxes.

Lombroso (1968), however, considered crime prevention to be "a dream of the idealist" (p. 331). For this reason, he said that we must consider the institution of the prison as the only social defense against crime. Although prison does not reform, the individual prison cell prevents the criminal from sinking further into crime and removes, at least in part, the possibility of the formation of associations of evil-doers.

Critique of Lombroso

In contrast to earlier theorists who based their assumptions about crime and the criminal on speculation, Lombroso was one of the first theorists to attempt to study the causes of crime using scientific methods. As a physician, he initially conducted research on the physical anomalies among military soldiers, mental patients, and prison inmates. The fact that Lombroso's theory is found in virtually every introduction to criminology and theory textbook is evidence of the recognition of the importance of his contributions. However, his works are not a theory as defined in Chapter 1 of this book. He does have a set of concepts that come close to creating a conceptual scheme, but like Merton's anomie concepts, they cannot be adequately tested as presented. Lombroso's theory certainly does not meet Homans' (1964) and Turner's (1978) social science definitions of theory. Although Lombroso has been given credit for his pioneering works in criminology, he has not been without his critics.

Research methods. Lombroso's works have been challenged by research conducted by Charles Goring (1870-1919) and Frances Alice Kellor (1873-1952). The most widely acknowledged criticism of Lombroso's works has been the refutation research conducted by Goring. Kellor's research on American women prisoners and college students has remained unknown to most current criminologists. Her contributions are presented in the next section of this chapter.

Goring, a contemporary of Lombroso, was an English psychiatrist, philosopher, and criminologist educated at the University of London. In his book, *The English Convict,* Goring (1913) praised Lombroso for his humanitarian efforts but attacked his methodology (Wolfgang, 1972, p. 263). Goring accused Lombroso of drawing fallacious conclusions based on anecdotes and leaps of the imagination. Goring further suggested that Lombroso did not arrive at his findings by "disinterested investigations." Goring challenged Lombroso's statistical methods and sampling techniques. He stated that Lombroso used both clinical and historical methods in the collection of data and that Lombroso crudely correlated a host of factors, such as education and wealth, with crime without much questioning of the presence or absence of the underlying cause-and-effect relationship.

Goring was assisted in his research by prison medical officers and by the statistician Karl Pearson. He collected and organized data on 96 traits of more than 3,000 English convicts, compared to a control sample of "normal Englishmen" composed of undergraduate university students, hospital patients, and army officers (Wolfgang, 1972, p. 264). Through this research, Goring was able to refute many of the propositions and findings claimed by Lombroso.

Racism and sexism. Although there generally is a consensus among scholars that Lombroso's research was biased partially due to his failure to have a meaningful control group, there has been little attention given to his racial and sexual biases. Much of this bias has its foundation in his atavistic perspective. One might argue that anyone different from Lombroso was a physical anomalie in his eyes.

Throughout his writing, Lombroso often contradicted himself. Yet, his biases regarding ethnicity and gender clearly can be found in his works.

In addition to his often quoted statements that women are like children with low intelligence and so forth, he advocated prostitution as a means to prevent certain types of crime. This approach suggests that he viewed women as merely sex objects and as property of men to be used for their pleasure.

Lombroso's influence on criminology. Despite the preceding criticisms of Lombroso, it must be recognized that he had a positive influence on criminology. His works advanced criminological theory by replacing the emphasis on punishment as a deterrent to crime with the emphasis on discovering physical and environmental differences that determine criminal behavior. Although he was primarily concerned with determining causes of crime, he also stressed the importance of prevention and rehabilitation. His works laid the foundation for replacing the legal policy of determinate sentencing for deterrence with indeterminate sentencing with an emphasis on rehabilitating the individual. He also laid the groundwork for a scientific research method in criminology. Finally, as suggested earlier, his analysis of the relationship of wealth and education to crime contains the seeds of modern conflict theory.

Frances Alice Kellor (1873-1952)

As stated in the biographical inset on Frances Kellor (Inset 3.2), she grew up in poverty. Because she assisted her mother by delivering the laundry, Frances had contact with the rich. Mary A. and Frances E. Eddy, two sisters mentioned in the biographical inset, provided financial support, access to books and libraries, and encouragement that created in Kellor a love of intellectual pursuits. With the help of these sisters and another wealthy Coldwater woman, Celia Parker Wooley, Kellor pursued and achieved a university education. Deegan (1991) also noted that Kellor was influenced by Henry P. Collin, pastor of the First Presbyterian Church in Coldwater (p. 309). Through his influence and as a result of her experiences with poverty as a child, Kellor became concerned with social problems, which she investigated as a reporter for the *Coldwater Republican.* Her sensitivity to and interest in the problems of the poor were manifested throughout her life, especially in her research on women prisoners and her activism on behalf of the downtrodden.

Kellor's formal studies in social science began at Cornell University, where she studied with Francis Sanborn, the university's first professor in the field. Sanborn introduced Kellor to a type of social inquiry that emphasized investigation of "practical" social problems (Fitzpatrick, 1990, p. 20). Her course work in law also heightened her fascination with crime. Kellor began her studies of crime with Charles Henderson (see Chapter 5) in the Department of Sociology at the University of Chicago in 1898. During her years of graduate study, Kellor tried to contribute to the theoretical foundations and methodology of sociology in research on crime. Her enthusiasm for criminology made Henderson the natural choice to guide her studies at the

| INSET 3.2 | **Frances Alice Kellor (1873-1952)** |

Frances Kellor was born in Columbus, Ohio, on October 20, 1873, the second daughter of Daniel and Mary Sprau Kellor (Deegan, 1991, p. 209). Her early childhood was financially difficult because her father abandoned the family and her mother assumed financial responsibility for the children. The family moved to Coldwater, Michigan, where Kellor's mother worked as a laundress. Kellor washed the clothes of the wealthy, and locals remembered her "as a little girl collecting and delivering laundry in a little wagon" (Fitzpatrick, 1990, p. 17). This work allowed her to complete 2 years of high school before she had to quit. One pupil recalled, "In the classroom, Kellor failed to keep up with her classmates but was often observed 'reading a book under her desk that was far beyond our interest' " (p. 17).

Kellor was described as a fearless tomboy, adept at using both a shotgun and a revolver, roaming the countryside hunting rabbits and other fur-bearing animals to augment the family income. It was an accident with a revolver that, according to Fitzpatrick (1990), altered the course of Kellor's life (p. 18). While target practicing with some local boys, her revolver misfired and injured her hand. Mary and Frances Eddy, the local librarians, spotted her on the way to the doctor and came to her aid. After this accident, the Eddy sisters took Kellor into their home and encouraged her social and intellectual development. They also freely shared their financial resources and their love of learning and books with Kellor.

Kellor, after quitting high school, was employed as a typesetter and then a reporter for the *Coldwater Republican*, a local newspaper. During her 2 years as a reporter, she seemed to relish the local crime stories, especially those involving thefts. She also was concerned about social problems and spread the word in her newspaper columns about local efforts to help the poor.

With the help of the Eddy sisters and another wealthy Coldwater woman, Celia Parker Wooley, Kellor set her sights on college. She studied and passed the entrance examinations for Cornell Law School and earned an LL.B. degree in 1897. With the continued help of Wooley and a special scholarship awarded by the Chicago Women's Club, Kellor enrolled as a graduate student in the Department of Sociology at the University of Chicago. Here, she studied with W. I. Thomas, Albion Small, and Charles Henderson from 1898 to 1900 (Deegan, 1991, p. 210). During this period, she lived at the Hull House. Her interest in social reform, race, and crime made Henderson a logical choice as her major adviser. Although she did not complete her graduate work at the University of Chicago, she made important contributions to criminology through her research on criminal anthropology.

Kellor was a major figure in New York's intellectual life and national politics. As the research director of the Progressive Party in 1912, Kellor raised women, social science, and policy planning to new heights. Her work with Afro-American women, especially domestic workers, ultimately led to her major role in founding the National Urban League. Kellor's studies on blacks, women laborers, immigrants, criminals, arbitration, and unemployment laid the foundation for present-day analyses (Deegan, 1991, p. 209). Kellor died in New York in 1952 at 78 years of age.

—*Shaun L. Gabbidon*
Pennsylvania State University at Harrisburg

SOURCE: Excerpted from the writings of Shaun L. Gabbidon with permission.

University of Chicago. He approached sociology with an open commitment to reform and had earned a reputation as an expert on social problems (p. 58).

From 1901 to 1905, Kellor lived intermittently at the Hull House in Chicago and the Rivington Street College Settlement in New York (Deegan, 1991, p. 210). At the Hull House, she was influenced by Edith Abbott, Sophonisba Breckinridge, and Katherine Bement Davis (see Chapters 5 and 10). Their efforts to fuse social science and social reform are noteworthy in Kellor's development. Kellor also made an impact on society through her research and reform activities. During her years in Chicago, Kellor conducted a series of research studies on female criminals, southern black migrants, and unemployed women, all of which supported her growing conviction of the causal connection between environmental factors and crime (O'Connell, 1980, p. 393). In 1905, Kellor moved permanently to New York, where she actively worked for black civil rights, especially black women's rights. Her efforts also resulted in legislation that remedied the most outrageous violations of workers' rights. During the Progressive party era, she influenced Theodore Roosevelt and was influenced by him. In fact, she chaired the Progressive Party's National Service in 1912 and actively campaigned for women's suffrage in that position. Under her leadership, Edith Abbott, Jane Addams, Emily Green Balch, and Mary McDowell worked on various committees for legislation, immigration, and suffrage (Deegan, 1991, p. 211). Following this, she worked on the Committee for Immigrants in America. Her major role from 1926 until her death in 1952 was as the vice president and chief administrator of the American Arbitration Association. This group worked to settle industrial disputes and organized for workers' rights throughout the world (p. 211).

Kellor's Critique of Previous Research

While a graduate student at the University of Chicago, Kellor published a series of articles discussing the state of contemporary research and presenting her own research on women criminals. In two of these articles (Kellor, 1900a, pp. 301-302; 1900d, pp. 528-529), she criticized many of her contemporaries. Kellor (1900a) chided Italian investigators for "neglecting the environment and such influences as training and associates" and the French for paying "too little heed to individual physical defects and inefficiencies" (p. 302). Both neglected physiological psychology and the functioning of the individual by means of his or her senses in response to stimuli. In her evaluation of criminal sociology being developed in the United States and in some European countries, she suggested that it

> means not only a study of criminals within prison walls—of their anatomy, craniums, and physiognomy—but [also] includes an investigation of the criminal's haunts, of his habits, amusements, [and] associates. Neither the psychology nor environmental forces are neglected. . . . The study of the life of the criminal in the community is more essential and yields richer results than the study within prison walls. Besides this knowledge, there must be possessed more adequate information of the so-called normal classes and the manner of their functioning in response to external stimuli— namely social forces. The criminal cannot, as has so often been done, be compared

with the ideal individual but [rather must be compared] with the one whose adjustment to society is better than his own. (Kellor, 1900a, p. 301)

Kellor (1900a) was much more critical of Lombroso, who, by emphasizing the anatomical and atavistic side, confined his observations to the structure of the criminal and neglected the psychological and environmental aspects (p. 302). She (1990b, p. 529) argued that Lombroso's conclusions about heredity and atavism were based on historic documents of 1492 and that his generalizations about criminals based on a few cases tended to mislead (Kellor, 1990d, p. 529). Kellor (1990a) further contended that Lombroso's works, which were largely confined to structural peculiarities, often were identified with race and must apply only to the race studied and not to the whole criminal class. Because of these methodological problems, Lombroso's "descriptions of typical murderers and of criminal expressions, such as heavy jaws and receding foreheads, cannot be duplicated into a general rule" (p. 305).

Kellor's Research on Women Criminals

In her own research on women offenders, Kellor (1900a) expanded her investigation to include anthropometrical, psychological, and sociological dimensions (p. 305). To study the individual (micro-level analysis) physical and psychological characteristics, she used measurements and observations. To examine the sociological dimensions, she used a more macro-level analysis by looking at the collective. This method consisted of questions, records, home visitations, inquiries of associates and officials, and observations of criminals in groups.

In 1899, Kellor began collecting data from five correctional institutions in Illinois, Ohio, and New York. In 1901, she extended her research to black criminals in the eight southern states of Mississippi, Louisiana, Alabama, Georgia, Florida, South Carolina, North Carolina, and Virginia as well as to black students in Tuskegee (Kellor, 1901a, p. 62).[2] The participants at these institutions were selected from among those who could read and write. Although only 10 were taken in each institution from populations of nearly 100, it was not always possible to secure literate participants. When illiterate ones were tested, the necessary recording was done by the experimenter (Kellor, 1901e, p. 510).

Data From Official Records

Types of offenses. Kellor (1900d) first considered the offenses of the women. She found that felonies are the crimes of those found in the penitentiaries, whereas misdemeanors are the crimes of those found in the workhouses (p. 516). She asserted that environmental conditions influence the nature of crimes.

In the workhouses, the crimes of women are not radically different from those of men. At Blackwell's Island, New York, out of 1,451 prisoners recorded, 948 were incarcerated for being disorderly, 369 for intoxication, 122 for vagrancy, 12 for petit larceny, and 3 for keeping a disorderly house. . . . Of 88 women in the penitentiaries, 19 were imprisoned for robbery, 28 for larceny, 17 for murder, 6 for manslaughter, 11 for burglary, 1 for receiving stolen goods, 2 for keeping girls, 2 for forgery, 1 for assault, and 1 for conspiracy. (pp. 516-517)

Kellor further proposed that the crimes of blacks are not different from those of whites, but their manners of commission vary. Blacks' crimes are simpler in execution. They more often are the result of uncontrolled impulse as opposed to deliberate planning and patience in execution (Kellor, 1901g, p. 525).

Education. Kellor indicated that the methods for ascertaining the degree of education are such that the facts gleaned from prison records are untrustworthy. Through her own tests, she was able to make some judgments regarding the educations of inmates. For example, Kellor (1900b) declared that her results suggest that the workhouse inmates in the North possessed more defective educations than did the penitentiary inmates in the North. She noticed that attention spans were limited and that few letters were written in proportion to the number incarcerated. She also examined the spelling, structure, and efficiency in writing and found few indications that the women were educated (p. 518).

Among the black inmates in southern institutions, Kellor (1901f) reported that "one-third of them had never read anything, and only 1 could describe a magazine clearly" (p. 306). She found that 37 stated that they had read the Bible, 22 had read novels, and 27 never had read a book. Kellor observed, however, that the range of available reading was so limited that little preference could be expressed. Furthermore, she found that there were no opportunities for obtaining reading matter in the prisons or in the county districts and only limited ones in the cities. Kellor (1901g) also noted, "It was impossible to secure the letters written to relatives and friends by the blacks for the purpose of comparison with those of the whites, for the former are seldom furnished materials, and in only a few instances can they write" (p. 524).

Marital status and occupation. Kellor (1900b) noted, "The ratio between married and unmarried is not so important as the fact that so many married women become inmates," which she attributed to "domestic troubles and . . . the struggle for existence" (p. 519). Almost without exception, the women in the northern prisons claimed occupations, showing that they were to a great extent dependent on their own efforts for subsistence. A high proportion of these women were domestics, housekeepers, laundresses, or cooks. These women also came from the lowest classes and from foreign origin. Kellor's (1901f) findings among the black prisoners in the South were similar, but these women also were found in occupations such as field hands, servants, and dressmakers (p. 307). She noted that the wage rate for black women was lower than that for whites and that on many plantations no regular wage was paid.

The records also showed that quite a number of these women had left home at early ages for various reasons including "too strict at home," "wanted to earn money for myself," "for excitement," "had to work," "ran away to marry," "hated school," and "too much church." Overall, these women appeared to be similar to women in today's prisons—low educational and professional skills, from the lower levels of society, and without strong family ties or support.

Psychological Tests

Kellor's studies in criminal sociology involved the application of psychological methods to sociology and sought to shed light on the influence of heredity and environment in producing crime.

Measurements. For these psychological tests, Kellor used the kymograph, a complicated instrument used for ascertaining emotional conditions. With reference to the kymograph, Pollock (1978) stated, "Evidently, it was a forerunner of the lie detector since it measured changes in a subject's respiration in reaction to stimuli" (p. 34). Kellor (1900c) described the kymograph as an instrument that forced air inhaled or exhaled up or down rubber tubing, which was attached to a pointer that drew corresponding lines/curves on smoked paper and showed any changes that occurred. The curves marked normal were secured first. This registration was taken without interruption, and the woman was told to keep her mind on subjects that were not markedly pleasant or unpleasant and to avoid thinking about her breathing (p. 1757).

The kymograph was set up in a quiet room, and the woman was seated with her back to the instrument so she could not see the registration. Every effort was made to prevent unintentional interruptions and to shut out any external suggestions or stimuli (Kellor, 1900c, p. 1757). Any emotion that was strongly felt influenced the rate and amplitude of breathing and also affected the circulation, all of which were recorded on the smoked paper by the kymograph (p. 1756).

The psychological tests included measurements of the five physical senses, of the mental faculties, of reactions and coordination, and of the emotions. Kellor (1900d) devised tests for the following emotions: surprise, pain, anger, hatred, love, vanity, sense of smell, joy, interest, modesty, reading aloud, and tickling. She also devised psychological tests for memory and color preferences (pp. 532-533).

Results. Anthropometric measures conducted by Kellor showed few significant differences between criminal women and college women. There were some differences between whites and blacks.[3] For example, the nasal index showed that blacks had much broader noses than did whites. In some instances, among the blacks, the width of their noses actually exceeded the length. The measurements of their mouths showed a similar divergence. In length, the differences were not so great. In thickness of lips, the differences were more evident (Kellor, 1901e, p. 513). The importance of these differences for determining crime were minimized by Kellor.

With regard to masculinity of the women's voices and features, on which emphases had been placed by other investigators, Kellor found only negative results. In comparing criminal women in the North and South to women of the same social and economic grades who were not criminal (i.e., students), she found no support for significant physical differences. Kellor (1901e) concluded,

> The faces of women from these classes, criminal or normal, are often harsh and uncultured; the voices are loud and frequently coarse, but they do not possess the peculiar quality of masculinity, which is not a synonym for harshness, coarseness, etc. The garb worn in prisons has a tendency to bring out the harshness rather than the softness of a personality, and this is often not taken into account in comparisons. (p. 514)

According to Kellor, there were few exceptions to the rule that in nutrition and physical strength, the black criminals surpassed the white criminals. Kellor explained the superior development of the strength of the hand grasps among the black women as "due to the nature of the labor both outside and within the prison" (p. 514). She also found anomalies in the imprints of the hands of blacks. She attributed all of this to the excessive farm labor of black women.

Kellor also explained many of the differences she observed between the criminal sample in the North and a group of northern college students as the result of situational factors associated with the environment. For example, the differences between northern delinquents and northern students were substantial in the tests for taste and smell. Kellor (1900d) noted,

> Instead of proving one of the current theories, that the criminal is allied to the savage and is more dependent upon physical senses than upon his intellect and thus has these more acutely developed, I found them to disprove it. In taste, the delinquents were only about two-thirds as accurate as the students, [and] in smell only about one-half. (p. 536)

Kellor explained her findings by suggesting that the eating of snuff by the delinquents, as well as excessive use of alcohol and tobacco, destroyed a fine sensibility to taste. Also, the coarse and strong foods used must have tended to render fine discriminations impossible, and bad sanitary conditions and unsavory odors in the districts from which most of the delinquents came must have affected the sense of smell (p. 536).

In tests of hearing and vision, differences were found between delinquents and students in both strength and acuteness. This might be due in part to the fact that the delinquents were older than the students. However, the physician at the reform school stated that among the girls received there, approximately two thirds had defective vision. The tests for pain revealed that whereas criminals had an extreme fear of pain, they endured it without complaint when it actually was applied (Kellor, 1900d, p. 538). For all of these differences, Kellor looked to the environment of the criminal to explain the results instead of the atavistic explanations proposed by Lombroso.

Abuses in Southern Penal Systems

Kellor (1901a) further noted that whereas the North had adopted the reformatory idea, the South still was in the age of revenge and punishment. The southern emphasis on corporal punishment and labor "attest[s] a stronger belief in heredity than does a more humane system, with more moral and mental instruction" (p. 61). Kellor (1901d) argued that the predominance of blacks in the southern prisons might be explained by inconsistencies in penalties for the same offenses. She quoted a southern officer as saying,

> If two white men quarrel and one *murders* the other, we imprison the culprit and in due season pardon him; if a white man *kills* a negro, we let him off; if a negro murders a white man, we like as not lynch him; if a negro kills a negro, we imprison him. (p. 420)

Kellor further indicated that within the previous 6 years, nearly 900 persons (including 5 women) had been lynched in the South for crimes such as rioting, incendiarism, robbery, stock poisoning, and barn stealing. Kellor (1901c) also declared,

> The pardoning power of the executives in the South is not equally applied. Data are exceedingly difficult to procure; but the last reports of Virginia and Louisiana show . . . [that] there [were] 29 pardons granted in a population of 132 white men and 17 to a population of 843 negroes. There are few or no white women in the penitentiaries. . . . In the course of inquiry, it appeared that convicted white women are pardoned as the accommodations, food, labor, and prison conditions generally are deemed unfit for them. (p. 312)

Kellor (1901d) also observed, "The criminal is first a negro and then a woman—in the whites' estimation. Their sympathy may be aroused, as when the woman is a mother, but rarely their chivalry" (p. 421).

Southern Conditions That Influence Black Criminality

Kellor was, indeed, a champion for the rights of blacks. She placed a strong emphasis on the prevention of crime through improved domestic life and training for the child. Kellor (1901b) argued,

> There is no race outside of barbarism where there is so low a grade of domestic life, and where the child receives so little training, as among the negroes. In slavery, the negro knew no domestic life. The continuance of family life depended upon the will of the master. (p. 190) . . .
> One of the primary needs of the South is enlightenment and ideals in domestic life, together with such knowledge as will secure training and discipline for the child. In the absence of other agencies, free public kindergartens are desirable for both mothers and children. Kindergartens will assist in supplying this need because the children are particularly deficient in the sense of responsibility. (p. 192)

Although Kellor was a strong advocate for blacks and a champion of their cause, she also was critical of their morals and their religion. In fact, some of her statements tended to sound racist. Kellor (1901b) continued her discussion of the needs of the child:

The training needed is one that will put the child in conscious control of himself. That the system of education is not accomplishing this is shown by the fact that negro teachers and ministers are frequently the most immoral of their race. This is true because the educational system gives so much knowledge of facts, while the moral and sympathetic sensibilities, the perceptions of domestic, social, and political life, in relation to the negro himself, are neglected. (p. 194)

With reference to religion, she declared,

Their religion is characteristic of an undeveloped race. This must be so, for slavery did nothing to change it. The slave's religion was not rational. . . . There can be no question that the negroes' religion is inferior and stands in the way of progress. (p. 196)

These are strong critical (many would say biased) statements about blacks' religion. Yet, she concluded her discussion of blacks' religion and social life by stating,

Contempt for the negroes' religion must be changed to respect. The negro's strong tendency to church affiliations can be used as a great educational and cultural agency. (p. 196) . . .

It matters not to God if the soul be negro or Chinese, but it *does* matter to *us* if the race is an integral part of our domestic and national life. If we have taken them from an environment in which they were functioning successfully and placed them in the midst of our own, which they as yet barely comprehend, there is a national duty added to the Christian duty. (p. 197)

Critique of Kellor

It is difficult to provide a meaningful critique of Kellor's contributions to criminology because her works have not been acknowledged by most criminologists. As indicated earlier, Kellor was the first American and the first woman to replicate Lombroso's research and to refute many of his conclusions. Furthermore, after completing this research, she left the University of Chicago and went to New York, where she worked in various social/political positions as an advocate for the poor, for blacks, for immigrants, for workers' rights, and for women's rights. Perhaps Kellor's childhood struggles with poverty influenced her research and works. Certainly, her works as a researcher and political activist suggest that she recognized the importance of the social and economic environment on various issues related to criminology. She also made policy suggestions that she insisted would help to prevent crime and delinquency.

Kellor's life and works have been studied by a few feminist sociologists and criminologists during recent years (Deegan, 1991; Fitzpatrick, 1990; Freedman, 1981; Pollock, 1978). These resources provide a basis for examining Kellor's contributions to theory, research methods, and impact on policy.

Methods

It is clear from reading Kellor's works that her efforts to replicate Lombroso's research used some of the same methods as did Lombroso. She examined the physical characteristics using instruments similar to those used by Lombroso. She also explored psychological and sociological explanations for women's criminal activities using methods that were innovative for her time and that were not used by Lombroso. These are evaluated next.

Kymograph. In examining the psychological characteristics of the women she studied, she used a kymograph. As described earlier, this machine was able to measure emotional responses of the women to specific stimuli. Pollock (1978) stated that this was a forerunner of the modern polygraph machine. Although Kellor must be credited for forging new ground, the accuracy of her findings are questionable. Evidence obtained from the use of the polygraph currently is not admissible in the courtrooms of America.

Control groups. One of the major criticisms of Lombroso's research was his failure to include a control group of citizens outside of the prison. He drew conclusions based only on his examination of prisoners. Kellor did not make this mistake. Her research was based on four groups of women: white prisoners, white students, black prisoners, and black students. This provides more credibility to her challenge of Lombroso's findings of physical stigmata among criminals. However, it is unlikely that her sampling techniques would meet the standards required for researchers today.

Multiple variables. Much to her credit, Kellor did not limit her research to physical characteristics of the women. Her psychological categories included issues of fear, love, anger, pain, and hatred. In the sociological area, she looked at marital status, education, occupation, and race. Thus, she used environmental factors to interpret her findings of physical and psychological differences between women prisoners and women students as well as between white women and black women.

Theory

Although Kellor broke new ground in the methods she used for her research, her theory (like that of Lombroso) does not meet the social science definitions of theory by Homans (1964) and Turner (1978) (see Chapter 1). Although she refuted much of Lombroso's claims about criminals, hers is more of an interpretation of findings. Kellor did make contributions to three of the current theoretical perspectives in criminology. What follows, then, is a critique of her works in terms of positivist, conflict, and feminist criminology.

Positivists. Positivism, as introduced by Lombroso, emphasized biological characteristics as the major determinant of crime. Kellor explored the physical causes of crime but also expanded the positivists' perspective by applying psychological and sociological criteria to interpret the physical differences between criminals and her control group of students. However, Kellor is remembered most as the first American using a positivist perspective to challenge Lombroso's conclusions on physical stigmata as the primary determinant of criminal behavior.

Conflict. Whereas Kellor clearly contributed to the positivists' theoretical perspective through her research, she also laid the groundwork for conflict theory. A major part of her works involved an interpretation of differences among women based on class and race. For example, her explanation of the anomalies in the hand imprints of black women was based on class and the type of work required of blacks in the South. She also called attention to inconsistencies in the application of the southern penal system on the basis of race. Although Kellor came across as a strong advocate for the poor and for blacks, some of her comments about black morality and religion sounded a bit racist.

Feminists. Feminist scholars have been at the forefront in recognizing Kellor's scholarship in criminology. Feminists also have been her greatest critics. Specifically, Freedman (1981) criticized Kellor for her "individualistic environmentalism" (p. 115) that focused too heavily on individual behavior as explanations of criminal involvement. Deegan (1991) also noted that Kellor exhibited "a strong antagonism to black churches and religion, and [she] blamed these institutions as well as white people for many problems that beset the black community" (p. 212). Yet, Kellor deserves recognition for her progressive approach to the study of crime. For example, Kellor's gender/class/race analysis, which was central to all of her research and theoretical explanations of crime, also is the foundation for the gender/class/race analysis advocated by current feminist scholars in criminology.

Kellor's works, then, are significant in the history of criminological research for her innovative challenge to Lombroso. Her explanations of criminal behavior can be seen as forerunners of aspects of today's positivist, conflict, and feminist criminological theories. Finally, Kellor serves as an example of a scholar whose research and theory helped to implement social and criminological policies that benefited women, immigrants, blacks, and workers during the Progressive Party era in America.

Summary and Conclusions

The positivist perspective that emerged during the 19th century established the importance of applying the scientific method in determining causes of crime. Although this early effort contained many weaknesses, it advanced criminological theory by replacing the Classical School model that was based on speculations and assumptions about the nature of society and people. In contrast to Goring and Kellor, who challenged Lombroso's findings and criticized his research methods, some 20th-century scholars[4] have continued to look for physical differences between criminals/delinquents and "normal" people. The positivist emphasis on an objective scientific approach to understanding causes of crime has dominated most

20th-century theories including the functionalists, control theory, and the Chicago School. The interactionist perspective, which emerged during the 1960s, was the first major effort to challenge the positivist theorists.

Notes

1. See Tarnowsky (1908). This is the reference cited by Lombroso and Ferrero (1958) in *The Female Offender*. Other references to Tarnowsky's research can be found in Pollak (1950), Pollock (1978), and Rasche (1974). Pollock (1978) cited Tarnowsky in discussing Lombroso's research, and Rasche (1974) cited her in the works of Pollak.

2. Kellor (1901a) suggested that the criminal class in the South is largely black. More specifically, she stated, "While the penitentiaries contain black women, there are rarely white women and at most but two or three" (p. 60). She explained the large number of black women in southern prisons by addressing southern conditions and influences.

3. However, Kellor (1901e) noted, "It is almost impossible among criminals under forty [years of age], which was my age limit, to secure blacks of a pure type. There is a large admixture of Indian blood as well as of white [blood]" (p. 513).

4. For the reader who would like to pursue the biological explanations, the following are some sources that he or she might want to explore: Goddard (1914), Herrnstein and Murray (1994), Hooten (1939), Sheldon (1949), and Wilson and Herrnstein (1985).

DISCUSSION QUESTIONS

1. How did Lombroso's biographical and historical background influence his theoretical perspective?

2. What were the strengths and weaknesses of Lombroso's research/theory and of Kellor's research/theory? How did the two theories differ?

3. Assume that you are a criminologist concerned with the overcrowding of American prisons. Apply the positivist perspective in discussing today's prisons. How would the positivist approach differ from the approach of the Classical School?

4. Assume that you have been appointed as a member of a special Task Force on Crime in America. Apply the main findings/concepts of the positivist perspective (using the theories of both Lombroso and Kellor) to explain America's crime problem today. What policy recommendations can you suggest from these theories?

5. One of the major issues in America today is the overrepresentation of minorities in criminal statistics and in prison populations. How would Lombroso account for this? In what ways would Kellor differ from Lombroso in explaining this phenomenon?

6. Considering all of the issues regarding crime in the world today, what does the positivist perspective have to offer with reference to (a) explanations of criminal behavior and (b) solutions to the crime problem?

CHAPTER 4

The Functionalist Perspective

Introduction and Historical Setting

The functionalist perspective emerged during the 19th century and has continued through the 21st century, although its popularity among criminologists has diminished somewhat. Whereas it built on the 19th-century positivists' scientific approach to the study of crime and criminals, it also emphasized the organic positivist approach of sociologists Auguste Comte and Herbert Spencer. That is, society was conceived as an organic whole, and the unit of sociological analysis is society (Martindale, 1960, pp. 62-63).

There are a variety of reasons for this emphasis on society. In part, it was a reaction against Cesare Lombroso's emphasis on the "born criminal" that stressed the innate physical characteristics of the individual as a cause of crime. Furthermore, sociology was trying to establish itself as a discipline separate from psychology that also studied the individual. Finally, the industrial and political revolutions in Europe and America had created a chaotic society that was perceived by functionalists as in a state of crisis.

The industrial revolution changed society from a rural and primarily agrarian society to a more urban and specialized society. During this process, the basic institutions of society (e.g., family, economic, religious, political) were disrupted. In an agrarian society, every member of the family was part of the production of the family subsistence. The family also was the major source of educational and religious instruction. As technology advanced and farmers began to produce a surplus, workers were released to pursue other professions (e.g., medical, legal, educational) or to enter military or political careers. The industrial revolution reduced the importance of the family unit as workers (mostly male) left their family farms to work in factories and other professions for wages. The functionalist theory of the 19th century was an effort to create an orderly and harmonious society out of this chaos.

Assumptions About People and Society

The functionalists used primarily a macro level of analysis with an emphasis on the structure of society. The 19th-century functionalist perspective was an effort to create an orderly and harmonious environment by establishing equilibrium in a society whose institutions had been disrupted and thrown out of balance by the changes resulting from the industrial revolution. Because of rapid changes, society was fluid and institutions no longer were integrated. There no longer was a consensus among individuals regarding the function of each of the institutions and the role of individuals within society. The theoretical model for a functional society, therefore, required a society in equilibrium. To have this equilibrium, there had to be integration and consensus, which would result in a stable society.

Once this stability had been achieved, the theoretical goal was to maintain this stability. Thus, the 20th-century functionalist emphasis was a conservative effort to maintain the status quo. Within this perspective, people were viewed as passive agents with social phenomena imposed on them by society, for example, Merton's argument that everyone was to strive for economic goals within a structure that did not provide equal opportunities for everyone to attain the goals. Similarly, Cloward and Ohlin (1960) contended that differential opportunities in neighborhoods resulted in three types of delinquent subcultures in the slums. The functionalist analysis is both objective overt and subjective covert. Émile Durkheim's solidarity and anomie, Robert K. Merton's goals and means, Ruth Shonle Cavan's overconformity, and Albert K. Cohen's reaction formation are subjective covert phenomena. Whereas the malicious feelings of Cohen's boys are subjective covert phenomena, the stealing of baskets of grapes and the breaking of milk bottles and other dirty tricks, as well as the suicides studied by Durkheim, are objective overt phenomena.

Émile Durkheim (1858-1917)

Émile Durkheim was a distinguished French sociologist who received the first doctor's degree in sociology in France and also taught the first sociology class in his country (see biographical Inset 4.1 on Durkheim for details). He also was the first sociologist to whom the term "functionalist" was applied. His importance to criminological theory stems from three of his major publications in which he discussed crime and deviance.

Crime as Social Fact

In *The Rules of Sociological Method,* Durkheim (1938) began the effort to separate sociology from psychology through the study of social facts. He stressed that social facts are objective phenomena to be treated as things external to the individual. Durkheim saw social facts as "a category of facts . . . that consists of ways of acting,

INSET 4.1

Émile Durkheim (1858-1917)

Émile Durkheim was born April 15, 1858, in Epinal, a small French town on the German border. Jews who lived in this eastern French province belonged to the Ashkenazi branch of Judaism. The Ashkenazi of Alsace and Lorraine had begun drifting into the region from Germany during the 16th century. They spoke almost exclusively Yiddish and Hebrew and were almost totally ignorant of French. Because Durkheim was the son of a rabbi and descended from a long line of Jewish rabbis, he decided early that he would become a rabbi himself. He studied Hebrew, the Old Testament, and the Talmud while at the same time following the regular course of instruction in secular schools.

Two significant events in his life changed the direction of the rest of Durkheim's life. The first was the fact that his native city was invaded and occupied by a German army on October 12, 1870, when he was 12 years old. Thus, at an early age, Durkheim came to experience the ravages of war in his own city. The second event occurred shortly after his traditional Jewish confirmation at 13 years of age. The influence of a Catholic woman teacher led to a short-lived mystical experience and an interest in Catholicism. Afterward, he turned away from all religious involvement and became an agnostic.

Coser (1977) indicated that Durkheim was a brilliant student who was awarded a variety of honors and prizes during his early education in the college of his native city (p. 143). Durkheim then transferred to one of the great French high schools, the Lycée Louis-le-Grand in Paris. After two unsuccessful attempts to pass the rigorous entrance examinations for the prestigious Ecole Normale Superieure, the traditional training ground for the intellectual elite of France, Durkheim finally was admitted in 1879.

After completing his formal education in 1882 at 24 years of age, Durkheim became a professor of philosophy at various academic institutions in France for several years. He then spent a year in Germany, where he studied social science under the famed experimental psychologist Wilhelm Wundt. In 1887, he taught the first French university course in sociology at the University of Bordeaux. In 1892, Durkheim received the first doctor's degree in sociology from the University of Paris. Ten years later, he returned to a teaching position at the University of Paris, where he dominated sociology until his death in 1917.

Three of Durkheim's major publications have significance for criminological theory. *The Division of Labor in Society* (Durkheim, 1933), his doctoral dissertation, was originally published in 1893. It was followed by *The Rules of Sociological Method* (Durkheim, 1938), originally published in 1895, and *Suicide* (Durkheim, 1951), orginally published in 1897. With these three major works, Durkheim moved into the forefront of the academic world, especially in France. In addition, he founded the important French sociological journal, *L'Annee Sociologique*, in 1898.

Lunden (1958) noted that Durkheim's intellectual heritage included Auguste Comte, the founder of organic positivism who died 1 year before Durkheim was born (pp. 3-4). Other influences in Durkheim's academic life were the French scholars Gustav Le Bon and Gabriel Tarde. Other contemporary scholars of Durkheim included the founder of the Italian School of Penology, Cesare Lombroso, and the German scholars George Simmel and Ferdinand Tonnies.

thinking, and feeling, external to the individual and endowed with a power of coercion, by reason of which they control him" (p. 13). Thus, social facts are imposed on the passive agent.

After stressing the importance of the study of social facts as a product of human activity and as things external to the individual to be defined and studied, Durkheim (1938, p. 17) moved on to crime. He argued that crime was defined in terms of punishment. That is, "punishment is not the essence of crime, but it does constitute a symptom thereof, and consequently, in order to understand crime, we must begin with punishment" (p. 42). Durkheim further stated, "An intimate bond must exist between punishment and the intrinsic attributes of these acts" (p. 43) defined as crimes.

Durkheim (1938) identified two types of social facts: normal (those that conform to given standards) and pathological (those that ought to be different) (p. 47). But as he continued to discuss social facts, he called normal "these social conditions that are most generally distributed" (p. 55). More specifically, Durkheim said that crime is normal because "crime is present not only in the majority of societies of one particular species but in all societies of all types. There is no society that is not confronted with the problem of criminality" (p. 65). What is normal simply is the existence of criminality. Furthermore, "crime is normal because a society exempt from it is utterly impossible" (p. 67) and "there is no society where the rule does not exist that the punishment must be proportional to the offense" (p. 73).

According to Durkheim (1938), "crime is, then, necessary; it is bound up with the fundamental conditions of all social life, and by that very fact it is useful because these conditions of which it is a part are themselves indispensable to the normal evolution of morality and law" (p. 70). Crime implies not only that the way remains open to necessary changes but also that in certain cases it directly prepares these changes. In fact, Durkheim suggested that crime often is an anticipation of future morality—a step toward what will be. He used the Greek philosopher Socrates as an example of this.

> According to Athenian law, Socrates was a criminal, and his condemnation was no more than just. However, his crime, namely, the independence of his thought, rendered a service not only to humanity but [also] to his country. It served to prepare a new morality and faith which the Athenians needed since the traditions by which they had lived until then were no longer in harmony with the current conditions of life. (p. 71)

Thus, Durkheim argued that Socrates' crime was useful as a prelude to reforms that became necessary on a daily basis.[1] Crime, then, is functional.

In the closing pages of *The Rules of Sociological Method*, Durkheim (1938) introduced a classification of societies based on their size and the degree of concentration of the group—dynamic density. His mechanical society and organic society in *The Division of Labor in Society* (Durkheim, 1933) were patterned on this classification.

Crime, Solidarity, and the Division of Labor

An understanding of Durkheim's personal life history, as explained in the biographical inset on Durkheim (Inset 4.1), and a knowledge of the chaotic society in which he lived are crucial in understanding the theoretical model that Durkheim developed. His goal was to create a mental construct or theoretical model that would restore order and harmony to this rapidly changing world. Using a macro level of analysis, Durkheim sought to explain how two different types of societies could attain solidarity. As a functionalist, he was concerned with establishing a society that was in equilibrium and with determining to what degree the solidarity that is produced contributes to the general integration of society (Durkheim, 1933, p. 64).

Mechanical solidarity. The mechanical society[2] that Durkheim described was patterned very much after the isolated Jewish community of his childhood. This was a small homogeneous society based on the family and the sacred/religion. The source of solidarity in this society was the collective conscience, which Durkheim (1933) defined as "the totality of beliefs and sentiment common to average citizens of the same society" (p. 79). This "totality of likenesses" (p. 81) is what encloses the individual more tightly into the society and establishes solidarity in the mechanical society.

Durkheim (1933) asserted that the collective conscience is the source of solidarity but that law produces solidarity (p. 69). It is the collective conscience that creates crime and leads to the necessity for law to produce solidarity.

> An act is criminal when it offends strong and defined states of the collective conscience. (p. 80) . . .
>
> The collective sentiments to which crime corresponds must, therefore, . . . have a certain average intensity. Not only are they engraven in all consciences, but they are strongly engraven. (p. 77) . . .
>
> In other words, we must not say that an action shocks the common conscience because it is criminal but rather that it is criminal because it shocks the common conscience. (p. 81)

When the crime occurs, it violates the collective conscience and disturbs the integration, consensus, and equilibrium of the society. It is necessary for the law to produce solidarity again. In the mechanical society, it is the repressive law that produces the solidarity through penal sanctions (Durkheim, 1933, p. 69). Durkheim (1933) argued that crime brings together upright consciences and concentrates them (pp. 102-103). That is, the crime/criminal must be expiated so that consensus—the totality of likeness (the collective conscience)—can function to put society back into equilibrium. He further stated that repressive law provides the punishment for society to avenge and defend itself (p. 86). The pain that repressive law inflicts no longer is anything but a methodical means of protection. At this point, Durkheim seemed to be saying that society must control the individual through punishment "so that the fear of punishment may paralyze those who contemplate evil" (p. 86).

Organic solidarity. The organic society as presented by Durkheim (1933) was the result of a slow evolutionary change brought about by the industrial revolution. He assumed that as the organic society progressed forward, the mechanical society would regress (p. 137). The organic society, as a result of the technical advances, was described by Durkheim as a large heterogeneous society with occupational specialization and an emphasis on the secular. Durkheim further stated that "great political societies can maintain themselves in equilibrium only thanks to the specialization of tasks [and] that the division of labor is the source, if not unique [then] at least principal, of social solidarity" (p. 62). Again, Durkheim stated,

> Social harmony comes essentially from the division of labor. It is characterized by co-operation which is automatically produced through the pursuit by each individual of his own interests. It suffices that each individual consecrate himself to a special function in order, by the force of events, to make himself solidary with others. (p. 200)

Durkheim summarized the solidarity produced by the division of labor as follows:

> We may say that the division of labor produces solidarity only if it is spontaneous and in proportion as it is simply the absence of all express violence but also of everything that can even indirectly shackle the free unfolding of the social force that each carries in himself. It supposes not only that individuals are not relegated to determinate functions by force but also that no obstacle, of whatever nature, prevents them from occupying the place in the social framework which is compatible with their faculties. In short, labor is divided spontaneously only if society is constituted in such a way that social inequalities exactly express natural inequalities. (p. 377)

Thus, Durkheim argued that equilibrium and solidarity are experienced through the division of labor because there is a continuous sentiment of mutual dependence. This occurs so long as there is spontaneity in the division of labor. However, Durkheim introduced the concept of anomie (i.e., lack of regulation) by stating, "If the division of labor does not produce solidarity in all these cases, it is because the relations of the organs are not regulated, [that is,] because they are in a state of *anomy*" (p. 368).

When there is force and coercion within the division of labor and anomie occurs, there is no solidarity in society. It is not in equilibrium. Then, law must be used to produce solidarity. In the organic society, Durkheim (1933) envisioned that the penal sanctions of repressive law have been replaced with restitutive law (pp. 142, 156). Restitutive law is separated from repressive law. Instead of penal sanctions, the purpose of restitutive law is the "return of things to [the] normal state" (p. 69). Restitutive law, according to Durkheim, includes civil law, commercial law, procedural law, administrative law, and constitutional law. These laws result in the "reestablishment of troubled relations to their normal state" (p. 69). Thus, equilibrium and solidarity are produced by restitutive law in the organic society.

The characteristics of Durkheim's mechanical and organic societies are summarized in the following table:

Characteristics of Mechanical and Organic Societies

Mechanical Society	Organic Society
Small population	Large population
Homogeneous	Heterogeneous
Family	Occupational specialization
Sacred/religion	Secular
Source of solidarity: Collective conscience	Source of solidarity: Division of labor
Crime	Anomie
Repressive law produces solidarity	Restitutive law produces solidarity

After developing his theory of solidarity in *The Division of Labor*, Durkheim (1951) tested his theory by studying the relationship between suicide and an individual's integration into society.

Suicide

In *The Division of Labor* (Durkheim, 1933), the pathological aspects of society were underplayed and a near unending faith that organic solidarity will ensure societal stability was affirmed. In *Suicide*, however, Durkheim (1951) gave a far more pessimistic picture of society: Anomie in general and chronic anomie in particular are ever-present forces that threaten the stability of society (Cullen, 1984, p. 61).

In *The Rules of Sociological Method*, Durkheim (1938) asserted that the sociologist must define the social facts that are studied. Thus, in defining suicide, Durkheim (1951) stated, "The term suicide is applied to all cases of death resulting directly or indirectly from a positive or negative act of the victim himself which he knows will produce this result" (p. 44). He hypothesized that suicide rates will vary with the degree of the individual's integration into society and the extent of society's regulation of the individual.[3]

In *Suicide*, Durkheim (1951) repeated what he had advocated in *The Rules of Sociological Method*—"that social facts must be studied as things, that is, as realities external to the individual" (p. 37). The early chapters of *Suicide* are devoted to the negation of doctrines that ascribe suicide to extra-social factors such as mental alienation, the characteristics of race as studied by anthropology, heredity, climate, temperatures, and a negation of the doctrine of "imitation" (p. 13). Suicide, then, must necessarily depend on social causes and be in itself a collective phenomenon.

Durkheim used official records of suicide in Western Europe during the 19th century to study suicide. He examined the individual's integration and the extent of society's regulation of the individual by using four major variables: religion, family, sex, and age.

Durkheim (1951) found that Protestants have a higher suicide rate than do Catholics and Jews. He explained this essential difference between Catholics and Protestants as the result of the free inquiry permitted of Protestants (p. 157). That is, Protestantism concedes a greater freedom to individual thought, whereas Catholicism provides a more unified and strongly integrated society. He also explained low suicide rates for Jews as deriving from the solidarity produced by hostilities of Christian religions. In sum, Durkheim stated that religion provides Jews and Catholics with solidarity and regulation that prevents suicide. With reference to the family, Durkheim (1951) reported that married people of both sexes have lower suicide rates than do widowed or divorced persons. An exception to this is for married men under 16 years of age, who have a higher suicide rate than do single men. Durkheim further stated, "Divorced men have a higher suicide rate than the undivorced men, divorced women a higher rate than undivorced women but lower than divorced men" (p. 30). He further reported that widowers with children have a lower suicide rate than do husbands without children (p. 187). His finding that Catholics and married persons over 20 years of age with children have a lower suicide rate provided support for his theory that persons integrated into society have a regulation and cohesion in their lives that keeps them from committing suicide.

A typology of suicide. Based on his findings of the relationship between integration and regulation and suicide, Durkheim (1951) proposed four types of suicide.

Egoistic suicide springs from excessive individualism of persons never integrated into society through religion and marriage (p. 209).

Altruistic suicide is a result of "insufficient individuation" (p. 217). This type of suicide is more apt to be found in primitive societies and is imposed by society for social ends "because it is their duty" (pp. 219-220). The individual is so completely absorbed in the group that it leads to obligatory altruistic suicide.

In explaining *anomic* suicide, Durkheim reintroduced the term "anomie" originally used in *The Division of Labor* (Durkheim, 1933, p. 368). Those who resort to anomic suicide once were integrated into society through marriage, children, and/or religion, but abrupt transitions (e.g., divorce, physical/economic disasters) have caused a loss of regulation of life (Durkheim, 1951, p. 252). Thus, the standards according to which needs were regulated no longer can remain the same. Disturbances of the collective order lead to an increase in suicides.

The fourth type of suicide mentioned by Durkheim (1951) is *fatalistic* (p. 276). It is the suicide deriving from excessive regulation, that of persons with futures pitilessly blocked and passions violently choked by oppressive discipline. It is the suicide of very young husbands and of married women who are childless. In sum, Durkheim argued that all suicides were a result of deficient collective activity. This involves a failure of society to influence and regulate the basically individual passions.

Critique of Durkheim

Durkheim, as the first sociologist to develop a theory of crime and then test the theory empirically, demonstrated the important interrelationship between theory and research. It should be noted that the theory developed in *The Division of Labor* (Durkheim, 1933) does not meet Homans' (1964) social science definition of theory (see Chapter 1) because Durkheim did not develop a set of propositions that form a logical deductive system. Yet, he has achieved recognition for his efforts to test his theory using methods available to him at that time. It should be acknowledged, however, that Durkheim's typology of suicide is a theoretical interpretation of data similar to Hirschi's bonding theory (see Chapter 6). Also, Durkheim's emphasis on regulation and integration of individuals into society seems to have influenced current control theory.

In *The Division of Labor,* Durkheim (1933) set forth a theory that societal integration, consensus, and equilibrium are essential to the solidarity of both the mechanical society and the organic society. He further developed a set of concepts as presented in this chapter. Then, Durkheim (1938) wrote *The Rules of Sociological Method,* in which he argued for the importance of treating social facts as things external to the individual and for the importance of defining social facts. In *Suicide,* Durkheim (1951) used many of the concepts contained in *The Division of Labor* to test his theory of the importance of integration and solidarity to the individual. Finally, he not only found support for his theory of solidarity but also expanded his theory using the data from his research to create a typology of suicide. One of these types of suicide, anomie, has been used extensively by 20th-century sociologists/criminologists to study crime and deviance.

Robert K. Merton (1910-)

The concept of anomie introduced by Durkheim in the organic society and used again later as a typology of suicide was mostly ignored in American criminology until Robert Merton revived the term 40 years later in his essay on "Social Structure and Anomie" (Merton, 1938). Although Merton was a student of Talcott Parsons at Harvard University, in his own structural functionalist theory, Merton reacted against Parsons' macrofunctionalist theories, which attempted an explanation of all social phenomena within a single theoretical framework.

Anomie and the Social Structure

Merton's conceptualization of anomie and the modes of adaptation represent a unidimensional[4] effort to explain why young, urban, poor, and minority males had high "crime rates" for property offenses. Merton, like many current criminologists, seemed to erroneously accept arrest rates reported in the Federal Bureau of Investigation's Uniform Crime Reports as accurate indicators of persons who commit these offenses. In Merton's case, he might have been influenced by his own background as the son of a carpenter and truck driver in the slums of South Philadelphia and by his experiences with juvenile gangs.

As a structural functionalist, Merton perceived crime as a result of a society that was in disequilibrium. Merton, like other functionalists, used a macro level of analysis suggesting that the phenomenon of crime is imposed on the actor by the social structure, which is out of balance.

Merton (1968b) argued that anomie occurs because of a "dissociation between culturally prescribed aspirations and socially structured avenues for realizing these aspirations" (p. 188). More specifically, he indicated that anomie is created within the structure of society when there is a disjunction or disparity between the goals emphasized within the cultural structure and the institutionalized means for attaining the goals within the social structure. This pressure is the result of the disproportionate accent on goals of economic success for everyone in American society without the social structure providing equal opportunity or means for everyone to attain the goals. Merton explained this emphasis as follows:

> Thus, the culture enjoins the acceptance of three cultural axioms: First, all should strive for the same lofty goals since these are open to all; second, present seeming failure is but a way-station to ultimate success; and third, genuine failure consists only in the lessening or withdrawal of ambitions. (p. 193)

Again, Merton observed,

> Anomie is conceived as a breakdown in the cultural structure, occurring particularly when there is an acute disjunction between the cultural norms and goals and the socially structured capacities of members of the group to act in accord with them. . . . Anomie refers to the state of confusion in a group or society which is subject to conflict between value systems. (pp. 216-217)

It is clear, then, that Merton perceived anomie as occurring within the social structure. Anomie is the strain, disjuncture, or gap that occurs between the goals and means within the structure of society.

Modes of Adaptation

Once this anomie occurs within the social structure, individuals experience the strain that is imposed on them and form modes of adaptation accordingly. Merton (1968b) described five modes of adaptation and set them out schematically in a table, where a plus sign (+) signifies acceptance, a minus sign (–) signifies rejection, and a plus-or-minus sign (±) signifies rejection of prevailing values and substitution of new values (pp. 193-194). Merton's table (p. 194) is presented here:

A Typology of Modes of Individual Adaptation

Modes of Adaptation	Cultural Goals	Institutionalized Means
I. Conformity	+	+
II. Innovation	+	–
III. Ritualism	–	+
IV. Retreatism	–	–
V. Rebellion	±	±

Merton emphasized that persons may shift from one alternative to another as they engage in different spheres of social and economic activities.

I. Conformity. To the extent that a society is stable, Merton (1968b) contended that Adaptation I (conformity to both cultural goals and institutionalized means) is the most common and widely diffused. Thus, conformity is the model response in American society, according to Merton (p. 195).

II. Innovation. This response occurs when the individual has assimilated the cultural emphasis on the goal without equally internalizing the institutional norms governing ways and means for its attainment.[5] Merton (1968b) suggested that the emphasis on economic success is especially problematic in a society with a class system that confines the occupational opportunities of large groups of people while it also stigmatizes manual and unskilled labor (p. 199). Thus, the innovator rejects the values of society and substitutes the innovator's own values in an effort to attain the economic goals of society. Merton summarized the stresses that lead to innovation as follows:

> It is when a system of cultural values extols, virtually above all else, certain *common* success goals *for the population at large* while the social structure rigorously restricts or completely closes access to approved modes of reaching these goals *for a considerable part of the same population* that deviant behavior ensues on a large scale. Otherwise said, our egalitarian ideology denies by implication the existence of noncompeting individuals and groups in the pursuit of pecuniary success. Instead, the same body of success symbols is held to apply to all. (p. 200)

III. Ritualism. The ritualistic type of adaptation involves the abandoning or scaling down of the lofty cultural goals of great monetary success and rapid social mobility to the point where one's aspirations can be satisfied. "But though one rejects the cultural obligation to attempt 'to get ahead in the world,' though one draws in one's horizons, one continues to abide almost compulsively by institutional norms" (Merton, 1968b, p. 204). Thus, according to Merton (1968b), a ritualist is one who realizes that he or she never will attain the lofty goal of economic success (e.g., a new house, an expensive car) but who continues to go to work each day and go through the motions of striving for economic success. Merton indicates that lower middle class Americans are the people predominantly in the ritualist mode of adaptation.

IV. Retreatism. Merton (1968b) stated,

> Just as Adaptation I (conformity) remains the most frequent, Adaptation IV (the rejection of cultural goals and institutionalized means) is probably the least common. People who adapt (or maladapt) in this fashion are, strictly speaking, *in* society but not *of* it. (p. 207)

Merton suggested that the retreatists are the true aliens. In this category, he included psychotics, outcasts, vagrants, vagabonds, tramps, chronic drunkards, and drug addicts. These people apply escape mechanisms that allow them to escape from the requirements of the society. By rejecting both the goals and the means, "the escape is complete, the conflict [is] eliminated, and the individual is asocialized" (p. 208). This fourth mode of adaptation, according to Merton, is that of the socially disinherited. Their adaptations are largely private and isolated.

V. Rebellion. Merton (1968b) explained that this adaptation leads people outside the environing social structure to envision and seek to bring into being a greatly modified social structure (p. 209). It presupposes alienation from reigning goals and standards, which are regarded as purely arbitrary. Merton suggested, "In our society, organized movements for rebellion apparently aim to introduce a social structure in which the cultural standards of success would be sharply modified and provision would be made for a closer correspondence between merit, effort, and reward" (p. 209).

Critique of Merton

Not a theory. One of the major criticisms of Merton has been his theory's failure to meet Homans' (1964) definition of a theory. That is, Merton did not operationally define his concepts and did not present a set of propositions that form a logical deductive system. Although Merton stated clearly that the social structure produces a strain toward anomie and deviant behavior, his critics contend that his theory is not testable as presented because he did not indicate how much strain is necessary for anomie to occur. Merton (1968b), however, has suggested that theories of the middle range (see details in Chapter 1) are stepping-stones in the middle distance

> that lie between the minor but necessary working hypotheses that evolve in abundance during day-to-day research and the all-inclusive systematic efforts to develop a unified theory that will explain all the observed uniformities of social behavior, social organization, and social change. (p. 39)

Thus, Merton's anomie theory could be regarded as a theory of the middle range. The fact that there have been so many research studies using anomie supports this claim.

Feminist criticism. Feminists (e.g., Leonard, 1982; Naffine, 1987) have noted that Merton made no attempt to apply his theory to women. Leonard (1982) stated that Merton "argues vigorously that the dominant goal in American society is monetary success, and yet he has forgotten at least half of the population with this formulation" (p. 57). The goal that women traditionally have been socialized to desire, above all else, is marriage and the family. Money and financial success are simply not as vital. This was especially true during the 1930s when Merton first introduced his conceptualization of anomie. Furthermore, the Uniform Crime Reports have reported low crime rates for women. For example, only 10% of all arrests reported in the Uniform Crime Reports during the 1950s were of women. Merton's anomie theory did not take this into account.

Interactionist criticism. Other criticisms have come from labeling/interactionist theorists (e.g., Lemert, Becker [see Chapter 7]), who noted that Merton treated behavior as abrupt change. That is, the person makes an abrupt decision to move from one mode of adaptation to another. They noted that the deviant is viewed as a passive agent who is acted on. Cohen (1966) specifically criticized Merton for his atomistic and individualistic approach that puts the individual in a box and ignores the process of interaction between the deviant and representatives of society (p. 113).

Addiction and retreatist. Lindesmith and Gagnon (1964) criticized Merton's assumption that drug addicts in the retreatist mode of adaptation had failed to attain economic success through institutionalized means. These authors pointed out that persons in many occupations, such as the medical profession, have ready access to drugs and continue to perform successfully and achieve economic success because they are using drugs. Cloward and Ohlin (1960) argued that the retreatists are double failures. They have failed to attain economic success by both illegitimate and legitimate means.

Expansions/revisions of anomie. Despite all of these criticisms, Merton's construction of anomie has been extremely successful. In addition to stimulating hundreds of research projects, there have been numerous efforts to extend and/or revise his conceptualization of anomie.

Srole (1956), for example, created the concept of "anomia," a psychological term to represent the anomic state of the individual. Srole developed a five-item scale to measure a person's sense of powerlessness, meaninglessness, normlessness, isolation, and self-estrangement. Seeman (1959) developed a similar scale to measure the psychological concept of "alienation." A third example of an expansion of the concept of anomie was an effort by Dubin (1959) to revise Merton's innovation and ritualism modes of adaptation by dividing them into behavioral innovation and normative innovation as well as behavioral ritualism and normative ritualism. Dubin eventually created 14 categories but provided little justification for this expansion.

The recent works of Agnew (1985, 1992) represent an effort to develop and test a new version of Merton's anomie. Agnew (1992) argued that the influence of Merton's strain theory has diminished since the 1970s (p. 47) and that, therefore, it must be revised. Agnew contended that although strain theory can be distinguished from control theory (see Chapter 6) and from differential association theory (see Chapter 5), they all explain delinquency and crime in terms of the individual's social relationships (pp. 48-49).[6] Strain theory emphasizes negative relationships, noxious stimuli, and stressful life events such as child abuse and neglect (Agnew, 1985).[7] Agnew (1992) further suggested cognitive coping strategies to this strain (pp. 66-68) that are similar to Merton's adaptations of ritualism and retreatism. Agnew's behavioral coping strategies, such as vengeful behavior and blaming adversity on others, are related to Merton's innovation and rebellion modes of adaptation (p. 69). Emotional coping strategies, as explained by Agnew (p. 70), focus on alleviating negative emotions through physical exercise, meditation, and use of stimulant and depressant drugs.

Agnew and White[8] (1992) used a Rutgers Health and Human Development database of 1,380 New Jersey adolescents to test Agnew's general strain theory of crime and delinquency (p. 479). Agnew and White focused on negative relationships that pressured the adolescents (12, 15, and 18 years of age) into delinquency and drug use (p. 476). In this research, they controlled for social control and differential association (p. 480). They reported finding the following support for Agnew's general strain theory. The strain variables of negative life events and life hassles were reported to be the most important ones related to delinquency and/or drug use. Also significant were parental fighting and negative relations with adults (p. 485). Four social control variables—parental attachment, school attachment, grades, and time spent on homework—were found to be negatively related to delinquency (p. 487). Drug use also was negatively related to parental and school attachment as well as time spent on homework. One variable from differential association theory, peer attachment, was found to have a positive effect on delinquency/drug use. Finally, Agnew and White reported that delinquent friends "strongly condition the impact of strain on delinquency and drug use" (p. 490) and that strain is more likely to lead to delinquency—but not to drug use—when self-efficacy is low (p. 491). These authors suggested that delinquent behavior also may lead to strain. They asserted that "these data provide support for the general strain theory of delinquency" (p. 493), although many measures of strain were not available.

Messner and Rosenfeld (1997) argued that the crime problem is related to the "American Dream," which they defined as "a commitment to the goal of material success, to be pursued by everyone in society under conditions of open, individual competition" (p. 62). This exerts pressure toward crime by encouraging an anomic environment that creates an "anything goes" mentality in the pursuit of personal goals. These authors further suggested that the American Dream emphasizes a "never-ending achievement" and glorifies economic success at the expense of other values and institutions such as family and education. Whereas Messner and Rosenfeld reviewed the social learning, control, and strain perspectives in criminology as well as cultural deviance, social disorganization, and anomie, they stated, "Anomie theory comes closest . . . to providing a compelling account of the American crime problem" (p. 39). In the closing chapter, Messner and Rosenfeld turned to policy issues by examining previous strategies for crime control. They indicated that both the conservative camp's war on crime, which defines the enemies as "wicked people," and the liberal camp's war on poverty and unequal opportunities, which defines the enemies as bad social conditions (pp. 88-95), have been failures because they "reinforce the very qualities of American culture that lead to high crime rates in the first place" (p. 88). These authors contended that because criminal activity is stimulated by strong cultural pressures for monetary success combined with anomie, crime reduction would require a change in policies that would vitalize families, schools, and the political system (p. 97). Messner and Rosenfeld summarized their policy proposals as follows:

> The structural changes that could lead to significant reduction in crime are those that promote a rebalancing of social institutions. These changes would involve reducing the subordination to the economy of the family, schools, the polity, and the general system of social stratification. (p. 103) . . .
>
> More specifically, social roles such as parenting, "spousing," teaching, learning, and serving the community will have to become, as ends in themselves, meaningful alternatives to material acquisition. (p. 104) . . .
>
> In short, it seems unlikely that a social change conducive to lower levels of crime will occur in the absence of a cultural reorientation that encompasses an enhanced emphasis on the importance of mutual support and collective obligations and a decreased emphasis on individual rights, interests, and privileges. (p. 105)

These are great ideas for crime policies, but specific proposals are needed to make these changes a reality.

The most important theoretical expansions of Merton's anomie have been studies of juvenile gangs by Cohen (1955) and Cloward and Ohlin (1960). These studies often have been referred to as subcultural studies. These works are not efforts to expand Merton's concept of anomie but rather are more concerned with his assumptions regarding the socialization of Americans toward economic success and the availability of institutionalized means for attaining that success for various classes of juvenile boys.

Studies of Subcultures/Juvenile Gangs

Albert Kircidel Cohen (1918-)

Albert Cohen is most well known among criminologists for his work, *Delinquent Boys* (Cohen, 1955). In that volume, one can readily see the influence of his Harvard professors, most notably Merton, as well as the influence of Edwin Sutherland, a graduate of the Chicago School and a professor at Indiana University (see biographical inset on Cohen [Inset 4.2] for details). In *Delinquent Boys,* Cohen (1955) accepted Merton's assumption that all classes are at some point confronted with the demand to strive for economic success. He also argued that the delinquent subculture is a product of the conflict between middle class values and working class values. Sutherland's influence can be seen in Cohen's use of examples from the works of numerous Chicago School ecological studies (e.g., Shaw and McKay, 1931; Thrasher, 1927) to support his premise.

Types of delinquent activities. Cohen (1955) described the activities of the delinquent boys as *nonutilitarian, malicious,* and *negativistic* (p. 25). He noted that people usually steal things because they want them to eat or wear. This is based on the assumption that stealing is a means to an end. In the case of the delinquent boys in Cohen's work, however, he claimed that they stole for "the hell of it" out of a type of *malice* (pp. 26-27). Cohen noted that there is no accounting, in rational and utilitarian terms, for the effort expended and the danger run in stealing things that often are discarded, destroyed, or casually given away. He supported his claims by explaining that a group of boys may enter a store and steal a hat, a ball, or a light bulb. The boys then move on to another store, where they covertly exchange this article for a similar item, and the game continues indefinitely.

Cohen (1955) then pointed to other malicious types of activities that are done for enjoyment in the discomfort of others, quoting one of the boys:

> We did all kinds of dirty tricks for fun. We'd see a sign, "Please Keep the Streets Clean," but we'd tear it down and say, "We don't feel like keeping it clean." One day, we put a can of glue in the engine of a man's car. We would always tear things down. That would make us laugh and feel good, to have so many jokes. (pp. 27-28)

Other types of destructive activities include those described in the following excerpt:

> We would get some milk bottles in front of the grocery store and break them in somebody's hallway. Then we would break windows or get some garbage cans and throw them down someone's front stairs. After doing all this dirty work and running through

INSET 4.2

Albert Kircidel Cohen (1918-)

Albert Cohen was born on June 15, 1918, in Boston. He grew up in the Boston area, where he has spent much of his adult life. He was 21 years of age when he completed his undergraduate work at Harvard University in 1939. Cohen was influenced by several prominent professors at Harvard including Talcott Parsons, Pitirim Sorokin, and the young instructor Robert K. Merton. After receiving his B.A. in sociology from Harvard, Cohen left the Boston area to begin graduate training at Indiana University. Here, Cohen came under the tutelage of Edwin Sutherland, a noted pioneer in criminological theory. In the preface of his work, Delinquent Boys, Cohen (1955) stated,

To enumerate all those on whose work I have built or who, through criticism and suggestion, have influenced the conception or the writing of this book would be impossible. I must, however, acknowledge my special indebtedness to the late Edwin H. Sutherland of Indiana University and to Talcott Parsons and Robert F. Bales of Harvard University.

After earning his M.A. from Indiana University in 1942, Cohen was director of orientation at the Indiana Boys School, the Indiana state institution for juvenile delinquents. A few years later, he returned to Harvard, where he received his Ph.D. in 1951. His dissertation, Juvenile Delinquency and the Social Structure, never was published. But his classic book, Delinquent Boys, undoubtedly was "a direct byproduct of his early writing while a doctoral student" (Martin, Mutchnick, and Austin, 1990, p. 240).

Cohen had taught at Indiana University in 1947 as an instructor prior to receiving his Ph.D. from Harvard. He continued to teach there until 1965, when he returned to the New England area of his childhood to teach at the University of Connecticut at Storrs. Although he remained at that university for more than two decades, he had several visiting professorships. These were at the University of California, Berkeley (1960-1961); the University of California, at Santa Cruz (1968-1969); and the Institute of Criminology in Cambridge, England (1972-1973). He also was designated as a fellow of the Center for Advanced Study in Behavioral Sciences at Stanford University (1961-1962).

Cohen served as editor of the American Sociological Review in 1967 and was the president of the Society for the Study of Social Problems during 1970-1971. In 1987, he received a Senior Fulbright award to the Philippines, where he studied and lectured on patterns of delinquent behavior. He also was honored as a fellow by the American Society of Criminology and received its Sutherland Award in 1993.

---

alleys and yards, we'd go over to a grocery store. There, some of the boys would hide in a hallway while I would get a basket of grapes. When the man came after me, . . . the boys would jump out of their places and each grab a basket of grapes. (p. 29)

Cohen referred to these delinquent acts as "short-run hedonism," that is, delinquency for the immediate pleasure. Although Cohen seemed to be suggesting that the boys were active agents in these acts, he also indicated that the reaction formation was imposed by the society's emphasis on middle class standards.

Reaction formation. The major point of Cohen's (1955) thesis was that this was a *reaction formation* (p. 132). The delinquent acts of the boys were the antithesis of middle class standards. Working class boys were reacting against middle class standards taught to them in schools. Cohen suggested that middle class norms are a tempered version of the Protestant ethic[9] that has played such an important part in shaping American character and society.

Cohen (1955) provided a summary description of these middle class standards "primarily applicable to the male role" and argued that the "middle class home is more likely to train the child to compete successfully for status" (pp. 88-91). Among the middle class values that Cohen contended the child is taught are ambition, long-run goals and long-deferred rewards, individual responsibility and self-reliance, cultivation and possession of skills, industry and thrift, forethought and planning, manners, control of physical aggression and violence, wholesome recreation, and respect for property (pp. 88-91).

Cohen (1955) argued that the "middle class home is more likely to train the child to compete successfully for status in terms of these norms than is the working class home" (pp. 94-95). The working class boy typically does not find these middle class values in his home and neighborhood. The aspirations for jobs and income are likely to be well below what a middle class person would consider necessary for respectability.

> "Planning" and "foresight" on the part of his parents are not so likely to be evident to the working class [child] as to the middle class child. It is good to have something "laid by for a rainy day," but the pinch of the present is a more potent stimulus than the threat or promise of the future. . . . A particularly significant contrast is that between what we have called the middle class "ethic of individual responsibility" and the "ethic of reciprocity" to which the working class, particularly its "lower lower" and "underprivileged" levels, tends. The ethic of reciprocity means a readiness to turn for aid to others toward whom one stands in a particularistic, primary-group relationship; a readiness to draw, with no feeling of guilt, upon their resources; and a corresponding sense of obligation to share one's own resources with them when they happen to be less fortunately situated. (p. 96)

It is when the working class child comes into the school system, Cohen contended, that the child confronts the middle class values that emphasize order, punctuality, and time consciousness. The conflict between the middle class norms and the working class values leads to the *reaction formation* that Cohen claims is manifested in the nonutilitarian malicious behavior defined as delinquency.

Gendered delinquency. Cohen (1955) seemed to have a certain affection for what he called the "rogue male." He described the delinquent as follows:

> His conduct may be viewed not only negatively, as a device for attacking and derogating the respectable culture; positively, it may be viewed as the exploitation of modes of behavior which are traditionally symbolic of untrammeled masculinity, which are renounced by middle class culture, . . . but which are not without a certain aura of

glamor and romance. . . . The important point for our purpose is that the delinquent response, "wrong" though it may be and "disreputable," is well within the range of responses that do not threaten his identification of himself as a male. (p. 140)

Unlike many other criminological theorists, Cohen did discuss girls. His comments, however, were very brief and placed girls in very stereotypical terms:

For the adolescent girl as well as for the adult woman, relationships with the opposite sex and those personal qualities which affect the ability to establish such relationships are central in importance. Dating, popularity, pulchritude, "charm," clothes, and dancing are preoccupations so central and so obvious that it would be useless pedantry to attempt to document them. . . . It is no accident that "boys collect stamps, girls collect boys." (pp. 141-142)

Cohen derived two major conclusions:

First, the problems of adjustment which we have described at such length in earlier chapters, and to which the delinquent subculture is, so to speak, a "tailor-made" solution, are primarily problems of the male role. Second, delinquency of the kind which is institutionalized in the delinquent subculture is *positively inappropriate* as a response to the problems which do arise in the female role.

This is not to deny that delinquency exists among girls also or even that female delinquency is subcultural. It does, however, imply that female delinquency is probably motivated by quite different problems than male delinquency and that the form it takes, whether institutionalized by a subculture or not, is likely to be different. . . . The most conspicuous difference is that male delinquency, particularly the subcultural kind, is versatile, whereas female delinquency is relatively specialized. It consists overwhelmingly of sexual delinquency. (pp. 143-144)

Critique of Cohen

Overall, Cohen's theory has received minimal criticism. It is at best a theory of the middle range and does not meet the criteria established in the classical definitions of theory by Homans (1964) and Turner (1978). Cohen relied heavily on previous ethnographic studies of delinquency. He used citations from these works very effectively to support his thesis. As one would expect from the preceding discussion of Cohen's treatment of girl delinquents, feminists (e.g., Leonard, 1982; Naffine, 1987) have criticized Cohen for his gender bias.

Finally, it should be noted that in a later publication, Cohen (1966) criticized Merton's discussion of his modes of adaptation for Merton's failure to consider the process of interaction between the deviant and the representative of society. Cohen, then, challenged the works of his former professor and seemed to be moving more into the interactionist perspective of crime and delinquency (see Chapter 7).

Richard A. Cloward (1926-) and Lloyd E. Ohlin (1918-)

As colleagues at Columbia University, Richard Cloward and Lloyd Ohlin conducted research on juvenile delinquency and published *Delinquency and Opportu-*

nity (Cloward and Ohlin, 1960). In addition to this study of delinquency, both scholars have conducted research and published in other areas. For example, Cloward has published in the areas of social behavior and the functions of public welfare, and Ohlin has published in the areas of adult corrections and probation and parole.

Delinquency and Opportunity: A Theory of Delinquent Subcultures

The theory of delinquency and opportunity is a major contribution to the theory of delinquency. The theory, referred to as "bridging theory" by Williams and McShane (1988, p. 76), is an attempt to integrate Merton's anomie theory and Sutherland's differential association theory to explain the evolution of delinquent subcultures. In Cloward and Ohlin's (1960) own words,

> The concept of differential opportunity structures permits us to unite the theory of anomie, which recognizes the concept of differentials in access to legitimate means, and the "Chicago tradition," in which the concept of differentials in access to illegitimate means is implicit. (p. 151)

This merger of the two theoretical approaches extends from the authors' personal experiences. Ohlin had studied under Sutherland at Indiana University and later received his Ph.D. from the University of Chicago. Cloward had been Merton's student at Columbia University, where he completed his dissertation, *Social Control and Anomie: A Study of the Prison Community* (Martin, Mutchnick, and Austin, 1990, pp. 262-263; Merton, 1997, p. 520). The theory also builds on the works of other theorists including Shaw and McKay, Cohen, and Durkheim.

The theory assumes, as Merton did, that everyone is socialized to want the goals of economic success. However, Cloward and Ohlin (1960) criticized Merton for assuming that those who do not have the opportunity to achieve economic success through institutionalized/legitimate means are able to turn to illegitimate means to achieve economic success. Instead, they argued that there are socially structured variations in the availability of illegitimate means as well as legitimate means (p. 146). Whereas Sutherland proposed that criminal behavior is learned through the process of differential association, Cloward and Ohlin suggested that delinquent subcultures arise based on differential opportunities within neighborhoods.

Cloward and Ohlin (1960) stated the purpose of their book quite clearly in the opening paragraph:

> This book is about delinquent gangs, or subcultures, as they are typically found among adolescent males in lower class areas of large urban centers. It is devoted to an exposition of how delinquent subcultures arise, develop various law-violating ways of life, and persist or change. (p. 1)

Cloward and Ohlin then defined a delinquent subculture as "one in which certain forms of delinquent activity are essential requirements for the performance of the dominant roles supported by the subculture" (p. 7). They also stated clearly that the evolution of specific subcultures depends on the opportunities available in specific neighborhoods. In discussing the types of subcultures, they were concerned with the dominant type of activity that is prominent in a given juvenile subculture. Three types of delinquent subcultures were proposed by Cloward and Ohlin: criminal, conflict/violent, and retreatist/drug subcultures.

The criminal subculture. Cloward and Ohlin (1960) indicated that the criminal subculture is the most stable and exhibits the greatest resistance to change of the three types of subcultures. They stated that this stability is the result of "integration of youthful delinquency and adult criminality" (p. 22). Therefore, delinquent and criminal behavior is accepted as a means of achieving success goals. In this culture, prestige is allocated to those who achieve material gain and power through means defined as illegitimate by the larger society.

> The means by which a member of a criminal subculture achieves success are clearly defined for the aspirant. At a young age, he learns to admire and respect older criminals and to adopt the "right guy" as his role model. Delinquent episodes help him to acquire mastery of the techniques and orientation of the criminal world and to learn how to cooperate successfully with others in criminal enterprises.... Close and dependable ties with income-producing outlets for stolen goods, such as the wagon peddler, the junkman, and the fence, are especially useful. (p. 23)

Cloward and Ohlin suggested that there is a close bond between different age levels of offenders—youth and adult criminals—that provides the means for juveniles to participate successfully in economic gain through criminal activities (p. 171). The process described here by these authors is similar to the process of recruitment and training that Sutherland (1937) suggested in *The Professional Thief.*

The conflict/violent subculture. The conflict subculture sometimes is referred to as the violent subculture because violent behavior is the dominant activity of this type of gang. This subculture arises in neighborhoods where transiency and instability are prominent as in unintegrated slums. According to Cloward and Ohlin (1960), communities unable to develop conventional forms of social organization and legitimate modes of access to culturally valued success goals become disorganized slums populated with failures (p. 173). They continued,

> Just as the unintegrated slum cannot mobilize legitimate resources for the young, neither can it provide them with access to stable criminal careers, for illegitimate learning and opportunity structures do not develop.... This is not to say that crime is nonexistent in such areas, but what crime there is tends to be individualistic, unorganized, petty, poorly paid, and unprotected. (p. 173)

Because social controls are not present to maintain order, violent behavior is more apt to occur.

Cloward and Ohlin (1960) explained that the role model in the conflict pattern of lower class culture is the "bopper" who swaggers with his gang, fights with weapons to win a wary respect from other gangs, and compels a fearful deference from the conventional adult world by his unpredictable and destructive assaults on persons and property (p. 24). They further noted,

The immediate aim in the world of fighting gangs is to acquire a reputation for toughness and destructive violence. A "rep" assures not only respectful behavior from peers and threatened adults but also admiration for the physical strength and masculinity it symbolizes. . . . Above all things, the bopper is valued for his "heart." He does not "chicken out," even when confronted by superior force. (p. 24)

Confronted with the apparent indifference and insincerity of the adult world, the ideal bopper seeks to win by coercion the attention and opportunities that he lacks and cannot otherwise attract. Violence is the dominant activity in the conflict subculture.

The retreatist/drug subculture. The retreatist subculture sometimes is called the drug subculture and often is conceived as an isolated adaptation, characterized by a breakdown in relationships with other persons. Its members are viewed as alienated from conventional society. Cloward and Ohlin (1960) also referred to members of this subculture as "double failures" (p. 183). They further stated,

It is our contention that retreatist behavior emerges among some lower class adolescents because they have failed to find a place for themselves in criminal or conflict subcultures. Consider the case of competition for membership in conflict gangs. To the extent that conflict activity—"bopping," street-fighting, "rumbling," and the like—is tolerated, it represents an alternative means by which adolescents in many relatively disorganized urban areas acquire status. . . . If the adolescent "failure" then turns to drugs as a solution to his status dilemma, his relationships with his peers become all the more attenuated. Habitual drug use is not generally a valued activity among juvenile gangs. (p. 183)

Cloward and Ohlin (1960) pointed out that although this often is true, the drug user must become affiliated with others so as to have access to a steady supply of drugs (pp. 178-179). That is, the opportunity to gain drugs is restricted. New users must learn the lore of drug use from old users and must acquire the necessary skills to make appropriate connections.

Critique of Cloward and Ohlin

The preceding discussion provides evidence that Cloward and Ohlin were reasonably successful in bridging or integrating Merton's anomie conceptualization and Sutherland's differential association theory. The theory has been criticized in many of the same ways as have the other strain/anomie theories. That is, Cloward and Ohlin in no way attempted to include women in their theory. In fact, they stated the narrow focus of their theory more clearly than did the other theorists. As indicated, they stated explicitly that they were focusing on adolescent males in lower class areas. Thus, these authors were subject to criticism for following the criminology tradition of ignoring girls and the upper class. They also accepted Merton's assumptions that everyone is socialized toward economic success and that the Uniform Crime Reports accurately identify delinquents and criminals.

However, Cloward and Ohlin, like Merton and Cohen, have received wide recognition by criminological theorists for their theories. Lilly, Cullen, and Ball (1989) claimed that "strain theory emerged in the early 1960s as the most prominent criminological explanation" (p. 75). But Lilly and colleagues did admit that this popularity has lessened (p. 77). It is more likely that strain theory was prominent among researchers but was not the dominant perspective among criminological theorists even during the 1960s.

Finally, it must be noted that Cloward and Ohlin seem to have had an impact on criminal justice policy. The research project on delinquency mentioned earlier was supported by the Ford Foundation. Ohlin served as a consultant on juvenile delinquency to the National Institute of Mental Health and to the Ford Foundation. While working on the Ford Foundation study, Ohlin and Cloward were asked by the coalition of the Lower East Side Community Settlement House in Manhattan to help the coalition develop a "saturation of service" project for youths (Martin et al., 1990, p. 263). This suggests that Ohlin and Cloward have the distinction of being among the few criminologists to influence the policy decision-making process and that their works tied together theory, research, and policy.

The legacy of anomie/strain/subculture theory may be illustrated through the flowchart displayed in Figure 4.1.

Ruth Shonle Cavan (1896-1993)

Although Ruth Shonle Cavan's theory of delinquency does not flow from the anomie/strain tradition, her conceptualization of delinquency does fit within the functionalist perspective of criminology. As indicated in the biographical inset on Cavan in Chapter 5 (Inset 5.1), Cavan received her Ph.D. from the University of Chicago in 1926 and studied criminology and juvenile delinquency with Ernest Burgess. The diversity found in her many research and publication projects reflects her training in the Chicago School. However, in her 1960 presidential address to the Midwest Sociological Society, she stated that she was attempting to "assign misbehavior to a place in the total social structure" (Cavan, 1961, p. 244). This emphasis on the social structure stresses the importance of integration and equilibrium of society and places this particular work within the functionalist perspective.

Delinquency as a continuum of behavior. In introducing her thesis that delinquency should be placed within the total social structure, Cavan (1961) pointed out that even though we know that behavior falls on a continuum, we often think in terms of dichotomies (p. 245). These dichotomies include the sinner and the saint, the devil and the angel, the criminal and upright citizen, the delinquent and the model child. Cavan used the normal curve (Figure 4.2) to illustrate that behavior falls into a continuum from condemnable behavior (Area A), through decreasing degrees of disapproved behavior, to the Central Area D, through increasing degrees of good behavior, to near perfection in Area G (p. 245).

Area D for Cavan (1961) represented an area of flexibility or tolerance, whereas one extreme (Area A) is labeled as underconformity and the other extreme (Area G) is

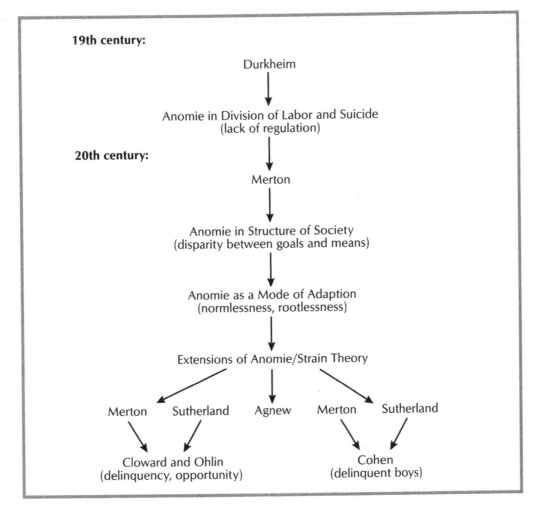

Figure 4.1. Anomie/Strain Theory

labeled as overconformity (p. 247). Although overconformity does not usually constitute delinquency or crime in the same degree as does underconformity, it must be included to provide a complete picture of the social structure. Cavan further stated that delinquency and crime are one type of deviation and that overconformity is the opposite type.

Cavan (1961) challenged other theorists who have assumed areas from D to G (to the right of the area of tolerance) as approved deviations that exceed the standard set by the group and receive public recognition for their overconformity. Instead, Cavan expressed doubt that so much admiration really is accorded the overconforming group (p. 250). She argued that the behavior and achievements that are rewarded by society are much more likely to be in Area D or E than in Area F or G. For example,

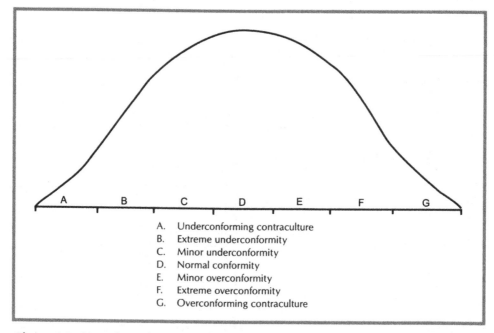

A. Underconforming contraculture
B. Extreme underconformity
C. Minor underconformity
D. Normal conformity
E. Minor overconformity
F. Extreme overconformity
G. Overconforming contraculture

Figure 4.2. Hypothetical Formulation of Behavior Continuum

Cavan pointed out that boys in Area A often are referred to as little savages, hood-lums, bums, or gangsters, whereas boys in Area G often are referred to as sissies, goody-goods, teacher's pets, drips, brains, fraidy-cats, wet blankets, or squares (p. 250). She further asserted that names such as sissy and goody-good are negative terms that indicate deviance from the accepted norms of society.

According to Cavan (1961), Areas A and G, in full development, are *contracultures*, one of which is built up around disregard for the norms, the other of which is built up around overcompliance with norms. She further stated that the contraculture has developed values and modes of behavior that are in conflict with the prevailing norms as represented in Area D (pp. 253-254). A contracultural orga-nization is not only a threat to the social norms but also an active disintegrative ele-ment in the total social structure. In the delinquent contraculture (Area A, extreme underconformity), the delinquent youth rejects the conforming groups of society. The youth's standard of measurement is the small, more restricted, less demanding standard of the delinquent contraculture. Here, the youth may be applauded for stealing, chronic truancy, or fighting.

In the overconforming contraculture, criticism, ostracism, and rejection of youths in Areas F and G also drive many of them into withdrawal into small closed groups with their own social organization and values and customs opposed to those of the central culture. Cavan (1961) provided the following examples of behavior in overconforming contracultures:

conscientious objection to war, refusal to salute the flag, rejection of medical care when ill or for ill children, refusal to have children vaccinated, refusal to send children to school for the number of years required by law, celibacy, and community ownership of property. (p. 255)

Each of these practices is an exaggeration of some value or social norm contained in the general culture. Each is socially disapproved according to the norms of Area D or is illegal.

To explain the continuum of behavior, Cavan (1961) used stealing as an example:

Pilfering of small objects was given as the modal type of behavior, falling within the area of tolerance although not rigidly conforming to the social norm of honesty. With this formulation, both the more serious forms of stealing and meticulous avoidance of taking things are deviations from the social norms and modal behavior. There is deviation in the nature of underconformity to the social norms, shown to the left on Figure [4.1] and deviation in the nature of overconformity to the social norms, shown to the right. Underconformity is an exaggeration of the tolerance allowed by the modal norms; for example, if the modal behavior permits a small amount of pilfering of candy and comic books in the corner store, the underconformer expands the tolerance to include stealing of more valuable objects. Overconformity is an exaggeration of the strict observance of formal social norms. Honesty may be exaggerated to the point where a person would not keep even a pencil that he found nor use an article belonging to someone else even in an emergency. (p. 247)

Either underconformity or overconformity that exceeds the limits of tolerance poses a threat to the operation of the social organization.

Although Cavan insisted that both conforming and nonconforming behavior may be thought of as falling into a continuum running from career-type criminal nonconforming, through conventional conformity, to ideological conformity, her 1964 article concentrated on the two extremes (Areas A and G). In this article, Cavan (1964) stated that tolerated crimes and idealized behavior are component forces in maintaining the balance of the social order (p. 236). Both extreme points on the continuum—the criminal underworld and the ideological deviators—are a threat to the social structure, although in different ways. In each case, the result is counter-rejection of conventional society by criminals or ideologists and withdrawal into a closed subsociety that is not fully responsive to legal standards. Cavan discussed organized crime as an example of the criminal underworld (Area A) and the Mormon church with its practice of polygamy as an example of the ideological underworld (Area G) (pp. 236-238). She further contrasted the key motives of the two contracultures. According to Cavan, organized criminals are motivated to exploit the conventional society, whereas the motivation for ideological deviants seems to be the desire to establish a better social order for themselves and often for the nation (p. 239).

Critique of Cavan. In sum, Cavan stated that criminologists, by concentrating only on the underconformists as delinquents, were ignoring half of the social structure and, therefore, half of the behavior. She argued for viewing delinquency as a continuum of behavior instead of as a dichotomy. Although Cavan stated that her continuum of behavior is an effort to include all behavior, her theory ignored the female half of the population. However, she did take class differences into account in defining tolerated behavior:

> Each social class or other large subcultural group has its own definition of what behavior falls into the area of tolerance, what is disapproved mildly or seriously, and what is condemned. Even when these groups share a basic culture and verbally accept the social norms, their concepts of approved and disapproved behavior may differ. (Cavan, 1961, p. 255)

Because Cavan's conceptualization of the continuum of behavior has been ignored by the vast majority of criminologists, it has not stimulated much research. A few graduate students during recent years have attempted to develop research projects for class papers using Cavan's continuum of behavior. Cavan, like the theorists discussed earlier in this chapter, has not explicitly operationally defined her concepts and has not formulated a set of propositions that form a logical deductive system. Thus, her works are more a theory of the middle range as proposed by Merton than a theory as defined by Homans (1964) and Turner (1978).

Summary

All of the theories presented in this chapter have emphasized the importance of the social structure of society and crime. Whereas Durkheim was trying to present a picture of how to take a chaotic society and create stability, each of the other theorists was concerned with crime as disturbing the stability of the status quo. All of the 20th-century theories had some gender bias, either by centering only on males (e.g., Merton, Cloward and Ohlin, Cavan) or by using stereotypical perspectives of females. However, Moyer (1996) argued that Cavan's continuum could be applied to examine issues of female crime and delinquency. The issue of class seems to dominate these theories, with Merton, Cloward and Ohlin, and Cohen seemingly assuming that most crime/delinquency occurs in the lower/working class. The Chicago School, discussed in Chapter 5, is more diverse in perspective and methodologies.

Notes

1. More recent examples of change through crime/deviance would include Susan B. Anthony, who was jailed for the crime of voting; Martin Luther King, Jr., who frequently was jailed during the civil rights protests of the 1960s; and Ida B. Wells, who led the anti-lynching protests at the turn of the 20th century.

2. Durkheim's mechanical society and organic society are very similar to the German sociologist Tonnies' (1957) Gemeinschaft and Gessellschaft.

3. Here, we see the early seeds of control theory (discussed in Chapter 6).

4. Merton's works are unidimensional in the sense that they concentrate on a select group of offenders (young, urban, poor, and minority males) while ignoring older, rural, and suburban women and most persons from the upper and middle classes.

5. Dubin (1959) correctly pointed out that the innovator would more accurately be presented with a minus sign (–) and a plus sign (+), indicating the rejection of prevailing values and the substitution of new values, instead of the simple minus sign (–) that Merton suggested (p. 150).

6. In accepting the American Society of Criminology's Sutherland Award, Merton (1997) himself stated, "I regard Sutherland's evolving idea of differential association and my evolving idea of anomie-and-opportunity structures as definite complementarities" (p. 518).

7. Agnew (1992) developed a typology of strain and its relationship to crime and delinquency (pp. 52-59).

8. The reader interested in more details of Agnew and White's research should see their 1992 article.

9. The concept of the "Protestant ethic" was introduced by the 19th-century German sociologist Max Weber. Weber (1958) created the term in explaining the emphasis on the work ethic—work for the sake of work, which Cohen was saying dominated the middle class value system. Weber suggested that the origin of the Protestant ethic was Calvinism, which stressed predestination. That is, God had selected a few people to be saved. If a person was not among those chosen few, then there was nothing he or she could do to achieve salvation. Weber suggested that people looked to material goods as an indication that God was blessing them and that they were predestined to be saved, hence the emphasis on hard work, thrift, saving, and the accumulation of wealth.

DISCUSSION QUESTIONS

1. How did Durkheim's personal background and the historical setting serve to bias/form his theory?

2. Durkheim stated that "social facts must be studied as things." What are the research issues involved in doing this?

3. Trace the development and influence of Durkheim's and Merton's anomie concept on criminological theory beginning during the 1960s. Support your answer.

4. Explain where you would place your juvenile behavior on Cavan's continuum of behavior, and indicate why you place your behavior where you do.

5. Why does Cavan's study of delinquency fall under the functionalist perspective? Are there ways in which it does not?

6. Which of the theories included in this chapter would best explain female delinquency? Justify your answer.

7. How is Cloward and Ohlin's theory like Cohen's theory? How is it different?

8. If you were asked to provide a report to the president of the United States on the causes of white collar crime, what specific theory in this chapter would be the basis? Keep in mind that the president does not know criminological theory, so you need to explain the theory to the president and why you have selected it. Which theory would you be least likely to select? Why?

CHAPTER 5

The Chicago School

Bulmer (1984) stated that the University of Chicago, which was established as a new foundation in 1892,[1] "has exercised a quite disproportionate influence upon the course of empirical social science" (p. xiii). He further noted that between 1914 and 1940, the university dominated sociology in the United States. The theories, concepts, and research studies that were developed by the early scholars at the University of Chicago also have had a lasting impact on criminological theory.

Historical Background

The University of Chicago was established in a city that was relatively young. Technological advances were rapidly transforming the United States, and especially the Midwest, from a land dominated by agricultural pursuits to a country with growing cities that served as centers of commerce and industrialization. According to J. John Palen, the city of Chicago was incorporated in 1833 with 4,100 residents (cited in Lilly, Cullen, and Ball, 1995, p. 38). The city expanded rapidly, reaching a population of 1 million by 1890 and more than 2 million by 1910. Many of those settling in Chicago and other urban areas carried little with them. They had high expectations for new lives and flocked to the cities seeking work. Although the cities were the industrial hubs of the nation, life in these cities was quite harsh.

Among those coming to Chicago were displaced farmworkers; poor blacks fleeing the rural South; and European immigrants whose skin colors, languages, and cultures set them apart from the "American mainstream" (Curran and Renzetti, 1994, p. 136; Lilly et al., 1995, pp. 38-39). They faced widespread prejudice and discrimination. Those who managed to work in the factories were paid low wages and worked long hours in hazardous conditions that jeopardized their health and safety. Their homes usually were unsafe and overcrowded tenement houses. Others unable to attain work became transients. As a result of these problems, many social work organizations and relief programs were established.

The Progressive movement, a broad liberal reform movement, emerged early in the 20th century. The Progressives did not accept the social Darwinists' view that the poor and the criminals were biologically inferior; instead, they claimed that the poor were pushed by their environment into a life of crime and argued that crime and poverty were the result of "America's unbridled industrial growth" (Lilly et al., 1995, p. 39). They proposed that social services such as schools, clinics, recreational facilities, foster homes, and reformatories would not only lessen the pains of poverty but also save the poor.

Emergence of the University of Chicago and Hull House

Within this urban context, the University of Chicago emerged and the Department of Sociology became "the first successful American program of collective sociological research" (Bulmer, 1984, p. xv). Deegan (1988) stated that the university "began on a desolate prairie" with William Rainey Harper as its first president (p. 1). Harper used persuasion, money, and promises of institutional power to lure prominent, but often young, scholars to the "wild West." His goal was for this university, located on the urban frontier, to rival the universities in the intellectually preeminent East. To accomplish this, Harper sought to establish new disciplines, such as sociology, by bringing ambitious and energetic faculty to the university. The early sociology professors who are not usually acknowledged in the history of the Chicago School include Albion Small, Charles Zeublin, Charles Henderson, and George Vincent.

Early Unrecognized Professors

Harper recruited Small, who was trained in both the ministry and history and was president of Colby College from 1889 to 1892, to be the first chair of the sociology department (Bulmer, 1984, pp. 33-34; Deegan, 1988, p. 17). Small became a major figure in defining a special area of expertise for sociology, which included using the city of Chicago as the center and subject of research. Small also helped the sociology department to achieve preeminence as the founder and editor of, and a major contributor to, the *American Journal of Sociology* and as a charter member and two-term president of the American Sociological Society (Bulmer, 1984, p. 34; Deegan, 1988, p. 18).

Harper also hired Zeublin and Henderson to teach in the sociology department. Both of these men have been ignored by most scholars' historical accounts of the Chicago School. They had a close affiliation with Jane Addams and Hull House, which was a settlement house and a center for a "women sociologists" network and research (Deegan, 1988, p. 34). This contact with Addams ultimately led to Zeublin making social settlement work one of his major interests (p. 19). But Deegan (1988) further noted of Zeublin: "Unfortunately for his academic career, his powerful and critical analysis of society, especially the work of businessmen, led to his ultimate removal from the University of Chicago" (p. 19).

Henderson. Although Henderson is almost entirely forgotten in the annals of sociology at the University of Chicago, Deegan (1988) claims that Henderson[2] "was one of the most far-thinking and influential men on the faculty" (p. 18). Henderson, who was a Baptist minister, served as a pastor for 19 years after graduating from the "old University of Chicago" (see Note 1) in 1870 (p. 18). While teaching at the University of Chicago, he also served as university chaplain. Courtright (1995) asserted the following about Henderson: "His religiosity, his association with Jane Addams (as well as other women researchers and sociologists from the University of Chicago and Hull House), and his insistence upon an applied or practical sociology have acted to keep him out of the 'Chicago limelight' " (p. 1).

Unlike Zeublin, Henderson made early contributions to criminology. Deegan (1988) noted that among Henderson's areas of specialization were criminology, prison reform, and juvenile delinquency (p. 18). In fact, Deegan asserted, "Henderson's early work with deviance led to the subsequent characterization of sociology as work with the 'three Ds': drunks, delinquents, and deviants" (p. 86). In 1914, Henderson published *The Cause and Cure of Crime,* in which he introduced the professional criminal as one of the more dangerous classes of criminals (Henderson, 1914). Courtright (1995) suggested,

> This classification, combined with Henderson's writings on the power and intelligence of businessmen in industry . . ., could have clearly influenced the later work of Edwin Sutherland in both his research on "Chic Conwell" of *The Professional Thief* (1937) and his later research on white collar criminality. (p. 16)

Henderson also influenced George E. Vincent, who studied at the University of Chicago with Small, Henderson, and the noted philosopher and educator John Dewey. Vincent received his Ph.D. from the University of Chicago in 1896 and continued as a faculty member until 1911. Vincent, whose father was the founder and first president of Chautauqua, a system of popular education and home study for adults, was more interested in education and administration. Deegan (1988) stated, however, that "from 1894 until 1900, he was at the forefront of sociological thought" (p. 20). Vincent left the University of Chicago in 1911 to accept the presidency of the University of Minnesota. Deegan also noted that Vincent "kept actively involved with sociology, but more as an avocation than as his major occupation" (p. 20).

Thomas and Mead. William I. Thomas and George H. Mead also came to the University of Chicago in 1894. Although these two men usually are not recognized in criminology, they have received a place of prominence among sociologists for their contributions. Thomas is most well known for *The Polish Peasant in Europe and America* (Thomas and Znaniecki, 1918). Also, for criminologists, Thomas's study of prostitution, *The Unadjusted Girl,* has significance (Thomas, 1923). Although Mead made no direct contribution to criminology, both Mead and Thomas emphasized process and socialization. Thus, the teachings and publications of both Mead and Thomas are important in the emergence of the interactionist perspective in criminology (see Chapter 7).

Park, Burgess, and Faris. Most scholars begin the history of the Chicago School with Robert E. Park, Ernest W. Burgess, and Ellsworth Faris. After Park graduated from the University of Michigan in 1887, he was a city newspaper reporter for more than a decade. Eventually, he became the secretary and companion of Booker T. Washington (Deegan, 1988, p. 23). Thomas recruited Park for the University of Chicago faculty in 1914.

Burgess, who received his Ph.D. from the University of Chicago in 1913, began teaching in 1916. Burgess has a more direct link to criminology in that he taught the first criminology and delinquency courses at the University of Chicago and developed the first parole prediction tables in the state of Illinois (Cavan, 1986).

Faris, who studied under Dewey and Mead, received his Ph.D. in psychology at the University of Chicago in 1914 and was appointed to teach Thomas's courses in social psychology (Bulmer, 1984, pp. 43, 109). Faris also replaced Small as chairman of the sociology department.

Park and Burgess (1921) coauthored what usually is defined as the first sociology text, *Introduction to the Science of Sociology,* in 1921. *The City,* originally published in 1925 and coedited by Park, Burgess, and McKenzie (1967), introduced the "concentric zone theory." In *The City,* Park and colleagues[3] noted that there had been numerous studies of the physical expansion of the city from the standpoint of the city plan (p. 48). The study by Park and colleagues was one of expansion as a process of growth illustrated by a series of concentric circles that designated "both the successive zones of urban expansion and the types of areas differentiated in the process of expansion" (p. 50). They represented this expansion through a chart as

> an ideal construction of the tendencies of any town or city to expand radially from its central business district—on the map "The Loop" (I). Encircling the downtown area that is normally an area in transition, which is being invaded by business and light manufacture (II). A third area (III) is inhabited by the workers in industries who have escaped from the area of deterioration (II) but who desire to live within easy access of their work. Beyond this zone is the "residential area" (IV) of high-class apartment buildings or of exclusive "restricted" districts of single-family dwellings. Still further out beyond the city limits is the commuters' zone—suburban areas or satellite cities—within a thirty- to sixty-minute ride of the central business district. (p. 50)

The chart further illustrated the tendency of each inner zone to extend its area by the invasion on the next outer zone. Park and colleagues called this aspect of expansion succession, a process that had been studied in detail in plant ecology. They also stated that the process of urban growth involved the complementary processes of centralization and decentralization. Chicago, according to Park and colleagues (p. 52), was in the process of changing from an agglomeration of country towns and immigrant colonies to a centralized/decentralized system of local communities blending into sub-business areas dominated by the central business district. The downtown sections of large cities included department stores, skyscraper office buildings, railroad stations, hotels, theaters, art museums, and city halls.

Addams, Kelley, and the Hull House maps. Deegan (1988) argued, however, that Park and Burgess failed to acknowledge their intellectual heritage from Jane Addams, Florence Kelley, and other women residents at Hull House (p. 55). Deegan stated that their book, *Hull House Papers and Maps* (Residents of Hull House, 1895), "had a monumental influence on Chicago sociology" (Deegan, 1988, p. 55). She claimed that this document was significant for the following reasons:

> First, it established the Chicago tradition of studying the city and its inhabitants. Second, its central chapters on immigrants, poverty, and occupational structures became the major substantive interests of Chicago sociologists. Third, it used the methodology of mapping demographic information on urban populations according to their geographic distribution. This "mapping" technique is now recognized as one of the major contributions of Chicago sociology in the 1920s and 1930s. Fourth, it undisputedly shows the intellectual influence of Addams on the men of the Chicago School. Fifth, it reveals the development of her social thought and intellectual antecedents. Sixth, it sharply illuminates the hostility of male sociologists who failed to acknowledge her groundbreaking work in founding the profession. (p. 55)

Research by early students. Deegan made a most convincing argument here. The influence of Park and Burgess on the research studies of students during the 1920s and 1930s, however, cannot be denied. Among the dissertations supervised by Park, Burgess, and Faris that based part of the research on the use of the concentric zone theory in the ecological distribution of people and specific behaviors were Thrasher's (1927) *The Gang,* Cavan's (1928) *Suicide,* Frazier's (1932) *The Negro Family in Chicago,* Reckless's (1933) *Vice in Chicago,*[4] and Hayner's (1936) *The Sociology of Hotel Life.*[5] Hayner's dissertation was published by the University of North Carolina Press, whereas the others were selected for publication in the University of Chicago's prestigious Sociological Series. Shaw and McKay later used the concentric zone theory to examine the distribution of delinquency in Chicago and other cities.

The emphasis in the Chicago School on process also is evident in the dissertations, for example, Thrasher's (1927) concern with the process whereby gangs developed and Cavan's (1928) analysis of the process whereby a person comes to the decision to commit suicide. Life histories, such as Sutherland's (1937) *The Professional Thief* and Shaw's (1966) *The Jackroller* (originally published in 1930), illustrate another approach to examining crime in the Chicago School. Field research (i.e., ethnographies), such as Anderson' (1923) *The Hobo,* was another frequently used methodology. Diversity of methodologies and theoretical perspectives was one of the many strengths of the Chicago School.

Assumptions About People and Society

The diversity of methodologies and theoretical perspectives within the early Chicago School makes an analysis of the assumptions of theorists regarding people and society somewhat complex. Within a given work, such as Cavan's (1928) *Suicide,* the scholar may present research using the ecological maps of Chicago to trace the geographic distribution of suicides in Chicago, life histories of persons who committed suicides, and an analysis of the process whereby a person reaches the point of committing suicide. Thus, those scholars using the ecological maps were using a macro level of analysis, whereas the life histories represent a micro level of analysis.

In a similar manner, Sutherland's differential association theory emphasized the objective overt phenomena in criminal behavior while also stressing the subjective covert process of learning. Sutherland further stated that the learning of criminal behavior involves the objective phenomena of techniques and skills for committing the crime as well as learning the motives, drives, and attitudes (subjective phenomena) necessary to justify the crime.

Because the scholars in the Chicago School were concerned with explaining what determines criminal/deviant behavior, they were primarily assuming that people are passive agents whose environment was largely imposed on them. The emphasis by Sutherland on the process of learning criminal behavior, by Thrasher on the development of delinquent gangs, and by Cavan in her study of suicide suggests that social phenomena are determined by society and that society is in a fluid state. This was especially true in the study of the distribution of delinquency in Chicago and other cities studied by Frazier and by Shaw and McKay. Frazier argued that Negro crime was the result of (or imposed by) a history of slavery and racial discrimination. These scholars viewed society as fluid and believed that change, which was imposed by society, also produced a conflict of values and cultures in the inner city. Shaw and McKay argued that this conflict of cultures was the basis for high delinquency in the inner cities.

Frederick M. Thrasher (1892-1962)

Frederick Thrasher was born in 1892 in Shelbyville, Indiana. He attended high school in Frankfort, Indiana, received his B.A. from DePauw University, and received both his M.A. and Ph.D. from the University of Chicago (Dodson, 1962). He was a student at the University of Chicago at the same time as Cavan, Reckless, and Hayner, and his research was influenced by Park, Burgess, and Faris. He taught at New York University from 1927 to 1960.

One of the most famous field studies by students at the Chicago School was Thrasher's[6] (1927) *The Gang.* Although the research primarily involved field observations, he relied on his personal observations as well as firsthand personal accounts from gang members, personal documents from persons who had observed the gangs in many contexts, and census and court records. Thrasher followed the Chicago tradition of including ecological maps demonstrating the distribution of the gangs in the city of Chicago. The theoretical thrust throughout the work emphasized "process," another traditional emphasis of Park, Burgess, and Faris. Cavan[7] remembered Thrasher and his work as follows:

> Thrasher was a small man and put on old clothes and interacted with gang members. He took lots of field notes and then analyzed them. He enlisted the assistance of some of the other graduate students from time to time. It took him years to do the research. (personal interview, March 9, 1989)

The Natural History of the Gang

In the first chapter of *The Gang,* Thrasher (1927) asserted,

> No less than 1,313[8] gangs have been discovered in Chicago and its environs! A conservative estimate of 25,000 members—boys and young men—is probably an understatement. . . .
>
> The favorite haunts and hang-outs of these 1,300 and more gangs have been definitely ascertained. Their distribution as shown on the accompanying map[9] makes it possible to visualize the typical areas of gangland and to indicate their place in the life and organization of Chicago. (p. 5)

Although Thrasher began the book with the ecological maps, the major emphasis of the book was on the ganging process and life of the gangs.

The Ganging Process

According to Thrasher (1927), the beginnings of gangs are most likely to occur in the slums of the city, where a large number of children are crowded into a limited area. In this pervasive crowd of children, "play groups are forming everywhere—gangs in embryo" (p. 26). This environment provides the opportunity for conflict, within or without the gangs' own social milieu, regarding territory, loot, and play spaces.

Thrasher (1927) asserted that play groups easily meet these hostile forces, which give their members a "we" feeling and start the process of ganging that is characteristic of the life of these unorganized areas. The majority of gangs develop from spontaneous play groups. Thrasher suggested that a play group emerges on the basis of interests and aptitudes and that the activities vary from "hide-and-go-seek" to crap-shooting (p. 29). This play group does not become a gang, however, until it begins to incite disapproval and opposition and, thereby, acquires a more definite group consciousness. Thrasher argued that this is the beginning of the gang, for now its members start to draw more closely together. It becomes a conflict group. The ganging process is a continuous flux and flow, and there is little permanence in most of the groups (p. 35).

Based on his study of 1,313 gangs, Thrasher (1927) defined the gang as follows:

> The gang is an interstitial group originally formed spontaneously and then integrated through conflict. It is characterized by the following types of behavior: meeting face to face, milling, movement through space as a unit, conflict, and planning. The result of this collective behavior is the development of tradition, unreflective internal structure, *esprit de corps,* solidarity, morale, group awareness, and attachment to a local territory. (p. 57)

Wide divergency in the character of its personnel, combined with differences of physical and social environment and of experience and tradition, give every gang its own peculiar character. Each gang may vary as to membership, type of leaders, mode of organization, interests and activities, and status in the community (p. 45). Movement through space in a concerted and cooperative way may include play, the commission of crimes (e.g., robbing, rum running), and migration from one place to another with changes of hangouts. Conflict comes in clashes with other gangs or with common enemies such as the police or park officials (p. 54).

Types of Gangs

Thrasher (1927) noted that if conditions are favorable to its continued existence, the gang tends to undergo a sort of natural evolution from a diffuse and loosely organized group into the solidified unit that represents the matured gang and that may take one of several forms.

The diffuse gang. This type of gang does not grow beyond a rudimentary stage. Its solidarity is not lasting, the loyalties of the members to each other and to the gang cannot be counted on too far, and the natural leaders might not be recognized definitely as such by the rest of the group (p. 59). Thrasher (1927) provided "Olaf's Crowd" as an example of the diffuse type of gang:

> Olaf's Crowd consists of about twenty members, ranging from twelve to sixteen years of age. It was never a real gang with an organization; some of its members associated somewhat with other crowds. There were no special meetings or meeting places; the boys congregated on the street corners, or in by-places, or in the neighborhood of poolrooms. There have been no recognized leaders, although some boys have naturally had more influence than others. . . .
> Not only the main but [also] apparently the sole bond that held these boys together has been the recounting and committing of delinquencies. . . . Thieving in stores was carried on extensively, at one time by a system—groups of three or four going into a store and getting away with anything they could. The articles were distributed or sold to the other boys; there was never any systematic sharing of booty. (pp. 60-61)

The solidified gang. The solidified gang is the result of a longer development and a more intense (or more extended) conflict. A high degree of loyalty and morale and a minimum of internal friction contribute to a well-integrated fighting machine, by means of which the gang presents a solid front against foes. "The Murderers" is an example of a solidified gang:

Shortly after the race riots of 1919, residents in the vicinity south of the stockyards were startled one morning by a number of placards bearing the inscription "The Murderers, 10,000 strong, 48th & Ada." In this way, attention was attracted to a gang of thirty Polish boys who [hung] out in a district known as the Bush.

The pastimes of the boys were loafing, smoking, chewing, crap-shooting, card-playing, pool, and bowling. Every evening, they would get together at their corner or in their shack nearby to "chew the rag" and talk over events of the day. . . .

A favorite rendezvous of the gang was a large sandpile near the railroad tracks. Here they had great fun camping, flipping freights, and pestering the railroad detectives. Most of them were "bumming away from home," sleeping under sidewalks or in the prairies. They had little difficulty swiping their food. . . .

They broke into boxcars and "robbed" bacon and other merchandise. They cut out wire cables to sell as junk. They broke open telephone boxes. They took autos for joyriding. They purloined several quarts of whiskey from a brewery to drink in their shack. . . .

A high degree of loyalty had developed within the gang, and its members repeatedly refused to peach on each other in the courts. They stuck close together in most of their exploits, for their enemies were many and dangerous. (Thrasher, 1927, p. 62)

The conventionalized gang. The dominant pattern for the conventionalized gang in Chicago is the athletic club. It may take other forms, however, such as dancing, social, or pleasure clubs; pool or billiard clubs; and benevolent associations or political societies. About one fourth (335) of the groups identified by Thrasher clearly were of the conventionalized type (p. 63). The tendency toward conventionalization usually manifests itself first during the period from 16 to 17 years of age. This type of gang attempts to achieve social standing and to make its activities legitimate in the eyes of the community. It sometimes adopts a constitution and bylaws, elects officers, and requires that members pay dues. It often incorporates, receiving its charter from the state or buying it from some defunct organization. If supervised and backed by some wholesome influences, the gang club may become thoroughly socialized. Or, it may function as a destructive and demoralizing agency in the community.

The criminal gang. If the gang does not become conventionalized or incorporated in some way into the structure of the community as its members grow older, then it often drifts into habitual crime and becomes completely delinquent. "Joe's Gang" is an example of a criminal type of gang:

Originating with a dozen adolescent truants in the vicinity of Halsted and Harrison streets, Joe's Gang has been a solid group for over ten years. Its members have initiative and a sense of honor toward each other and those who have befriended them. They went straight for some time, owing to the efforts of teachers and social workers, but they have now become a hold-up and beer-running outfit.

One of the members was shot by his own father. Several of them pulled off a $100,000 robbery in a Loop jewelry store. Joe drove a wagon that bombed a building under construction on the North Side. . . .

The gang has dealt summary justice to its own members, having killed two of them on account of internal friction. Joe was shot recently and later died from the wound, but he declined to give the name of his assassin or any other clue. The Black Hand would have dealt cruelly with his sister, he said, had he squealed. (Thrasher, 1927, pp. 67-68)

The Roles of Girls in the Gangs

In some of the younger gangs, a girl may play the same role as that of a boy. Among the younger adolescents, there is a definite indifference or hostility toward girls. The members of the older adolescent or young adult gang usually have a definite, if half-concealed, interest in girls. Dates and dancing become important. Girls' groups may enter into alliance with the gang, and certain girls may be taken under its protection or actually may become members of the gang in their sexual capacity (Thrasher, 1927, p. 221).

Thrasher (1927) explained that the reason why younger adolescent gang members have hostility toward girls is that girls interfere with the enterprises of the group. Involvement with girls weakens the loyalties of its members. Thus, gang tradition discourages any but the most casual contacts (p. 223). If a boy's clandestine interest in girls becomes manifest, then he often is subjected to unpleasant ridicule. Although the adolescent gang would appear to despise girls, it has its own code of chivalry, as indicated by the following:

The boy who attempted to fight with a girl was punished by the other boys. A girl might slap a boy in the face, and all he could honorably do was to dodge the second blow, or if he was very religious, as was seldom the case, he might turn his head around and ask to have the inequality rectified by a similar blow on the other side. (p. 223)

However, Thrasher (1927) noted that the gang also may have a girl as a member. He explained this as the girl taking the role of a boy and noted that the girl is accepted on equal terms with the others. Such a girl probably is a tomboy in the neighborhood. "She dares to follow anywhere, and she is ill at ease with those of her own sex who have become characteristically feminine" (p. 224). One girl described her membership in a gang as follows:

My entrance into the alley gang occurred soon after my family moved to a small town of five thousand population. I was eight years of age at the time, a small but strong and agile girl quite capable of taking care of myself and of my younger brothers and sister.

The first few days, I watched the boys playing in the alley beside the church where my father was to act as pastor. One morning, I found one of the boys, surrounded by a delighted group of onlookers, torturing a frog. I could not countenance such cruelty, and I squirmed my way into the group.

"Stop that!" I commanded.

The boy looked up in astonishment, grinned, and continued his activity. I sailed into him and soon sat astride his stomach, directing vicious jabs at his head.

"Say 'enough'!" I demanded. He wiggled uncomfortably and looked sheepishly at the interested circle of boys.

"Nuff!" he said, and I let him go. The next day, I was invited to take part in a game of Piggy; I had made my debut into the gang as an equal. (p. 224)

Thrasher (1927) noted that there was a gang composed largely of girls who had transferred their interests from sewing to playing in a large sandpile with a protruding plank. Forced to defend their play space against other gangs, they waged wars in which combat took the form of rock battles. They took the role of boys until they began to wear their hair up and put on long skirts (p. 227). Thrasher noted, however, that gangs composed entirely of girls are very rare.

Older gangs are more apt to have sexual delinquencies. Among members of the older gangs, Thrasher (1927) contended, there sometimes is evidence of looseness and promiscuity involving an obliging sweetheart or a clandestine prostitute (p. 236). Some of the clubs have been accused of harboring women in their rooms. The semi-criminal gangs and clubs of older adolescents and young men sometimes are guilty of attacks on women.

Thrasher (1927) also claimed that women have come to play an increasingly important role in the criminal gang (p. 239). Although wives of successful gangsters are well protected, sweethearts and paramours often take part in criminal enterprises, sometimes acting as lures and sometimes actually holding guns and participating like other gangsters in holdups. Thrasher further argued that a girl sometimes plays the gangster role so well that she may qualify for a share in the leadership of such a group.

Other Research on Delinquency

After receiving his Ph.D. from Chicago in 1927, Thrasher accepted a position at New York University in the Department of Educational Sociology. Seddon (1995) noted,

Thrasher, like so many other Chicago alumni, blended scholarship and teaching with service and always maintained contact with the community in which he studied and taught. He served on a variety of committees dealing with delinquency and children throughout his career including being a member of President Hoover's White House Conference on Child Health and Protection. (p. 4)

Thus, Thrasher was among the first theorists in the Chicago School to combine research, theory, and policy. He continued to explore issues of delinquency initially raised in his dissertation.

Perhaps Thrasher's most important research after *The Gang* was his study of the Boys' Club of New York City. The purpose of the Boys' Club was to prevent boys from becoming delinquent by providing guided leisure time activities. His longitudinal study of the club indicated that delinquency rates of members of the club did not differ significantly from those of boys within the surrounding community who were not involved in the club (Thrasher, 1936, p. 68). Thrasher (1936) suggested that the club was not successful because boys' involvement with the club was sporadic, few activities were offered during the summer, and the club was not seen as an integral part of the community.

> Obviously, the general conclusion is that the club did not succeed in reaching a large number of boys whom it was designed to serve.
>
> A study of the distribution of club members indicates that large numbers were drawn from outside the forty city blocks originally conceived to be the club's area of service.... The club, during its first three years, never enrolled more than 59 percent of the eligible boys in the thirty city blocks in its immediate area. . . . A comparatively small percentage of boys remained members year after year. . . . This instability of membership constituted a failure to achieve a continuous influence through critical adolescent years. (p. 67)

Seddon (1995) suggested that this research served as a model for future program evaluations (p. 8). According to Seddon, Thrasher stressed the importance of coordinating programs with the social milieu of the community so as to serve all children, with a particular effort to reach those who are at higher risk for delinquency. In other research, Thrasher concluded that delinquency was the result of numerous factors and that looking for a one-factor cause of delinquency was futile.

Critique of Thrasher

Thrasher's research studies of delinquency were based on Chicago School concentric zone theory of the city and on the process of the formation of gangs. Although he did not have a set of propositions that formed a logical deductive system (as Homans [1964] and Turner [1978] indicated are necessary for a social science theory [see Chapter 1]), he did have a set of concepts and outlined the process whereby gangs develop. Thrasher, then, developed a typology and an explanation of delinquent gangs that may meet Merton's criteria for a theory of the middle range or may be considered a sociological/criminological interpretation of data. His application of the theory to issues of delinquency also made important contributions to policy and to delinquency programs.

In contrast to most early researchers on delinquency, Thrasher did include girls in a basically nonsexist way. Although he noted that girls often fulfill a sex role in the gang, he also recognized leadership roles of some of the girls in the gang. Criminologists have given virtually no recognition to Thrasher's delinquency research after the publication of *The Gang*.

Thrasher's (1927) *The Gang* was selected for the prestigious Sociological Series published by the University of Chicago Press and was reissued as a paperback by the University of Chicago Press in 1963. Thus, it has been recognized as one of the classics in criminology. Furthermore, Rogers and Mays (1987) stated, "Without question, the 'father' of juvenile gang research is Frederick Thrasher" (p. 216). The importance of this work also was noted by Cavan, who suggested in 1948, "Although now twenty years old, this book is still the one authoritative study of boy-gang life" (Cavan, 1948, p. 74). It is puzzling to note, therefore, that most of the current criminological theory texts (Akers, 1994; Curran and Renzetti, 1994; Leonard, 1982; Lilly et al., 1995; Naffine, 1987; Williams and McShane, 1988, 1994) either totally ignore Thrasher's works or mention them in bibliographies only.

Ruth Shonle Cavan (1896-1993)

Ruth Shonle Cavan was perhaps the only woman from the early Chicago School to receive national recognition for her works in sociology and criminology. As indicated in the biographical inset on Cavan (Inset 5.1), she had a long and productive career. Many current students of criminology, however, are not aware of her many scholarly contributions. Her continuum of behavior conceptual scheme was presented in Chapter 4. Her study of suicide and other major works in delinquency and criminology are discussed here.

Suicide

Although Cavan was a student of Park and Burgess, Faris was the director of her master's thesis and her doctoral dissertation. Cavan explained the selection of her dissertation topic, suicide, as follows:

> I had to select something for a doctor's dissertation. Dr. Faris suggested several things to me, and one of them was suicide, and we talked about suicide and the different aspects of it. . . . So, I decided to do that. Thereafter, almost every course I took, I managed somehow to do a term paper on suicide until Professor Robert E. Park, who had many students and would have liked to have had me in his collection, became kind of exasperated because I would never take his suggestions. He said he thought, if I took a course in astronomy, I would somehow write a paper on suicide. (cited in Moyer, 1990, p. 139)

Cavan's dissertation was composed of these various class papers that she revised and integrated into a lengthy manuscript. Although the book contained 14 chapters, only the most pertinent chapters for theory are discussed here.

Religion. An early chapter in *Suicide* (Cavan, 1928) examined the statistical trends of suicide for Europe and the United States prior to 1923. Cavan used variables similar to those used by the sociologists Durkheim (1897) and Morselli (1897). Her findings concurred with those of Durkheim and Morselli with reference to religion. That is, she also found that Protestants have higher suicide rates than do Catholics and Jews. She stated that the low suicide rates of Catholics and Jews are explained in part by the fact that these religions forbid and condemn suicide as a sin. Cavan (1928) further argued,

> Religions such as the Catholic and the Jewish are more than religions; they are systems of social organization which (1) mold the personalities and dictate the dominant interests of their members; (2) furnish the means of satisfying the needs thus created; and

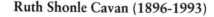

INSET 5.1   **Ruth Shonle Cavan (1896-1993)**

Ruth Shonle Cavan was born August 28, 1896, in the small town of Tuscola, Illinois. She was the third child born to Annie and Charles Shonle, who owned a tailor shop. Her love for reading and writing developed early in her childhood, when she read and reread all the books in her home and at 12 years of age spent Saturday afternoons in the public library reading *National Geographic* magazines. Her teachers and high school principal encouraged her intellectual interests. The high school principal suggested that she enter an essay competition for high school students sponsored by the Carnegie Foundation for Peace. She won third place and a $50 prize (Moyer, 1991, p. 91).

She completed high school in 3 years and immediately moved to Decatur, Illinois, to work and save money for college. After 2 years, she saved enough money to enroll at Millikin University, where she majored in English. Eventually, she was able to transfer to the University of Chicago, where she received three degrees: Ph.D. in English and economics, M.A. in sociology, and Ph.D. in sociology.

Her dissertation, *Suicide* (1928), was selected by her committee—Robert E. Park, Ernest W. Burgess, and Ellsworth Faris (chair)—for the prestigious Sociological Series of the University of Chicago Press. She met Jordan True Cavan in 1926 when they both were student residents at Jane Addams' Hull House. The two were married in June 1927. Ruth continued at the University of Chicago as a research associate for several years while Jordan returned to Rockford, Illinois, to continue teaching in the Department of Education at Rockford College. Jordan traveled to Chicago on weekends to visit Ruth during the first year of their marriage. This was a somewhat unusual arrangement at that time and indicated her independence and commitment to her career.

For several years, Cavan worked with Burgess on several research projects including *The Adolescent in the Family* (Cavan, 1934), which was conducted for a White House Conference on Child Health and Protection and included the research on juvenile delinquency discussed in this chapter. During this period, Ruth and Jordan had a daughter, Anna-Lee, and Cavan worked intermittently in Chicago and in the Department of Sociology at Rockford College. From 1947 to 1962, she taught full-time in sociology at Rockford and retired professor emerita. During these years at Rockford, she also had visiting appointments at other universities in Washington, Utah, Michigan, Pennsylvania, and Illinois. In 1964, she was invited to teach at Northern Illinois University, where she taught full-time until her second retirement in 1971. In 1977, she was designated professor emerita at Northern Illinois.

Cavan's career spanned more than 60 years, and she published eight scholarly books in addition to co-editing or coauthoring 10 others. She also published approximately 80 articles in professional journals. Her first article was published in *The Journal of Religion* in 1924 while she still was a graduate student, and her final article was published in the *Criminal Justice Policy Review* in 1987. During these years, Cavan demonstrated a sustained interest in historical/religious communes, suicide, family, criminology, juvenile delinquency, old age, and women (Moyer, 1991, pp. 94-96).

Ferdinand (1988) suggested that Cavan's contributions to the discipline "reflect a fine blend of talent, virtuosity, receptiveness, versatility, and resourcefulness. . . . Such versatility has been richly rewarded" (pp. 340-341). Cavan received many honors. She was the first woman elected president of the Midwest Sociological Society in 1960. She was made a fellow of the American Sociological Society in 1959 and of the American Society of Criminology in 1961. She received two awards of appreciation from the John Howard Association in 1961 and 1967, a distinguished scholar award from the National Historical Communal Societies in 1987, and the Illinois Governor's Award for Unique Achievement in 1988. A Ruth Shonle Cavan Young Scholars Award has been established in her honor by the American Society of Criminology.

(3) provide means for reorganizing the few individuals who do become disorganized. (p. 42)

Cavan suggested that the peculiarity of Protestantism contributes to the high Protestant suicide rate:

> Protestantism is an individualistic religion. Theoretically, anyone may interpret the Bible according to his own intellect and interests. Thus, the individual does not have his attitudes firmly set by an institution which in the case of the Catholics and Jews not only saves the person from becoming confused and disorganized but also fosters homogeneity of beliefs throughout the group. (p. 43)

Suicide among preliterate cultures. Cavan's analysis of suicide and religion suggested that lack of social organization fosters suicide. In the subsequent chapter, Cavan (1928) continued to explore the importance of social organization and developed a typology of suicides as (a) institutionalized suicides and (b) suicides for personal motives.

Institutionalized suicides are found in preliterate societies, but not all suicides that occur at the command of a group have reached the stage of complete institutionalization, especially among preliterates. Completely institutionalized suicides have group approval and usually participation of the group in the commission of the suicides. The ritual of the performance of the suicides is specified according to some concept or attitude of a traditional group character (Cavan, 1928, p. 70). Cavan (1928) explained,

> Institutionalized suicides imply first a scale of values which places the life of the individual lower than certain other values. . . . Such scales of values are held by the entire group and are a part of the group tradition, but they are accepted implicitly by each member to such a degree that individuals willingly give up their lives to support and maintain these values.
>
> For this complete acceptance of group values, a well-integrated and functioning social organization is necessary. It seems almost a paradox to assert . . . that suicides from personal motives do not exist among preliterates because of the complete control of the group over the individual and that institutional suicides do exist because of this same complete social control. (p. 74)

Institutionalized suicides, however, are disrupted when groups of dissimilar traditions meet and contradictory ideals of life become disseminated. The days of isolation and complete submission of the individual to one set of group customs and ideals are gone. Social control has been weakened, and individual interests have arisen and take precedence over social values. Individualism has developed (Cavan, 1928, p. 75). Cavan (1928) stated that institutionalized suicides do not exist under these circumstances but that suicides from personal motives occur. She devoted several chapters to the discussion of this type of suicide in Chicago.

Suicide in Chicago. In the remainder of *Suicide,* Cavan (1928) demonstrated the Chicago School influence. Her data on suicides in Chicago came from the coroner's records, diaries, life histories, and newspaper articles. Furthermore, she illustrated her data by using the concentric zone maps, reflecting the influence of Park and Burgess. Finally, her theoretical analysis of the case histories stressed the process by which a person comes to commit suicide.

Cavan used small questionnaire cards to record data for more than 1,000 suicide cases from the coroner's records in Chicago for the 1919-1921 period. Cavan used these data to trace the distribution of suicide in Chicago on the ecological maps. Cavan (1972) described the task as follows:

> Another approach was to assemble incidences of some kind of behavior, e.g., alcoholic deaths, suicides, welfare cases, delinquencies, crime; . . . compute rates by using census data for small communities; and construct maps. The method was arduous. We first located each address on a large street map of Chicago, making a colored dot for each case. We then counted the dots in each area and computed a rate. Finally, we made a rate map with different kinds of cross-hatching for each rate. I cannot tell you how many hours I spent locating some thousand cases of suicide. (p. 10)

After computing the rates of suicide by hand, Cavan proceeded to trace the distribution of the incidents of suicide in Chicago. Cavan's (1928) data indicated the following:

> Chicago has four suicidal areas: the "Loop" or central business district and its periphery of cheap hotels for men and sooty flats over stores (No. 1 on Map II); the Lower North Side, particularly the central part of this district, which includes a shifting population of young men and women in the rooming-house area (No. 64 on the map); the Near South Side linking the Loop on the north with the Negro area to the south and having one-fourth of its population Negro (No. 2 on the map); and the West Madison area, with its womanless street of flophouses, missions, cheap restaurants, and hundreds of men who drift in aimless, bleary-eyed abandon (No. 40 on the map). (p. 81)

Cavan noted that these areas had a heavy concentration of rooming and lodging houses as well as homeless men. She stated that "lodging-house people are a restless, moving throng" with a striking lack of the type of intimate group life considered by some sociologists to be fundamental for control of individuals and for the establishment of conventional norms (pp. 91-92). She further explained,

> Unincorporated into family groups, the lodging-house people are also without neighborhood life. People living in the same house scarcely come to know each other due to the rapidity with which roomers move in and out and also to the lack of opportunity for contacts. The old-time boarding house with a common parlor and front porch and meals served in one large dining room is gone. Chicago roomers in these areas usually see their fellow roomers only in passing in the halls or on the stairway, if they see them at all. This condition means that the lodging house has no standards and no traditions. (p. 92)

The suicide process. Cavan also used diaries obtained from charities, life histories, and newspaper stories to explore the process by which suicide occurs. Whereas Cavan used these cases to develop a general typology of the process of suicide,[10] she analyzed the process of suicide based on two lengthy diaries of suicide. One of those involved a young woman whose marriage had failed and who had an unfulfilled desire to be loved. The woman's diary traced the details of her relationship with a married man and her unfulfilled hopes that he eventually would divorce his wife and marry her. Her crisis came when she realized that the man never would leave his wife. The last entry in her diary read as follows:

> May 6, Saturday, 9:40 a.m. Bert phoned, swore at me furiously about phoning the night before. Marjorie's raised Cain, he said. I listened to nothing but oaths and hung up. I did not phone yesterday, nor did he. I thought I'd let him cool down, and he knew I had only $6 Tuesday night. Just now he phoned and said he wanted to send me some money, and I said I was going downtown and would meet him for lunch. I'm glad I didn't phone first. I am all broken up about Bert. My sense of honor (Oh, God, how ridiculous that sounds about me) tells me to leave my Bert, who belongs to another. Some day I will have the strength. (Cavan, 1928, p. 218)

Cavan (1928) indicated, "What happened between Marion and Bert when they met is not known, but Bert stayed with her the night of May 6 and sometime while he slept Marion shot and killed him and then killed herself" (p. 218). Based on her analysis of these cases of suicide in Chicago, Cavan theorized that suicide is "the process whereby the person experiences an unfulfilled need that creates a crisis that cannot be adjusted and ends in defeat, 'I can't stand it any longer' " (p. 177).

Cavan indicated the importance of this study of suicide to her career in a personal autographed statement in the book that she gave to the present author:

> This book is my doctoral dissertation selected by Ellsworth Faris, Robert E. Park, and Ernest W. Burgess, editors, to be included in the University of Chicago Sociological Series. It was a great honor to have my dissertation included. This publication in 1928 marked my transition from a graduate student to a professional sociologist and set me on the path of publications that has continued until the present. . . . RSC, December 25, 1986.

Major Works in Crime and Delinquency

After receiving her Ph.D., Cavan continued her affiliation with the University of Chicago as a research associate for various projects. One of these studies, *The Adolescent in the Family* (Cavan, 1934), was completed for the White House Conference on Child Health and Protection. This publication is important to criminology because of the chapter on delinquent children. For this study, Cavan administered questionnaires to predelinquents, delinquents, and a control group of boys from schools in the Chicago area. She compiled data on the responses of 163 boys from Montefiore School in Chicago; 265 girls from the State Training School for Girls in Geneva, Illinois; 324 boys from the St. Charles School for Boys in St. Charles, Illinois; and a control group of 127 boys selected randomly from public schools in the community in which predelinquent boys lived (p. 213). Cavan's interest in the family is evidenced here.

> Homes of delinquent children differ from the homes of public school children in that a much larger proportion of them are broken homes; parents are dead or separated in one-half to two-thirds of the homes. More mothers of delinquent children are employed outside the home, and there is a rather high percentage of homes with roomers in addition to the family. (p. 231)

Cavan was the first researcher to distinguish between homes broken by death of a parent (or of both parents) and homes broken by divorce or separation of parents. She also examined the quality of relationships between children and their families: "As judged by the degree to which children confide in their parents, the delinquent children are on less friendly and intimate terms with their parents than are public school children" (p. 224). Although these findings might seem trite in the new millennium, this early project marked an important contribution to the field of crime and delinquency. This study also is significant in that it marked Cavan's first research project in delinquency.

After leaving the University of Chicago during the mid-1940s, Cavan published texts in the areas of marriage and the family, criminology, and juvenile delinquency. It is for these texts that she is most well known by current criminologists. Cavan also published in the area of international crime and delinquency. Much of this interest was stimulated by her summer travels to Europe and Asia as well as by her attendance at the First United Nations Congress on the Prevention of Crime and Treatment of Offenders in 1955 (Moyer, 1990, p. 148). With reference to this, Cavan indicated that "the cluster of books on criminology and delinquency was completed by a book on *Delinquency and Crime: Cross-Cultural Perspectives* [Cavan and Cavan, 1968], written by myself and my husband, Jordan True Cavan, and published by [J. B.] Lippincott in 1968" (personal communication, November 25, 1986).

Cavan and Cavan (1968) began the book by stating that delinquency and crime are defined differently in every society based on its culture's own values. Crime and delinquency, then, are violations of those values (pp. 2-3). The authors continued the introduction to the book along a theme common to the Chicago School of sociology:

> From this point of view, delinquency and crime are the result of the failure of a society to completely socialize children into the values and behavior deemed important for the preservation of the society. Delinquency and crime indicate a failure of the educational mechanisms of society rather than a shortcoming of the individual. (p. 3)

Cavan and Cavan stated, "A crime is an act that violates a value considered vital for physical or cultural survival of a society, is recognized by that society as a violation, and is officially enforced by established penalties" (p. 7). The chapters that followed in their book examined crime and delinquency among the Eskimos as well as in Mexico, India, the Soviet Union, Sicily, and England. There also was a chapter exploring crime and delinquency in eight Western European countries during and after World War II.

Cavan also was interested in, and conducted research on, prison reform policy. In a chapter in *The Future of Imprisonment in a Free Society*, Cavan (1965) argued against the isolating conditions of current prisons because they tend to cut off contact with the family and outside world in general (p. 49). She urged a change in policy that would lead to a reduction of imprisonment that could be accomplished by increased use of probation and other community-based programs as well as shorter prison sentences (pp. 50-51).

As indicated in the biographical inset on Cavan (Inset 5.1), she also was involved with the John Howard Association in conducting research and publications. This combined her various interests in criminology, the family, and international studies. Cavan published two articles with Eugene Zemans, executive director of the John Howard Association, on marital relationships of prisoners in the United States and in 28 countries. The first article (Zemans and Cavan, 1958) used data collected by the John Howard Association on contacts permitted between prisoners and their spouses in the United States. The second article (Cavan and Zemans, 1958) was based on data on visitation policies of 28 countries collected at the United Nations conference attended by Cavan.

Zemans and Cavan (1958) stated that in the United States,

> In general, the purpose of visiting does not seem to be part of a clear-cut policy. In all except a few prison systems, visiting seems to be regarded as a technique to reduce tensions or as a disciplinary device to be manipulated as the warden sees fit. . . . A newer point of view that is gaining ground is that marital contacts may be used as a rehabilitative technique in a treatment program. (p. 56)

Zemans and Cavan recommended policy changes that enhanced visitation in prisons as a prisoner's right as well as the implementation of home furloughs and other community programs (p. 57).

Cavan and Zemans (1958) reported great variation in visitation practices among the 28 countries studied (pp. 134-137). Whereas some countries (e.g., Turkey, Cambodia) had fewer visitation privileges than did the United States, other countries provided greater use of private visits in prison and home visits. A few countries even allowed families to live with their spouses in the prison environment.

Critique of Cavan

Cavan's success as a criminologist/sociologist may be attributed to her ability to respond to an intellectual challenge, her resourcefulness as a researcher, her creative mind, and her love for writing. With reference to her extensive publication record, Cavan stated,

> Throughout my lifetime, my interest has shifted from marriage and the family, to delinquency and crime, to historical communes and utopias. . . . My life has been a succession of changes, with writing as the occupation that has given it continuity. (personal communication, March 20, 1986)

These characteristics were nurtured and stimulated at the University of Chicago, where a diversity of theoretical perspectives and methodologies were advocated by the faculty. The Chicago School influence on Cavan's scholarship may be illustrated

---

INSET 5.2

Edward Franklin Frazier (1894-1962)

E. Franklin Frazier was born on September 24, 1894, in Baltimore, Maryland. Frazier was born to Mary and James Frazier. Edwards (1974) noted that "Frazier was an extremely bright student" (p. 89). While at Baltimore High School, Frazier performed so well that he was recommended for a scholarship to Howard University. During his tenure at Howard, Frazier took courses in languages (Greek, Latin, German, and French), literature, natural sciences, and social sciences. In 1916, he graduated cum laude, receiving his bachelor's degree.

After graduation, Frazier taught high school mathematics, English, and French. During his years teaching in high schools, he became interested in socialism and sociology (Edwards, 1974, p. 91). His interest in sociology led him to graduate studies at Clark University in Worcester, Massachusetts, where he received his M.A. in 1920.

After leaving Clark, Frazier accepted a research fellowship at the New York School of Social Work. Following this appointment, he received a 1-year fellowship to study in Denmark. On returning to the United States, he became a professor of sociology at Morehouse College in Atlanta, Georgia. There, he organized the Atlanta School of Social Work and served as its director (Platt, 1991, pp. 72-73).

From 1922 to 1927, Frazier established himself as a prolific researcher and writer. During this period, he also managed to take his first graduate courses at the University of Chicago (Platt, 1991, p. 62). In 1927, he published a controversial article and subsequently was forced out of Atlanta. In leaving, he headed to Chicago to pursue his dream of attaining his Ph.D. During this period, the Department of Sociology at the University of Chicago was highly respected under the guidance of Robert E. Park, Ernest W. Burgess, and others. In fact, Park referred to Frazier as his most complete student (Platt, 1991, p. 89). Frazier graduated in 1931, having completed his dissertation, *The Negro Family in Chicago* (Edwards, 1974, p. 94; Frazier, 1932).

After graduating from the University of Chicago, Frazier taught at Fisk University and later at Howard University. In 1948, while at Howard, Frazier became the first African American to head the American Sociological Association (Edwards, 1974, p. 85). Throughout his academic life, Frazier published numerous books, articles, and reports.

—Shaun L. Gabbidon
Pennsylvania State University at Harrisburg

SOURCE: Excerpted from the writings of Shaun L. Gabbidon with permission.

---

in the variety of research methodologies found in her works. In *Suicide*, for example, she conducted descriptive statistical analyses of official suicide records in the United States and Europe, did historical analyses of suicide in primitive cultures, used ecological maps to explore the distribution of suicides in Chicago, and conducted analyses of life histories (diaries) of persons who had committed suicide in Chicago. In later works, she gathered data through the administration of questionnaires on a variety of topics. Although none of Cavan's works meets the classical definitions of theory of Homans (1964) and Turner (1978), her sociological/criminological interpretations of data, as well as her conceptual schemes and typologies, have made important contributions to criminological theory that should not be ignored. Many current criminologists credit Cavan with making contributions as the author of texts only. As noted previously, Cavan made important policy recommendations, especially with regard to prisons, that should provide valuable insights for those making corrections policy decisions today.

The current lack of recognition of Cavan's outstanding contributions to criminology could be partially explained by the fact that Cavan taught for most of her career at Rockford College, a small undergraduate college in Illinois, and did not have graduate students to carry on her research. However, as indicated in the biographical inset on Cavan (Inset 5.1), she has received recognition and numerous awards throughout the years from various professional associations at the national, regional, state, and local levels. The American Society of Criminology recently established the Ruth Shonle Cavan Young Scholars Award to be awarded annually.

In evaluating her own works, Cavan indicated that her greatest contributions were her early research books and her texts on the family, criminology, and delinquency. With reference to her texts, Cavan stated, "I found my niche in textbooks, which I could write and which were widely used" (cited in Kuhn, 1987). It is important to recognize that Cavan introduced thousands of students to criminology and juvenile delinquency through her texts. Cavan also was one of the first to include women and girls in her criminology and juvenile delinquency texts. But to limit her contribution to that of a great textbook writer who synthesized other people's research is to do a disservice both to her and to the discipline of criminology.

Edward Franklin Frazier (1894-1962)

E. Franklin Frazier was the first social scientist to fully document the history, variety, and status of the Afro-American family in the United States (Platt, 1991, p. 12). He wrote extensively about the effect of slavery on the family and about the impact of family disorganization, poverty, and unemployment on delinquency and crime. Yet, he left few autobiographical remnants of his childhood and family in Baltimore, Maryland. According to Platt (1991), Marie Brown Frazier, Frazier's wife of 40 years, explained that the social scientist's father was a bank messenger, his paternal grandfather was a self-emancipated slave who had bought his family's freedom, and his mother had been born a slave (p. 13). Frazier was 33 years of age when he was recruited by Park as a doctoral student at the University of Chicago. Platt suggested that when Frazier arrived in 1927, "he was an experienced and traveled intellectual and an independent and strong-willed thinker who had already formulated his initial ideas about the family" (p. 4). Persons (1987) indicated that Frazier had become a socialist during his undergraduate studies at Howard University (p. 131). These socialist ideas convinced him that "politics expresses the interests of the dominant economic forces." These ideas can be found today among many conflict theorists in criminology. Persons further stated that Frazier, during his graduate studies at Clark University, was persuaded of the value of theory in analyzing the social problems of the disadvantaged minority.

Research and Professional Activities
Prior to the Chicago School

While he was a research fellow in the Department of Social Research at the New York School of Social Work (see biographical inset on Frazier [Inset 5.2] for details), he broke new ground by conducting "one of the first empirical investigations of black industrial workers in the North" (Platt, 1991, p. 53). Frazier spent a great deal of time talking to men and their families in bars, on street corners, in union halls, and in their homes. Platt (1991) noted that Frazier described the working conditions on the docks and presented a demographic profile of 82 Afro-American longshoremen (p. 54). Frazier was discouraged by his findings:

> The men as a whole live under the domination of fear and hopelessness. . . . Further-
> more, racism had implanted such a legacy of "diffidence and self-abasement" that col-
> ored longshoremen expressed the opinion on every side that their fate is adverse be-
> cause they are colored, and colored people in America are impotent and cannot strike
> back at their oppressors except at the price of annihilation. (p. 55)

Frazier was the first Afro-American applicant for the fellowship awarded by the American-Scandinavian Foundation. Although he was awarded the fellowship with a stipend of $1,000, his name and photograph were not included in the foundation's announcement of fellows for 1921-1922 (Platt, 1991, p. 56). He was to study "co-operative agriculture" and rural folk high schools in Denmark. Frazier was well prepared for this endeavor. While a student at Howard, he had studied French, German, Latin, and Greek and was able to "develop a fairly good speaking knowledge of Danish" (p. 57).

This experience was a much more positive one for Frazier than was his research in New York. The folk high schools were set up in the countryside to give agricultural workers a broad cultural education. This experience, along with his exposure to the self-help programs advocated by Booker T. Washington, influenced Frazier. His publications suggest that this brief experience with the cooperatives in Denmark guided his political and economic views for several years.

Prior to beginning his studies at the University of Chicago, Frazier also had developed a somewhat "militant spirit" and participated in various protests. Before going to Denmark, for example,

> he joined a small group of former servicemen and YMCA war secretaries on an
> NAACP [National Association for the Advancement of Colored People]-organized
> picket line protesting the re-release of *The Birth of a Nation*, which in Frazier's words
> was a "vicious anti-Negro film" or, as Du Bois put it, was a "cruel and indefensible li-
> bel of the Negro and glorification of the mob in the Ku Klux Klan." Frazier was among
> those arrested for disorderly conduct, and though he received a suspended sentence, he
> spent a few hours in jail. (Platt, 1991, p. 57)

During his years as a professor of sociology at Morehouse College and acting director of the Atlanta School of Social Work, Frazier established his reputation as a leading Afro-American scholar and activist (Platt, 1991, pp. 62-63). Among his accomplishments was the publication of 33 articles in leading academic, professional, and civil rights journals as well as the completion of many administrative duties such as recruitment of students and curriculum revisions and teaching courses (p. 72).

Frazier and the Chicago School

Frazier actually began his studies at the University of Chicago during a summer session in 1923, when he completed three classes in sociology and passed his doctoral language examination in French and German (Platt, 1991, p. 86). He returned to Chicago in 1927 to complete his doctoral work. Although Platt (1991) noted that Frazier's reputation for a lack of "interracial diplomacy" (p. 75), as well as some of his controversial publications on race issues, caused some members of the Rockefeller Foundation to have serious reservations about him, Frazier did receive an $1,800 scholarship from the Rockefeller Foundation for his studies at the University of Chicago. This was supplemented by a part-time job with the Chicago Urban League (p. 85).

Frazier arrived at the University of Chicago in 1927, just as Cavan, Reckless, and Thrasher were completing their doctorates. The sociology department still was built around Park, Burgess, and Faris, and it was rigorous and demanding. After completing his doctorate there, Frazier continued his copious publication record including his dissertation, *The Negro Family in Chicago* (Frazier, 1932), *The Negro Family in the United States* (Frazier, 1939), and *The Negro in the United States* (Frazier, 1949).

Frazier's Major Publications on Slavery, the Family, and Delinquency/Crime

Frazier's (1932) study *The Negro Family in Chicago* followed an ecological analysis that was the trademark of the Chicago School during this period. In fact, he expanded the concentric zone to include seven zones in his analysis of the family in Chicago. He was primarily interested in refuting the prevailing stereotype of the widespread family disorganization and sexual immorality of the Negro family and the belief that the Negro was either inherently or culturally unable to be assimilated into Western civilization. Platt (1991) noted that Frazier was the first intellectual to seriously challenge these racist theories of Negro culture and family life (p. 137). Frazier's research, then, combined the Chicago tradition of ecological studies with a heavy reliance on historical research to trace the impact of slavery and racial discrimination on the Afro-American family and its involvement in crime and delinquency.

Impact of slavery on the Negro family. Frazier (1949) challenged the assumption of some scholars that the matriarchal family is a continuation of African traditions in a diluted form and that loose and unregulated sexual behavior among American Negroes is the same as the polygynous customs and practices of African Negroes (p. 12). Instead, Frazier argued,

The important position of the mother in the Negro family in the United States has developed out of the exigencies of life in the new environment. In the absence of institutional controls, the relationship between mother and child has become the essential social bond in the family, and the woman's economic position has developed in her those qualities which are associated with a "matriarchal" organization. On the other hand, the Negro family has developed as a patriarchal organization or similar to the American family, as the male has acquired property and an interest in his family and as the assimilation of American attitudes and patterns of behavior has been accelerated by the breaking down of social isolation. (p. 14)

These variations in family patterns have their roots in the Negroes' experiences as slaves on the southern plantations. Because plantations were capitalist undertakings dependent on the forced labor of slaves for the production of the commercial staples of cotton, tobacco, sugar, indigo, and rice, slaves were regarded as instruments of production to be used for the maximum profit (p. 44). Frazier asserted that "the most dehumanizing aspect of slavery was the trade in human beings" (p. 47). The slave traders, who had only a temporary monetary interest in slaves, viewed slaves as commodities.

Frazier suggested, therefore, that slavery was not conducive to the development of stable families for most blacks. The character of the sexual contacts and family life of slaves was determined, to some extent, by their masters' attitudes toward the slaves. Frazier (1949) noted the variety of ways in which slavery influenced family stability/instability for blacks:

Some masters with no regard for the preference of their slaves mated them as they did their stock. There were instances where Negro males were used as stallions. In a world where patriarchal traditions were firmly established, even less consideration was shown for the wishes of the female slaves. But this was not the whole story, for the majority of masters, either through necessity or because of their humanity, showed some regard for the wishes of the slaves in their mating. (p. 307) . . .

Under the most favorable conditions of slavery, the Negro family did, among certain elements of the slave population, acquire considerable stability. But very often the exigencies of the slave system, such as the settlement of an estate, might destroy the toughest bonds of conjugal affection and parental love. Because of the conditions imposed by the slave system, the mother was the most dependable and the most important member of the Negro family. . . . A Negro father might be sold and separated from his family, but when the Negro mother was sold, the master was forced to take into account her relation to her children. (p. 309)

The Emancipation Proclamation of 1862, which freed the slaves, created a state of bewilderment among the vast majority of illiterate slaves on southern plantations (Frazier, 1949, p. 109). The collapse of the traditional forms of control that had developed under the slave regime tended to demoralize the freed slave. In every state, thousands were found without employment, without homes, without means of subsistence, crowding into towns and about military posts, where they hoped to find protection and supplies (pp. 112-117). Among the better situated emancipated slaves, the family had acquired considerable stability and the transition to freedom did not result in disorganization. In acquiring land, the Negro husband and father laid the foundation for patriarchal authority in the family (p. 314). The point that Frazier was making is that there was not just one type of Negro response to slavery and to emancipation. Rather, there was a substantial amount of variation regarding family stability and participation in crime and delinquency. A major key to this diversity was the social and economic status of the freedmen.

Social and economic stratification. According to Frazier (1949), the roots of the social and economic stratification among the black population were related to the social distinctions of the individual roles of the slave in the social and economic organization of the plantation (p. 273). The main distinctions were between those who served in the house and those who labored in the fields. This division of labor on the plantation provided an outlet for individual talent and skill that continued to play a role among the freedmen.

Frazier (1949) indicated that the economic and social stratification of blacks after emancipation varied geographically. Those in the North and South, as well as those in rural and urban environments, had different social and economic opportunities. He illustrated the variation in class structure among Negroes by describing the social stratification for Washington, D.C., as follows:

> *Lower Class.* The lower class has a larger proportion of dark or black Negroes. . . . Many of them are recent migrants from the rural South. Among this class, there is considerable family disorganization. The lower class includes laborers, many service workers (barbers, charwomen, porters, janitors, etc.), many domestic workers, and semi-skilled workers. The group is characterized by a high rate of illiteracy, low incomes, and poverty. The social life of the more stable elements evolves about the church and the lodge. The less stable elements account for the high degree of criminality in the Negro community.
>
> *Middle Class.* The middle class includes a larger proportion of Negroes of lighter complexion who have had a longer residence in the city. . . . The middle class exhibits considerable "race pride" and strives to be respectable. Members of this class maintain a stable family life and place considerable value upon conventional sex behavior. For a livelihood, middle class families depend upon wage earners in skilled and semi-skilled occupations, domestic service, and the service occupations. . . .
>
> *Upper Class.* The upper class in the Negro community has long had a reputation for snobbishness toward dark or pure-blooded Negroes. . . . Such factors as family and general culture, occupation and income, and personal achievement and morals help to determine membership in this class. (pp. 286-287)

Frazier presented a strong argument for the relationship between the economic and social stratification among blacks and the degree of family disorganization, crime, and delinquency.

Crime and delinquency. Frazier's concern with family disorganization and poverty as they relate to crime and delinquency is evidenced in all three of the studies considered here (Frazier, 1932, 1939, 1949). He also briefly explored crime during slavery as well as in a large number of cities including Chicago (Frazier, 1932).

With reference to crime and slavery, Frazier (1949) wrote,

Throughout slavery, there were recalcitrant slaves who were beaten into submission or even killed. The idea once current that there was scarcely any crime among slaves has been shown to be false. Many of the crimes of the Negro slaves were aggressions or retaliations against whites if the record of Virginia is typical of the South. . . . Of the 1,117 convictions stating the offense, 346 were for murder, [with] 194 of the murdered persons being whites, characterized as follows: master, 56; overseer, 7; white man, 98; mistress, 11; other white woman, 13; master's child, 2; other white child, 7. . . . For other assaults, such as attempts to murder, there were 111 convictions, only two of which were assaults against Negroes. (p. 90)

Frazier further discussed several slave revolts[11] during the early part of the 19th century as well as the Underground Railroad[12] that provided for passage of the slaves to freedom in the North.

After emancipation in 1862, lynching of blacks became a common practice. "[When] the Negro failed to observe the traditional forms of etiquette toward the whites, when he exercised his right to vote, even when he acquired land and attended school, such actions were an indication that the Negro was 'getting out of his place' " (Frazier, 1949, p. 143). The Ku Klux Klan developed as the result of an organized attempt on the part of southern whites to force the blacks to accept a subordinate status in the social organization.

Juvenile delinquency in the cities. Frazier examined the delinquency rates of the black youths in cities in both the North and the South. He noted the overrepresentation of black children in court records in northern cities such as Indianapolis, Indiana; Gary, Indiana; and Dayton, Ohio (Frazier, 1932, p. 204; 1939, p. 359) as well as in southern cities such as Richmond, Virginia; Memphis, Tennessee; Nashville, Tennessee; and Charleston, South Carolina (Frazier, 1932, p. 204; 1939, pp. 359-360).

Frazier (1939) suggested that to understand the problem of Negro delinquency in southern cities, it was necessary to study the delinquent boys or girls in relation to their families and community settings (p. 360). To accomplish this, Frazier used several cases from a master's thesis written by one of his students (Mary LaVerta Huff) at Fisk University in Nashville. In this study, "nearly a half of the boys were charged with stealing, whereas the majority of the girls were charged with incorrigibility and disorderly conduct" in 1929 (p. 360).

These boys often are picked up for acts of theft, ranging from petty stealing to burglaries. Frazier (1939) presented the record of an 11-year-old boy charged with larceny to illustrate this:

The boy's father came in court and made [a] complaint that the boy would not work or go to school but was stealing all around the neighborhood and was teaching the small boys with whom he associates to steal. His mother brought him to court this day and made the same complaint. . . . From the statements of both parents and after talking to the boy, the court is satisfied that he is a truant and delinquent and is stealing. (p. 362)

The charges of incorrigibility against girls involved offenses such as sexual delinquency, truancy, ungovernability, running away, and continued association with vicious companions (Frazier, 1939, p. 363). Frazier (1939) found that, in some cases, the delinquent behavior of these girls is their response to what is held up to them as their expected role in life. A woman who called the probation officer for aid in managing her 13-year-old niece illustrated this:

> But I know Mary. I ought to when I have had her ever since she was five months old. . . . She is exactly like her mama. Her mama is my baby sister. . . . She had Mary when she was only 15 by an old nigger that didn't have a dime to his name. . . . I kept her in my house until Mary was born and treated her good and helped her with the baby. Then when Mary was five months old, this gal ups and runs off with another nigger, and I ain't laid eyes on her from that day to this. Mary has never seen her mama to remember. So this gal has just done like her mama. I understand alright. (p. 364)

Frazier's use of the ecological analysis and case history approach to studying delinquency was applied to Chicago (Frazier, 1932), which also was his dissertation.

With reference to delinquency in Chicago,[13] Frazier (1932) stated that the increase in the proportion of black cases had been most marked since the migrations from the South during and since World War I (p. 204). This increase in the number of black delinquents had followed the movement of the black population into the areas that have been characterized by a high rate of delinquency. The high delinquency rate that has characterized the area near the Loop in Chicago, "where a large part of the Negro population has found a foothold in the city, has existed over a period of thirty years 'notwithstanding the fact that the [racial] composition has changed markedly' " (p. 206). According to Frazier,

> In the first zone near the "Loop," where deterioration and the encroachment of business and industry were forcing the Negro families further south, the thirty-three boys who were arrested for juvenile delinquency in 1926 represented over two-fifths of the boys from ten to seventeen years of age in the area. . . . The next three zones showed only a slight improvement over the first in regard to juvenile delinquency. Three boys out of ten in these areas were arrested for juvenile delinquency, and some of these boys were arrested three and four times during the year. A decided decrease in the delinquency rate appeared in the fifth zone, where police probation officers had complaints against 15 percent of the boys. In the sixth zone, as in the case of family desertion and illegitimacy, the delinquency rate continued to decline sharply, and in the seventh zone less than 2 percent of the boys had complaints brought against them for delinquency. (pp. 209-210)

Frazier (1932) indicated that the highest rates of juvenile delinquency were in those areas of the black community that were characterized by deterioration and social disorganization (p. 211). In these areas, the customary forms of social control in the black group tended to decay, family discipline disappeared (especially in the cases of the many broken homes), and even the well-organized families lost much of their influence over the behavior of the children. Frazier quoted a black social worker from a good family background about the influence of the vicious behavior in the community where she was reared on her younger sisters:

> When our neighborhood began to be more thickly populated, it became known as the "red light district" for white sporting people. As the city grew, they were always being forced farther out, and as this was the edge of the city, they were permitted to live in this vicinity. I remember when my mother would go away from home, my sisters would make believe they were sporting people and roll up newspapers and pretend they were smoking cigarettes and even try to imitate their language by swearing. (pp. 211-212)

Frazier further indicated that one of these sisters became delinquent.

The case of a delinquent boy in the third zone shows the relationship between the family situation and community background and the high delinquency rate in this area. The boy was born in Jackson, Mississippi, and was taken to Washington, D.C., when he was 5 years old. After 6 years, the family moved to Chicago, and his delinquency began soon after coming to Chicago. The father was employed at unskilled work, and the mother was engaged in day work. Neither parent was at home from 6 a.m. until 5:30 p.m. The mother told the following story of the beginning of the boy's delinquency:

> We were living at [_____], and there was a boy who used to come over to see [M_____]. Him and this boy was great friends, so one day—one Sunday it was—I had gone to church and was on my way back, and when they saw me coming they ran. I had about fifteen dollars in a little bank, and they had thrown it out of the back window in the alley and ran down the stairs and got it and went off. . . . That was about a year after we came to Chicago, and ever since then [M_____] has been doing something. He has a gang of boys that he goes around with, and I can't do anything with him. He began when he was about twelve years old to stay away from home and school. (Frazier, 1932, p. 213)

Frazier used these cases to illustrate the close relationship between the community situation and juvenile delinquency. He argued that this relationship was further emphasized by the fact that the rates of delinquency showed wide variations in the black community. It was high in the areas of deterioration, where the poorer migrants from the South settled chiefly and in the area that was distinguished by crime, vice, and other forms of social disorganization. The rate of delinquency decreased considerably for the successive zones marking the expansion of the black community (p. 218).

Critique of Frazier

Frazier made many significant contributions to both sociology and criminology. The inclusion of his research and theoretical perspective of black delinquency during the early part of the 20th century provides a more accurate perspective of African American crime and delinquency than that usually included in theory texts limited to mainstream criminological theorists. Yet, his works are not found in current criminological theory texts (Akers, 1994; Cullen, 1984; Lilly et al., 1995; Martin, Mutchnick, and Austin, 1990; Williams and McShane, 1994).

When Frazier's works have been recognized by current scholars, they often have been distorted and misrepresented. The Moynihan Report is one such example. Platt (1991) suggested,

> Frazier plays an important symbolic role in the Moynihan Report in that he is quoted extensively on one page and quoted again in a highly visible place in the conclusion. Aside from the fact that Moynihan was selective in his use of Frazier's writings and ignored his contemporary works, the specific quotes used in the report were also surgically abstracted from Frazier's writings and quoted totally out of context. . . . When they are read out of their original context and abstracted from their situated meanings, one might easily conclude that Frazier regarded most black family life as disorganized, chaotic, and pathological. (p. 116)

The material presented from three of Frazier's major works provides evidence that Frazier had a much more complex vision of the black family and its relationship to crime and delinquency.

By developing a historical analysis of the experiences of blacks in America from slavery through emancipation, Frazier was able to demonstrate the diversity of experience among blacks during the early part of the 20th century. That is, Frazier provided evidence that the family stability, economic status, and delinquent behavior of blacks varied according to various roles in slavery, geographical locations, and the occupational and economic opportunities provided for them in their social environments.

Finally, Frazier, like other scholars discussed in this chapter, applied the diverse methodologies and theories of the Chicago School. Specifically, his theoretical analysis of the ecological distribution of black crime and delinquency used Park and Burgess's concentric zone theory, and his historical analysis of the impact of slavery on the black family and delinquency used a Chicago School theoretical perspective. Although these conceptual analyses do not have a set of propositions that form a logical deductive system that can be tested (as required by the classical definitions of theory), they could fit into Merton's theories of the middle range. They also use many of the theoretical arguments of conflict theory (see Chapter 8). Platt (1991) stated that Frazier's research and theoretical analyses were distorted in the Moynihan Report for political purposes, but this work certainly has the potential to inform policy in the current political world.

Clifford R. Shaw (1895-1957) and Henry D. McKay (1899-1980)

Clifford Shaw and Henry McKay both were graduate students at the University of Chicago during the 1920s. Although neither Shaw nor McKay completed the Ph.D., they worked together as a team for more than 30 years at the Institute for Ju-

---

INSET 5.3   ### Clifford R. Shaw (1895-1957)

Clifford Shaw was born in August 1895 in Luray, Indiana. He was the 5th of 10 children. At 14 years of age, he left school to assist his father with the farming duties. After becoming bored with farming, Shaw began to work on his vocabulary while completing his duties. In addition to working on his vocabulary, he read at night. Shaw persisted at these things because he was intent on eventually joining the ministry (Snodgrass, 1976).

When Shaw turned 15 years of age, he met a minister who encouraged him to pursue his interest in the ministry. Later that year, Shaw enrolled in the ministry program at Adrian College in Michigan. During his junior year, he recalled, "my attitude toward religion [became] very hostile" (Snodgrass, 1976, p. 4). Because of this change in sentiment, Shaw left school for a 1-year stint in the military. In 1918, Shaw returned to Adrian and completed his A.B. degree. Soon after completing his degree, he enrolled in the graduate program in sociology at the University of Chicago.

In addition to his graduate studies, Shaw worked as a parole officer from 1921 to 1923 and as a probation officer from 1924 to 1926. In 1924, he discontinued his graduate studies due to his inability to pass the language requirement for the Ph.D. Although he never completed his Ph.D., he was awarded an honorary doctorate of law from his alma mater (Adrian) in 1939 (Snodgrass, 1976, p. 4). Throughout his life, Shaw was very productive, most notably while working for the Institute for Juvenile Research at the University of Chicago. Some of Shaw's most notable publications include *Delinquency Areas* (Shaw and McKay, 1929), *The Jackroller* (Shaw, 1966, originally published in 1930), *The Natural History of a Delinquent Career* (Shaw, 1931); *Brothers in Crime* (Shaw, McKay, McDonald, and Hanson, 1938), and *Juvenile Delinquency and Urban Areas* (1972, originally published in 1942).

Henry D. McKay (1899-1980)

Henry McKay was born in Hand County, South Dakota, in December 1899. He was the fifth of seven children. During his youth, McKay worked on the farm with his father and attended public schools. He later went on to receive his A.B. from Dakota Wesleyan University (Snodgrass, 1976). In 1923, McKay enrolled in graduate school at the University of Chicago, where he remained for 1 year before heading to the University of Illinois to teach and study (p. 5).

During his term at Illinois, he met and became close friends with Edwin Sutherland. McKay left Illinois and headed back to the University of Chicago in 1926. Although he remained there for 3 years, he was unable to complete his degree due to the language requirement (p. 5). McKay, in conjunction with Clifford R. Shaw, published numerous studies showing that the primary cause of crime was social conditions.

—Shaun L. Gabbidon
Pennsylvania State University at Harrisburg

SOURCE: Excerpted from the writings of Shaun L. Gabbidon with permission.

venile Research near the Chicago Loop (Snodgrass, 1976, p. 2). Shaw was appointed director of the institute in 1926, and McKay was employed as a clerical research assistant in January 1927 (p. 5). By 1938, McKay had become the senior assistant research sociologist at the institute, and Shaw was director of both the institute and the Chicago Area Project. As indicated in the biographical inset on Shaw and McKay (Inset 5.3), they came from similar social backgrounds. Although their social origins were quite similar, Snodgrass (1976) described the personalities of the two men as strikingly different:

> McKay was the quiet statistician, a man who stayed removed at the institute and plotted the maps, calculated the rates, ran the correlations, and described the findings which located empirically and depicted cartographically the distribution of crime and delinquency in Chicago. Shaw, on the other hand, was an activist, who "related" to delinquents and got their life stories, and an organizer, who attempted to create a community reform movement. McKay was the professional scholar and gentleman—polite, kind, thoughtful—an academic out to prove his position with empirical evidence. Shaw was the more emotional practitioner, a professional administrator and organizer—talkative, friendly, personable, persuasive, energetic, and quixotic—out to make his case through action and participation. (pp. 2-3)

Together, Shaw and McKay produced contributions in three main areas of sociology. The ecological studies analyzed the distribution of delinquency in Chicago and other cities. They were followed by the creation of a delinquency prevention program known as the Chicago Area Project. The third contribution was a collection of autobiographies of delinquents that produced three life histories: *The Jackroller* (Shaw, 1966, originally published in 1930), *The Natural History of a Delinquent Career* (Shaw, 1931), and *Brothers in Crime* (Shaw, McKay, McDonald, and Hanson, 1938).

Ecological Studies of Delinquency

Shaw and McKay (1931) published their findings on the distribution of delinquency in American cities in 1931 as a report for the National Commission on Law Observance and Enforcement. A second study with updated data was published in 1942 with a revised edition in 1969 and a "second impression" published in 1972 (Shaw and McKay, 1972). The ecological studies of delinquency reported by Shaw and McKay include research in Chicago (1931, 1972); Boston (1972); Philadelphia (1931, 1972); Richmond (1931, 1972); Cleveland, Ohio (1931, 1972); Cincinnati, Ohio (1972); Birmingham, Alabama (1931); Denver, Colorado (1931); and Seattle, Washington (1931).[14] Although they reported some discrepancies between cities in definitions of delinquency and police dealing with juvenile offenders as well as some differences in their own methodologies,[15] their overall findings were quite similar in all of the cities. Shaw and McKay concentrated on their research in Chicago in both books and included only brief discussions of the other cities. Therefore, the present discussion concentrates on the Chicago study.

In both the 1931 and 1942 studies, Shaw and McKay created spot maps to show the distribution by place of residence of juvenile delinquents at various stages of the justice system. They also developed spot maps to show distribution of railroads, industrial parks, and residences (Shaw and McKay, 1931, p. 40); school truants (Shaw and McKay, 1972, p. 91); and tuberculosis cases (p. 102). In addition, they developed rate maps to demonstrate the rate of delinquency, truancy, infant mortality, insanity, and tuberculosis cases in specified areas in the city.[16] Finally, Shaw and McKay (1931, 1972) used Park and Burgess's concentric zones to illustrate the distribution of delinquency in each of the zones of the city.

Findings on Distribution of Delinquency in Chicago

Shaw and McKay (1931, p. 68; 1972, p. 143) noted that the highest rates of delinquency most frequently are found in areas in or adjacent to the districts zoned for industry and commerce. These are areas of physical deterioration and decreasing residential populations. Shaw and McKay (1931) explained,

> As the city grows, the areas of light industry and commerce near the center of the city expand and encroach upon the areas used for residential purposes. The dwellings in such areas, already undesirable because of age, are allowed to deteriorate under the threat of invasion because further investment in them is unprofitable. Others are junked to make way for new industrial or commercial structures. The effect of these changes is that the areas become increasingly undesirable through general depreciation. . . .
>
> Likewise, the areas that are slowly increasing in population tend to be the areas with medium rates of delinquents, while the areas of more rapid increases tend to be the low-rate areas. (pp. 69, 71)

However, Shaw and McKay went on to state that "decreasing population, rather than contributing to delinquency, is a symptom of the more basic changes that are taking place in those areas of the city that are subject to invasion by industry and commerce" (p. 73). For example, the districts near the center of the city that show a decreasing population have the greatest density of population as measured by the number of inhabitants per acre. This density is greatest in the areas within 2 miles of the central district and tends to decrease with considerable regularity out from the inner zone (p. 74).

Shaw and McKay (1972) suggested that areas adjacent to industry and commerce also are characterized by low rents and low family income, which are complementary characteristics. The rents in old dilapidated buildings in deteriorated neighborhoods are naturally low, and these low rents attract the population group of the lowest economic status. The areas of lowest rentals correspond quite closely with those of high delinquency rates (p. 148). There also is a relationship between families on relief and rates of delinquency (Shaw and McKay, 1931, p. 77; 1972, p. 147). Median rentals and home ownership, on the other hand, both are inversely related to delinquency (Shaw and McKay, 1972, p. 149). Another characteristic of the areas of decreasing population, physical deterioration, and economic dependency is the high percentage of foreign and black population (Shaw and McKay, 1931, p. 79). That is, the most recent arrivals—persons of foreign birth and those who have migrated from other sections of this country—find it necessary to make their homes in neighborhoods of low economic status. The data from both studies (1931 and 1942) suggest that the foreign born and blacks are concentrated in the areas of high rates of delinquency. Shaw and McKay (1972), however, presented an extensive argument against assuming that delinquency was an inherent trait of the foreign born and blacks.

> While it is apparent from these data that the foreign born and the Negroes are concentrated in the areas of high rates of delinquents, the meaning of this association is not easily determined. One might be led to assume that the relatively large number of boys brought into court is due to the presence of certain racial or national groups were it not for the fact that the population composition of many of these neighborhoods has changed completely without appreciable change in their rank as to rates of delinquents. Clearly, one must beware of attaching causal significance to race or nativity. For, in the present social and economic system, it is the Negroes and the foreign born, or at least the newest immigrants, who have least access to the necessities of life and who are therefore least prepared for the competitive struggle. It is they who are forced to live in the worst slum areas and who are least able to organize against the effects of such living. (pp. 154-155) . . .
>
> Within the same type of social area, the foreign born and the natives, recent immigrant nationalities, and older immigrants produced very similar rates of delinquents. Those among the foreign born and among the recent immigrants who . . . lived in physically adequate residential areas of higher economic status displayed low rates of delinquents, while conversely, those among the native born and among the older immigrants who . . . occupied physically deteriorated areas of low economic status displayed high rates of delinquents. Negroes living in the most deteriorated and disorganized portions of the Negro community possessed the highest Negro rate of delinquents, just as whites living in comparable white areas showed the highest white rates. (pp. 160-161)

Theoretical Interpretation of Findings

Shaw and McKay (1931) continued their discussion of the distribution of delinquency in Chicago by claiming that percentage of families owning their homes, percentage of foreign born, and so forth, may serve as formal indexes for making distinctions among the areas of the city (p. 109). Yet, the traditions, standards, and moral sentiments that characterize the neighborhood life may be more important in explaining the distinctions among the various communities. The authors further suggested that children living in middle class areas, where delinquency rates are lower, are insulated from direct contact with delinquency through the shared traditions and values within the neighborhood. By contrast, Shaw and McKay (1972) argued that areas of low-income status, where rates of delinquency are high, are characterized by wide diversity in norms and standards of behavior (p. 171).

After reporting similar findings from the research conducted in the other American cities, Shaw and McKay (1972) concluded that delinquency "has its roots in the dynamic life of the community" (p. 315). They summarized their analysis as follows:

> In the low-income areas, where there is the greatest deprivation and frustration; where, in the history of the city, immigrant and migrant groups have brought together the widest variety of divergent cultural traditions and institutions; and where there exists the greatest disparity between the social values to which the people aspire and the availability of facilities for acquiring these values in conventional ways, the development of crime as an organized way of life is most marked. (p. 319)

Based on these findings and the theoretical interpretations of these findings, Shaw set out to establish a prevention program known as the Chicago Area Project.

The Chicago Area Project

Following Shaw and McKay's (1972) conclusion that "the delinquency-producing factors are inherent in the community" (p. 315), they[17] determined that reduction in the volume of delinquency probably would not occur without changes in the economic and social conditions surrounding children in high-delinquency areas. Thus, Shaw set out to develop a program of community action, initiated and carried on by the concerted efforts of citizens and the local residents' interest in improvement in all aspects of community life.

> It was for the purpose of assisting in the development of such programs of community action in low-income areas that in 1932 the Institute for Juvenile Research and the Behavior Research Fund initiated the work of what is now known as the Chicago Area Project, a private corporation with a board of directors made up of prominent citizens interested in delinquency prevention. (p. 322)

The Chicago Area Project was begun with the "local community area or neighborhood as the unit of operation" (p. 322). The work was developed on a neighborhood basis because it was assumed that "delinquency is a product chiefly of community forces and conditions and must be dealt with, therefore, as a community problem" (p. 322).

Shaw and McKay believed that for a prevention program to be successful, the planning and management must be done by local residents. Therefore, the activities in each area were planned and implemented by a committee composed of representative local citizens. These committees included members of churches, societies, labor unions, trades and professions, business groups, athletic clubs, and the like. The committees functioned as boards of directors and assumed full responsibility for sponsoring and managing all aspects of the community program. Shaw and McKay (1972) contended that the local residents would achieve a sense of self-reliance, preserve their self-respect, and enhance their status among their neighbors by contributing time and energy to the creation of better opportunities for children (p. 323). Shaw also advocated the employment of local workers to staff each neighborhood program, noting that "indigenous workers have intimate and significant relationships with local organizations, institutions, groups, and persons which are of great value in promoting programs of social action" (p. 323). However, it also was argued that professional workers were an important part of the project because they can translate their special knowledge into the thinking, planning, and practices of the local residents.

The use and coordination of community resources also was considered an indispensable part of the success of the project. Whereas the local residents often had been isolated from community organizations/resources, Shaw envisioned that the committee of local residents would seek the cooperation of churches, schools, recreation centers, labor unions, industries, societies, clubs, and other social groups in developing action programs for the improvement of the neighborhood. Through this process, a great variety of activities—recreation programs, summer camps, scouting, handicraft forums, trips, projects to improve the housing and physical conditions in the neighborhoods, and so forth—were organized. Parent-teacher groups were established to effect a more satisfactory working relationship between the school and community (Shaw and McKay, 1972, p. 324). It was important to the success of the Chicago Area Project that these program activities be controlled by the local communities and that they receive the credit for the success of the activities.

Shaw and McKay (1972) concluded their discussion of the Chicago Area Project by claiming that the local residents have successfully demonstrated that they possess the talents and capabilities necessary to effectively participate in the planning and management of welfare institutions, agencies, and programs (p. 325). They claimed that the residents have planned, developed, and implemented summer camps, community centers, and health and sanitation programs and also have effectively functioned in the improvement of their schools and contributed to the adjustment of juvenile and adult offenders. Although current criminologists might question the actual success of the program, one cannot deny the effectiveness and, therefore, the importance of this policy on delinquency and crime in these Chicago neighborhoods.

The Life Histories of Delinquent Boys

The third contribution, autobiographies or life histories, also was predominantly the work of Shaw, who enjoyed the social work aspect of research and interacted frequently with those whom he studied. A large portion of the report on *Social Factors in Juvenile Delinquency* (Shaw and McKay, 1931) was devoted to brief excerpts from various case histories of delinquents to augment the ecological analysis of the distribution of delinquency. Each life history was based on the "boy's own story" as written by the boy or as obtained through interviews with the boy and others acquainted with him. Each autobiography also was supplemented by official records. In discussing the value of the delinquent boy's own story, Shaw (1966) indicated,

> The life record itself is the delinquent's own account of his experiences, written as an autobiography, as a diary, or presented in the course of a series of interviews. The unique feature of such documents is that they are recorded in the first person, in the boy's own words.... Each case study should include, along with the life history document, the usual family history; the medical, psychiatric, and psychological findings;

the official record of arrest, offenses, and commitments; [and] the description of the play-group relationships. . . .

His story will reflect his own personal attitudes and interpretations, for it is just these personal factors which are so important in the study and treatment of the case. Thus, rationalizations, fabrications, prejudices, [and] exaggerations are quite as valuable as objective descriptions, provided, of course, that these reactions be properly identified and classified. (pp. 1-3)

The Jackroller

This boy's story originally was published in 1930 by Shaw (1966). Stanley was 22 years of age at the time his story was published. The account of this boy's delinquency begins with a history of the official record of arrests and commitments as well as his employment and school history. His first contact with police was at 6 years of age, when he was found sleeping on the street, having run away from home 2 days earlier. The police took him home. His delinquent acts consisted mostly of truancy, running away from home, shoplifting, and stealing from drunks during the first 17½ years of his life. The official records indicate that he was in and out of foster homes, detention homes, and reformatories, and also had a record of sporadic employment and school attendance, during these years.

In his story, Stanley blamed his stepmother for much of his behavior. He gave the following account of his relationship with her:

From a quiet woman, the stepmother changed to a hell-cat full of venom and spite. The first time she struck me was when I was in my favorite nook behind the stove, playing with the cat. She pulled me out and beat me, striking me in the face and on the back with her hard and bony hand. That was the first time that I ever knew fear. After many beatings, I became more and more afraid. (Shaw, 1966, p. 49) . . .

My fear and hatred made me avoid her. . . . So I grew old enough to go out on the street. The life in the streets and alleys became fascinating and enticing. (p. 50)

Despite his fascination with the streets and his fear of his stepmother, Stanley frequently returned home. Usually, he was taken home by the police. He claimed that his stepmother sent him out to steal from stores (from the market where he would steal vegetables for her) and to break into boxcars. He stated that he was so afraid of her that "I couldn't do anything but obey" (p. 53). Stanley gave the following account of his experience in a detention home, the St. Charles School for Boys, and then at the Illinois State Reformatory:

The detention home at first seemed like a palace to me. It was clean and in order. The very first night, I took a nice bath (the first one I ever had), had a change of clothes, and [ate] a good meal. (p. 57) . . .

I was awed by the sight of the St. Charles School for Boys, for it is a beautiful landscape to gaze upon from the outside. But it is quite a different place on the inside, as I learned during fifty months of incarceration there. (p. 65)

After having my hair shaved off [and being] given a number for a name and a large tablespoon to eat with, I was assigned to a cell [at the Illinois State Reformatory].

The cell was bare, hard, and drab. As I sat on my bunk thinking, a great wave of feeling shook me.... There, for the first time in my life, I realized I was a criminal. Before, I had been just a mischievous lad, a poor city waif, a petty thief, a habitual runaway.... That night I tried to sleep, but instead I only tossed on my bunk, disturbed by my new life.... When the whistle blew for breakfast the next morning, I was heartsick and weak. (p. 103)

While in these institutions, Stanley heard stories of the crimes of other boys and men. Although he often resolved to get a job and not continue to steal, he usually became dissatisfied with the job and returned to the streets and stealing. He gave the following account of "jackrolling":

This first night, we were walking along the street and spied a drunk who appeared to be a "live one." We waited until he got near a dark spot and then surrounded him. He was very drunk.... My nerves were a little shaky at first, but throwing caution to the wind, I sprang at him.... An alley was close by, so we dragged him into it and proceeded to search him.... Making sure that no one saw us, we left the bum in the alley and went to my room. We were overjoyed to find ninety-six dollars in the money belt. (p. 140)

The Natural History of a Delinquent Career and Brothers in Crime

These two case studies followed the same basic format as that of *The Jackroller*. The second life history in Shaw's series, *The Natural History of a Delinquent Career* (Shaw, 1931), is the study of a young male recidivist who was sentenced to a state penal institution after being convicted of robbery with a gun and rape. In the news, he was characterized as a "young brute," "moron," and "beast." Shaw saw the act of robbery as a symptom of the types of social experiences that had characterized the life history of this boy throughout his childhood and early adolescence. Thus, Shaw used the youth's own story to tell of his experiences in his family, delinquent play groups, and criminal gangs as well as his contacts with junk dealers, fences, and residents who purchased his stolen merchandise and so forth to understand the process of social conditioning that led to his life of crime.

The third life history, by Shaw and colleagues (1938), is a study of the social background and delinquent careers of five brothers[18]: John Martin (the oldest), Edward Martin, James Martin, Michael Martin, and Carl Martin (the youngest). This case study followed the same basic format of the two previous life histories except that it involved five brothers. It began by presenting the official arrest and commitment history of each of the brothers, followed by excerpts from the boys' accounts of their first steps in their careers (tracing their movement in delinquency from begging to burglaries), the social background and life history for each boy, and methods of treatment. The process by which the younger brothers became involved in delinquency and crime was demonstrated by the official records of their early contacts with the police and by their life stories. The two oldest boys were first picked up by police at 8 years of age (pp. 6, 10). The younger brothers had their first contacts with police at progressively younger ages and in the company of the older brothers, with the youngest brother being picked up by police at 2 years and 10 months of age (p. 43).

Critique of Shaw and McKay

The importance of Shaw and McKay's works is evidenced on several accounts. First, these authors made contributions to research, theory, and policy through their three projects. In the ecological studies, they conducted extensive research on the distribution of delinquency in numerous cities. They presented a theoretical explanation for their findings that emphasize process, social control, and cultural conflict. Shaw, as director of the Chicago Area Project, then developed policy based on the research and theory intended to rectify the problems in these urban neighborhoods. Shaw and McKay were among the first criminologists to incorporate theory, research, and policy into their scholarship. Although their theory does not meet the classical definitions of theory, this contribution cannot be ignored.

Shaw and McKay's works also are significant as an example of the diversity of methodology that is useful in studying crime. To examine the distribution of delinquency, they relied on official records and ecological maps through the use of quantitative data and analysis. But they also explored the process by which individuals become delinquent by combining the qualitative methods of diaries or the boys' own stories and interviews and the quantitative methods of official records to acquire life histories/autobiographies of delinquent boys.

Thus, in the spirit of the Chicago School, Shaw and McKay used a diversity of methodological and theoretical approaches to the study of delinquency. As a result of their diverse theoretical analyses, one can find the early development of the interactionist perspective, control theory, and conflict theory in their works. These authors also followed the Chicago School perspective of concentrating on male delinquents even when they had data on female delinquents.

Edwin Hardin Sutherland (1883-1950)

Edwin Sutherland was born into a deeply religious fundamentalist Baptist family. Schuessler wrote that Sutherland's parents "presided over a Protestant parsonage in a rural community, and in that setting they succeeded in giving their son a sense of the moral importance of carrying out one's duties" (cited in Gaylord and Galliher, 1988, p. 7). Although Sutherland had a falling out with his father and broke with the Baptist church, he retained his father's fundamental ethical values throughout his life. He was an outstanding student and acquired a classical education in languages, history, literature, natural science, and religion (pp. 8-9).

| INSET 5.4 | Edwin Hardin Sutherland (1883-1950) |

Edwin Sutherland was born on August 13, 1883, in Gibbon, Nebraska. He was the fourth child in a family of five boys and three girls. All accounts indicate that Sutherland came from a family with a strong religious background (Martin, Mutchnick, and Austin, 1990; Gaylord and Galliher, 1988). He attended school at Grand Island College in Grand Island, Nebraska. In 1904, Sutherland received an A.B. degree and accepted a teaching position at Sioux Falls College in South Dakota.

In 1905, Sutherland enrolled in a correspondence course in sociology offered by the University of Chicago. The course was offered by the university's home study department and was supervised by Annie Marion. Marion, a graduate of the University of Chicago, encouraged Sutherland to take a course on the "Treatment of Crime" (Gaylord and Galliher, 1988, p. 17).

In 1906, Sutherland left Grand Island College and enrolled at the University of Chicago. After taking the course recommended by Marion, Sutherland became interested in criminology. However, 3 years later, he left Chicago to teach at Grand Island College. On returning to Chicago in 1911, Sutherland resumed his studies and changed his major to political economy. It was there where he developed a close relationship with Paul Hoxie in the political economy department. This influ-ence led Sutherland to graduate with a dual major of so-ciology and political economy.

After completing his doctorate, Sutherland accepted a teaching position at William Jewell College in Mis-souri. Six years later, he moved on to the University of Illi-nois. It was there where the chairperson of the sociology department encouraged Sutherland to write *Criminol-ogy* (Sutherland, 1924; see also Gaylord and Galliher, 1988, p. 53).

By 1926, Sutherland was off again, this time to the University of Minnesota. Three years later, he again was on the move to the Bureau of Social Hygiene in New York City. Sutherland returned to the University of Chi-cago in 1930, accepting a research professorship. This position resulted in two later publications: *Twenty Thou-sand Homeless Men* (Sutherland and Locke, 1936) and *The Professional Thief* (Sutherland, 1937). Also, in the 1939 edition of *Principles of Criminology*, Sutherland made the first "explicit statement of the theory of differen-tial association" (Gaylord and Galliher, 1988, p. 132).

In 1935, Sutherland moved on to Indiana University, which was his final academic appointment. At Indiana, he flourished and became the preeminent criminologist of his day. This is evidenced by his election to the presi-dency of the American Sociological Society in 1939 and to the presidency of the Sociological Research Asso-ciation in 1940 (Gaylord and Galliher, 1988, p. 123). During the latter years of his life, Sutherland continued his productive ways in publishing another version of *Princi-ples of Criminology*. His final publication, *White Collar Crime* (Sutherland, 1949), was published just prior to his untimely death in 1950 (Martin et al., 1990, p. 143).

—*Shaun L. Gabbidon*
Pennsylvania State University at Harrisburg

SOURCE: Excerpted from the writings of Shaun L. Gabbidon with permission.

Sutherland began his graduate studies at the University of Chicago in 1906 and was influenced by several professors including Henderson, Mead, Small, and Thomas from sociology. Gaylord and Galliher (1988) stated, "Henderson was re-sponsible for Sutherland's changing his major from history to the 'type of sociology' that Dr. Henderson presented" (p. 19). Henderson also was his adviser. As indicated in the biographical inset on Sutherland (Inset 5.4), he had several teaching positions between 1913 and 1935, when he began his 15-year stay at Indiana University. In 1914, Sutherland was quoted as saying, "My interests are confined almost entirely to investigation of such things as farmers' organizations, trade unions, socialism, and similar movements of 'the people' to improve themselves" (p. 48). While teaching at William Jewell College during the mid- to late 1910s, he wrote just one article, "What Rural Health Surveys Have Revealed." It was published in 1916 in the *Monthly Bulletin: State Board of Charities and Corrections* (p. 50). This is not a very impressive publication record for a scholar who was to be ranked "among the most prominent, if not as the most prominent, of American criminologists" (Martin et al., 1990, p. 139).

Sutherland made three major contributions to criminology that have earned him this place of prominence. His earliest contribution on the topic of crime was a *Criminology* text (Sutherland, 1924) that Burgess called "the first sociological textbook in the field" of criminology (Gaylord and Galliher, 1988, p. 62). This contained his differential association theory, and the text dominated the field of criminology for 45 years (Schuessler, 1973, p. xiii). His second contribution was *The Professional Thief* (Sutherland, 1937), based on the account of Chic Conway, a professional thief. Finally, Sutherland (1949) laid the groundwork for conflict theory with his research on white collar crime, which is discussed in detail in Chapter 8.

Differential Association Theory

Schuessler (1973) suggested that "the publication in 1924 of *Criminology*, as the first edition of *Principles* was titled, marks Sutherland's official entry into the field" of criminology (p. xii). According to Schuessler (p. xii) and Gaylord and Galliher (1988, p. 53), the idea for the criminology text came from Edward C. Hayes, who was the chair of the Department of Sociology at the University of Illinois, where Sutherland taught from 1919 to 1926. In 1921, Hayes, who was the editor of the Lippincott Sociological Series, asked Sutherland to write a criminology textbook for the Lippincott series. Hayes believed that the younger faculty should be engaged in some major project for their own good. Until this time, Sutherland's professional identity had oscillated between sociology and political economy. From this point onward, Sutherland began to devote himself to criminology almost exclusively (p. 53).

What set Sutherland's text apart from other works was its avoidance of the pitfalls of biological theories of crime and its attempt to promote a sociological definition of crime and use of sociological concepts then common within the discipline. In an address given as retiring president of the Ohio Valley Sociological Society in 1942, Sutherland explained the development of the theory of differential association theory as follows:

> My principal interest in criminology at that time was the controversy between heredity and environment. . . . I made some effort from the first to apply sociological concepts to criminal behavior, especially Thomas's attitude value and four wishes, but also imi-

tation, culture-conflict (implicitly rather than explicitly), and a little later Park's and Burgess's four processes. . . . Almost all the ideas in the 1939 edition of my *Criminology* are present in the 1924 edition, but they are implicit rather than explicit, appear[ing] in connection with criticisms of other theories rather than as organized constructive statements. (Schuessler, 1973, pp. 14-15)

Sutherland noted in this speech that the second edition of his *Criminology* in 1934 showed some progress toward a point of view and a general hypothesis (Sutherland, 1934). He further stated that he was surprised when McKay referred to his theory of criminal behavior, and Sutherland asked McKay what his theory was. McKay referred Sutherland to the following quotation:

> The hypotheses of this book are as follows. First, any person can be trained to adopt and follow any pattern of behavior which he is able to execute. Second, failure to follow a prescribed pattern of behavior is due to the inconsistencies and lack of harmony in the influences which direct the individual. Third, the conflict of cultures is therefore the fundamental principle in the explanation of crime. (pp. 15-16)

In the third edition of *Principles of Criminology* in 1939, Sutherland developed his differential association theory into seven hypotheses. He placed it in the first chapter "under the insistent prodding of Henry McKay, Hans Riemer, and Harvey Locke" (p. 17). Sutherland continued to discuss the theory with his graduate students and colleagues, and by 1947 he published the theory of differential association in its final form in the fourth edition of his *Principles of Criminology* (Sutherland, 1947). Sutherland suggested that these nine propositions, shown in Inset 5.5, presented a general theory of criminal behavior.[19] He further stated that the theory of differential association of criminal behavior is based on the assumption that a criminal act occurs when a situation appropriate for it, as defined by a person, is present.

In discussing the development of his theory in his 1942 address, Sutherland argued that culture conflict is the basic principle in the explanation of crime. Differential association may be a statement of cultural conflict in relation to religion, politics, standard of living, or other things. It also may be a statement of conflict from the point of view of the person who commits the crime. The two types of culture impinge on the person, or he or she has associations with the two types of cultures, and this is differential association. Sutherland also used the concept of differential group organization. He stated, "Differential group organization . . . should explain the crime rate, while differential association should explain the criminal behavior of a person" (Schuessler, 1973, pp. 20-21).

The Professional Thief

The Professional Thief (Sutherland, 1937) is a description of the profession of theft by a person, Chic Conwell, who had been engaged in that profession almost continuously for more than 25 years. In contrast to the life histories/autobiographies

Sutherland's Differential Association Theory

(1) *Criminal behavior is learned.* Negatively, this means that criminal behavior is not inherited. . . .

(2) *Criminal behavior is learned in interaction with other persons in a process of communication.*

(3) *The principal part of the learning of criminal behavior occurs within intimate personal groups.* Negatively, this means that the impersonal agencies of communication, such as picture shows and newspapers, play a relatively unimportant part in the genesis of criminal behavior.

(4) *When criminal behavior is learned, the learning includes (a) techniques of committing the crime, which are sometimes very complicated, sometimes very simple; (b) the specific direction of motives, drives, rationalizations, and attitudes.*

(5) *The specific direction of motives and drives is learned from definitions of legal codes as favorable or unfavorable.* In some societies, an individual is surrounded by persons who invariably define the legal codes as rules to be observed, whereas in others, he is surrounded by persons whose definitions are favorable to the violation of the legal codes. In our American society, these definitions are almost always mixed, and consequently we have culture conflict in relation to the legal codes.

(6) *A person becomes delinquent because of an excess of definitions favorable to violation of law over definitions unfavorable to violation of law.* This is the principle of differential association. It refers to both criminal and anti-criminal associations and has to do with counteracting forces. When persons become criminals, they do so because of contacts with criminal patterns and also because of isolation from anti-criminal patterns. . . .

(7) *Differential associations may vary in frequency, duration, priority, and intensity.* . . . "Frequency" and "duration" modalities of associations are obvious and need no explanation. "Priority" is assumed to be important in the sense that lawful behavior developed in early childhood may persist throughout life and also that delinquent behavior developed in early childhood may persist throughout life. . . . "Intensity" is not precisely defined, but it has to do with such things as the prestige of the source of a criminal or anti-criminal pattern and with emotional reactions related to the associations. . . .

(8) *The process of learning criminal behavior by association with criminal and anti-criminal patterns involves all of the mechanisms that are involved in any other learning.* Negatively, this means that the learning of criminal behavior is not restricted to the process of imitation. . . .

(9) *Though criminal behavior is an expression of general needs and values, it is not explained by those general needs and values since noncriminal behavior is an expression of the same needs and values.* Thieves generally steal in order to secure money, but likewise honest laborers work in order to secure money.

SOURCE: Sutherland (1947, pp. 5-7).

of delinquent boys by Shaw, Sutherland's *The Professional Thief* uses the knowledge of a professional thief to describe the life and culture of this profession.

Definition. According to Conwell,

> The professional thief is one who . . . makes a regular business of stealing. He devotes his entire working time and energy to larceny and may steal three hundred and sixty-five days a year. . . . Every act is carefully planned. . . . The professional thief has technical skills and methods which are different from those of other professional crim-

inals. Manual skill is important in some of the rackets, but the most important thing in all the rackets is the ability to manipulate people. The thief depends on his approach, front, wits, and in many instances his talking ability. . . . The professional thief is generally migratory and may work in all the cities of the United States. He generally uses a particular city as headquarters. (Sutherland, 1937, p. 3)

The principal rackets of the professional thief are

the cannon (picking pockets), the heel (sneak-thieving from stores, banks, and offices), the boost (shoplifting), penny-weighting (stealing from jewelry stores by substitution), hotel prowling (stealing from hotel rooms), the con (confidence game), some miscellaneous rackets related in certain respects to the confidence games, laying paper (passing illegal checks, money orders, and other papers), and the shake (the shakedown of, or extortion from, persons engaged in, or about to engage in, illegal acts). (p. 43)

All of these rackets involve manipulation of suckers by nonviolent methods.

Recruitment. The professional thief has no policy of recruiting for the profession. Such a person always can obtain adequate partners from among the thieves who already are professionals. A person can become a professional thief only if he or she is selected and trained by those who already are professionals (Sutherland, 1937, p. 21). There are few limits on the types of people who become professional thieves. Professional female thieves usually are recruited from the ranks of prostitutes, waitresses, cashiers, and hotel or restaurant employees (p. 23). In rare instances, legitimate workers in other lines of work started by boosting clothes for their own use and continued boosting. Contacts between female amateurs and female professionals are much more frequently and easily made than those between male amateurs and male professionals. Conwell stated that "this is because most female thieves start at boosting and, upon arrest, are placed in contact with professional boosters"[20] (p. 24).

The mob. The working group of professional thieves is known as a mob, troupe, or outfit. Although the lives of most mobs are comparatively short—for a season or for a trip or two—many have grifted intact for years (Sutherland, 1937, p. 27). Just as professional thieves have a code of ethics, the mob also has many codes or rules. Among these are that the division of all gains in all rackets is to be even, the nut (i.e., expenses) must come off the top of every touch, and all loans must be repaid out of the first knock-up money. A major understanding among the mob is "in on the good, in on the bad." That is, if one member of a mob gets a pinch and the case costs $500, then each member of the mob contributes his share of it (p. 36). Members of the mob also are expected to deal honestly with one another.

It also is understood that one member of a mob should not cut in on another member. Each member is given his part to do and is expected to handle that part, except in the case of an inexperienced person who has been taken on for a minor part. In case any member of a mob is pinched or arrested in connection with the mob activities, it is the responsibility of every member of the mob to do everything possible to fix the case. These codes may be summed up in the statement, "A mob must be a unit and work as a unit" (Sutherland, 1937, p. 38).

Code of ethics. Professional thieves also have a strong code of ethics that is much more binding than those among legitimate commercial firms (Sutherland, 1937, p. 9). One of the first rules of ethics is that no thief may squawk (i.e., inform) on another thief. A professional thief must not squawk on another even when he or she has been beat by the other. A professional thief reported the following experience:

> I was riding on a streetcar in Chicago when I felt someone put his hand in my prat [i.e., hip pocket] clear up to the elbow. I turned and saw that it was Eddie Jackson, whom I knew and who knew me. When he saw who it was, he asked in friendly sarcasm, "What in hell are you doing here? Why can't you stay out of the way?" He led his mob away knowing that there was absolutely no danger from me. (p. 11)

Another rule among all thieves except cannons is that if one mob comes into a place and finds another mob already at work, then it will leave at once. It will do so partly out of professional courtesy and partly for safety. Also, there are other rules that can be illustrated by the maxim, "Never grift on the way out" (p. 13). The following is an example of what this means:

> Two thieves recently went down into southern Indiana. During the week, they picked up a whole carload of junk which must have been worth $10,000, though they would not be able to sell it for more than a fourth of that amount. They stopped on the way back at Fort Wayne to work some more, though they already had a full load. The coppers caught them there, and they had to turn over to the coppers their car and everything they had in it and wire to Chicago for $500 more. The coppers got the car, the stuff, and the money, and the grifters got the debt. (p. 13)

The fix. The professional thief usually has a long record of arrests in the Bureau of Identification, but after most of the cases, "dismissed" or "no disposition" is entered. This is because of the thief's ability to fix cases. Sometimes, the thief fixes his own cases, or a member of the mob fixes his cases. Sometimes, the thief employees a fixer. In every large city, there is a regular fixer for professional thieves. Also, police and court officials often will accept a fix. Conwell explained,

> In most cases, the fixers use the coppers. The copper knows that if he does not take the money, someone else will, and that he himself gets no money but he gets in bad. The copper can be influenced to do two things: first, to hold up or be uncertain about his own testimony; second, to advise the complainant that the case will probably take a long time and cause him many inconveniences and that he would be wise, if he gets a chance, to get his money back and forget about the prosecution. (Sutherland, 1937, pp. 89-90)

The social life of the thief. The personal life of the professional thief is somewhat distinct from his professional life. The professional thief has a wife or a longtime relationship with the same woman. This wife or live-in companion does not work while she is living with the professional thief. The thief who grifts a winter resort generally takes this woman with him and establishes a home there for the winter (Sutherland, 1937, pp. 155-156). The woman has a strictly social life and must depend on her own man for financial support.

Conwell suggested that the social life of the professional thief is not much different from that in conventional society. The thief goes to movies, theaters, and restaurants. He vacations at the lakes during the summer. The one personal characteristic of the thief is extreme suspicion (Sutherland, 1937, p. 168). The thief does not like to see his name in the newspaper or to have bank accounts that would call attention to him. The thief also has a huge ego. The successful one lets his accomplishments be known among other professional thieves. But Conwell asserted that hundreds of thieves do not like any feature of their lives: "Every thief has an ambition to get out of stealing and get into a legitimate occupation" (p. 181), and some thieves accomplish this. However, "no thief ever decided that he would not grift any more simply because he felt that he might get arrested. Arrests and a bit are always a possibility in the life of the professional thief" (p. 191).

The Professional Thief and Differential Theory

Sutherland (1937) contended that professional thieves illustrate differential association. The differential element in the association of thieves is primarily functional rather than geographical. Their personal association is limited by barriers that are maintained principally by the thieves themselves. These barriers are based on their community of interests including security or safety (pp. 206-207).

Furthermore, the group defines its own membership. According to Sutherland (1937), professional theft is a group way of life. One can enter the group and remain in it only if accepted by those already in the group. Recognition as a professional by other professional thieves is the "absolutely necessary, universal, and definitive characteristic" of the professional thief (p. 211). Sutherland also explained that "selection and tutelage" are the two necessary elements in the process of acquiring recognition as a professional thief. Furthermore, "an inclination to steal is not a sufficient explanation of the genesis of the professional thief. . . . The person must be appreciated by professional thieves" (p. 212). He must demonstrate that he has "an adequate equipment of wits, front, talking ability, honesty, reliability, nerve, and determination" (p. 213).

White-Collar Crime and Differential Association

Sutherland developed his theory of differential association largely because he was dissatisfied with conventional explanations of crime. Sutherland did not accept the emphasis on poverty and other conditions concentrated in the lower socioeconomic classes. He argued that this emphasis obstructed the development of a theory sufficiently general to cover the whole range of crime. Sutherland contended that criminology should study all violations of criminal law no matter how processed or named. Thus, he coined the term "white-collar crime" for the elite crime committed by those who are in positions of power. He argued that differential association as a general theory of crime could explain the criminal behavior of the upper class as well as that of the lower classes. Sutherland's theory of white-collar crime is a forerunner of current conflict theory (see Chapter 8).

Critique of Sutherland

Sutherland's differential association theory and Merton's anomie (see Chapter 4) were developed and published during the same time period (1938-1947). Both of these works have stimulated extensive research and criticism. Merton's anomie is basically a conceptual scheme, whereas Sutherland developed a logical deductive system by stating his nine propositions so that each proposition built on the previous one. Sutherland's differential association theory was the first and one of the few criminological theories to approach Homan's (1964) social science definition of a theory (see Chapter 1).

Yet, Sutherland has been criticized for not stating his propositions so that they are testable, which was the last requirement in Homan's definition of a theory. Sutherland did not operationally define concepts such as excess, priority, duration, frequency, and intensity. Several scholars (Burgess and Akers, 1966; De Fleur and Quinney, 1966; Jeffrey, 1965) have attempted to modify or reformulate Sutherland's nine propositions. For example, Burgess and Akers (1966), in their "differential association-reinforcement" theory, produced a "reformulation that retained the principles of differential association, combining them with, and restating them in terms of, the learning principles of operant and respondent conditioning that had been developed by behavioral psychologists" (Akers, 1994, p. 94). Akers has continued to develop and test this theory, which he refers to as social learning theory. Although the following quote suggests that Sutherland recognized that his propositions did not formulate a scientific theory, Sutherland's statement suggests that he did not think that criminology was ready for this:

> I am opposed to an effort at this time to make criminology highly scientific (in the sense of universal propositions) because I think we will be trying to define things about which we do not have enough information. . . . [My] theory should have been called a point of view or at least no more than a hypothesis. (cited in Schuessler, 1973, p. xvi)

It is a tribute to Sutherland that his *Principles of Criminology* (which contained his theory) dominated criminology for more than 40 years and that virtually every criminological theory text today includes a discussion of differential association theory. Gaylord and Galliher (1988) stated, "Among sociological students of criminal behavior, there is considerable agreement that this is the single most important innovation during the past fifty years" (p. 1). They further quoted Chambliss as stating, "Edwin Sutherland . . . developed the most influential of all sociological perspectives

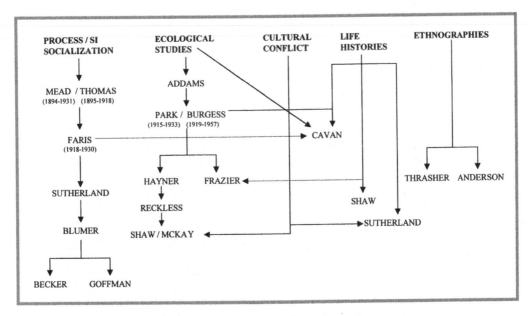

Figure 5.1. Flowchart of Chicago School Scholars

on criminal behavior: the differential association theory" (p. 1). Furthermore, Sutherland's application of differential association theory to the professional thief and white collar crime has earned him widespread recognition. Lindesmith reported in the foreword to Gaylord and Galliher's (1988) book, "The author of the screenplay for *The Sting* used Sutherland's book, *The Professional Thief*, to learn the details of the 'con game' and did a good job of it" (p. xiii). With reference to Sutherland's monograph on white collar crime, Lindesmith noted, "A survey of 1940-1950 publications selected Sutherland's study as the most important one of the decade" (p. xvii).

Summary

The scholars of the Chicago School have provided a rich legacy of research, theory, and policy for today's criminologists (Figure 5.1). The scholarship of the Chicago School used a diversity of methodologies and theories. These works examined crime at the macro level through the ecological studies that dominated the early years and at the micro level through the case studies used in examining the process of suicide and delinquent gangs as well as the life histories of the jackroller and the professional thief. The impact of the Chicago School on current criminological theories is seen in the chapters that follow. The interactionist perspective (see Chapter 7) has its historical seeds in the emphasis on process in the theories and research that permeated most of the writings of the Chicago School. It also is true that the emphases on cultural conflict found in the works of Shaw and McKay and

Sutherland, and to some extent Cavan and Frazier, were forerunners of conflict theory (see Chapter 8). Finally, to some extent, the peacemaking perspective (see Chapter 10) can be traced to the works of early Chicago School scholars such as Addams and Henderson.

Notes

1. According to Cavan (1986), the University of Chicago originally was intended as a Baptist seminary to be funded by a grant. However, it became a private university funded by John D. Rockefeller, Sr. (Bulmer, 1984, p. 135). Cavan (1986) further stated that there was a Divinity School during the early days and that various departments were built around the Divinity School.

2. Henderson also was a mentor to Frances Kellor, who was a graduate student at the Chicago School from 1898 to 1900. Her specific works in criminology were discussed in Chapter 3.

3. "The Growth of the City," the chapter that contains the concentric zone theory, actually was written by Burgess. The book, *The City*, was edited by Park, Burgess, and McKenzie (1967).

4. The major contribution of Walter C. Reckless to criminological theory was his containment theory of delinquency (see Chapter 6).

5. Although Hayner's dissertation on hotels did involve the study of crime and/or deviance, he made important contributions to the field of corrections while a professor at the University of Washington. His research and his teaching had a major impact on the development of the field of criminology.

6. As was true with many of the publications that came out of the Chicago School during the 1930s, this study originally was Thrasher's dissertation.

7. Cavan indicated that she remembered Thrasher's research because she had edited his manuscript, *The Gang*, before it was published. She stated, "Thrasher was very verbose. Park asked me to edit the book and cut it by twenty-five percent. He told me what types of things to delete, etc. I got paid for doing it, and I learned a lot from Park about writing that helped me in my future publications" (personal interview, March 9, 1989).

8. Cavan suggested that Thrasher made up this number (personal interview, March 9, 1989).

9. At this point in the text, Thrasher had a footnote that read, "The gangs and the cultural areas of the city are indicated on the map folded in the pocket at the back of the book. Chap[ter] 1 should be read with this map at hand."

10. The classification based on unselected cases for 1923 included suicides from (a) the unidentified craving, (b) the recognized wish, (c) the specific wish, (d) mental conflicts, and (e) the broken life organization (Cavan, 1928, pp. 148-170).

11. Frazier (1949) noted the well-planned insurrection under the direction of a slave known as Gabriel near Richmond, Virginia, in 1800; a slave uprising planned by Denmark Vesey in Charleston, South Carolina, in 1822; and an insurrection led by Nat Turner in Southampton County, Virginia, in 1831 (pp. 87-89).

12. Frazier (1949) also noted that the role of the Negro in the abolitionist movement generally has been discounted or ignored, although free Negroes of the North and runaway

slaves often risked their lives to assist other slaves in escaping to freedom. There were many undistinguished Negroes who acted as guides along the routes of the Underground Railroad. But there also were Negroes of distinction who had escaped from slavery and played important parts in the movement. Among those mentioned by Frazier were William Still, David Ruggles, Frederick Douglass, and Harriet Tubman, the latter of whom acquired the title of "the Moses of Her People" for her heroic efforts to free other slaves. After escaping from slavery in Maryland in 1849, Tubman made 19 trips to the South and helped 300 slaves escape to freedom. She did this in defiance of the slaveholders when rewards amounting to $40,000 were offered for her capture (pp. 97-98).

13. Frazier relied heavily on the preliminary data collected by Shaw for his analysis of delinquency in Chicago.

14. It should be noted that data for some of these ecological studies included delinquent girls. Shaw and McKay did mention these data but provided only minimal discussion. Overall, their studies were gender biased in that the analysis was limited to delinquent boys.

15. In the research reported in 1931, Shaw and McKay examined three types of cases in their Chicago study: (a) a series of 9,243 alleged delinquent boys (10 to 16 years of age) dealt with by the juvenile police probation officers during the year 1926, (b) a series of 8,141 alleged delinquent boys (10 to 16 years of age) brought before the juvenile court of Cook County during the 1917-1923 period, and (c) a series of 2,596 delinquent boys (10 to 16 years of age) committed to correctional institutions by the juvenile court of Cook County during the 1917-1923 period (Shaw and McKay, 1931, p. 26). The edition published in 1972 examined delinquent boys, school truants, and recidivism in Chicago for three groups: (a) series of alleged delinquents brought before the juvenile court on delinquency petitions, (b) series of delinquents committed by the juvenile court to correctional institutions, and (c) series of alleged delinquents dealt with by police probation officers with or without court appearances (Shaw and McKay, 1972, p. 43). The study further looked at the distribution of delinquents in Chicago based on juvenile court cases and commitments for periods roughly centered around 1900, 1920, and 1930 as well as series of police cases for 3 different years around 1930 (p. 46). Place of residence of the boys was used to establish the distribution of delinquency in each of the cities studied (p. 50). The research reported in the 1972 publication also extended the dates of delinquencies to the 1930s for Philadelphia, Cleveland, and Richmond (the three studies also included in the report published in 1931). It should be noted that Shaw and McKay provided much more information about their methodology than did many of the early studies conducted at the Chicago School.

16. The rate in a given area is the ratio of the number of delinquent boys (or truants) during a specific period and the number of 10- to 16-year-old boys in that area for the same period of time (Shaw and McKay, 1931, p. 41).

17. Although Shaw and McKay functioned as a research team, it was Shaw who went out into the community and interacted with the local residents. The Chicago Area Project actually was the work of Shaw.

18. To preserve anonymity, fictitious names, dates, and places were used.

19. Feminists such as Leonard (1982), Messerschmidt (1993), and Naffine (1987) have criticized Sutherland's "general theory" for its failure to explain female crime and delinquency.

20. There was no effort to explain the logic of this statement. It is just assumed to be true, which is another example of gender stereotyping and bias.

DISCUSSION QUESTIONS

1. Albert Cohen (discussed in Chapter 4) cited Thrasher's works to illustrate his delinquency theory. Compare and contrast Cohen's theory of delinquent boys and Thrasher's theory of delinquent gangs. What makes Cohen's theory functionalist? What makes Thrasher's study fall within the Chicago School tradition?

2. What were the contributions of women at the Chicago School to the disciplines of sociology and criminology? How do you explain their lack of recognition by today's scholars?

3. What are the similarities and differences between Cavan's study of suicide and Shaw and McKay's study of delinquencies? What can those making policy decisions about crime and delinquency today learn from the works of Cavan and Shaw and McKay?

4. What makes Cavan's continuum of delinquent behavior functionalist? Why isn't her suicide study functionalist? Or, what makes both of them functionalist theories?

5. What are the major themes and contributions of Frazier to criminology? How important are his works to understanding today's crime problem? Why do you think his works are not included in other criminological theory books?

6. Some scholars argue that Sutherland was the most important American criminologist of the 20th century. Do you agree with this? If yes, then justify your answer by comparing his works to those of other scholars of the 20th century. If no, then why not? If not Sutherland, then who would you suggest was the most important American criminologist? Justify your choice.

7. What are the three most significant contributions to criminology from the Chicago School? Explain and justify your choices.

8. Feminists in criminology have stated that "malestream" criminology is gender biased and narrow focused because research is conducted on males and theories are developed based on this research. How would you evaluate the theorists in this chapter from this feminist perspective? To what extent do they include women? Do they do so objectively? What difference would it make to these theorists' works if women really mattered in their studies?

9. Assume that you have been appointed by the president of the United States to a committee to make criminal justice policy recommendations. Make a series of policy suggestions to the president, and support your policies using the research and theories in this chapter. Be specific.

CHAPTER 6

The Control Theorists

on and Historical Setting

Control theory arose from seeds sewn by the Classical School, the Chicago School, and the functionalists, in particular Émile Durkheim. Because a large part of control theory deals with the development of self-control, the influence of psychology, especially Freudian theory and Piaget's cognitive-developmental approach, is important.

Edward A. Ross (1866-1951)

The term "social control" first appeared in a series of articles written by Edward Ross for the *American Journal of Sociology* between 1896 and 1898 (Ross, 1939). Ross is considered by some to be one of the founders of sociology. He used the term "social control" in much the same way as did later control theorists, although not quite as precisely, to refer to the ways in which society ensures that its members behave in a like fashion. These writings were the basis of his later book, *Social Control* (Ross, 1901; see also Stark, 1987).

These early articles were written just prior to the end of the 19th century, during a time of much social change and upheaval. (This is the same time frame in which many of the early Chicago School theorists were working.) The last half of the 19th century saw numerous technological advances and the shift for most Americans from a more rural agrarian lifestyle to an urban city-dwelling lifestyle. The decades directly preceding and following the end of the 19th century also saw the most massive influx of European immigrants into the country. These factors, among others, accounted for the social changes that were occurring at the time when Ross was writing his initial articles concerning social control.

Ross (1939) explained, in the preface to his book, how his study of social control fits into the larger study of social psychology:

> Social psychology . . . falls into two subdivisions. One of these, social ascendency, deals with the domination of society over the individual; the other, individual ascendency, . . . deals with the domination of the individual over society. Social ascendency is fur-

ther divided into social influence—mob mind, fashion, convention, custom, public opinion, and the like—and social control. The former is occupied with the social domination, which is without intention or purpose; the latter is concerned with that domination which is intended and which fulfills a function in the life of society. (pp. vii-viii)

Ross then explained what he was investigating regarding social control:

I seek to determine how far the order we see all about us is due to influences that reach men and women from without, that is, social influences. I began the work . . . with the idea that nearly all the goodness and conscientiousness by which a social group is enabled to hold together can be traced to such influences. It seemed to me, then, that the individual contributed very little to social order, while society contributed almost everything. Further investigation, however, appears to show that the personality freely unfolding under conditions of healthy fellowship may arrive at a goodness all its own and that order is explained partly by this streak in human nature and partly by the influence of social surroundings. (p. viii)

In Ross's writings, we can clearly see the seeds of later formulations of control theory. He discussed both internal and external forces affecting social control. His mentioning of "the personality freely unfolding under conditions of healthy fellowship," although not clarified by Ross, could be taken to mean under appropriate guidance from parents and elders.

If Ross is considered to be one of the founders of sociology, then he also can be considered to be one of the founders of control theory.

The development of control theory can be dated to the 1950s, with the theory being most influential by the middle of the 1960s and then receding somewhat into the background until the 1990s, when Gottfredson and Hirschi (1990) published their *General Theory of Crime*. It is of interest to note that just as the Chicago School was fed by the change and disruption occurring in the city of Chicago, and just as Durkheim was influenced by the strife created during war in his own France, the 1950s and 1960s were times of great social and political change in the United States, and control theory was nurtured by these changes. Although popular media at the time portrayed life during the 1950s as idyllic—every family living in a fashionable suburb, the father traveling to the city every day in his "gray flannel suit" to a well-paying job, the mother remaining at home to cook wholesome and nutritious meals for the children, and all of the children doing very well in school—this was not the case.

Popular media were accurate in their portrayals of several things. First, the 1950s saw the first wave of city dwellers make their way to the brand-new suburbs, causing the beginnings of decay in some urban areas. Second, although it is true that a mass of men in their gray flannel suits suddenly headed out their doors each day to go to work, they were not necessarily as content as they were portrayed on television. In addition, although a significant portion of mothers with children remained at home to care for them, this was not necessarily done by choice, and the early rumblings of the modern feminist movement could be heard during the 1950s. Popular television also made no mention of McCarthyism or segregation.

Because these three schools—the Chicago School theorists, Durkheim, and the control theorists—were created and grew during times of great upheaval, change, and "social disorganization," this may be one reason for the common thread among them concerning how social solidarity, or the lack thereof, affects people.

Influences on Control Theory

Influence of the Classical School

Control theory does not mark a return to Classical School criminological thought. But control theorists, like their Classical School predecessors (discussed in Chapter 2), do believe in the rationality of the criminal act. That is, the individual behaves in a criminal manner for ordinary rational reasons, and this behavior arises out of the person's own free will. This point of view—that crime involves free will—had largely been abandoned by the Positivist School theorists (discussed in Chapter 3), who searched for biological and physiological explanations for crime. The Positivist School theorists looked for what it is that *makes* an individual become a criminal. Rather than look toward criminogenic factors in a person's environment, Classical School and control theorists looked toward the individual's ability to choose a course of action.

Control theory shares another common theme with Classical School thought. Not only do both schools see criminal action as arising out of personal choice, they also see criminal action, or any action, as arising out of the need for humans to seek pleasure and avoid pain. In this way, both schools see criminal actions as being like any other actions in that they are undertaken to maximize pleasure and avoid pain (Gottfredson and Hirschi, 1990).

Also, the Classical School viewed laws as uniting a group of individuals into a society, and for the individual to reap the benefits of that society, he or she had to relinquish certain freedoms and behave in a more restrained manner than if there were no society at all.

Influence of Durkheim

Perhaps the most important contribution to control theory by Durkheim (discussed in Chapter 4) lay in his conception of anomie. For Durkheim (1933), anomie was a lack of regulation (p. 368). He addressed how this anomie arose out of a division of labor, where the individual worker performed an isolated task removed from the final product and removed from others. Durkheim (1951) also spoke of anomic suicide, where the individual became isolated from society and social controls. When social solidarity dissolves, anomie results; individuals may become free from the bonds of social control and are more likely to behave in deviant ways.

Durkheim's view of human nature also influenced control theorists. Durkheim saw each human as being comprised of a social self and an egoistic self. The social self was the product of socialization by parents, school, neighborhood, and religion. The egoistic self was comprised of animal urges and was not controlled by society's rules. Through proper socialization, the egoistic self could become integrated into the social self. Without this integration, deviance—whether in the form of crime, suicide, or some other socially unacceptable behavior—results (Durkheim, 1938, 1951).

Durkheim (1938) believed that crime was not only a natural and normal form of behavior but also necessary:

> Crime is present not only in the majority of societies of one particular species but in all societies of all types. There is no society that is not confronted with the problem of criminality. Its form changes; the acts thus characterized are not the same everywhere; but, everywhere and always, there have been men who have behaved in such a way as to draw upon themselves penal repression. . . . What is normal, simply, is the existence of criminality. . . . To classify crime amongst the phenomena of normal sociology is not to say merely that it is an inevitable, although regrettable, phenomenon. . . . It is to affirm that it is a factor in public health and [an] integral part of all healthy societies. (pp. 65-67)

Durkheim viewed crime not only as normal but also as necessary:

> Crime is, then, necessary; it is bound up with the fundamental conditions of all social life, and by that very fact it is useful because these conditions of which it is a part are themselves indispensable to the normal evolution of morality and law. . . . Crime implies not only that the way remains open to necessary changes but that in certain cases it directly prepares for these changes. . . . Crime, for its part, must no longer be conceived as an evil that cannot be too much suppressed. (pp. 70-72)

Influence of the Chicago School

The Chicago School influenced control theory not only through its ideas but also due to the fact that several control theorists had their beginnings in the Chicago School.

The influence of the Chicago School echoes that of Durkheim. Chicago School sociologists contributed much work on social disorganization (which may be considered as a cause of anomie) and a dual conceptualization of the self (Lilly, Cullen, and Ball, 1995). The city of Chicago, like Durkheim's war-torn France, was in a state of great upheaval when the University of Chicago, and subsequently its Department of Sociology, was founded. The upheaval was due to large masses of immigrants flooding into the city, making it the largest metropolis west of New York. Between the years 1820 and 1920, Chicago saw its population increase from less than 50,000 to well over 2 million (Androit, 1983). This influx of immigration created a number of problems including overcrowding (especially in the center of the city), unemployment, crime, and vice. Because these immigrants were from several European countries and not just one, there also was a clash of values and customs. It was amid this atmosphere of great disruption that the Chicago School of sociology was born and flourished.

Owing to the massive population increase that occurred right before their eyes, it is no wonder that members of the Chicago School—including Robert E. Park, Ernest W. Burgess, Florence Kelly, and Jane Addams—studied the effects of the growth and expansion of the city. They termed the disruption that resulted from the massive immigration, and the resulting values clash, as "social disorganization." Numerous Chicago School researchers from the Hull House and the university studied both the causes and the effects of this disorganization. Not unlike Durkheim, they found that the areas of the city with the highest rates of social disorganization also had higher rates of crime, delinquency (Clifford R. Shaw and Henry D. McKay), gangs (Frederick Thrasher), suicide (Ruth Shonle Cavan), divorce, homelessness (Nels Anderson), and so forth.

The Chicago School's conception of human nature also had a pronounced effect on control theory. The Chicago School, much like Durkheim, saw the self as a blend of the social self and the primal self. This conception of self is evident not only in Chicago School sociology but also in Chicago School psychology. The influence of Charles H. Cooley[1] and George H. Mead are of particular importance.

Cooley (1902), a social psychologist, coined the term "looking-glass self" to denote how a person's conception of self comes about through interaction and the responses of others:

> The social reference takes the form of a somewhat definite imagination of how one's self ... appears in a particular mind, and the kind of self feeling one has is determined by the attitude toward this attributed to that other mind. A social self of this sort might be called the reflected or looking-glass self. (pp. 151-152)

It is because of this looking-glass self that the individual comes to see himself or herself as worthy or worthless, good or bad, powerful or powerless. In turn, the individual behaves in such a way as to act the part of the worthy or worthless, and so forth.

Cooley (1983, originally published in 1963) discussed the development of the looking-glass self as taking place within a person's primary groups, which are the groups that the child is surrounded by early in life such as the family and, later on, school and peers:

> By primary groups, I mean those characterized by intimate face-to-face association and cooperation. They are primary in several senses, but chiefly in that they are fundamental in forming the social nature and ideals of the individual. ... The most important spheres of this intimate association and cooperation—though by no means the only ones—are the family, the play group of children, and the neighborhood or community of elders. (pp. 23-24)

This conceptualization of primary groups will prove especially useful to control theorists.

Interestingly, Cooley (1983) also used the term "drift" to describe how individuals in society were becoming distant from traditional ideas and constraints:

> Evidently, the drift of modern life is away from this state of things. The decay of settled traditions, embracing not only those relating directly to the family but also the religious and economic ideas by which these were supported, has thrown us back upon the unschooled impulses of human nature. (p. 357)

Mead's (1955) system of social psychology, like Cooley's looking-glass self, built on the idea of the self arising out of the perceptions of others. This self is not innate; rather, it develops over time.

> The self is something which has a development; it is not initially there at birth but arises in the process of social experience and activity, that is, develops in the given individual as a result of his relations to that process as a whole and to other individuals within that process. (p. 135)

Furthermore, the individual's perception of self is indirect; that is, the self is perceived through the other. It is from other people that the child learns who he or she is.

> The individual experiences himself as such, not directly but only indirectly, from the particular standpoints of other individual members of the same social group or from the generalized standpoint of the social group as a whole to which he belongs. . . . The self is essentially a social structure, and it arises in social experience. (pp. 138-140)

Mead (1955) termed the group from which the individual received his or her view of self as the "generalized other." The generalized other may be comprised of parents, other family members, neighbors, teachers, classmates, and so forth.

> The organized community or social group which gives to the individual his unity of self may be called "the generalized other." The attitude of the generalized other is the attitude of the whole community. (p. 154)

Mead (1934) saw the self as divided into the "I" and the "me":

> The "I" is the response of the organism to the attitudes of the others; the "me" is the organized set of attitudes of others which one himself assumes. The attitudes of the others constitute the organized "me," and then one reacts toward that as an "I." (p. 175)

Although the "I" and the "me" seem confusing, they are not. The "I" represents how the individual presents himself or herself to others, that is, her outward appearance and actions. The "me" is the internalized attitudes of others.

Influence of Psychology

The influence of one discipline on another often is ignored, especially with universities set up by department. Because control theory deals so explicitly with the self and with concepts such as "self-control," the influence of psychology cannot be discounted. It is important to keep in mind that Cooley often is viewed as a social psychologist and that Mead, who produced a number of important works in sociology, also was a well-known psychologist and philosopher. In addition to these influences, the influences of Freudian (and neo-Freudian) theory and the works of Piaget have been important to the development of control theory.

Although some control theorists used terminology more particular to sociology, several of them (especially Reckless, 1961) used terms such as "ego" and "superego," taken directly from Sigmund Freud. Unlike the dual conceptualization of human nature that Durkheim and Mead proposed, Freud proposed a tripartite human nature consisting of the id, the ego, and the superego—literally the "it," the "I," and the "above I," respectively. The id is comprised of animal instincts and urges, the superego is the conscience, and the ego mediates between the two. When a child is born, only the id functions. The id strives to maximize pleasure and avoid pain; it signals the child when hunger strikes or when it is cold. It is the responsibility of the parents to develop the superego, which initially is comprised of parental values. Later on, the superego also will represent the values of the larger society of which the child is a part. The ego arises between these two extremes and is the self that society sees (Freud, 1962).

It is readily apparent how Freud's conceptualization fits into control theory. The superego represents internalized constraints, the id represents the self that seeks to maximize pleasure and avoid pain, and the ego moderates between the two. When a child has been properly instructed during childhood, there is a balance among these three forces.

Piaget and his works on the moral development of children also influenced the control theorists. Of particular interest are *The Moral Judgment of the Child* (Piaget, 1969) and *The Psychology of the Child* (Piaget and Inhelder, 1969). Piaget's theory had as its focus, first, how the child internalizes the rules of his or her parents and, second, the various moral stages through which children pass. Furthermore, Piaget's (1969) *The Moral Judgment of the Child* drew quite heavily on Durkheim's *Sociologie et Philosophie* and *Education Morale* and the works of Freud. Piaget (1969) stated,

> We have recognized the existence of two moralities in the child, that of constraint and that of cooperation. The morality of constraint is that of duty pure and simple. . . . The child accepts from the adult a certain number of commands to which [the child] must submit. . . . Right is what conforms with these commands; wrong is what fails to do so; the intention plays a very small part in this conception. . . . Parallel with this morality, and . . . in contrast to it, there is gradually developed a morality of cooperation. (p. 335)

The Search for Self-Control

The major difficulty with the theories that preceded control theory, according to control theorists, was not that they did not explain why crime occurred but rather that they seemed to over-explain it. Indeed, if subcultural theory is correct, then why is it that not everyone born in a lower class neighborhood becomes some type of criminal? What is it that accounts for the good child in the bad neighborhood? Control theory asks the question, "Why do people *not* commit crimes?"

Likewise, if the Chicago School view of crime causation is complete, then why is it that so many individuals in "areas of social disorganization" actually were happy, well-adjusted individuals? Why was there not more divorce, more suicide, and more crime?

The control theorists argued that the chief factor leading to a person not becoming criminal, no matter where the person lived, was self-control, that is, the ability to restrain one's self from illegal actions. Control theory stresses free will among individuals to choose their own actions.

Assumptions About People and Society

The cornerstone of control theory is the assumption that self-control serves as a restraint from criminal actions, and this self-control arises out of a positive self-concept. A child's self-concept develops, first, through interaction with parents and family members and, later on, through interaction with teachers and peers.

Control theory's emphasis on free will denotes that criminal behavior, like any other type of behavior, is a result of rational choice. Control theory devotes much time to the study of both internal controls (e.g., a well-developed conscience) and external controls (e.g., parental discipline, parental monitoring, laws). When these controls are properly in place, an individual is less likely to commit a crime—indeed, less likely to commit nonsanctioned actions. Because of their emphasis on free will, the control theorists view individuals as active rather than passive agents. That is, the individual must choose to commit the criminal act.

Although control theory emphasizes free will, control theorists also see behavior as imposed. Gottfredson and Hirschi (1990) stated this most clearly when they held parents responsible for children learning self-control. For parents to be responsible, they must do three things. First, they must monitor their children's behavior. Second, they must recognize deviant behavior. Third, they must punish deviant behavior. In other words, parents should be imposing proper forms of behavior on their children. Looking at it in this way, although an individual chooses his or her actions, behavior also is the result of coercion. This is especially apparent where Gottfredson and Hirschi stated that parents must punish behavior that is wrong. Punishment clearly is coercion.

Like Classical School theory, control theory views society as stable. The vast majority of individuals are not criminals. Also, because control theory states that internalizing the norms of the larger society is an important part in not becoming a criminal, there must be a general set of norms that are agreed on in that larger society. Control theory also views the acceptance of the norms of the larger society as a process whereby, over a considerable amount of time during childhood, the individual accepts the norms and morals of his or her parents and the larger society.

Control theorists conceptualize crime as not being extraordinary. That is, crime and deviance are normal behaviors. This is vastly different from the Positivist School conception of crime, or the subcultural conception, which views crime as an aberration arising either out of some biological or psychological fault or out of a faulty society. If crime is a "normal" behavior, then we need not employ special measures to study it. We can study it along with other behaviors. Control theorists ask the question, "Why don't all people commit crimes?" This changes the focus from crime being abnormal to crime being the expected result of a loss of societal constraints. Criminal actions also are not extraordinary in that they do not differ significantly from other deviant actions that are not classified as criminal. Both criminal and noncriminal deviant actions share many properties. The most important of these is that they are the result of low self-control.

Control theory can be considered to be both a macro theory and a micro theory. As a macro theory, control tries to discover how society "hangs together"—how it remains cohesive, keeping all of the individuals who make up that society in their respective places, that is, conforming to the rules. It also holds that society agrees on a general set of norms. As a micro theory, control looks toward self-control. It has as its concern how the individuals in society learn, through parental monitoring and discipline, how to regulate their behavior.

Control theory is interested in self-control. Self-control is a subjective concept. That is, it is not something that can be pointed to; one cannot take a picture of self-control. Self-control, or the lack thereof, is manifested in observable behaviors that seem to be objective. But a particular behavior can indicate low self-control to one observer while merely indicating a high level of curiosity to another observer. In other words, there is a certain amount of subjectivity even in observable behaviors.

Containment Theory

One of the major contributions to control theory was made by Walter Reckless and Simon Dinitz[2] while they were colleagues at Ohio State University. As indicated in the biographical inset on Reckless (Inset 6.1), Reckless studied with Park and Burgess at the University of Chicago, where he received his Ph.D. in sociology. Dinitz's multidisciplinary interests also had a strong effect on containment theory as a theory that crosses the lines among sociology, psychology, and psychiatry.

Reckless and Dinitz conducted their initial research in Columbus, Ohio, during the 1950s.[3] At that time, Columbus was a city of less than a half million inhabitants (471,316 in 1960, according to the Bureau of the Census, 1962). It was a sizable city by Ohio standards, but not when compared to New York or Chicago. Reckless and Dinitz focused their attention on trying to discover what factors could insulate (or

> **INSET 6.1**   **Walter Cade Reckless (1899-1988)**
>
>
>
> Walter Reckless was born in Philadelphia on January 19, 1899. His first love was music, but a car accident that injured his finger made a career as a professional musician impossible, although he used his musical talent as a participant-observer when he studied the roadhouses operated by organized crime during prohibition. He did his undergraduate work at the University of Chicago in the social science program. Reckless majored in history, and his interests included Middle Eastern archaeology, Egyptology, and comparative religions. Reckless was given the chance to go to Egypt to study Tutankhamen's tomb but passed on the opportunity because Park and Burgess offered him a graduate assistantship in the Department of Sociology. Reckless's interest in religion was not aban-
>
> doned. He later investigated how religion could insulate a person against deviance (Martin, Mutchnick, and Austin, 1990, pp. 179-180).
>
> Reckless took a position at Vanderbilt University shortly before he completed his degree in 1925. His dissertation, *Vice in Chicago*, was published in 1933 under the same title (Reckless, 1933). While at Vanderbilt, he published numerous articles, chapters, and books. He also was a force in establishing the university's criminology program.
>
> Because of his success in creating Vanderbilt's program, Reckless was offered a position at the Ohio State University in 1940 to create a criminology/corrections program. It was at Ohio State that he collaborated with Simon Dinitz and the research for containment theory was conducted. He remained at Ohio State until he retired. In addition to teaching and recruiting graduate students, he was responsible for the development of the criminology graduate and undergraduate programs. It also was at Ohio State that the research leading to the creation of containment theory was conducted over the course of 15 years (Martin et al., 1990, pp. 180-181).

contain) a youth in a high-delinquency area from becoming delinquent. They highlighted the inner containment of self-control as an insulator against delinquency.

The first group of boys in their study consisted of 125 nominated "good boys." They were studied to see what it was that served to insulate these boys from becoming delinquent, even though they lived in the highest white delinquency area in Ohio (Reckless, Dinitz, and Murray, 1956, p. 744). Reckless and colleagues (1956), in the initial article, made particular mention of the boys' family situations:

> The 125 families were stable maritally, residentially, and economically. There appeared to be close parental supervision of the boys' activities and associates, an intense parental interest in the welfare of the children, and a desire to indoctrinate them with nondeviant attitudes and patterns. This parental supervision and interest seemed to be the outstanding characteristic of the family profiles. (p. 745)

Reckless and colleagues stressed the importance of parental supervision in the development of these boys' self-concepts as "good boys": " 'Insulation' against delinquency on the part of these boys may be viewed as an ongoing process reflecting an internalization of nondelinquent values and conformity to the expectations of significant others" (p. 746). Appropriate parental supervision, it seems, leads to a boy's internalizing the values of his parents. It further leads him to live up to the expectations of his parents.

The second group of boys, those nominated as "likely to have contact with the law," had family situations that were very different from those of the "good boys" insulated against delinquency.

> Those differences between the "insulated" and potentially delinquent boys were, if anything, magnified by their respective parents. . . . All but one of the mothers of the potentially delinquent boys thought their sons could have selected better friends. These mothers also indicated significantly more frequently than their counterparts in the insulated group that they were often unaware of their sons' whereabouts, that they did not know very many of the friends with whom their boys associated, and that their sons did not very often bring their friends home. . . . [They also] stated that the family situation[s] [were] characterized by conflict and that there was not very much family participation in leisure and other activities. (Reckless, Dinitz, and Kay, 1957, p. 569)

Here again, parental supervision is the key. The mothers of the boys who were nominated as likely to become delinquent were less aware of what their sons were doing and who they were with and also reported more conflicts in their homes than did the mothers of the insulated boys. Whereas the positive self-concept helps to insulate against delinquency, the negative self-concept moves an individual toward delinquency.

Reckless (1961) noted a number of the advantages of control theory, which he referred to as "containment theory" because it has as its concern how delinquency is contained. There is a general "goodness of fit" to control theory.

> If criminology must have a general theory, containment theory is proposed as a theory of best fit to explain the bulk of crime and delinquency. . . . Containment theory applies to the delinquent and the nondelinquent. . . . Containment theory explains crimes against the person as well as crimes against property. Weak self-control, weak indirect control, [and] poor self-concept are as important in assault, murder, and statutory rape as they are in robbery and burglary. (p. 356)

Reckless (1961) also noted that control theory is multidisciplinary. Unlike other criminological theories that do not cross disciplinary lines, control theory can be used to draw the behavioral sciences together:

> It is a formulation with which psychiatrists [and] psychologists can agree. . . . All three fields [psychiatry, psychology, and sociology] agree that there are self-images or self-concepts and that the self-image or self-concept is developed in interaction with significant others (figures) in a person's social world. They all agree that the self is a directional agent [and] that it can steer the person toward goals. They all agree that the self is a control agent—a containment. . . . These three behavioral sciences can join together in recognizing [the] self as a controlling agent. (p. 357)

Control theory also be researched and used for constructing treatment.

> It is possible to assess inner and external containment. . . . Containment theory consti-
> tutes an effective operational theory for treatment of offenders. Treatment can consist
> of manipulating an environment or changing an environment. . . . Effective treatment
> of juvenile and adult offenders involves getting the person to attach himself to effective
> reference groups for him. (Reckless, 1961, pp. 357-358)

Critique of Reckless and Dinitz

Containment theory was presented in a series of articles that were resultant of a
longitudinal study. This enabled Reckless and Dinitz to make predictions about their
study groups and conduct follow-up. Initially, containment theory spawned several
research studies using other groups (e.g., black children, females), but beyond those,
there has been little other research.

Containment theory has been subjected to much criticism. Several authors
(Brown, Esbensen, and Geis, 1991; Schrag, 1971) have noted that a significant drawback to this theory lies in the fact that because its concepts are not operationally well
defined, it cannot be empirically tested. The fact that it is difficult to test this theory
might account for the lack of further research.

Brown and colleagues (1991) stated that the importance of containment theory,
despite its drawbacks, might lie not so much in the theory itself as in its contribution
to the development of control theory:

> [Containment theory] did, however, contribute to the theoretical framework of con-
> trol theory, which Gresham Sykes, David Matza, Travis Hirschi, and others have suc-
> ceeded in advancing to a more sophisticated level. Their versions of control theory,
> however, shift focus to outer containments or social control factors. (p. 364)

Techniques of Neutralization

Based on the biographical inset on Gresham Sykes (Inset 6.2) and the biographical
sketch on David Matza,[4] the collaboration of these two scholars discussed in what
follows occurred during the mid-1950s when Sykes was a professor and Matza was
a graduate student at Princeton University. Sykes and Matza (1957) introduced
their theory by contrasting it with the dominant approach of the day, subcultural
theory. According to subcultural theory, delinquents and criminals are able to commit their crimes because they have rejected the norms and values of the larger,
law-abiding society for another set of values that, in many ways, is the antithesis of
mainstream values. Embracing this other set of values allows them to commit
crimes without guilt because they are obeying their own set of rules and, therefore,
feel no guilt. Sykes and Matza stated, "The basic characteristic of the delinquent
subculture . . . is a system of values that represents an inversion of the values held by
respectable, law-abiding society" (p. 664). Whereas the law-abiding society values

INSET 6.2

Gresham Sykes (1922-)

Gresham Sykes was born in Plainfield, New Jersey, in 1922. Although little is known about his childhood, we know that he entered World War II in 1942 and served time in England, Belgium, and Germany (Martin, Mutchnick, and Austin, 1990, p. 299). He married Carla Adelt in 1946 and then attended Princeton University, where he received his B.A. in sociology in 1951 and his Ph.D. in sociology in 1954.

Sykes's first teaching appointment was at Princeton. After leaving that university, he moved to at least a dozen institutions for varying periods of time. "For this reason, it is rather difficult to determine his institutional affiliation when he was inspired to write some of his major works or to determine from whom he received scholarly encouragement" (Martin et al., 1990, p. 300). As a result, it is difficult to state where or from whom the ideas he conceptualized into the "techniques of neutralization"

might have originated. Sykes had several visiting professorships during his career, but in 1974 he "found a home at the University of Virginia in Charlottesville" (p. 301). He retired from the University of Virginia in 1988 as a professor emeritus of sociology.

Sykes has a distinguished publication record. He published five books including *The Society of Captives* (Sykes, 1958), an analysis of a men's maximum-security prison. This book was a great success nationally and internationally, and it has become a classic in the area of penology. In addition, he has published about 30 articles and book chapters including the classic theoretical work with David Matza examined in the present chapter. In his teaching, publications, and service, Sykes has combined theory and policy.

In addition to teaching and publishing, Sykes has served on numerous state and national advisory boards concerned with penological issues, behavioral science research, and education. He has received several awards and honors. As an undergraduate at Princeton, he received three scholarly grants. In 1961, while Sykes was a professor of sociology at Dartmouth College, he was awarded an honorary master of arts degree. In 1980, Sykes received the Edward H. Sutherland Award from the American Society of Criminology.

hard work, the delinquent subculture values taking the easy way. Whereas the law-abiding society values education, the delinquent subculture first encourages low achievement and later encourages dropping out. It is this rejection of society's values for another set of values that is the crux of subcultural theory. Sykes and Matza maintained that, contrary to subcultural theory, delinquents have not rejected the values of the larger society; rather, they simply "get around" them:

> It is our argument that much delinquency is based on what is essentially an unrecognized extension of defenses to crimes in the form of justifications for deviance that are seen as valid by the delinquent but not by the legal system or society at large. (p. 666)

The delinquent is able to violate the rules of society without rejecting them by a series of rationalization techniques that Sykes and Matza (1957) termed "techniques of neutralization." Each technique enables the delinquent to "get around" the law. Although society in general would not condone the delinquent's use of neutralization, to some extent, each technique is used, or has been used, by lawmakers, the courts, and ordinary noncriminal individuals. It is a way of saying, "Yes, it should be wrong, and normally it would be, *but* . . ." Sykes and Matza stated that the techniques of neutralization are "critical in lessening the effectiveness of social controls and that they lie behind a large share of delinquent behavior" (p. 669).

Sykes and Matza (1957) outlined five techniques of neutralization: denial of responsibility, denial of injury, denial of the victim, condemnation of the condemners, and appeal to higher loyalties.

Denial of responsibility. The delinquent sees his or her actions more as reactions to some external person or situation. "It may also be asserted that delinquent acts are due to forces outside of the individual and beyond his control such as unloving parents, bad companions, or a slum neighborhood" (Sykes and Matza, 1957, p. 667). This has been a popular technique that receives support from numerous criminological theories. For example, the Chicago School might explain delinquency in terms of the area in which a child lived. "By learning to view himself as more acted upon than acting, the delinquent prepares the way for deviance from the dominant normative system without the necessity of a frontal assault on the norms themselves" (p. 667).

Denial of injury. The delinquent may consider his or her actions to be victimless: "Wrongfulness may turn on the question of whether or not anyone has clearly been hurt by his deviance" (Sykes and Matza, 1957, p. 667). Society in general recognizes a class of "victimless crimes" such as drug use, prostitution, and gambling. These actions are crimes because the government is trying to legislate morality, not because the acts themselves harm others, and the delinquent takes advantage of this. The delinquent also may add to these victimless crimes actions such as vandalism (because the victim seems far removed) and petty theft from stores (because the "victim" is a company and can afford it).

Denial of the victim. With this technique, the crime is viewed as either something the victim "asked for" or something the victim "had coming to him or her" in retaliation: "The injury, it may be claimed, is not really an injury; rather, it is a form of rightful retaliation or punishment" (Sykes and Matza, 1957, p. 668). Stating that the victim was "asking for it" historically has been an accused male rapist's best defense. If the female victim was out too late, was dressed too provocatively, or had gone out with the perpetrator before, then she could not possibly be a victim. This technique can be used to rationalize hate crimes (e.g., "gay bashing") or violence against racial minorities (e.g., African Americans, Asians, Hispanics, Jews). Denial of the victim also can be used to rationalize actions against another individual who has caused the offender some type of harm, whether real or imagined. The perpetrator might see himself or herself as the "true victim" and, for example, use this excuse to vandalize the car of the person who fired him or her.

Condemnation of the condemners. "The delinquent shifts the focus of attention from his own deviant acts to the motives and behavior of those who disapprove of his violations" (Sykes and Matza, 1957, p. 668). The focus then becomes, for example, the corruptness of the police, or the incompetence of parents, rather than the delinquent's actions. Think of how the focus of O. J. Simpson's criminal trial changed once it appeared that Mark Fuhrman had lied under oath. Suddenly, people were not as interested in whether or not Simpson was a murderer as in whether or not the police were corrupt and racist.

Appeal to higher loyalties. "Internal and external social controls may be neutralized by sacrificing the demands of the larger society for the demands of the smaller groups to which the delinquent belongs" (Sykes and Matza, 1957, p. 669). The crime had to be committed because something far more important was at stake. The delinquent committed his crime because he or she owed allegiance to a fellow gang member or because the delinquent had to defend the reputation of a sister or brother. This technique also is commonly used by governments to justify wars. The United States had to drop that bomb on Hiroshima to save the lives of U.S. soldiers.

Next, let us examine how the techniques of neutralization have stood up against scrutiny.

Critique of the Techniques of Neutralization

One difficulty with the techniques of neutralization is that they fail to take into account how the use of these techniques may be fostered and condoned by membership in certain social classes, subcultures, or neighborhoods (Sykes, 1978). It is easy to see how anyone can use these techniques to justify his or her actions. But are certain groups (e.g., poor, minorities, government officials) more likely to use certain rationalizations?

In their original article, Sykes and Matza (1957) admitted that research supporting the techniques of neutralization is sparse. And although there has been some research conducted since the 1950s, it still is the case that the techniques lack a solid empirical background. Those studies that have attempted to test the techniques have found little support (Ball, 1983; Minor, 1981), or no support (Hamlin, 1988, Minor, 1980), for them.

Perhaps the most important criticism that can be leveled against the techniques of neutralization is that they do not constitute a theory (as discussed in Chapter 1). Although the initial article touted the techniques as a "theory" of delinquency, they really work better as a smaller part of a more general theory, serving to explain how an individual can commit a criminal act and still see himself or herself as upholding the morals and values of the larger society. Matza himself tried to address this with his "drift theory." We can see that, similar to containment theory, the techniques of neutralization, rather than being a complete theory, may be better conceptualized as building blocks in the development of control theory.

Delinquency and Drift

Matza built on the techniques of neutralization with his more general drift theory. He considered the techniques to be the tools with which the delinquent was able to begin to free himself or herself from the constraints of social control. They did not necessarily result in a delinquent act. They merely made that act more of a possibility or made it more of a possibility that the delinquent could "drift" away from social control. But for a delinquent act to be committed, the individual must choose that act. Free will is a key factor. Matza (1964) set his drift theory in opposition to the delinquent subculture theories of Albert K. Cohen, Richard A. Cloward, and Lloyd E. Ohlin (discussed in Chapter 4). Unlike delinquent subculture theories, drift theory is not a Positivist School theory.

> There is a subculture of delinquency, but it is not a delinquent subculture.... A subculture of delinquency is a setting in which the commission of delinquency is common knowledge among a group of juveniles. . . . The delinquent subculture is the modern sociological rendition of the positivist assumptions regarding delinquency and crime. (p. 33)

If there were a delinquent subculture, then the delinquent, when apprehended, would react not with guilt but rather with indignation. This simply is not the case.

> Delinquents do frequently voice indignation in the situation of apprehension, but mainly because they believe or pretend to believe themselves [to be] unjustly accused. . . . Once the delinquent has expressed his wrongful indignation, he proceeds to either contriteness or defensive explanations. (p. 41)

This clearly is not the reaction of a person who believes the correctness of his or her actions. Matza (1964) also pointed out that delinquents are quick to take offense when negative traits or deeds are attributed to family members. Like everyone else, the delinquent takes offense if his or her father or sibling is called a "crook." If the delinquent truly were a member of a delinquent subculture that condoned criminal activity, then being called a crook would be more of a badge of honor than an insult. This is another good indication that there is not a delinquent subculture.

> The subculture of delinquency consists of precepts and customs that are delicately balanced between convention and crime. The subculture posits objectives that may be attained through delinquency but also by other means. Its customs allow delinquency and even suggest it, but delinquency is neither demanded nor necessarily considered a preferred path. The norms and sentiments of the subculture are beliefs that function as the extenuating conditions under which delinquency is permissible. (p. 59)

Matza went on to state that the subculture of delinquency, far from being particularly special, actually is one of many subcultures that exist within the structure of the larger society:

The subculture of delinquency is one of many. It shares with other subcultures certain general characteristics. Foremost among these general characteristics is some degree of differentiation from the parent culture and some degree of provisional utility or function. . . . Each subculture has special characteristics that reflect its constituency and its position in society. (pp. 59-60)

Delinquent subculture theory posits that for the delinquent to violate the norms of society, these norms must be rejected. Matza (1964) maintained that total rejection of norms is not necessary for the violation of those norms: "Norms may be violated without surrendering allegiance to them. . . . They may be evaded rather than radically rejected. . . . Most, if not all, norms in society are conditioned" (p. 60). Of course, it is at this point that the techniques of neutralization fit in. It is with the techniques of neutralization that the delinquent can violate norms without completely abandoning them.

Matza (1964) was careful to point out that whereas drift is necessary for delinquency, it is not sufficient. Drift merely makes delinquency possible.

The period breaking of the moral bind to law arising from neutralization and resulting in drift does not assure the commission of a delinquent act. Drift makes delinquency possible or permissible by temporarily removing the restraints that ordinarily control members of society, but of itself it supplies no irreversible commitment or compulsion that would suffice to thrust the person into the act. . . . I wish to suggest that the missing element which provides the thrust or impetus by which the delinquent act is realized is will. (p. 181)

Here, Matza moved to a statement about human nature. He affirmed that individuals have a choice in how they act and that they can choose noncriminal actions or criminal actions. Matza highlighted the concept of free will in his theory, mentioning that free will also was the cornerstone of classical theory, thus linking his theory to Classical School theory.

Matza (1964) further stressed that there is nothing particularly special about this will:

The will to repeat old infractions requires nothing very dramatic or forceful. Once the bind of law has been neutralized and the delinquent [has been] put in drift, all that seems necessary to provide the will to repeat old infractions is preparation [i.e., learning that it can be done]. (p. 184)

Critique of Matza

Matza's works evolved considerably during the 1950s and 1960s. This is to his credit. After the work he did in collaboration with Sykes on the techniques of neutralization, Matza went on to incorporate those techniques into his drift theory, noting that on their own, the techniques were not a theory. After publishing *Delinquency and Drift* (Matza, 1964), he continued to refine his theory and went on to write *Be-*

coming Deviant (Matza, 1969), in which he moved away from control theory and into Interactionist School theory.

As with the techniques of neutralization, drift theory does not have a solid foundation in empirical research, and this is a serious drawback. The concept of drift, in and of itself, presents a number of problems to the would-be researcher. Whereas an individual's use of the techniques could be discerned during an interview when he or she uses a phrase such as "they deserved it," drift is much more subtle. How would a researcher uncover the temporary removing of society's restraints? Even more difficult, how would the researcher prove that free will is what allows a person to be or not be deviant? The problem of creating a good operational definition for drift presents quite a research problem. If an operational definition cannot be constructed, then research cannot be conducted.

Social Bond Theory

Travis Hirschi[5] outlined the basis for social bond theory in *Causes of Delinquency.* Hirschi (1969) stated, "Control theories assume that delinquent acts result when an individual's bond to society is weak or broken" (p. 16). In this work, Hirschi focused on this bond and posited four elements of the bond: attachment, commitment, involvement, and belief. These four elements, when taken together, will either create a weak bond between the individual and society (which makes delinquency more likely) or create a strong bond (which makes delinquency less likely).

Attachment. Attachment refers to the connection that exists between one person and another, or between one person and society, that compels the individual to behave in a moral fashion. An individual who is attached to another will value the opinions of that other person and will behave in such a way as to please that other person. When an individual is attached to society, or connected to the whole of society, he or she will behave in such a manner as to not offend other members of that society. The individual will behave morally.

Hirschi (1969) explained,

> We are moral beings to the extent that we have "internalized the norms" of society. But what does it mean to say that a person has internalized the norms of society? The norms of society are, by definition, shared by the members of society. To violate a norm is, therefore, to act contrary to the wishes and expectations of other people. If a person does not care about the wishes and expectations of other people—that is, if he is insensitive to the opinions of others—then he is, to that extent, not bound by the norms. He is free to deviate. (p. 18)

Commitment. Commitment refers to how invested the individual is in conforming to the rules of society. Hirschi (1969) stated,

> The concept of commitment assumes that the organization of society is such that the interests of most persons would be endangered if they were to engage in criminal acts. Most people, simply by the process of living in an organized society, acquire goods, reputations, [and] prospects that they do not want to risk losing. These accumulations are society's insurance that they will abide by the rules. . . . One is committed to conformity not only by what one has but also by what one hopes to obtain. Thus, "ambition" and/or "aspiration" play an important role in producing conformity. (p. 21)

So, the successful investment banker is more committed to conventional society than is the drifter. The investment banker has money, power, and status in the community that he or she does not want to lose, so the investment banker does not steal from stores and risk being caught. The drifter has no money, power, or status, so the drifter does not have as much at stake if he or she chooses to steal.

Ambition and aspiration help to produce conformity among younger people. Hirschi (1969) pointed out, however, that a certain amount of rebellion is expected and condoned among the young (p. 21). So, a teenager can behave in a somewhat delinquent fashion and not risk his or her future status as a doctor or lawyer because he or she is a teenager.

Involvement. The more involved an individual is in conventional work, actions, and pastimes, the less time there is for nonconventional lawbreaking behavior: "A person may be simply too busy doing conventional things to find time to engage in deviant behavior" (p. 22). Individuals trying to thwart delinquency often address the issue of involvement by providing after-school programs, sports, and church activities in which young people may become involved.

Belief. Unlike subcultural theories, which maintain that the delinquent and nondelinquent are operating from different systems of values, control theories state that both the delinquent and nondelinquent share a common system and values. Control theories, then, explain why the delinquent chooses to behave in a way that is contrary to this value system.

> Control theories have taken two approaches to this problem. In one approach, beliefs are treated as mere words that mean little or nothing if other forms of control are missing. . . . The second approach argues that the deviant rationalizes his behavior so that he can at once violate the rule and maintain his belief in it. (Hirschi, 1969, p. 24)

Hirschi (1969) pointed out that the second approach, which refers specifically to Sykes and Matza's techniques of neutralization, is problematic because it pushes the question back a step. Rather than asking why a delinquent goes against his or her value system, the new question asks why the delinquent neutralizes. Hirschi explained the difference between the value systems of the delinquent and nondelinquent in the following way:

> We assume . . . that there is variation in the extent to which people believe they should obey the rules of society and, furthermore, that the less a person believes he should obey the rules, the more likely he is to violate them. (p. 26)

Hirschi also explained that it is not merely the elements of attachment, commitment, involvement, and belief that create either a weak or strong bond between the individual and society. Another factor is the relationship among these four elements.

Attachment and commitment. Hirschi (1969) pointed out that "it is frequently suggested that attachment and commitment . . . tend to vary inversely" (p. 27). That is, the more attached a lower class adolescent is to family and peers, the less committed the adolescent is to the conventional goals of getting ahead. This almost feels like a support of subcultural theory. Hirschi, however, believed that just the opposite is true. The more attached an individual is to conventional others, the more committed the individual will be to conventional goals.

Commitment and involvement. Hirschi (1969) stated that commitment can be understood to affect the probability that a person will give in to the temptation to act in a delinquent manner. The more committed a person is to conventional actions, the less likely the person will jeopardize what he or she has by stealing a car. Involvement, on the other hand, affects the probability that a person will be exposed to temptations. The more involved the person is in traditional activities, church functions, family picnics, and/or playing soccer, the fewer opportunities the person will have to steal a car.

Attachment and belief. Hirschi (1969) explained,

> There is a more or less straightforward connection between attachment to others, and belief in the moral validity of rules appears evident. . . . Insofar as the child respects (loves and fears) his parents and adults in general, he will accept their rules. Conversely, insofar as this respect is undermined, the rules will tend to lose their obligatory character. It is assumed that belief in the obligatory character of rules will, to some extent, maintain its efficacy in producing conformity, even if the respect which brought it into being no longer exists. (pp. 29-30)

Here, the more attached the child is to the parents, the more the child will accept the parents' rules. And if the individual accepts those rules as a child when he or she "loves and fears" the parents, then the individual still will accept those rules as an adult, even though he or she might no longer "love and fear" the parents.

Critique of Hirschi

Social bond theory has been subjected to considerable scrutiny and testing. It is the most complete of the control theories presented thus far, and it has generated a considerable amount of research, as noted by Brown and colleagues (1991):

Hirschi is one of the few theorists to have proposed a theory of crime or delinquency that was subjected to substantial empirical testing during its developmental stages. . . . The theory has since been buttressed by empirical testing undertaken by many criminologists. . . . The basic framework of the theory has been challenged by only a few criminologists. . . . A number of criminologists have since tested the tenets of Hirschi's version of control theory among females . . . [and] across various age groups. . . . In short, social control or bond theory has fared very well in empirical tests. (p. 373)

Another benefit of Hirschi's theory is its intuitive appeal.

Social bonding theory is intuitively appealing because it focuses on the relationship between the individual and social institutions that should have an influence on constraining criminal behavior. It is a flexible theoretical perspective in that it is not class based. . . . The theory should be as applicable to middle class crime as it is to that of the lower class. (Sheley, 1991, pp. 304-305)

Much to Hirschi's credit is the fact that he was not satisfied to let his theory stand, and he continued to develop it in collaboration with Michael R. Gottfredson.[6]

A General Theory of Crime

Gottfredson and Hirschi (1990) proposed their *General Theory of Crime* as an all-encompassing theory to explain not only all types of crimes but also many other deviant actions. They began by asking the question, "What is crime?" They touted this as a unique approach for a criminology text given that most accept the legal definition of crime; that is, crime is whatever is not permitted by the law. Gottfredson and Hirschi argued, however, that this sort of definition is unnecessarily limiting. They stated that "crime is a form of behavior, but it is not separate or distinct from other behaviors" (p. 10). Unlike drift theory or containment theory, which were constructed to explain only criminal actions, the general theory seeks to unite criminal actions with other deviant behaviors with which they share commonalities.

Gottfredson and Hirschi (1990) saw their theory as a return to "classical-like" theory because it has at its roots many of the same assumptions that classical theory does, but it also takes into account research generated by the Positivist School and other theories since the Classical School. In keeping with the Classical School tradition, the general theory views crime as rational, that is, the result of the offender's choice: "People behave rationally when they commit crimes and when they do not" (p. 5). Also, crime and all other actions are the result of the natural human desire to maximize pleasure and avoid pain.

Gottfredson and Hirschi (1990) defined crimes as "acts of force or fraud undertaken in pursuit of self-interest" (p. 15). So, whereas all human actions may be considered to be undertaken "in pursuit of self-interest" (i.e., to maximize pleasure and avoid pain), crimes also involve the use of force or fraud.

[Criminal actions] will tend, on the whole, to require little foresight, planning, or effort.... Carefully planned and executed crimes are rare.... Crimes will tend to take place at little remove from the offender's usual location.... Potential targets will be selected based on the ease with which they can be victimized.... Criminal acts [are] governed primarily by short-term pleasures. (pp. 12-13)

The general theory, then, sees the majority of crime as being mundane and poorly thought out, resulting in little profit for the offender and little loss for the victim, and occurring near the offender's home. Most crimes are committed on the spur of the moment. Contrary to popular law enforcement and Hollywood portrayals, career criminals are very rare, and when they do exist, these individuals seem to be involved in many types of crime during their lifetimes and do not specialize in one particular criminal action.

Gottfredson and Hirschi (1990) used this conceptualization of criminal actions and the Federal Bureau of Investigation's (FBI) Uniform Crime Reports to present portraits of "typical" offenses and offenders. In considering burglaries, Gottfredson and Hirschi found that most burglaries take place in empty dwellings along major streets that the offenders pass through often. Items taken are quickly consumed, used, given away, or discarded. These offenders are young, male, and disproportionately non-white. For a burglary to occur, there must be a building or dwelling that is not monitored and that has contents that the offender desires. Also, the would-be burglar must be "insufficiently restrained from taking advantage of these conditions" (p. 27). This last point—that the offender must be "insufficiently restrained"—was seen by Gottfredson and Hirschi as the common thread among all criminal activities.

Likewise, in considering robberies, Gottfredson and Hirschi (1990) found that most robberies involve losses of less than $250, half involve weapons, and most involve a lone victim but multiple offenders. Again, the offenders are young, male, and disproportionately non-white, with varied prior records. For a robbery to occur, there must be an attractive target, the offender must have the advantage by show of weapon or force, and the offender must be unrestrained. Another common thread among all criminal activities seems to be that the offender is young, male, and disproportionately non-white (pp. 29-31).

When considering homicides, Gottfredson and Hirschi (1990) found that homicide victims usually are male and that nearly half are black. Homicides occur "on weekends, at night, indoors, and in front of an audience" (p. 32). Drugs and/or alcohol often are involved. The offenders and victims are very similar and tend to be young, male, and disproportionately non-white.

When auto thefts were examined, Gottfredson and Hirschi (1990) found that most occur at night and that most autos are recovered. Contrary to popular belief, most stolen cars are not sold for parts; rather, joyriding is the most common use of stolen vehicles. Again, offenders tend to be young, male, and disproportionately non-white (pp. 34-35).

In the case of rapes, Gottfredson and Hirschi (1990) stated that most occur outside of the home and that few involve weapons. Arrestees usually are young and disproportionately non-white with priors for a number of crimes. Victims also are young and disproportionately non-white. Family violence and date rape are rare, as is gang rape. Most often, a lone woman is attacked in a deserted area by a stranger. When the victim and offender are known to each other, the attack usually takes place in a vulnerable setting such as a car. For a rape to occur, a female victim must be attractive to the offender, available to him, and both unwilling to have sex with him and unable to resist. Of course, the offender also must be insufficiently restrained (pp. 36-37).

In considering embezzlement cases, offenders typically are young, male, and non-white. There must be "money or goods that are attractive to the offender, available to the offender, and not rightfully the property of the offender" (Gottfredson and Hirschi, 1990, p. 39). The offender also is insufficiently restrained.

The term "white collar crime" was invented by Sutherland to denote crimes committed by respectable individuals. According to Gottfredson and Hirschi (1990), "The idea that such people have crimes unique to them is directly contrary to the idea of crime used throughout [their] book" (p. 38). They saw no difference between white collar crime and any other type of crime. White collar crime still requires an individual that is insufficiently restrained and an attractive target.

Gottfredson and Hirschi (1990) saw the nature of criminality as low self-control: "Self-control suggests that people differ in the extent to which they are restrained from criminal acts" (p. 88). Individuals with low self-control want instant gratification, lack patience, are adventuresome and active, and possess few cognitive skills. Those individuals who possess more self-control will commit fewer criminal acts, whereas those individuals who possess less self-control will commit more criminal acts.

Gottfredson and Hirschi (1990) explained that criminal acts satisfy the needs of individuals who have low self-control:

> [These] acts provide immediate ... easy gratification of desires. ... [They] are exciting, risky, or thrilling. ... Crimes provide few or meager long-term benefits. ... [They] require little skill or planning ... [and] often result in pain or discomfort for the victim. (p. 89)

The authors pointed out that "the variety of manifestations of low self-control is immense" (p. 91). Not only do offenders tend to engage in different types of crimes, but they also tend to engage in other deviant, yet not criminal, behaviors that provide the same quick rewards as do criminal activities (p. 92).

Gottfredson and Hirschi (1990) attributed self-control, or the lack thereof, to child-rearing practices: "The minimum conditions seem to be these: in order to teach the child self-control, someone must (1) monitor the child's behavior, (2) recognize deviant behavior when it occurs, and (3) punish such behavior" (p. 97). These conditions most often are missing in the backgrounds of delinquents.

Gottfredson and Hirschi (1990) also saw a significant link between parental criminality and delinquency, as criminal parents tend not to supervise their children well, cannot recognize criminal behavior in their children, and do not punish appropriately (pp. 100-101). Children from larger families also are more likely to be delinquent given that the time and energy of the parents must be divided among a greater number of children. Children who come from single-parent families are more likely to be delinquent, as are children of working mothers.

Critique of Gottfredson and Hirschi

Gottfredson and Hirschi approached the explanation of crime and the creation of their theory in a unique way. They began by defining crime rather than by accepting the legal definition that most theorists do. This means that their theory encompasses more than just illegal actions; it also includes other forms of deviance that do not fall outside of the law.

Constructing a theory that encompasses not only all criminal acts but also all deviant behaviors is not a simple task. Gottfredson and Hirschi fell short of their proposed goal. Miller and Burack (1993) summarized the likely shortcomings of a general theory as follows:

> General theories tend to assume the homogeneity of the study population and, hence, leave out too much or speak only to hegemonic values, interests, activities, or social goals. Often, general social theories are developed in the absence of a consideration of differences among individuals. The elimination of social, psychological, political, economic, and historical differences serves to reinforce dominant cultural values and ideological beliefs, erasing the divergent experiences of women and members of minority groups. (p. 116)

There are a number of serious drawbacks to the general theory. First, and most glaringly, is the way in which Gottfredson and Hirschi discussed the crime of rape. They claimed that the Uniform Crime Reports show that date rape and family violence are rare occurrences, as is gang rape. Contrary to what Gottfredson and Hirschi stated, approximately 683,000 adult women are raped each year, and 13% of women will be victims at some point in their lives. Approximately one in four girls and one in seven boys will be sexually abused by 18 years of age (National Victims Center and Crime Victims Research and Treatment Center, 1992). Gottfredson and Hirschi made no mention of the fact that rapes are underreported, with only an estimated 10% to 16% of all rapes being reported (Pittsburgh Action Against Rape, personal communication, April 1996), or of how the Uniform Crime Reports might be wrong or misleading.

Miller and Burack (1993) stated,

> Recent empirical research suggests that acquaintance rape is much more common than [Gottfredson and Hirschi] conclude. A national study of 6,100 students on 32 college campuses reports that one of four women had an experience that would legally qualify as rape or attempted rape by a date or acquaintance. . . . These high numbers are consistent with findings from other victimization surveys. (p. 121)

Gottfredson and Hirschi also did not clarify the use of the phrase "attractive to the offender." This may be read by some to mean that the victim is a physically attractive person, that is, a beautiful girl or woman. Even the Uniform Crime Reports show that not all rape victims are young and beautiful; victims can be any age and have any physical appearance. The authors did not attempt to explain crimes such as child molestation and rape when the victim is a male.

Gottfredson and Hirschi stated that the commission of deviant and criminal acts is resultant of an inability to exercise proper self-control, that is, of being unrestrained. This explanation has a great intuitive appeal and works nicely for many types of crimes and deviant actions. But this explanation does not work for domestic violence. Miller and Burack (1993) stated,

> Research conducted on batterers suggests [that the] battering cycle becomes increasingly more violent, frequent, and injurious, resulting in long-term benefits of absolute power, authority, and control exercised by the offender over the victim/household. (p. 122)

So, for the husband who abuses his wife, the benefits are not constrained to her obedience at the present time; they include her continued fear and obedience. This does not fit neatly into the conception of criminal actions as "providing only short-term gain" that Gottfredson and Hirschi presented.

For all crimes that Gottfredson and Hirschi investigated, the perpetrators were overwhelmingly young, male, and non-white. Are we to assume that although minorities comprise a small portion of the entire population, they are responsible for most of the crimes? Gottfredson and Hirschi made no mention of the fact that there are biases in the criminal justice system and that these biases are responsible, at least in part, for the overrepresentation of minorities among arrestees, defendants, and convicts.

Gottfredson and Hirschi used the Uniform Crime Reports as the empirical basis for their theorizing. There is nothing wrong with using the Uniform Crime Reports in research so long as their limitations are fully explicated. The authors made no mention of the possibility that certain crimes may be underreported or how official reporting of crimes differs from jurisdiction to jurisdiction. And although they purported that their theory explains not only criminal behaviors but also all deviant behaviors, the Uniform Crime Reports deal only with criminal behaviors that have been detected by or reported to law enforcement. The FBI gathers no empirical evidence dealing with other deviant actions.

Gottfredson and Hirschi's theory also is open to charges of "mother blaming." The authors mentioned that delinquents are more likely to come from single-parent and female-headed households. They did not place any blame for delinquency on the father who leaves the home and does not provide adequate guidance for his children. They also cited the rise in the number of women who work outside the home as a factor in delinquency. To support this statement, they cited a study conducted at mid-century by Glueck and Glueck (1950). Is it possible that they needed to return to the paternalistic attitude of the 1950s to find support for their statement? They did not mention that many women, especially women who are single parents, work out of necessity because their former mates are irresponsible and do not support their children. Nor did the authors mention the fact that the current tax structure often necessitates both parents working to adequately provide for their children.

Miller and Burack (1993) observed that Gottfredson and Hirschi, in their discussion of rape, engaged in victim blaming: "The responsibility of rape prevention remains squarely placed on women. . . . Women (who are potential victims) must restrict their freedom of movement; women (as parents) must adequately socialize (male) children to have self-control" (p. 121).

Gottfredson and Hirschi also ignored race and class differences. Miller and Burack (1993) stated,

> [Gottfredson and Hirschi] are either blithely unaware of, or unmoved by, race, class, and gender differences in society that do not buttress their arguments. . . . The differential risk of violent victimization is virtually ignored. . . . The fact that poorer people, members of racial minority groups, and (with rape) women are disproportionately victimized does not figure in the general theory. (p. 119)

In addition to ignoring the fact that the poor and minorities are more frequently victimized, Gottfredson and Hirschi never questioned why it is that so many minority males end up in the criminal justice system. Could it be that there are other prejudices operating within the system itself?

Since the initial appearance of Gottfredson and Hirschi's (1990) book, the general theory has generated a significant amount of research. Although the initial presentation of the theory had significant gaps in it, much of the research conducted since that time has helped to fill in the gaps and bolster support for the theory. Work has been done in examining and explicating what exactly self-control is, how to measure self-control, and behaviors that frequently can be found alongside low self-control (Arneklev, Grasmick, Tittle, and Bursik, 1993; Barlow, 1991; Gibbs and Giever, 1995; Keane, Maxim, and Tevan, 1993). Schreck (1999) even extended the theory as an explanation of victimization. The advantage of much of the research spawned by the general theory is that it does not rest on the Uniform Crime Reports and, therefore, is not hindered by their limitations, as was Gottfredson and Hirschi's original work.

Summary

Control theory is a Classical School–type theory that stands in direct opposition to Positivist School theories. For control theorists, crime is the result of free will. Crime is not out of the ordinary, nor does it differ from other noncriminal deviant acts. Rather than ask the question, "Why do people commit crimes?," control theorists ask, "Why doesn't everyone commit crimes?" The answer to this question is *self-control*. Individuals with high self-control do not commit crimes, nor do they engage in other deviant acts. Self-control is the result of parental training. Control theory was mentioned as far back as 1901 in a series of articles by Ross. It generated a considerable amount of research and attention during the 1950s and 1960s, with contributions from Sykes and Matza as well as Reckless and Dinitz. With Gottfredson and Hirschi's publication of their *General Theory of Crime* in 1990, interest in control theory was reawakened, and even though their original conceptualization had limitations, much of the research and further theorizing that it has generated shows great promise.

In Chapter 7, we turn our attention to the Interactionist School perspective. Interactionism sees crime as something that is created in an interaction between society and the criminal. In other words, there are no criminals until society chooses who will be criminals.

Notes

1. Cooley himself was not at the University of Chicago; rather, he was at the University of Michigan. His works, however, are closely tied to those of Mead. Therefore, he is discussed in this section.

2. Simon Dinitz was born in New York City on October 29, 1926, to Morris Dinitz and Dinah Schulman Dinitz. In 1949, he married Mildred H. Stern, and the couple subsequently had three children. Dinitz received his B.A. from Vanderbilt University in 1949 and received his M.A. and Ph.D. from the University of Wisconsin in 1949 and 1951, respectively. He began his career in 1951 at Ohio State University, where he taught for 40 years and currently is a professor emeritus. Dinitz had numerous visiting professorships including those at the University of South Florida, Indiana University of Pennsylvania, the University of Tel Aviv, and the University of Haifa. He has distinguished himself in the fields of criminological and psychiatric research and has published numerous books, articles, and research reports. He also has been active in many professional associations in sociology, psychopathology, criminology, and delinquency.

3. In a series of articles, Reckless, Dinitz, and colleagues (Dinitz, Reckless, and Kay, 1958; Dinitz, Scarpitti, and Reckless, 1962; Reckless and Dinitz, 1967; Reckless, Dinitz, and Kay, 1957; Reckless, Dinitz, and Murray, 1956; Scarpitti, Murray, Dinitz, and Reckless, 1960) followed a group of white sixth-grade males living in a high-delinquency area who had been selected by their teachers as either "not likely to have contact with the law" or "likely to have contact with the law." Each of the boys chosen completed four self-administered scales designed to measure delinquency proneness, social responsibility, general personality, and a measure of the boy's self-concept. Each boy and his mother also were interviewed.

4. David Matza was born May 1, 1930, in New York City. He received his A.B. from the City University of New York in 1953, the same year in which he married. He received his M.A. and Ph.D. in sociology from Princeton University in 1957 and 1960, respectively. He began his teaching career at Temple University in 1957. He then taught at the University of Chicago from 1960 to 1974. He currently is a professor emeritus of sociology at the University of California, Berkeley (Jaques Cattell Press, 1978).

5. Travis Hirschi was born April 15, 1935, in Rockville, Utah, to Warren G. and Orra Terry Hirschi. In 1955, he married Anna Yergensen. They subsequently had three children: Kendal, Nathan, and Justine. Hirschi received his B.S. in 1957 and his M.S. in 1958 from the University of Utah. He served in the army from 1958 to 1960 and then returned to his studies

at the University of California, Berkley, where he received his Ph.D. in 1968. Hirschi's first teaching appointment was at the University of California, Davis. He then taught at the State University of New York. Currently, he is a professor in the Department of Management and Policy at the University of Arizona (Metzger, 1984, p. 255).

6. Michael R. Gottfredson received his A.B. degree in psychology from the University of California, Davis, in 1973. He received his M.A. in 1974 and his Ph.D. in 1976, both in criminal justice, from the State University of New York at Albany. He has been a member of the Department of Management and Policy at the University of Arizona since 1985, where he collaborated with fellow faculty member Travis Hirschi on the general theory. Gottfredson has published six books, numerous articles and book chapters, and several government publications.

DISCUSSION QUESTIONS

1. Show that you understand how psychology influenced the development of control theory and discuss the importance of an interdisciplinary approach.

2. Compare and contrast two theorists' (or sets of theorists') conceptualizations of internal and external social control.

3. Take each technique of neutralization and provide an example of its use either from your own experience or from the media. Then, try to find another likely explanation for each of those examples that does not use the techniques.

4. In the critique of Gottfredson and Hirschi, it was pointed out that their discussion of rape and domestic violence was not satisfactory. How could you better address these issues within the confines of their theory?

5. How would you fit the contributions of Sykes and Matza, as well as those of Reckless and Dinitz, into Gottfredson and Hirschi's general theory?

6. Discuss how Gottfredson and Hirschi's general theory could be viewed as being sexist, classist, and racist.

CHAPTER 7

The Interactionist School

Cavit S. Cooley

Introduction and Historical Setting

For several decades following World War II, tranquillity appeared the norm throughout the majority of modern societies. Political stability, economic opportunity and growth, and social peace were characteristics that could have been applied to many countries throughout the world. However, the 1960s evolved into a period of extreme social disillusionment and change, especially in the United States. What began as a stable and progressive decade of social, economic, and political stability would end in bitter turmoil. The assassinations of important political figures; the Vietnam War; the Cuban missile crisis; the Watergate scandal; and the exposure of gender, class, and racial inequality during the civil rights movement provided a social atmosphere in which individuals began to question the legitimacy of government action including the creation and enforcement of rules, laws, and policies. The social environment was right for the acceptance of new theoretical foundations and policies in criminal justice that removed, to some degree, the responsibility from the individual and placed it more on the actions of questionable government entities. The time was right for social change grounded in the Interactionist School of criminology (Lilly, Cullen, and Ball, 1989).

According to the Interactionist School, crime and deviance can be explained as the result of a social reaction process that individuals go through to become deviant. Cooley (1902), Mead (1934), and other early symbolic interactionists discussed in Chapter 6 provided the foundation for this process. Tannenbaum (1922, 1938), Lemert (1951, 1972), Becker (1963), Goffman (1961, 1963), and Schur (1965, 1971, 1984) later expanded and applied this reaction process to deviance and crime. Figure

159

Early Pioneers → Contemporary Theorists
(1900-1940s) (1950s-1990s)
↓↓

Charles H. Cooley   Edwin M. Lemert
"looking-glass self-concept"   "primary and secondary deviance"
↓↓

George H. Mead   Erving Goffman
"development of self"   "total institution"
"moral career"
"stigma"
↓↓

Frank Tannenbaum   Howard S. Becker
"dramatization of evil"   "moral entrepreneurs"
"process of tagging"   "outsiders"
"sequential model of deviant behavior"
"master status"
↓

Edwin M. Schur
"crimes without victims"
"radical intervention"
"women as deviants"
"devaluation process"

Figure 7.1. Historical Development of Symbolic Interactionism

7.1 provides a brief historical description of these theorists and their major concepts. In summary, the Interactionist School suggests that individuals are constantly changing beings capable of altering behavior in response to characteristics of their real or perceived social environment. For this reason, the application of real or perceived positive or negative labels to individuals may, over time, cause individuals to alter behaviors to those defined by such labels. Hence, individuals identify with the applied labels, alter their behaviors to those defined by the labels, and possibly embark on careers of deviance or crime.

Assumptions About People and Society

Applying the sociology of knowledge approach to the writings of the 20th-century interactionists, one may conclude that such works are grounded in several major theoretical assumptions. The social phenomenon being analyzed in this case is the social process that one goes through to become a career deviant or criminal. The criminal or deviant acts of check forging (Demert, 1951, 1967) are objective overt behavior, while the concepts of "stigma" (Goffman, 1963) and "tagging" (Tanenbaum, 1938) are subjective covert phenomenon. These cognitive processes become one of the primary factors in the origin of the individual's behavior.

Unlike many other theoretical perspectives, the focus of the Interactionist School may be either the individual (micro) or the group (macro). For example, one variation of the Interactionist School focuses not on the organization or structure of society but rather on the process of individual change from conformity to career deviancy. Examples include Lemert's (1951) discussion of the career development process from the primary deviant to the secondary deviant and Goffman's (1961) discussion of the "moral career" of the mental patient. Ironically, this same focus on the individual's behavior development has been criticized by Becker (1963) and Schur (1979), who suggested that the group must be considered in the identification of any behavior. Examples include Becker's (1963) discussion of the politicization of deviance through "moral entrepreneurs" and Schur's (1979) discussion of the social definition of deviance and collective rule making.

Another theoretical assumption underlying the Interactionist School perspective involves viewing the individual as a passive agent of his or her label. More specifically, once the individual has incorporated into his or her identity the social stigma and the labeling process has become complete, the individual is almost powerless as to the effects of the label on his or her behavior; the individual becomes a victim of his or her social environment and no longer acts with free will. For this reason, major policy proposals derived from the Interactionist School of thought often would suggest less involvement by society and the criminal justice system toward the individual deviant or criminal so as to avoid the greater evil of an uncontrollable label (Schur, 1973; Tannenbaum, 1938).

Another theoretical assumption suggests that the social phenomenon, in this case career deviant behavior or crime, is a generated phenomenon. More specifically, the process that one goes through to become labeled is not directly imposed. Instead, the process occurs over time. A description of this process typically is associated with Tannenbaum's (1938) discussion of "tagging" and Lemert's (1951) discussion of becoming a secondary deviant.

The final theoretical assumption proposed by the Interactionist School suggests that society is not stable or made up of a consensus of beliefs; societies typically are conflict oriented. The work of Becker (1963) illustrates this assumption, with his suggestions regarding the politicizing of deviance and the concept of moral entrepreneurs. Specifically, Becker believed that society creates deviance through a nonconsensual political process that may change depending on who is holding power. Consequently, a wide variety of legal changes will occur and are expected from the group in any political entity that holds the power to create and impose its idea of appropriate or inappropriate behavior on the entire population through the creation and enforcement of rules and sanctions.

The Rise of Symbolic Interactionism

The Interactionist School of criminology, often referred to as labeling theory, typically is grounded in the works of two early 20th-century sociologists mentioned briefly in Chapter 6: Charles H. Cooley (1864-1929) and George H. Mead (1863-1931). The works of Cooley, a professor of sociology at the University of Michigan from 1892 until his death in 1929, traditionally are associated with *Social Organization* (Cooley, 1909), in which he discussed the primary group concept and described its importance in influencing individual behavior.

More important to the Interactionist School tradition, however, was *Human Nature and the Social Order,* in which Cooley (1902) introduced the "looking-glass self" concept. According to Cooley, individuals develop an image of self from the perspective of others or continually see a reflection of self as they believe others view them.

> As we see . . . our face, figure, and dress in the glass, and are interested in them because they are ours, and pleased or otherwise with them according to as they do or do not answer to what we should like them to be, so in imagination we perceive in another's mind some thought of our appearance, manners, aims, deeds, character, friends, and so on, and are variously affected by it. (p. 184)

Conclusively, Cooley believed that the social setting provides the individual with an image of how he or she is perceived by others. It is the processing of this image that could affect or change behavior, a type of self-fulfilling prophecy in which the individual's behavior is altered to meet the expectations of the perceived other.

Similar to Cooley, Mead was a foundational inspiration in the Interactionist School tradition. Mead, a professor who taught philosophy at the University of Chicago from 1894 until his death in 1931, traditionally has been described as a social behaviorist and, along with Cooley, as a primary originator of the symbolic interactionist approach to sociology (Deegan, 1988).

In *Mind, Self, and Society,* Mead (1934) stressed the importance of symbols including gestures and especially language in the development of one's self-image and accompanying behavior. As stated in Chapter 6, one may remember that the self was not initially present at birth but rather developed over time through social experiences. In fact, Mead suggested that the process of developing a self is merely learning to assume the role of others. More specifically, Mead suggested that the self develops in levels of sophistication as the individual grows from a child into an adult. A summary of Mead's description of self development is as follows:

1. The individual in the infant stage does not posses a self. The infant's actions are only imitations of others without any underlying motives. At this stage, the individual is not viewing himself or herself through the eyes of others.

2. As the child learns language and other symbols, he or she begins to model individuals who are significant in the child's life (often parents). This often is exemplified by the child play-acting one parental role in a specific playtime activity.

3. As the child matures, the child further develops his or her self, becoming capable of assuming the role of several others in an individual situation. For example, the child is capable of assuming the role of all players in a group activity (e.g., baseball).

4. The self further develops as the individual continues to grow and mature. This allows the individual to assume the role of many others in many situations. It is at this point that the self has recognized the generalized other. Thus, the individual now recognizes that there are specific cultural norms and values that exist and begins to view himself or herself from this generalized perspective.

It should be noted that Mead believed that the socialization process did not stop with the development of the self. In fact, the self will continue to change, depending on the circumstances and occurrences in one's life.

In conclusion, the works of Cooley and Mead did not specifically attempt to explain the origin of deviance or the development of a criminal career. Instead, their ideas provided a foundation regarding the process that all individuals go through in the development of self. As stated earlier, these early symbolic interactionists believed that individual perceptions of self and accompanying behavior may be influenced by one's social environment. In other words, behavior results from a process in which individual actions may be caused by the actions or perceived actions of others. These behaviors could be either deviant or nondeviant. Thus, at this time, one should focus beyond the aforementioned general explanations of behavior and instead examine the issues of deviance and crime themselves. Specifically, what is the process of development for the career criminal? The remainder of this chapter focuses on this question as we turn from the general interactionist theories of behavior to the specific interactionist theories of career criminality and deviance.

Frank Tannenbaum (1893-1969)

The formal origin of contemporary Interactionist School theory in criminology may be credited to the historian Frank Tannenbaum. Tannenbaum was born in Poland in 1893. He received his A.B. degree from Columbia College and his Ph.D. from the Robert Brookings Graduate School in Economic and Political Science in 1927. He was a professor of Latin American history at Columbia University from 1936 until his retirement in 1961 (Tannenbaum, 1964).

The personal background of Tannenbaum provided much assistance to his work and association with criminology. He personally served 1 year of imprisonment for unlawful assembly during the unemployment unrest of 1913. He also focused much of his research on prison and its reform, visiting more than 70 institutions including Sing Sing and Auburn prisons. In sum, Tannenbaum believed that the penal system took everything from the inmate and gave nothing in return (Tannenbaum, 1975).

Tannenbaum's Early Works

The time served in prison by Tannenbaum and his research provided the ideas that later led to the creation of contemporary interactionist criminology. As Tannenbaum (1922) suggested in *Wall Shadows,* there often is very little separating the individuals labeled as criminals and those who are law abiding.

> To justify punishment, we develop false standards of good and bad. We caricature and distort both our victims and ourselves. They must be all black, we all white; if not, how could we impose upon others what we would not admit as applicable to our own flesh and blood? But that is not true. The difference between us and them is mainly relative and accidental. (p. 148)

Thus, the characteristics and social backgrounds of most criminals are the same as those of the common citizen. One of the few things distinguishing criminals is that they were brought into the criminal justice system. If they had not been arrested, prosecuted, and sent to prison, then most of their lives would continue in a manner similar to that of the rest of society.

Tannenbaum (1922) further reiterated that prison is not necessarily the best solution to a problem as common in occurrence as crime. Once the crime is committed, the offender is "stamped" as a criminal and subjected to all of the negative ramifications associated with the offender label.

> The prison is a great equalizer. All men are fit for it; all they need is to break the law. That done, one is stamped as a criminal, and all criminals are sent to similar places, as if all crimes were alike, and as if all men who committed them were cast in the same mold. . . . Break the law, and you are fit to abide with all men who have done the same, be the mood and temper as varied as the shadows that creep over the earth. (p. 149) . . .
>
> Imprisonment is negative. It takes all. It gives nothing. It takes from the prisoners every interest, every ambition, every hope; it cuts away, with a coarse disregard for personality, all that a man did and loved, all his work and his contacts, and gives nothing in return. (pp. 154-155)

Therefore, Tannenbaum suggested that regardless of the crime committed, the offender is stamped as an offender, thereby losing his or her identity and left to face the world as a labeled criminal.

Tannenbaum's "Tagging" Process

Tannenbaum later expanded the aforementioned stamping process and the accompanying negative ramifications of official criminal justice response and imprisonment policy into his most cited works in criminology. In *Crime and the Community,* Tannenbaum (1938) suggested that the individual becomes deviant through a tagging process following his or her involvement in an "innocent misadjustment" that has been dramaticized by society. To exemplify, the individual, for the most part nondeviant in nature, becomes involved in some form of deviant behavior. When identified, this act of deviance may be dramaticized by society, creating a label that differentiates the individual from the majority of the population. Once labeled (or tagged), the individual may incorporate this deviant label into his or her identity and become the very thing that society finds repugnant.

> The first dramatization of the "evil" which separates the child out of his group for specialized treatment plays a greater role in making the criminal than perhaps any other experience. It cannot be too often emphasized that for the child the whole situation has become different. He now lives in a different world. He has been tagged. A new and hitherto nonexistent environment has been precipitated out for him.
>
> The process of making the criminal, therefore, is a process of tagging, defining, identifying, segregating, describing, emphasizing, making conscious and self-conscious; it becomes a way of stimulating, suggesting, emphasizing, and evoking the very traits that are complained of. If the theory of relation of response to stimulus has any meaning, the entire process of dealing with the young delinquent is mischievous in so far as it identifies him to himself or to the environment as a delinquent person.
>
> The person becomes the thing he is described as being. . . . The dramatization of the evil therefore tends to precipitate the conflict situation which was first created through some innocent maladjustment. The child's isolation forces him into companionship with other children similarly defined, and the gang becomes his means of escape, his security. The life of the gang gives it special mores, and the attack by the community upon these mores merely overemphasizes the conflict already in existence and makes it the source of a new series of experiences that lead directly to a criminal career. (pp. 19-20)

In summary, Tannenbaum (1938) suggested that society creates the criminal, often through official criminal justice policy by a reaction process involving the separation of the child from conventional society. It is this societal reaction process, or "dramatization of evil" (p. 19), that labels the individual and pushes him into a career of deviance.

Negative Effects of the Criminal Justice System

In accordance with the Interactionist School, Tannenbaum (1938) suggested that society creates deviants through a labeling process. It must be reiterated, however, that the society discussed by Tannenbaum is not limited to individuals, peers, and so forth. It also may include government entities and official criminal justice policies, concepts that were not widely appreciated until after World War II when the Interactionist School formally was established as an independent area in the field of criminology. As Tannenbaum reiterated regarding the criminal justice system and the process that occurs therein,

> No more self-defeating device could be discovered than the one society has developed in dealing with the criminal. It proclaims his career in such loud and dramatic forms

that both he and the community accept the judgment as a fixed description. He becomes conscious of himself as a criminal, and the community expects him to live up to his reputation and will not credit him if he does not live up to it. (p. 477)

Thus, Tannenbaum (1938) stated that society, including the criminal justice system, should take special caution when creating policy that attempts to sanction or correct deviants or criminals.

In dealing with the delinquent [or] the criminal, therefore, the important thing to remember is that we are dealing with a human being who is responding normally to the demands, stimuli, approval, [and] expectancy of the group with whom he is associated. We are dealing not with an individual but [rather] with a group. (pp. 19-20)

Critique of Tannenbaum

It is difficult to determine the criticisms associated with the works of Tannenbaum. In fact, few textbooks in criminology make reference to his works with any great detail. When criticisms are found, they primarily focus on the fact that Tannenbaum exaggerated the tagging process. This seems appropriate when one considers the social context of the times. Tannenbaum's major publication of *Crime and the Community* was published in 1938. Tensions were mounting in Europe as Hitler and Mussolini were beginning to attain power. In addition, through government assistance, the United States was beginning to make positive advances from the Great Depression that began in 1929. It seems almost obvious that a society would be very unaccepting of writings that criticized government policies and programs when they appeared to be in great demand and depended on by a large proportion of the population.

Edwin M. Lemert (1912-1996)

The works of the early symbolic interactionists and Tannenbaum were further expanded by the sociologist/anthropologist Lemert. Similar to Tannenbaum, Edwin Lemert's personal and professional background provided much insight into his later writings. Hence, he worked for 1 year as a welfare worker prior to attending graduate school and was exposed to the works of the early symbolic interactionists while pursuing his graduate education (Martin, Mutchnick, and Austin, 1990). After obtaining his Ph.D. at the Ohio State University in 1939 (Anderson Publishing, 1997), Lemert eventually published several major works criticizing past sociological research and further expanding the interactionist/labeling tradition. As Lemert (1967) stated,

[The] concern is with social control and its consequences for deviance. This is a large turn away from older sociology, which tended to rest heavily upon the idea that deviance leads to social control. I have come to believe that the reverse idea, i.e., social control leads to deviance, is equally tenable and the potentially richer premise for studying deviance in modern society. (p. v)

Lemert's Concepts of Primary and Secondary Deviance

One of the foremost contributions of Lemert to the Interactionist School was his introduction of and distinction between primary and secondary deviance in *Social Pathology* (Lemert, 1951). It is the understanding between these concepts, according to Lemert (1967), that is "indispensable to a complete understanding of deviation in modern pluralistic society" (pp. 17-18).

According to Lemert (1951), primary deviance is occasional deviant behavior, often situational in nature, that is excused, rationalized, or otherwise socially acceptable. He added,

> [Primary deviance] is assumed to arise in a wide variety of social, cultural, and psychological contexts, and at best [it] has only marginal implications for the psychic structure of the individual; it does not lead to symbolic reorganization at the level of self regarding attitudes and social roles. (Lemert, 1967, p. 17)

For example, the excessive use of alcohol is considered deviant in many social settings. However, in other diversified social settings such as following the death of a loved one, participating in an organized group activity that promotes heavy drinking, and following the loss of a job, such behavior may be excused or deemed socially acceptable. Such "deviations remain primary deviations or symptomatic or situational as long as they are rationalized or otherwise dealt with as functions of a socially acceptable role" (Lemert, 1951, p. 75).

Most important to the Interactionist School, however, was Lemert's concept of secondary deviance, which he clarified in *Human Deviance, Social Problems, and Social Control.* According to Lemert (1967),

> Secondary deviation refers to a special class of socially defined responses which people make to problems created by the societal reaction to their deviance. These problems are essentially moral problems which revolve around stigmatization, punishments, segregation, and social control. Their general effect is to differentiate the symbolic and interactional environment to which the person responds, so that early or adult socialization is categorically affected. They become central facts of existence for those experiencing them, altering psychic structure [and] producing specialized organization of social roles and self-regarding attitudes. Actions which have these roles and self attitudes as their referents make up secondary deviance. The secondary deviant, as opposed to his actions, is a person whose life and identity are organized around the facts of deviance. (pp. 40-41)

Thus, the secondary deviant is the deviant who has received severe societal reaction to repeated primary deviance. The societal reaction has been so severe that through a process of identification, the secondary deviant has adjusted and incorporated a new identity into his or her image of self that is grounded in a deviant lifestyle. The secondary deviant has become a career deviant.

The Process of Becoming a Secondary Deviant

It should be noted that an individual does not become a secondary deviant through one act of primary deviance. Instead, for the process to be complete, there must be repetitive primary deviance and accompanying societal reaction. According to Lemert (1951), a rough description of the process includes

1. primary deviation;

2. societal penalties;

3. further primary deviation;

4. stronger penalties and rejections;

5. further deviation, perhaps with hostilities and resentments beginning to focus upon those doing the penalizing;

6. crisis reached in the tolerance quotient, expressed in formal action by the community stigmatizing of the deviant;

7. strengthening of the deviant conduct as a reaction to the stigmatizing and penalties; and

8. ultimate acceptance of deviant social status and efforts at adjustment on the basis of the associated role. (p. 77)

Lemert's Discussion on the
Naive and Secondary Check Forger

To distinguish between primary and secondary deviance, Lemert researched the offense of check forgery and suggested that differences did exist among individual offenders. According to Lemert (1972), most check forgeries are naive or criminally unsophisticated and situational in nature.

Naive forgery is a crime of persons who are unacquainted with criminal techniques; but aside from this, the persons involved would appear to have acquired normal attitudes and habits of law observance. It follows that naive forgery emerges as behavior which is out of character or "other than usual" for the persons involved. In the act of forging an ephemeral, personal reorganization occurs in response to situational interactors which may be recognized as a special symbolic process conceived to cover aspects of motivation, feeling, emotion, and the choice of adjustment alternatives. The personal differentiae we have set down here are the original broad limits within which a certain class of situations can impinge upon the person with the possibility of emergent forgery. (p. 142)

Thus, the individual may become involved in the offense of check forgery without the development of a criminal career. Unlike the secondary deviant, the primary deviant has not incorporated this deviant lifestyle into his or her identity. In the words of Lemert, such situational offenders include

> [offenders who] pass worthless checks only once and quit; others, casual offenders, intersperse periods of stable employment with check writing sorties quickly followed by arrest. Some people imprisoned for bad checks are alcoholics who have unwisely passed worthless checks during a drinking spree, drug addicts "supporting a habit," or gamblers desperately trying to cover losses. (p. 165)

The secondary deviant or systematic check forger, however, is different. This individual ultimately has accepted the deviant social status with efforts of adjustment on the basis of the associated role. More specifically, the systematic offender has a commitment to check forgery as a way of life, having developed an individual system of passing bad checks that revolves around pseudonymity, mobility, and seclusion.

Lemert described the life of the secondary check forger as one of great anxiety, loneliness, and lacking individual identity. Hence, for the professional check forger to avoid arrest, this individual becomes a real-life actor hiding his or her true self, maintaining constant mobility, and often caught up in a life that is out of his or her control. The secondary check forger also avoids progressive involvement in social relationships because such intimate interchange of experiences comes with a danger of inadvertent or deliberate exposure of his or her offenses by others.

According to Lemert (1972), maintaining a life at the aforementioned pace necessary for a successful check forger contains the seeds of its own destruction. The offender, left without an outlet for true identity,

> [reaches] a point at which he can no longer define himself in relation to others on any basis. The self becomes amorphous, without boundaries; the identity substructure is lost. Apathy replaces motivation, and in phenomenological terms, "life" or "this way of life" is no longer worth living. This is the common prelude to the forger's arrest. (p. 180)

Therefore, by society's including criminal justice authorities reacting to the professional check forger, the latter is forced into a deviant lifestyle of continued offenses. The person has employed his or her deviant behavior, or a role based on it, as a means of defense, attack, and adjustment to the problems created by societal reaction and policy to him or her. The professional check forger is the secondary deviant.

Critique of Lemert

There are several criticisms associated with Lemert's attempt to explain social deviance and the development of a deviant career. The first involves his attempt to explain the origin of deviance. More specifically, while attempting to explain the process that one goes through in becoming a secondary deviant, Lemert did not explain the actual origin of deviant behavior; the origin of primary deviance is avoided

(Gibbs, 1966). Second, Lemert provided an explanation as to why individuals get involved in secondary deviance or become career criminals. Such an explanation, however, does not include much corporate and white collar crime or many violent offenses (e.g., spouse abuse, acquaintance rape). Such crimes often are committed by career offenders who never have been the recipients of the application of public labels (Mankoff, 1971). Third, Lemert has been criticized for failing to provide a systematic analysis of female criminality. For example, Heidensohn (1968) suggested that the works of Lemert viewed prostitution as a form of sexual deviance instead of as a rational economic crime, a description often used by the prostitutes themselves. Such a position clearly is at odds with the interactionist/labeling tradition—understanding behavior from the individual deviant's perspective (Leonard, 1982). This contradictory position also complicates the creation of programs and policies through a lack of clarity. According to Akers (2000), such a characteristic is not found in the preferable theory. A final criticism of Lemert includes a lack of empirical support regarding the individual's identity changing in a negative manner as he or she moves from the primary deviant to the secondary deviant (Shoemaker, 1996).

It also should also be noted that a legitimate argument could be presented that the works of Lemert do not, in and of themselves, constitute a theory by definition. As suggested by Homans (1962, 1974) and Turner (1991), a theory must have propositions stating the relationship between two or more variables, must form a logical deductive system in which each proposition builds on previous propositions, and must have concepts defined in a manner to be empirically tested. It appears arguable that the works of Lemert are lacking in such higher-order propositions and, therefore, lack true theoretical explanatory power.

Howard S. Becker (1928-)

A review of the Interactionist School of criminology never could be considered complete without a discussion of Howard S. Becker. Although failing to acknowledge that he is a criminologist, the works of Becker have had a "considerable impact on criminological thought and theory," having started "somewhat of a revolution" in the discipline (Martin et al., 1990, pp. 352-355).

Contemporary Influences

As mentioned in the biographical inset on Becker (Inset 7.1), many individuals had the potential to influence his works. He was educated at the University of Chicago under the guidance of Ernest Burgess, Everett Hughes, Lloyd Warner, and Herbert Blumer. In fact, a required graduate class in advanced field studies taught by Burgess eventually associated Becker with Hughes (Martin et al., 1990). Hughes's research interest in occupations and methods of data collection would influence Becker

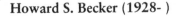

| INSET 7.1 | Howard S. Becker (1928-) |

Howard S. Becker was born in Chicago in 1928. During his early years, he was particularly interested in music, especially jazz. This interest remained with Becker through the early 1970s, when he continued to play in jazz clubs throughout Chicago (Martin, Mutchnick, and Austin, 1990, p. 349). Becker began his pursuits of higher education while in high school. He took college course work at the University of Chicago and later completed his degree at the University of Chicago. Becker's father encouraged him to enroll in the master's program in sociology. He took his father's advice. However, he also continued to pursue his musical interests.

While taking an advanced field studies course under Ernest Burgess, Becker decided to take field notes during his work as a pianist in the jazz clubs of Chicago. Later, Burgess encouraged Becker to work with Everette Hughes, another faculty member in the Department of Sociology (Martin et al., 1990, p. 350). This research subsequently was turned into his master's thesis and part of his book, *Outsiders* (Becker, 1963).

Following the completion of his thesis, Becker was encouraged by Hughes to apply for a fellowship to pursue doctoral studies. On receipt of the fellowship, Becker began research that materialized into his dissertation thesis. Having completed his dissertation in 1951 at 23 years of age, Becker had limited opportunities. He stayed at the University of Chicago and taught for 2 years. In addition, he served as a research associate at the Institute for Juvenile Research.

From 1953 to 1955, Becker completed a postdoctoral fellowship for the Ford Foundation. The fellowship provided funding for him to conduct personality research at the University of Illinois. After completing this postdoctorate, Becker was contacted by Hughes to participate in a study on the University of Kansas medical school. This research led to the collaboration with several others and the classic publication, *Boys in White* (Becker, 1961). After completing this research, Becker accepted a position at the Stanford University Institute for the Study of Human Problems.

In 1965, Becker accepted a position as a professor in the Department of Sociology at Northwestern University. Throughout his life, Becker has published numerous scholarly articles and books. However, his most notable contributions to criminology have been his theoretical writings related to the labeling perspective.

—Shaun L. Gabbidon
Pennsylvania State University at Harrisburg

SOURCE: Excerpted from the writings of Shaun L. Gabbidon with permission.

throughout his career, especially in his study of jazz musicians and the publication of *Outsiders* (Becker, 1963).

Many other individuals had the potential to influence the theoretical thoughts and beliefs of Becker during his tenure as a graduate student. There were more than 200 graduate students pursuing degrees at the University of Chicago during the 1940s including Erving Goffman, James Short, and David Gold (Martin et al., 1990). To say that such prominent students did not influence Becker in any way would be erroneous.

Becker's Critique of Previous Research

While acknowledging the difficulty in scientifically studying deviant behavior, Becker (1963) suggested that flaws are all too common in the literature pertaining to deviance. Hence, one should not attempt to theorize from the literature for two specific reasons.

> First, there simply are not enough studies that provide us with facts about the lives of deviants as they live them. Although there are a great many studies of juvenile delinquency, they are more likely to be based on court records than on direct observation. . . . Very few tell us in detail what a juvenile delinquent does in his daily round of activity and what he thinks about himself, society, and his activities. When we theorize about juvenile delinquency, we are therefore in the position of having to infer the way of life of the delinquent boy from fragmentary studies and journalistic accounts instead of being able to base our theories on adequate knowledge of the phenomenon we are trying to explain. (p. 166)

The second, and less complex, reason is as follows:

> There are not enough of them [scientific research studies]. Many kinds of deviance have never been scientifically described, or the studies are so few in number as to be a bare beginning. . . . For instance, . . . an area of deviance of utmost importance for sociological theorists has hardly been studied at all. This is the area of professional misconduct. It is well known . . . that the ethics committees of legal and medical professional associations have plenty of business to occupy them. Yet, for all the wealth of sociological descriptions of professional behavior and culture, we have few, if any, studies of unethical behavior by professionals. (pp. 166-167)

Becker concluded that the problems associated with research on deviance will lead to the "construction of faulty or inadequate theories" (p. 167). Few could disagree that such scenarios must be avoided if a thorough understanding of deviance and crime is to occur.

Politicizing Deviance: Labeling the Outsider

The works of Becker provided much insight to those of earlier Interactionist School criminologists. To exemplify, Becker was very critical of the traditional sociological view of deviance and law creation that previously had proposed that such concepts were the result of a consensus of the population as to what was functional for the group as a whole. To Becker, such actions only labeled individuals as "outsiders" and as those whose behavior was dysfunctional with regard to the group's best interests. In the words of Becker (1963), "Such an assumption seems to me to ignore the central fact about deviance" (p. 8). One must realize that all that constitutes deviant behavior—all rules, laws, policies, and the like—are "the products of someone's initiative" (p. 147). Therefore, the behavior that society defines as deviant or criminal is ever changing and always open for debate—a never-ending political decision.

> It is harder in practice than it appears to be in theory to specify what is functional and what [is] dysfunctional for a society or social group. The question of what the purpose or goal (function) of a group is and, consequently, what things will help or hinder the achievement of that purpose is very often a political question. Factions within the group disagree and maneuver to have their own definition of the group's function accepted. The function of the group or organization, then, is decided in political conflict, not given in the nature of the organization. If this is true, then it is likewise true that the questions of what rules are to be enforced, what behavior regarded as deviant, and which people labeled as outsiders must also be regarded as political. (p. 7)

To summarize, Becker suggested that the creation of rules and their enforcement is not necessarily a universally agreed-on phenomenon: "Instead, [it is] the object of conflict and disagreement, part of the political process of society" (p. 18).[1]

Moral Entrepreneurs and the Definition of Deviance

Believing that rules and sanctions were not necessarily the result of consensus, Becker (1963), in the interactionist tradition, developed the concept of "moral entrepreneurs" to further exemplify his belief that deviance is created through a nonconsensual political process. More specifically, Becker suggested that both law creators and law enforcers were only moral entrepreneurs who believed that society was the victim of various social problems that, in their judgment, could be corrected only through their political action.

> Moral crusaders typically want to help those beneath them to achieve a better status. That those beneath them do not always like the means proposed for their salvation is another matter. But this fact—that moral crusaders are typically dominated by those in the upper levels of the social structure—means that they add to the power they derive from the legitimacy of their moral position, the power they derive from their superior position in society. (p. 149)

Hence, moral entrepreneurs, often believing that they have taken society's best interests into consideration, create and enforce rules that label particular individuals as outsiders. Becker (1963) stated this proposition better, perhaps, with one of the most frequently cited passages in the Interactionist School:

> Social groups create deviance by making the rules whose infraction constitutes deviance and by applying those rules to particular people and labeling them as outsiders. From this point of view, deviance is not a quality of the act the person commits but rather a consequence of the application by others of rules and sanctions to an "offender." The deviant is one to whom that label has successfully been applied; deviant behavior is behavior that people so label. (p. 9)

Becker's Sequential Model of Deviant Behavior

In an attempt to better explain society's political creation of deviance and crime and to expand the issue that such behaviors are not the quality of the act but rather the application of labels, Becker (1963) proposed a typology commonly known as the sequential model of deviant behavior (p. 20). This typology depicts four types of behavior with accompanying societal perceptions that may occur when discussing deviance:

Becker's Sequential Model of Deviant Behavior		
	Obedient Behavior	Rule-Breaking Behavior
Perceived as deviant	Falsely accused	Pure deviant
Not perceived as deviant	Conforming	Secret deviant

In explaining this typology of deviant behavior, Becker (1963) defined the conformist as one who "obeys the rule and which others perceive as obeying the rule" (p. 19). To exemplify, the conformist does not engage in deviance and has been accurately perceived or labeled by society as an individual who is not deviant. The pure deviant "is that which both disobeys the rule and is perceived as doing so" (p. 20). In other words, the pure deviant engages in deviance and has been accurately perceived or labeled by society as deviant.

Perhaps more interesting to Becker (1963), however, was the falsely accused individual and the secret deviant. The falsely accused individual is the person who is "seen by others as having committed an improper action, although in fact he has not done so" (p. 20). Hence, the falsely accused individual has been misjudged or incorrectly labeled as deviant. On the contrary, the secret deviant is the individual who has committed improper behavior, "yet no one notices it or reacts to it as a violation" (p. 20). This individual also has been misjudged or incorrectly labeled as nondeviant.

In conclusion, Becker's sequential model of deviant behavior depicts his proposition that the quality of the acts does not matter; it is the application of the label that determines whether an individual is deviant. More specifically, the secret deviant engages in the same behavior as does the pure deviant but has not been defined or labeled deviant. In addition, the falsely accused person is engaged in the same behavior as is the conformist but also has been labeled inaccurately. Consequently, in Becker's view, the application of the label—not one's actual behavior—characterizes the individual. Ironic as this may be, it signifies the power of labels in society.

Acceptance of the Label as One's Master Status

According to Becker (1963), once an individual has been successfully labeled, he or she is subjected to the positive and negative effects of the label itself. Thus, Becker suggested that the label eventually will become the individual's "master status," a term borrowed from earlier work published by Hughes (1945), forcing the individual into a future deviant career. The concept of master status may be defined as the process in which a particular trait becomes the individual's central identifying characteristic (Becker, 1963). To exemplify, a "falsely accused" individual identifies with, alters his or her behavior, and lives up to the deviant label placed on him or her by others—a type of self-fulfilling prophecy. The individual now possesses deviant behavior as his or her master status, quite possibly resulting in a career of deviant or criminal behavior.

Critique of Becker

The works of Becker are fundamentally plagued with the same criticisms often associated with the earlier works of Lemert. How does one explain the initial deviant act that occurs prior to becoming labeled (Gibbs, 1966)? In addition, as mentioned earlier in this chapter, empirical support is lacking regarding the identity change that one goes through in accepting a new master status (Shoemaker, 1996). Such criticisms still would apply to the works of Becker (1963) and most theorists in the interactionist/labeling perspective. In sum, Becker's (1963) work does not appear to meet the definition of theory as discussed by Homans (1962, 1974) and Turner (1991) earlier in this chapter. Without a set of general propositions about the relationship among variables and the specific definition of concepts, empirical testing cannot occur in the manner required of scientific theory. Unfortunately, this is a devastating strike for any theoretical explanation because, according to Homans (1974), such limitations make the explanation of social behavior impossible.

There are several additional criticisms that may be associated with the works of Becker. First, according to Becker's (1963) perspective, deviant behavior is relative; no behavior is deviant unless defined as such by society. As Wellford (1975) suggested, such a statement should be considered very naive given that many crimes, including rape and homicide, are universally sanctioned.[2] A second criticism of Becker's (1963) work involves the deterministic nature of his perspective. As Akers (1968) suggested, individuals who read this literature might be led to believe that those involved in "deviant" behavior are only "minding their own business" until a "moral entrepreneur" comes along and places a negative label on them. Finally, Becker's (1963) work has been criticized by several writers (Liazos, 1972; Taylor, Walton, and Young, 1973; Young, 1981) for his focusing too much on the individual labeling process (micro) and not emphasizing the structural organization of society (macro) as the more important origin of deviant behavior. In sum, it appears that there may be several unanswered questions associated with Becker's (1963) work. Such criticisms, however, should not negate the impact of his works on criminology. Perhaps Becker (1973) said it best when he responded to his critics as follows:

> [The process of labeling], as carried out by moral entrepreneurs, while important, cannot possibly be conceived as the sole explanation of what alleged deviants actually do. It would be foolish to propose that stick-up men stick people up simply because some-

one has labeled them stick-up men or that everything a homosexual does results from someone having called him homosexual. Nevertheless, one of the most important contributions of this approach has been to focus attention on the way labeling places the actor in circumstances which make it harder for him to continue the normal routines of everyday life and thus provoke him to [engage in] "abnormal" actions (as when a prison record makes it harder to earn a living at a conventional occupation and so disposes its possessor to move into an illegal one). The degree to which labeling has such effects is, however, an empirical one, to be settled by research into specific cases rather than by theoretical fiat. (p. 179) . . .

Labeling theory, then, is neither a theory, with all the achievements and obligations that go with the title, nor focused so exclusively on the act of labeling as some have thought. It is, rather, a way of looking at a general area of human activity, a perspective whose value will appear, if at all, in increased understanding of things formerly obscure. (p. 181)

Erving Goffman (1922-1982)

Erving Goffman provided several contributions to the underlying foundations of the Interactionist School of criminology. As discussed in the biographical inset on Goffman (Inset 7.2), he held numerous academic/research positions that would have significant influence on his theoretical writing including his most significant works related to criminology, *Asylums* (Goffman, 1961) and *Stigma* (Goffman, 1963). Described in life as a very particular and opinionated individual, Goffman passed away following a long battle with cancer in 1982 (Manning, 1992).

Contemporary Influences

Many individuals had the potential to influence the works of Goffman. Similar to Becker, Goffman was educated at the University of Chicago during the tenure of Burgess, Hughes, Warner, and Blumer. In addition, in *Asylums,* Goffman (1961) footnoted the works of Edwin Sutherland, Donald Cressey, and Lloyd Ohlin, suggesting at least partial influence on Goffman's thoughts and writings. Finally, the works of sociologists Émile Durkheim and Louis Wirth and anthropologist A. R. Radcliffe-Brown traditionally have been cited as significant influences on the works of Goffman (Martin et al., 1990).

Goffman's View of the Study of Deviance

The works of Goffman have been very important to the study of criminology despite his personal view toward the discipline. To Goffman, there was little reason to individually study deviant behavior because there was not, and probably never would be, a general theory of deviance. In his opinion, the study of deviance was an

INSET 7.2

Erving Goffman (1922-1982)

Erving Goffman was born June 11, 1922, in Manville, Alberta, the son of Max and Ann Goffman. He was educated at the University of Toronto, graduating with an A.B. degree in 1945. After graduating, Goffman headed to the University of Chicago, where he received both his M.A. and his Ph.D. (Martin, Mutchnick, and Austin, 1990).

During his professional career, Goffman held numerous positions. He taught at the University of Edinburgh from 1949 to 1951. He returned to the University of Chicago from 1953 to 1954, serving as a resident associate. It was through his next position, as research associate in the visiting scientist program of the Laboratory of Socio-Environmental Studies, National Institute of Mental Health, that Goffman conducted the research for his classic publication, *Asylums* (Goffman, 1961; see also Martin et al., 1990, p. 322).

From 1958 to 1968, Goffman was a professor at the University of California, Berkeley. During his tenure at Berkeley, he rose to the status of full professor and developed a stellar reputation. This reputation initially was perpetuated through his publication of *Presentation of Self in Everyday Life* (Goffman, 1959), *Asylums* (Goffman, 1961), and *Stigma* (Goffman, 1963).

During his life, Goffman received numerous awards for his work. Starting in 1961, Goffman received the McIver Award from the American Sociological Association. Goffman was awarded a Guggenheim fellowship during 1977-1978. In 1979, he was awarded the Mead-Cooley Award and the George Orwell Award presented by the Harvard University Press. In addition, he received numerous honorary degrees (Martin et al., 1990, p. 323).

In 1980, Goffman became president-elect of the American Sociological Association. However, he was unable to deliver his presidential address due to illness. Martin and colleagues (1990) noted that the address was published posthumously by the *American Sociological Review* in February 1983 (p. 323).

—*Shaun L. Gabbidon*
Pennsylvania State University at Harrisburg

SOURCE: Excerpted from the writings of Shaun L. Gabbidon with permission.

extension of sociology's broad concern with all social problems and only devised to keep such researchers busy. As Goffman (1963) stated,

> It is remarkable that those of us who live around the social sciences have so quickly become comfortable in using the term "deviant," as if those to whom the term is applied have enough in common so that significant things can be said about them as a whole. Just as there are iatrogenic disorders caused by the work that physicians do (which gives them more work to do), so there are categories of persons who are created by students of society and then studied by them. (p. 140)

Despite this opinion, Goffman's works would have a major impact on criminological thinking, especially in relation to prison and changes that occur in the personal identities of inmates.

Goffman's Discussion of the Total Institution

Asylums (Goffman, 1961) was the result of research conducted between 1954 and 1957 as a visiting member of the National Institute of Mental Health. It included small research studies of ward behavior in the National Institute of Health Clinical Center and 1 year of field research at St. Elizabeth Hospital in Washington, D.C. In summary, Goffman analyzed life inside a mental hospital suggesting that the critical factor shaping an individual in a closed environment was not the person's reason for institutional entrance but rather the institution itself.

In analyzing this work as it relates to criminology, one may conclude that Goffman's discussion of the total institution is very important to the discipline. In the words of Goffman (1961), such places were those "where a large number of like-situated individuals, cut off from the wider society for an appreciable period of time, together lead an enclosed, formally administered round of life" (p. xii). More specifically, he describes such institutions as places where the following situation exists:

1. All aspects of life are conducted in the same place and under the same single authority.

2. Each phase of the member's daily activity is carried on in the immediate company of a large batch of others, all of whom are treated alike and required to do the same thing together.

3. All phases of the day's activities are tightly scheduled, with one activity leading at a pre-arranged time into the next, the whole sequence of activities being imposed from above by a system of explicit formal rulings and a body of officials.

4. The various enforced activities are brought together into a single rational plan purportedly designed to fulfill the official aims of the institution. (p. 6)

Hence, jails, prisons, drug and alcohol treatment centers, and any other places of confinement often associated with the criminal justice system could be considered total institutions. Goffman (1961) made such a suggestion as he defined the five types of total institutions traditionally operating in society.

First, there are institutions established to care for persons felt to be both incapable and harmless; these are the homes for the blind, the aged, the orphaned, and the indigent. Second, there are places established to care for persons felt to be both incapable of looking after themselves and a threat to the community, albeit an unintended one: TB [tuberculosis] sanitaria, mental hospitals, and leprosaria. A third type of total institution is organized to protect the community against what are felt to be intentional dangers to it, with the welfare of the persons thus sequestered not the immediate issue: jails, penitentiaries, P.O.W. [prisoner of war] camps, and concentration camps. Fourth, there are institutions purportedly established the better to pursue some worklike task and justifying themselves only on these instrumental grounds: army barracks, ships, boarding schools, work camps, colonial compounds, and large mansions from the point of view of those who live in the servants' quarters. Finally, there are those establishments designed as retreats from the world even while often serving also as training stations for the religious; examples are abbeys, monasteries, convents, and other cloisters. (pp. 4-5)

The Moral Career of the Mental Patient

As mentioned in the aforementioned paragraphs, Goffman's works can be applied to any total institutions including those associated with the criminal justice system. This becomes increasingly important to the Interactionist School in his description of the life or career of the inmate.

Goffman (1961) referred to the inmate's life as his or her "moral career," the "regular sequence of changes that [occur] in the person's self and in his framework of imagery for judging himself and others" (p. 128). Goffman further related that this career occurs in three primary phases. The first is the pre-patient phase, involving the period of time before institutional entrance. This phase is very important because it initiates the process in which the inmate will question or possibly begin to lose his or her identity. More specifically, society has identified the inmate as an individual failing to meet its minimum standards. This could include being charged and convicted of a crime, hearing voices, talking to oneself, and so forth. Regardless of the societal standard that the individual has broken or has been accused of breaking, the inmate begins to reevaluate himself or herself—Goffman referred to this as "disintegrative reevaluation" (p. 123)—from the perspective of society.

The second phase in the inmate's career is the inpatient phase. This is the time period when the individual is a resident of the institution. According to Goffman, all inmates in total institutions experience a similar situation on entry. This includes the loss of most rights and freedoms and the loss of most possessions typically associated with one's individual identity including personal effects, clothes, and relationships. Goffman (1961) referred to this process as the loss of one's "identity kit" (p. 21). The inmate also is forcibly provided with very little privacy as he or she typically must live as a group with other inmates.[3] Thus, the inmate is stripped of his or her personal identity without a means of escape. Such a situation exemplifies a tremendous loss of personal identity given that individuals in the free world at least have the choice of leaving an uncomfortable situation.

During the inpatient phase and after the inmate has been stripped of most of his or her personal identity, the institution attempts to provide the inmate with a new identity kit. This new identity, however, is limited in that inmates now are controlled as a "batch" with the selective allocation of privileges to ensure obedience to or compliance with the institution. Goffman suggested that such a process further removes the inmate's identity as he or she loses self-respect by being forced to comply with the rules of the institution so as to receive items that most individuals in society take for granted (e.g., letters, visitation rights, snacks). As a consequence, the inmate's identity is further removed as he or she is forced to adapt to the new environment.

According to Goffman (1961), the inpatient inmate employs four personal lines of adaptation in an attempt to maintain his or her identity in the new environment. Such means of adaptation may opportunistically occur at different times during the inmate's career, or the inmate may alternate among different tactics at the same time. The first is referred to as "situational withdrawal," in which "the inmate withdraws apparent attention from everything except events immediately around his body and sees these in a perspective not employed by others present" (p. 61). Thus, the inmate may fantasize and appear to have lost touch with reality. A second possible means of adaptation is the "intransigent line," whereby "the inmate intentionally challenges the institution by flagrantly refusing to cooperate with staff" (p. 62). Hunger strikes, complete disregard for institutional order, and violence may exemplify inmates following this means of adaptation. Third, is "colonization," in which the inmate identifies with the favorable conditions of the institution. Hence, the inmate may believe that the institution offers a better life than that on "the outside," quite possibly planning ways in which to be readmitted following release (pp. 62-63). The final mode of adaptation is "conversion," where "the inmate appears to take over the official or staff view of himself and tries to act out the role of the perfect inmate" (pp. 63-64). Although pleasurable for the staff, one must reiterate that this is only an act—a cynical form of rehabilitation. In conclusion, Goffman (1961) suggested that none of the adaptation strategies assists with maintaining the self. In fact, each strategy removes the individual's identity, creating complementary symptoms that the institution was designed to treat.

The third and final phase in the career of the inmate is that of the ex-patient or the time period following discharge (Goffman, 1961). Although one would assume that such a period is a time for celebration, it is ironic to note that the individual's identity has been irrevocably changed. The former inmate has been labeled and forced to face the consequences that society has placed on him or her. In the words of Goffman (1961),

> Although some roles can be reestablished by the inmate if and when he returns to the world, it is plain that other losses are irrevocable and may be painfully experienced as such. It may not be possible to make up, at a later phase of the life cycle, the time not now spent in educational or job advancement, in courting, or in rearing one's children. A legal aspect of this permanent dispossession is found in the concept of "civil death"; prison inmates may face not only a temporary loss of the rights to will money and write checks, to contest divorce or adoption proceedings, and to vote, but [also] may have some of these rights permanently abrogated. (pp. 15-16)

Goffman's Discussion of Stigma

Following the aforementioned discussion regarding the difficulty associated with inmates becoming reintegrated back into society following release from the institution, it appears most appropriate to provide a brief analysis of Goffman's second major contribution to the Interactionist School of criminology. *Stigma* (Goffman, 1963) applied the social psychological literature pertaining to stigma to the field of sociology. Consequently, Goffman analyzed numerous case studies and autobiographies regarding the self-image of the stigmatized individual, the relationship of the stigmatized individual to "normal" society, and the strategies of adaptation that a stigmatized individual must go through to reduce stigma in a world traditionally nonaccepting of those labeled as different.

According to Goffman (1963), a stigma is any of three "attribute[s] that [are] deeply discrediting" to an individual (p. 3). Thus, "abominations of the body" are physical deformities of any type. Second, "blemishes of individual character" represent society's labeling of individuals with records of unemployment, imprisonment, mental illness, homosexuality, and so forth and as being weak-willed, treacherous, and/or dishonest. Finally, "tribal stigma[ta] of race, nation, and religion" suggest contamination of all members of the particular "family" through lineages (p. 4). Taken in total, all three types of stigma possess the same sociological features.

> An individual who might have been received easily in ordinary social intercourse possesses a trait that can obtrude itself upon attention and turn those of us whom he meets away from him, breaking the claim that his other attributes have on us. He possesses a stigma, an undesired differentness. (p. 5)

In describing the aforementioned "differentness" associated with those who possess a stigma, Goffman (1963) further expanded the thoughts underlying the Interactionist School in a manner similar to that proposed by Becker (1963). More specifically, it is not necessarily the quality of the attribute that is discrediting to the individual so much as the application (by others) of negative connotations to the individual who possesses such characteristics.

> A language of relationships, not attributes, is really needed [for a person to become stigmatized]. An attribute that stigmatizes one type of possessor can confirm the usualness of another and therefore is neither creditable nor discreditable as a thing in itself. For example, some jobs in America cause holders without the expected college education to conceal this fact; other jobs, however, can lead the few of their holders who have a higher education to keep this a secret, lest they be marked as failures and outsiders. (p. 3)

As already mentioned, Goffman (1963) suggested that individuals do not automatically become associated with a stigma; for one to possess a stigma, there must be a "language of relationships" that identifies the individual as not being "normal" (p. 3). Thus, in the interactionist tradition, for one to acquire a stigma, a reaction process must occur. Goffman related this as he described such a two-step process. First, the stigmatized person "learns and incorporates the standpoint of the normal, acquiring thereby the identity beliefs of the wider society and a general idea of what it would be like to possess a particular stigma" (p. 32). Second, the stigmatized person "learns that he possesses a particular stigma and, this time in detail, the consequence of possessing it" (p. 32). Thus, the process of acquiring a stigma has been completed. The individual has accepted the view of society regarding his or her possession of a stigma. The individual now must face the consequences of such a negative label or adapt to the stigma that society has placed on him or her.

To conclude Goffman's discussion of stigma, one should note that once a stigma is acquired, it is very difficult to overcome. However, some individuals do attempt to mitigate or alter the attributes associated with the possession of a stigma so as to better cope with the accompanying consequences. This is exemplified by Goffman's (1963) suggestion that individuals possessing a stigma may conceal or disguise negative attributes through physical or environmental changes. Examples include surgery for the removal of physical deformities and restricting social engagements to those only including other stigmatized individuals. Ironically, such attempts might only intensify the individual's problems if they result in an increased loss of personal identity and self-respect.

Critique of Goffman

There are numerous criticisms typically associated with the works of Goffman. The first, and perhaps most important, applies to his methodology, which typically was based on unsystematic observation (Kuper and Kuper, 1985), a travesty to any scientific theory evaluation (Babbie, 1989). Goffman, while acknowledging that serious limitations were associated with his works (Goffman, 1971), defended his research by identifying the numerous problems associated with all scientific thinking (Goffman, 1983).

A second major criticism of the works of Goffman involves the usefulness of the total institution concept. According to Mouzelis (1971) and Perry (1974), such a concept and its definition as proposed by Goffman (1961) are too general and do not identify important distinctions that must be considered such as size of institution and type of commitment (i.e., voluntary or involuntary). The importance of such distinctions is further exemplified by the work of Delaney (1977), who found that not all life in total institutions is necessarily negative.

A third criticism of the works of Goffman suggests that it is too simple to offer realistic policy proposals for positive change in total institutions (Sedgwick, 1982). It is debatable whether or not the policy changes that occurred pertaining to total institutions following the publication of Goffman's works were positive. Throughout the late 1960s and early 1970s, deinstitutionalization and decarceration movements attempted to reduce total institution populations by correcting/treating various problems in the community. However, to say that such movements were not in any way affected by the works of Goffman would be erroneous.

In conclusion, the works of Goffman have been described as frustrating reading due to their lack of direction and their focusing on social situations in general (Manning, 1992). Regardless of this and the other aforementioned criticisms, the works of Goffman, although personally very critical of the study of deviance as a discipline, played a significant role in the attempt to understand and further develop the Interactionist School of criminology.

Edwin M. Schur (1930-)

The final individual to be discussed pertaining to the Interactionist School tradition is Edwin Schur. As suggested in the biographical inset on Schur (Inset 7.3), he developed a very productive career of contributions including many writings in both the interactionist and feminist criminological traditions. He also became an early critic of abortion laws and other "victimless" crimes, seeking policy change including decriminalization or the removal of a particular type of conduct from the control of criminal law. Consequently, his major works in the Interactionist School

INSET 7.3

Edwin M. Schur (1930-)

Edwin Schur was born on October 18, 1930, in New York City. He attended Williams College and graduated cum laude in 1952. He graduated from Yale Law school in 1955 and was admitted to the Connecticut bar in the same year. Schur returned to school and received an M.A. in sociology in 1957. He completed his education by enrolling at the London School of Economics and receiving his Ph.D. in 1959.

Throughout his career, Schur held numerous academic positions. His appointments began with an instructor in sociology position at Wellesley College from 1959 to 1961. From 1961 to 1971, he was a professor of sociology at Tufts University, serving as chair from 1966 to 1971. In 1971, Schur left Tufts and accepted a position as chair of the Department of Sociology at New York University. He remained chair until 1975 and retired from that university in August 1993.

In addition to his numerous academic appointments, Schur consistently was a productive scholar. Throughout his career, he published an abundance of articles and books. He wrote several important criminological books including *Crimes Without Victims* (Schur, 1965), *Law and Society* (Schur, 1968), *Our Criminal Society* (Schur, 1969), *Labeling Deviant Behavior* (Schur, 1971), *Radical Non-Intervention* (Schur, 1973), *Interpreting Deviance* (Schur, 1979), *The Politics of Deviance* (Schur, 1980), and *Labeling Women Deviant* (Schur, 1984).

Throughout his academic life, Schur held numerous prestigious appointments. Most notably, he served as a member of the Governor's Special Commission on Crime and Violence in Massachusetts from 1966 to 1968, as president of the Massachusetts Sociological Association during the 1968-1969 period, and as associate editor of the *American Sociological Review* from 1971 to 1974.

—Shaun L. Gabbidon
Pennsylvania State University at Harrisburg

SOURCE: Excerpted from the writings of Shaun L. Gabbidon with permission.

of thought eventually provided much assistance in the development of feminist criminology (see Chapter 9).

Schur's Critique of Previous Research

Similar to past writers in the Interactionist School, Schur criticized the works of prior researchers. One of his larger criticisms involved the failure of prior research to emphasize the creation and enforcement of legal norms and their importance in explaining deviant or criminal behavior. In the words of Schur (1965),

There has been a general tendency for sociologists to focus greater attention on informal mechanisms of social control. In many instances, however, no real sociological understanding of the deviance problem being considered is possible unless the role of legal norms is examined. This is not to suggest that the sociologist need engage himself in detailed or technical legal analysis; rather, he must consider the important ways in which specific legal definitions and law enforcement policies influence the development of such problems. . . . Thus, the very existence of a particular deviant behavior pattern in a society is an important datum for research, as is the social reaction to that behavior and the interplay between the two. (pp. 1-2)

Such insight was further reiterated as Schur (1979) discussed the importance of official statistics to research, criminological theory, and the origin of crime and deviance.

Official statistics should be considered an object of investigation to be explained in their own right. Our primary interest should not be in what they might tell us about the causation of deviance but rather in exploring the causation of the rates themselves. (p. 363)

Consequently, such thoughts and criticisms were the underlying foundation for one of his most significant contributions to the interactionist perspective, *Crimes Without Victims,* in which Schur (1965) discussed the problems associated with the creation and enforcement of laws pertaining to abortion, homosexuality, and drug addiction.

A final criticism suggested by Schur, quite possibly influenced by his legal background, involved his confrontation of earlier critics of the interactionist perspective. As noted earlier in this chapter, a major criticism of the Interactionist School involves its focusing too much on the individual labeling process (microanalysis of deviance and crime). To this, Schur (1979) related,

The twin emphases in such an approach are on definition and process at all the levels that are involved in the production of deviant situations and outcomes. Thus, the perspective is concerned not only with what happens to specific individuals when they are branded with deviantness ("labeling," in the narrow sense) but also with the wider domains and processes of social definitions and collective rule-making that frequently lie behind such concrete applications of negative labels. (p. 160)

In sum, Schur (1979) further suggested that the organization of society does have an impact on the origin of deviant or criminal behavior, with the Interactionist School incorporating this factor into its foundation. One who believes otherwise is failing to take the complete perspective into consideration.

Schur's Definition of Deviance

There is no doubt that Schur's early works were grounded in the interactionist tradition. Perhaps this is most exemplified by his definition of deviance and its similarities to that of Becker (1963). In the words of Schur (1971),

Human behavior is deviant to the extent that it comes to be viewed as involving a personally discreditable departure from a group's normative expectation, and it elicits interpersonal and collective reactions that serve to "isolate," "treat," "correct," or "punish" individuals engaged in such behavior. (p. 21)

Similar to Becker (1963) and other Interactionist School criminologists, Schur suggested that the social reaction of others (including criminal justice practitioners) to a particular behavior and the incorporation of that reaction into subsequent behavior defines the individual as a deviant, not the behavior itself.

Schur's Discussion of Crimes Without Victims

As mentioned earlier, Schur's (1965) major work in the interactionist tradition, *Crimes Without Victims*, discussed problems typically associated with the creation and enforcement of particular crimes including abortion, homosexuality, and drug addition. Such offenses, according to Schur, were victimless and merely involved the "willing exchange, among adults, of strongly demanded but legally proscribed goods or services" (p. 169).

According to Schur (1965), the problems associated with enforcing laws pertaining to this type of crime are numerous. Included is the difficulty with actual law enforcement, a situation that could potentially lead to police corruption.

> Every criminal law represents a societal judgment establishing both an offender and an individual or collective victim. Where there is direct offense by one person against another person or his property, the victim and victimizer are easily identified. On the other hand, in a crime against the state or a crime against morals [i.e., crimes without victims], the victim becomes more elusive.... One feature which seems to characterize all crimes without victims is the unenforceability of the laws surrounding them. Such unenforceability stems directly from the lack of a complainant and the consequent difficulty in obtaining evidence. Also significant is the low visibility of these offenses. (pp. 170-171)

Additional problems associated with the enforcement of laws pertaining to crimes without victims include an increased disrespect for the law by those seeking goods and services that are in great demand and, in the interactionist tradition, an increased potential for secondary offending. Schur (1965) related such insight as he described the lives of those involved in illegal abortion, homosexual activity, and drug abuse.

> In all three cases, the individuals involved tend to develop, in some degree, a deviant self-image. This is largely the result of the dominant social definition of their behavior as being outside the pale of respectability, and the more specific labeling of the behavior as "criminal" reinforces and heightens this process.... [The] criminalization of deviance may have an especially crucial influence on the individual's view of himself. Thus, the realization that they are considered criminals and—even more significantly—the need to act like criminals causes most [individuals involved in deviant behavior] to develop—at the very least—a pronouncedly antisocial outlook.... The ex-

tent of deviant self-image seems, then, to be directly related to the degree of primacy taken on by the deviant role or the extent to which the deviant behavior comes to be elaborated into a role at all. And primacy relates closely to the extent to which the deviant must, in order to satisfy the proscribed demand, engage himself in various instrumental and supportive activities. (pp. 171-172)

Therefore, the effects of the label become so significant that those individuals who might want to return to the conventional world are unable to do so.

Schur's Radical Nonintervention Policy Proposal

An additional contribution of Schur to the Interactionist School of criminology involved social policy. In *Radical Nonintervention*, Schur (1973) suggested that society's response toward juvenile crime was excessive and that society should "leave kids alone whenever possible" (p. 155). Schur was adamant about this position because, in his opinion, the majority of juvenile crime involved only minor offenses; the negative effects typically associated with official labeling far outweighed the need to incarcerate our nation's youths. This proposal included the abolition of juvenile correctional facilities and the legalization of many types of delinquent behavior. One can imagine the criticisms of such policy following the anti-establishment movement of the 1960s.

Schur's Discussion of Women as Deviant

A final contribution of Schur to the interactionist/labeling tradition eventually provided much assistance in the development of feminist criminology. Specifically, Schur provided insight to Goffman's (1963) previously mentioned concept of stigma further associating gender with deviance. In the words of Schur (1984),

In our society, being treated as deviant has been a standard feature of life as a female. With great regularity, women have been labeled—and still are being labeled—"aggressive," "bitchy," "hysterical," "fat," "homely," "masculine," and "promiscuous." Judgments such as these, and the social reactions that accompany them, represent a very potent kind of deviance-defining. They may not put the presumed "offender" in jail, but they do typically damage her reputation, induce shame, and lower her "life chances." (p. 3)

As a result, according to Schur, the mere status of being female is devalued.

To what extent, overall, are we justified in viewing femaleness as a devalued or "deviant" status . . ., one that carries a stigma in and of itself? . . . It seems clear that the devaluation of women is not total. On the other hand, there is massive evidence showing that it is indeed very substantial and that its manifestations are extremely widespread.

[Specifically, there are] four major grounds for accepting the notion that womanhood is, on balance, a devalued status. [First is] the well-documented existence of pronounced sex inequality within our social and economic system. . . .Highly valued persons are not systematically relegated (in the way women have been) to the lower echelons of the socioeconomic and occupational prestige ladders. . . . [Second,] it should be apparent that some measure of devaluation is always present in [the] modes of perceiving and responding to women. . . . Women are routinely—and to an extent that we cannot simply attribute to the general impersonality of modern life—treated in ways that suggest they are being little valued for their own selves. . . . [Third] is the pervasive devaluation of women in "cultural symbolism." . . . Common language usage often trivializes, slights, derogates, or unnecessarily sexualizes women. . . . The same can be said about images of women in the mass media and advertising. . . . The fourth, and perhaps overriding, reason to view femaleness as devalued is reflected in the central concern of this text—namely women's relation to definitions of deviance. Both the multitude of specific "deviances" imputed to women under our gender system and the failure to strongly condemn male offenses against women illustrate the low value placed on femaleness. (pp. 34-36)

In conclusion, Schur attempted to demonstrate that in contemporary society, the female attribute is a deviant characteristic. Although this thesis might not be proven, there is considerable evidence supporting it. Regardless of this debate, individuals studying the Interactionist School perspective cannot underestimate the importance of Schur's works to traditional criminology as well as to the studies of deviance, gender, sex roles, and contemporary American society.

Critique of Schur

There are two major criticisms pertaining to the works of Schur. The first involves Schur's (1965) concept of "crimes without victims." Numerous authors have challenged this major construct by stating that no such thing exists. For example, drug addicts might not be capable of engaging in legitimate occupations because of their habits. According to criminalization proponents, one negative consequence associated with drug legalization is the potential to create a "societal victim" through additional medical, safety, and financial burdens. Although such conclusions should be open to debate and considered in any discussion of legalization/criminalization, the answer, if attainable, goes beyond the realm of this chapter.

A second criticism involves Schur's (1973) proposal of "radical nonintervention." Although intervention has the potential for negative consequences, policy changes suggesting little or lesser intervention into the lives of troublesome youths could have serious negative consequences as well. Hands-off approaches devalue the impact of state intervention (e.g., incapacitation, deterrence) on the crime rate, whereas diversionary programs run the risk of including only those who would not originally have been in the criminal justice system (i.e., net widening) (Binder and Geis, 1984).

Summary

The Interactionist School has had a substantial effect on criminological thinking through the provision of insight in several critical areas. First, the Interactionist School developed the premise that crime or deviance is socially constructed through the selective creation and enforcement of both formal and informal means of social control. Second, this perspective suggested that criminal justice policy and state intervention may have unanticipated and even contradictory consequences. Third, the Interactionist School provided a significant precursor to future criminological thinking including conflict theory (see Chapter 8) and feminist criminology (see Chapter 9). Finally, the Interactionist School created a foundation for criminological thinking as to the complexities surrounding the creation and enforcement of criminal law. This is perhaps most important given that advances can be made in the reduction of crime or deviance only through the development of a complete and thorough understanding of the problem and its context.

The Interactionist School, however, has not been without its critics. Perhaps most important are the suggestions pertaining to this perspective not meeting the definition of theory as discussed by Homans (1962, 1974) and Turner (1991). As mentioned earlier in the chapter, several factors must be present in the formulation of a theory. First, the theory must have propositions stating the relationship between two or more variables (concepts). Second, the propositions of each theory must occur in a logical fashion; each proposition must build on previous propositions. Finally, each concept must be defined in a very specific manner so as to be empirically tested. Although the Interactionist School may have a system of categories that fit different aspects of social behavior, none of the theorists discussed in this chapter specifically proposed a set of general propositions, nor did any define specific concepts that can be empirically tested. As a result, the Interactionist School appears significantly limited so far as meeting the requirements of an explanatory theory.

Although not meeting the criteria of a scientific theory, the Interactionist School has had, and will continue to have, a significant impact on criminological thinking. As mentioned in Chapter 1, Merton (1968b) suggested the concept of a middle range theory as a guide to empirical inquiry, a stepping-stone in the middle distance between research and theory. Although not meeting the definition of a scientific theory, these criminological orientations are, by all accounts, truly important in understanding human behavior. Only through continued research and the development of interconnecting planes between orientations, such as the Interactionist School and other schools of criminological thought, will a comprehensive explanation of human behavior be possible.

Notes

1. It should be noted that some similarity does exist between the interactionist/labeling perspective and conflict theory (see Chapter 8).

2. Although rape, homicide, and the like often are universally sanctioned offenses, one must note that universal agreement regarding the specific definitions of these behaviors does not exist. The behaviors defined as rape, homicide, and the like vary cross-culturally.

3. Goffman (1961) referred to these groups as "batches" of people (p. 6).

DISCUSSION QUESTIONS

1. The works of Cooley and Mead were mentioned in Chapter 6. Why are they also important to the Interactionist School of criminology? Describe and discuss these authors' contributions. How do these contributions provide a better understanding of the labeling process?

2. This chapter has described the contributions of Tannenbaum as the formal origin of contemporary interactionist criminology. Why is this statement appropriate? How do his contributions provide insight to the works of future theorists from the Interactionist School perspective?

3. What is the difference between primary and secondary deviance? According to Lemert, what process does an individual go through to become a secondary deviant?

4. The major contribution of Becker to the Interactionist School was titled *Outsiders*. Describe and discuss the significance of this title.

5. Explain Becker's typology of deviant behavior including the four types of deviants and nondeviants. How do moral entrepreneurs relate to this typology?

6. Describe and discuss the moral career of the inmate as proposed by Goffman. Include a detailed description of the three phases of the career as well as the four modes of adaptation used by the inmate in his or her attempt to preserve personal identity.

7. Describe Schur's work regarding "crimes without victims." What is the significance of this work to the Interactionist School?

8. Although referenced in much criminological research, Becker, Lemert, and Goffman traditionally have resisted being defined as criminologists. Why are their works a valuable contribution to the Interactionist School?

CHAPTER

Conflict/Radical/Marxist Theory

As indicated in Chapter 7, the Interactionist School perspective was the dominant theory used by criminologists during the 1960s. One of the most influential interactionist theorists, Howard S. Becker, stressed the arbitrary definitions of deviance and the importance of societal reactions in the development of deviant careers. Becker (1973) also mentioned the "moral entrepreneurs" as rule creators and rule enforcers but did not emphasize the power differentials.

The conflict theorists, who came to the forefront of criminological theory during the 1970s and 1980s, shared with the interactionists the emphasis on arbitrary definitions of deviance and crime as well as the emphasis on the process of interaction and the importance of societal reaction to the deviant or criminal act. Although the conflict/radical theorists in criminology shared the interactionists' emphasis on arbitrary definitions of deviance or crime and the emergence of deviant or criminal careers, the conflict theorists criticized the interactionists for not emphasizing the power differentials based on race and class. Thus, conflict theory focused on the political and economic nature of crime. The capitalistic system was identified as a major source of conflict and crime.

Although current conflict theory can be traced historically to the 19th and early 20th centuries through the works of Karl Marx, Willem Bonger, W. E. B. Du Bois, and Edwin Sutherland, it was not until the 1970s and 1980s that it became a major criminological theory. As indicated in what follows, much of this can be credited to Quinney's (1970b) *The Social Reality of Crime*. But the political activism of the 1960s—with the civil rights and women's movements, the Vietnam War protests, and the offenders' and prisoners' rights debates—did much to set the stage for the dominance of conflict theory among criminological theorists beginning during the 1970s.

Defining the Perspective

Although the theories of conflict, radical, and Marxist criminology often are referred to as one and the same, Bohm (1982) argued that there are fundamental differences among them.[1] He noted, "Radical criminologists are more specific than conflict criminologists in their identification of the explanatory variables that presumably account for crime" (p. 566). Bohm supported his argument by citing Beirne (1979) as follows:

> The conflict theorists were rarely precise in delineating quite in what "power" and "conflict" consisted, how power manifested itself, how conflict was resolved, and why it was resolved at all; but they nevertheless agreed that power and conflict were at the root of social organization. . . . Conflict theory was generally so vague in its basic assumptions, and so wide-ranging in its scope, that it might easily incorporate (or co-opt) a variety of different perspectives, including Marxism, within the compass of its structure. (pp. 375-377)

Bohm (1982) further noted that the crucial difference between the conflict and radical theorists is the degree to which they focus on the political and economic structures of society as explanations of crime (p. 567). Bohm cited Keller (1976) as follows:

> While the conflict school specifies stratification as a criminogenic factor, the critical [i.e., radical] school specifies the political economy of capitalism as the criminogenic factor. Only the critical school specifies the political and economic structures that promote conflict and therefore produce crime. (p. 283)

Both radical theorists and conflict theorists assume that the fundamental basis of society is conflict. However, radical criminologists assert that the particular nature of society is fundamentally related to the historical and social distribution of productive private property in that society (Bohm, 1982, p. 568). It is the "competitive and exploitative inter- and intraclass relations of capitalism that engender income or property inequality [and] poverty" (p. 570).

For radical criminologists, therefore, it is the struggle both among and between those who own and control the means of production and distribution and those who do not that is the source of all crime in capitalist societies. Thus, a radical definition of crime includes imperialism, racism, capitalism, sexism, and other systems of exploitation. Radical criminologists argue that this exploitation contributes to human misery and deprives people of their human potential and rights. The radical definition of crime would reconceptualize crime in terms of violations of human rights (Bohm, 1982, p. 571).

There also are differences between conflict and radical theorists with reference to policy implications. Conflict criminologists tend to advocate reform, but radical criminologists can more accurately be described as revolutionary (Bohm, 1982, p. 568). The distinguishing characteristic of radical criminology is its emphasis on "praxis" or human action as a means of bringing about changes in society (p. 578).

Noting that Marx actually wrote very little about crime and criminal justice, Bohm (1982) suggested, "In other ways, Marxist criminology is perhaps the most appropriate metonym for radical criminology" (pp. 572-573). Bohm stated that "a Marxist is always radical (i.e., revolutionary)" (p. 578).

Marxist analysis provides an explanation of the reality of crime and crime control under capitalism, and Marxist analysis further explains the functions of an inaccurate portrayal of crime in a capitalist society (p. 573). Bohm further argued that Marxism provides radical criminologists with a theoretical framework that interrelates the capitalist mode of production, the state, law, crime control, and crime.

The Historical Background

Although conflict/radical/Marxist theory did not emerge as an important criminological perspective until the 1970s and 1980s, several scholars from the 19th and early 20th centuries laid the foundation for its eventual development. Chapter 5 pointed to several research studies, such as Shaw and McKay's (1972) study of delinquency in large urban areas, that contained the seeds of conflict theory. However, the present chapter concentrates on the early contributions that Marx, Bonger, Du Bois, and Sutherland made to conflict theory.

Karl Marx (1818-1883)

Karl Marx, the eldest son of Heinrich and Henrietta Marx, was born May 5, 1818, in Trier, Germany (Coser, 1977, p. 58). Because his father was a lawyer who "rose to become head of the bar," Marx was reared in a bourgeois household. However, the family had a marginal status because both the mother and father came from a long line of Jewish rabbis. Marx's father was the first in his line to receive a secular education and eventually converted to the mildly liberal Lutheran church "as an act of expediency" (p. 58).[2]

Marx was repelled by his father's subservience to governmental authority. Despite the strain this caused in the father-son relationship, Marx remained close to his father until the latter's death. After finishing the Trier Gymnasium at 17 years of age, Marx registered at the University of Bonn to study law. In 1836, he transferred to the University of Berlin, where he was exposed to the ideas of the philosopher Hegel. Reacting to his early training and bourgeois background, Marx "interpreted Hegelianism in a militant atheistic form" (Martindale, 1960, p. 156).

While in Paris from 1843 to 1845, Marx met Friedrich Engels, the son of a British textile manufacturer, who had turned socialist. Engels and Marx shared a revulsion to the misery of working class life and became lifelong friends. Engels returned to England, and Marx continued his studies with the financial support of Engels (Coser, 1977, p. 61; Martindale, 1960, p. 157). Despite the financial contributions from Engels, Marx lived a life of poverty for most of his adult life and only occasionally was employed. According to Mehring (1951), "Marx's scientific studies were a never-failing source of consolation to him. He sat from nine o'clock in the morning to seven o'clock in the evening in the British Museum" (p. 212). Marx continued to dedicate himself to his library research. But over the years,

Marx was no longer able "to live from hand to mouth." . . . He had no prospects, and his family expenditure was steadily increasing. On the 20th of January 1857, he wrote to Engels: "I really don't know what to do next; in fact, my situation is more desperate than it was five years ago. (p. 253)

Marx's wife died in 1881. Mehring reported that Marx "was still so weak that the doctor forbade him to accompany his beloved wife on her last journey" (p. 528). Marx survived his wife little more than a year. He died in 1883.

Marx wrote little about crime. Taylor, Walton, and Young (1973, pp. 209-218) and Leonard (1982, pp. 143-145) included some obscure references to crime made by Marx in *The German Ideology* (Marx and Engels, 1965) and *Theories of Surplus Value* (Marx, 1964) and in a few articles written for the *New York Daily Tribune*. One statement from Marx's *Theories of Surplus Value* quoted by both books was the following: "A philosopher produces ideas, a poet poems, a clergyman sermons, a professor compendia, and so on. . . . The criminal produces not only crimes but also criminal law" (Leonard, 1982, p. 143; Taylor et al., 1973, p. 210). Marx further argued against capital punishment and asserted that crime was the struggle of the isolated individual against poverty. Marx advocated a revolution that would overthrow the capitalist system. This was his greatest contribution to criminology.

Marx first was exposed to the Hegelian dialectic at the University of Berlin in 1836. From then on, much of his research was dedicated to supporting this dialectic and advocating a revolution. Marx (1959) stated in his *Communist Manifesto*, originally published in 1932, that "the history of all hitherto existing society is the history of class struggles" (p. 321). Marx further declared that this struggle was between the bourgeoisie (the "haves") and the proletarians (the "have-nots"). His years of study were an effort to document his claim for this struggle.

Hitherto every form of society has been based . . . on the antagonism of oppressing and oppressed classes. But in order to oppress a class, certain conditions must be assured to it under which it can at least continue its slavish existence. The serf, in the period of serfdom, raised himself to membership in the commune, just as the petty bourgeois[ie], under the yoke of feudal absolutism, managed to develop into a bourgeois[ie]. The modern laborer, on the contrary, instead of rising with the progress of industry, sinks deeper and deeper below the conditions of existence of his own class. . . . Society can no longer live under this bourgeoisie. . . . Its existence is no longer compatible with society. (p. 333)

The revolution that Marx (1959) advocated was spelled out in his *Communist Manifesto*. He asserted, "The immediate aim of the Communists is the same as that of all other proletarian parties: formation of the proletariat into a class, overthrow of the bourgeois[ie] of supremacy, [and] conquest of political power by the proletariat" (p. 335). He also claimed,

The distinguishing feature of communism is not the abolition of property generally but [rather] the absolution of bourgeois property. (p. 335) . . .

> You are horrified at our intending to do away with private property. But in your existing society, private property is already done away with for nine-tenths of the population; its existence for the few is solely due to its nonexistence in the hands of nine-tenths. . . . Communism deprives no man of the power to appropriate the products of society: all that it does is to deprive him of the power to subjugate the labor of others by means of such appropriation. (p. 337)

Marx further claimed that communism is not opposed to private property but rather is opposed to the accumulation of private property that allows the bourgeoisie to oppress the proletariat. Among the suggestions Marx (1959) made in the *Communist Manifesto* for achieving equality of classes are as follows:

1. Abolition of property in land and application of all rents of land to public purposes

2. A heavy progressive or graduated income tax

3. Abolition of all right of inheritance

4. Centralization of credit in the hands of the state

5. Centralization of the means of communication and transport in the hands of the state

6. Extension of factories and instruments of production by the state

7. Equal liability of all to labor

8. Free education for all children in public schools (pp. 342-343)

Marx contended that these changes would lead to a classless society. The conflict theories of crime that emerged during the 1970s had much of their foundation in Marx's theory of the class struggle.

Willem Adrian Bonger (1876-1940)

Willem Bonger, a Marxist Dutch criminologist, was born September 16, 1876, and died May 15, 1940. Austin Turk, in his introduction to Bonger's (1969a) *Criminality and Economic Conditions,* wrote that Bonger chose "suicide rather than submission to the Nazi scum" (p. 3). In 1905, Bonger received his doctorate from the University of Amsterdam with a specialization in criminal sociology. His dissertation, *Criminality and Economic Conditions,* was a Marxist socialist treatise on crime that was enlarged and originally published in English in the United States in 1916.

In 1922, he was appointed as a professor of sociology and criminology at the University of Amsterdam and was a distinguished professor at that university at the time of his death. He was the prime leader of criminology in the Netherlands, publishing several books and articles including *An Introduction to Criminology* (Bonger, 1932) and *Race and Crime* (Bonger, 1969a, p. 3; 1969b, pp. v-vi) during the 1930s. He was the founder of the Netherlands Sociological Association and became editor-in-chief of the *Sociological Guide* in 1915 (Bonger, 1969b, p. v). He achieved international eminence for his contributions to criminological knowledge (Bonger, 1969a, p. 3).

Like Marx, Bonger argued that capitalism produced crime. He asserted that the primitive mode of production results in altruism and that the capitalist mode of production causes egoism. Bonger further contended that egoistic tendencies, and thereby crime, result from the capitalist economic system.

According to Bonger, an economic system based on exchange cannot fail to have an egoistic character that isolates the individuals by weakening the bond that unites them. The owner of the means of production takes into account exclusively his or her own interests in making a profit. The workers, then, sell their labor only so as not to die of hunger. The capitalist takes advantage of the workers and exploits them. Thus, Bonger (1969a) noted, "Little by little, one class of men has become accustomed to think that the others are destined to amass wealth for them and to be subservient to them in every way" (p. 44). This demoralizes both the workers and the owner of the means of production. The owner develops cupidity and the imperious character that sees in the workers beings only fit to satisfy the owner's desires.

Race and crime. Bonger (1969b), in his discussions of race, also attacked Lombroso's claim that criminals are atavistic throwbacks (see Chapter 3). Bonger noted that physical qualities of race are without any importance in the relationship between race and crime. He credited other factors, such as physical milieu and economic relations, as more relevant to criminal behavior. "The individual differences between members of the same race are so great that those between races themselves are small by comparison" (p. 9).

Bonger (1969b) originally published *Race and Crime* in 1939 during the Nazi regime, and his antagonism toward the Nazis is evident in this work. He rejected the idea that race should be the decisive factor in history and noted, "Since the Nazi regime, this race doctrine has been developed especially along anti-Semitic lines" (p. 10). He further declared that these things were not proved but simply alleged. He illustrated his points by making references to various races internationally, and he made some insightful points about African Americans and crime in the United States.[3]

Bonger (1969b) was among the first to point out the following:

> The amount of crime actually punished in different classes or communities may not bear a fixed or unvarying ratio to the amount of crime committed. Crimes committed by Negroes are more frequently prosecuted than those committed by whites. Negroes are less well able to defend themselves legally, they are less often in a position to secure a good lawyer, and they are more promptly sentenced to prison. (p. 43)

He also noted,

> The circumstances in which the Negroes live are very different from those of the whites and are strongly conducive to crime. When they were freed from slavery after the Civil War (1861-65), the Negroes were left to their fate under the most difficult conditions. Unadjusted to their entirely new surroundings, [they were] despised and oppressed by whites. . . . In spite of the greatest difficulties, they have worked themselves a little way up but are still held back in every respect by the whites. (pp. 45-46)

Bonger concluded his book on race by stating,

> Consequently, to speak of criminal races (in which all individuals would be criminal) is pure nonsense. No person comes into the world a criminal. . . . Crime is always limited to a (comparatively) small number of individuals in a race. (p. 105)

Sex and crime. Based on Bonger's examination of international data, he found that the criminality of women does not differ much among various countries. Also, women participate less in sexual crimes and in crimes that require strength and courage. Bonger (1969a) was the first to recognize that women's motive for prostitution is economic and not moral depravity. He stated, "The part played by women in economic crimes committed because of poverty, or even of greed, is explained by prostitution" (p. 60). But he did recognize that prostitution has a very demoralizing effect on those that practice it. Bonger argued that women's lower involvement in crime is the result of their social position and social environment, which provide women with limited opportunities to commit economic crimes.

Classification of economic crimes. Bonger (1969a) presented four types of economic crimes: vagrancy and mendacity; theft and analogous crimes; robbery and homicide for economic reasons; and fraudulent bankruptcy, adulteration of food, and the like (p. 92). The first three categories, he asserted, are committed almost exclusively by the poor.

Vagrancy and mendacity are committed by the poor and unemployed because under capitalism, there always are workers who cannot sell their labor (Bonger, 1969a, p. 93). This behavior rises considerably during economic crises and falls as economic situations improve. Bonger (1969a) argued that under capitalism, "vagrancy and mendacity would be no less extensive even if all the workers knew a trade and were equal in zeal and energy" (p. 96). He explained,

> If these people are blamed, blame must be attached also to a state of society in which honest labor is so poorly paid that begging is often more lucrative. . . . These people are cunning egoists, and as long as society is organized as it is, they are right from their point of view. (p. 101)

Bonger (1969a) asserted that simple thefts are committed out of poverty because poverty directly incites the appropriation of the property of others and exercises a demoralizing influence (p. 106). Embezzlement, fraud, and aggravated theft, however, are committed out of cupidity or greed and the desire for wealth (p. 107). These crimes are most numerous in countries where manufacturing and commerce are most developed and where the contrasts of fortune are the greatest. Bonger also noted that the way in which commercial capital tries to encourage buyers results in the public's desire to buy. Thus, those without the means to buy the beautifully displayed items steal them (p. 108).

However, the thefts of large sums of money are committed by employees of banks who have the opportunity, by the nature of their work, to appropriate other people's money.[4] Bonger (1969a) suggested, "Nine times out of ten, . . . the criminal is a speculator who has lost, or perhaps an individual who visits prostitutes, and hence has great need of money" (p. 109). Again, Bonger declared that the principal cause of these crimes is the cupidity awakened by the environment.

He asserted that at one time, robbery and similar acts of violence were the ordinary forms of professional crime but that these crimes have been replaced, in large measure, by less serious crimes such as theft and fraud (p. 124). Whereas he stated that economic criminality takes a more violent form among the poorer classes, he explained the decrease in violent economic crimes as changes in the opportunity to commit violent crimes and the increasing opportunity to commit other economic crimes such as theft, embezzlement, and fraud. He further asserted that the accumulation of wealth in the cities, the development of credit, and the extension of capitalism have multiplied the opportunities for committing economic crimes without violence (p. 125).

Whereas most of the previously discussed crimes are committed due to poverty, fraudulent bankruptcy, adulteration of food, and similar crimes are committed by the bourgeoisie due to business decline or failure (Bonger, 1969a, p. 134). Bonger (1969a) suggested that capitalism is the source of these crimes:

> It is the present organization of society which makes it possible for a man to be in charge of an enterprise which he is not fitted to conduct, while another who is fitted for it cannot find employment for his talents. It is only in a society where complete anarchy reigns in the economic life that it is possible for a man to think he is capable of directing a business merely because he happens to have capital. (p. 135)

A second type of bourgeois economic crime, according to Bonger (1969a), occurs from cupidity. Business might be flourishing, but what is attained from honest business is not enough; one wants to become richer. The opportunities to commit crimes, such as adulteration of food, without detection are enormous. For example, "they put fuchsine in our wine, margarine in our butter, chicory in our coffee, tallow in our chocolate, and we swallow it in perfect good humor" (p. 139). Bonger suggested that protesting is of little or no help. This is the way things are, and business could not be carried on if really pure food were served. "So we swallow it all without gagging or moving a muscle" (p. 139).

The final group of economic crimes from cupidity are committed by "those who throw themselves into gigantic enterprises while knowing beforehand that these will certainly or probably fail, or those who make great purchases of stock and afterward cause a rise in price through the dissemination of false news, etc." (Bonger, 1969a, p. 140). Such crimes can arise only in a society with an insatiable thirst for economic gain and with unlimited opportunities to deceive the public in one's greed for great profits. Crimes of this type are committed by those with excessive cupidity.

William Edward Burghardt Du Bois (1868-1963)

Du Bois, an African American scholar at the turn of the 20th century (see biographical inset on Du Bois [Inset 8.1] for details), did not identify himself as a crimi-

INSET 8.1   William Edward Burghardt Du Bois (1868-1963)

W. E. B. Du Bois was born on February 23, 1868, in the small town of Great Barrington, Massachusetts. School records and personal accounts suggest that he was an outstanding student who left a lasting impression on the residents of Great Barrington (Lewis, 1993). Because of his outstanding performance, Du Bois was selected as the speaker for his high school graduation. By all accounts, he gave a well-articulated and highly regarded speech.

After graduating from high school, Du Bois attended Fisk University in Nashville, Tennessee. While at Fisk, he majored in philosophy and received his A.B. degree in 1888. On graduation from Fisk, Du Bois fulfilled his childhood dream and enrolled at Harvard University, where he completed a second A.B. degree in 1890. He completed his master's degree in 1892 and immediately enrolled in the Ph.D. program in history.

Du Bois went for additional study overseas at the University of Berlin. He studied there from 1892 to 1894 and was heavily influenced by Gustav Von Schollmer, leader of the influential "Historical School of Economics" (Boston, 1991). Du Bois returned to America in 1894 and, while completing his doctorate at Harvard, inquired about employment at numerous universities. He was unable to secure a position at a major university, so he accepted a position at Wilberforce University in Ohio. In 1895, Du Bois completed his doctorate in history at Harvard. This made him the first African American to receive a doctorate at Harvard (Huggins, 1986). Du Bois's dissertation, *The Suppression of the Slave Trade to the United States of America*, originally was published in 1896 in the Harvard Historical Publications Series (Du Bois, 1986).

Du Bois then accepted a 1-year position at the University of Pennsylvania. While at that institution, he was expected to focus exclusively on conducting a study on the Negroes in Philadelphia. This research culminated in the sociological/criminological classic, *The Philadelphia Negro: A Social Study* (Du Bois, 1899b).

Du Bois's well-received work in Philadelphia led to his recruitment by Horace Bumstead, president of Atlanta University, to serve as chair of the Department of Sociology and to carry out annual research on problems concerning the American Negro. From 1897 to 1913, Du Bois carried out highly acclaimed studies on the American Negro. He focused on Negro crime (Du Bois, 1904; Du Bois and Dill, 1913).

During the early part of the 20th century, Du Bois became disenchanted with scholarship and decided that activism would be the most logical way in which to improve the condition of Negroes in America. He embarked on this activism by starting the radical "Niagara Movement." This movement sought to fight injustices against the American Negro. In 1909, this movement eventually merged with the National Association for the Advancement of Colored People (NAACP). Besides being a founding member of the NAACP, Du Bois served as the director of publicity and research. In this position, he founded and edited *The Crisis*, the NAACP's monthly magazine.

After resigning from the NAACP, Du Bois returned to Atlanta University, where he served as chairperson of the sociology department. He remained at that university for 10 more years before deciding to return to the NAACP as director of special research. During the late 1940s, he traveled abroad in support of international peace efforts. But during the 1950s, Du Bois came under increasing scrutiny by the federal government because of his support of communism. In 1961, at 93 years of age, Du Bois joined the Communist Party and moved to Ghana, Africa, at the invitation of its president, Kwame Nkrumah. Du Bois died in Ghana on August 23, 1963.

—Shaun L. Gabbidon
Pennsylvania State University at Harrisburg

SOURCE: Excerpted from the writings of Shaun L. Gabbidon with permission.

nologist, and his contributions have been ignored by most current criminologists. Many of his publications did not concern crime, but he has made important contributions to criminology, and the seeds of conflict theory are found in his works. This chapter examines his most significant works on crime, with a special emphasis on the Philadelphia study (Du Bois, 1899b).[5]

The Philadelphia research study. In this study, Du Bois (1899b) examined the problems of poverty, crime, and labor as well as the physical environment of the city and the social environment that he defined as the "surrounding world of custom, wish, whim, and thought which envelops this group and powerfully influences its social development" (p. 7). He also studied the occupations, income, property, and family life of the Negroes in the city. Du Bois noted that not all Negroes lived in poverty:

> The best class of Philadelphia Negroes, though sometimes forgotten and ignored in discussing the Negro problems, is nevertheless known to many Philadelphians. Scattered throughout the better parts of the Seventh Ward . . . and here and there in the residence wards of the northern, southern, and western sections of the city is a class of caterers, clerks, teachers, professional men, small merchants, etc., who constitute the aristocracy of the Negroes. Many are well-to-do, some are wealthy, all are fairly well educated and some liberally trained. (p. 7)

In a chapter titled "The Negro Criminal," Du Bois (1899b) used both arrest and penitentiary data to explore the amount of crime committed by Negroes in Philadelphia during the 19th century. Using these data, he suggested,

> From this study, we may conclude that young men are the perpetrators of the serious crime among Negroes; that this crime consists mainly of stealing and assault; that ignorance and immigration to the temptations of city life are responsible for much of this crime but not for all; that deep social causes underlie this prevalence of crime, and they have so worked as to form, among Negroes since 1864, a distinct class of habitual criminals; [and] that to this criminal class, and not to the great mass of Negroes, the bulk of the serious crime perpetrated by this race should be charged. (p. 259)

With reference to women criminals, Du Bois noted that "women are nearly all committed for stealing and fighting." He further stated that women generally are "prostitutes from the worst slums" (p. 255). Then, he presented a "few typical cases of the crimes of Negroes" (p. 259). The subsequent 10 pages of the chapter provide accounts of cases of larceny, fighting and quarreling, servants caught pilfering, pocketbook snatching, confidence men, pickpocketing, robbery, gambling, and assaults.

The convict lease system in the South. Du Bois (1901) referred to the convict lease system as "a modified form of slavery" and as "slavery in [the] private hands of persons convicted of crimes and misdemeanors in the courts" (pp. 737-738). He suggested that before the Civil War, crime was less prevalent in the South than in the North because the system of slavery modified the situation. That is, the punishment and trial of nearly all ordinary misdemeanors and crimes lay in the hands of the masters. Consequently, so far as the state was concerned, there was no crime of any consequence among African Americans.

The war and emancipation of slaves changed this. When the masters' power was broken, the control of African Americans was easily transmuted into a lawless and illegal mob known to history as the Ku Klux Klan (Du Bois, 1901, p. 738). Amid this chaos, the courts sought to do by judicial decisions what the legislatures formerly had sought to do by specific law—namely, reduce the freedmen to serfdom.

> As a result, the small peccadillos of a careless untrained class made the excuse for severe sentences. The courts and jails became filled with the careless and ignorant, with those who sought to emphasize their new-found freedom, and too often with innocent victims of oppression. . . . The result of this was a sudden large increase in the apparent criminal population of southern states—an increase so large that there was no way for the state to house it or watch it even had the state wished to. And the state did not wish to. Throughout the South, laws were immediately passed authorizing public officials to lease the labor of convicts to the highest bidder. The lessee then took charge of the convicts—worked them as he wished under the nominal control of the state. Thus, a new slavery and new slave trade was established. (p. 740)

Theoretical explanations of crime. Like current conflict theorists such as Richard Quinney, William Chambliss, and Jeffrey Reiman, Du Bois (1899a) explored historical documents to explain the origins of crime. He began with the following general statement:

> The development of a Negro criminal class after emancipation was to be expected. . . . Indeed, it is astounding that a body of people whose family life had been so nearly destroyed, whose women had been forced into concubinage, whose labor had been enslaved and then set adrift penniless, that such a nation should in a single generation be able to point to so many pure homes, so many property holders, so many striving law-abiding citizens. (p. 1355)

More specifically, Du Bois (1899b) examined the various historical laws and court decisions in Pennsylvania in *The Philadelphia Negro.* He began this historical documentation with 1638 and noted,

> Negroes were brought here early [and] were held as slaves along with many white serfs. They became the subjects of a protracted abolition controversy and were finally emancipated by gradual process. Although, for the most part, in a low and degraded condition, and thrown upon their own resources in competition with white labor, they were nevertheless so inspired by their new freedom and so guided by able leaders that for something like forty years they made commendable progress. (p. 10)

Du Bois examined the development of Quaker decisions, beginning in 1696, to regulate slavery and discouraged the importation and trading of slaves (p. 12). He also documented the first laws passed, in 1726, for the "better regulation of Negroes," that were for the "punishment of crime, the suppression of pauperism, [and] the prevention of intermarriage," that is, the regulating of the social and economic status of Negroes, both free and enslaved (p. 13). Du Bois also indicated that "the right of suffrage to free Negro property holders" in Pennsylvania was given in 1790 and exercised in most counties until 1837. When the freed slaves began to exercise their rights and compete with white labor, a series of riots began in 1829 directed chiefly against Negroes, and these recurred frequently until 1840 (p. 26). Du Bois documented this struggle of the Negroes against discrimination in Pennsylvania through 1896.

Du Bois (1899a) provided four explanations for the development of a Negro criminal class after emancipation. For Du Bois, "the first and greatest cause of Negro crime" (p. 1356) in the South was the convict lease system described earlier.

> States which use their criminals as sources of revenue in the hands of irresponsible speculators; who herd girls, boys, men, and women promiscuously together without distinction or protection; who parade chained convicts in public, guarded by staves and pistols; and then plunge into this abyss of degradation the ignorant little black boy who steals a chicken or a handful of peanuts—what can such states expect but a harvest of criminals and prostitutes? (p. 1356)

The next greatest cause of Negro crime in the South, according to Du Bois, was the attitude of the courts. Here again, we see the forerunner of current conflict theory, as Du Bois declared,

> The southern courts have erred in two ways. One, in treating the crime of whites so leniently that red-handed murderers walk scot-free and the public has lost faith in methods of justice. The other, in treating the crimes and misdemeanors of negroes with such severity that the lesson of punishment is lost through pity for the punished. . . . Students must not forget this double standard of justice, which can by illustrated by the following clippings from *The Atlanta Constitution* of January 22d:
> "Egbert Jackson [colored], aged thirteen, was given a sentence of $50, or ten months in the chain gang, for larceny from the house.
> "The most affecting scene of all was the sentencing of Joe Redding, a white man, for the killing of his brother, John Redding. . . . Judge ____ is a most tender-hearted man, and heard the prayers and saw the tears, and tempered justice with moderation, and gave the modern Cain two years in the penitentiary." (p. 1356)

The third cause of crime identified by Du Bois was lynching, which he referred to as "the increasing lawlessness and barbarity of mobs." He continued,

> Let a negro be simply accused of any crime from barn-burning to rape and he is liable to be seized by a mob; given no chance to defend himself; given neither trial, judge, nor jury; and killed. Passing over the acknowledged fact that many innocent negroes have thus been murdered, the point that is of greater gravity is that lawlessness is a direct encouragement to crime. It shatters the faith of the mass of negroes to justice; it leads

them to shield criminals; it makes race hatred fiercer; it discourages honest effort; and it transforms horror at crime into sympathy for the tortured victim. (p. 1357)

The fourth cause of Negro crime suggested by Du Bois (1899a) was the exaggerated and unnatural separation in the South of the best classes of whites and blacks, that is, the drawing of the color line that extended to streetcars, elevators, and cemeteries and that left no common ground for meeting and no medium for communication. He further noted that this was dangerous because "it makes it possible for the mass of whites to misinterpret the aims and aspirations of negroes; to mistake self-reliance for insolence and condemnation of lynch law for sympathy with crime" (p. 1357).

Finally, Du Bois (1899b) provided some early evidence of the seeds of current conflict theory when he noted that using Philadelphia arrest and penitentiary data to examine the proportion of crimes committed by African Americans assumes that those arrested and the convicts in the penitentiary "represent with a fair degree of accuracy the crime[s] committed" (p. 249). He argued,

> The assumption is not wholly true: In convictions by human courts, the rich always are favored somewhat at the expense of the poor, the upper classes at the expense of the unfortunate classes, and whites at the expense of Negroes. We know that certain crimes are not punished in Philadelphia because the public opinion is lenient, as for instance embezzlement, forgery, and certain sorts of stealing; on the other hand, a commercial community is apt to punish with severity petty thieving, breaches of the peace, and personal assault or burglary. It happens, too, that the prevailing weakness of ex-slaves brought up in the communal life of the slave plantation, without acquaintanceship with the institution of private property, is to commit the very crimes which a great center of commerce like Philadelphia especially abhors. We must add to this the influences of social position and connections in procuring whites pardons or lighter sentences. (p. 249)

Although Sutherland did not acknowledge this early contribution to conflict theory by Du Bois, Sutherland's study of white collar crime came after Du Bois's analysis.

Edwin Hardin Sutherland (1883-1950)

As discussed in Chapter 5, Edwin Sutherland made three major contributions to criminology: differential association theory, the professional thief, and white collar crime.[6] Sutherland saw differential association theory as a general theory of crime, which he illustrated with his study of the professional thief. The white collar crime work was an effort to apply his theory to upper class behavior. Thus, Sutherland's conceptualization of white collar crime was a forerunner of current conflict theory.

In Sutherland's original publication in the *American Sociological Review* (Sutherland, 1940), he expanded the definition of crime to include the illegal behavior of the "upper class, composed of respectable or at least respected business and professional men" (Sutherland, 1973, p. 46). Sutherland (1973, originally published in 1942) asserted,

> The criminal statistics show unequivocally that crime, *as popularly conceived and officially measured,* has a high incidence in the lower class and a low incidence in the upper class; less than two percent of the persons committed to prisons in a year belong to the upper class. These statistics refer to criminals handled by the police, the criminal and juvenile courts, and the prisons. (p. 47) . . .
>
> The crimes of the upper class either result in no official action at all or result in suits for damages in civil courts or are handled by inspectors and by administrative boards or commissions with penal sanctions in the form of warnings, orders to cease and desist, occasional rescinding of a license, and in extreme cases with fines or prison sentences. (p. 55)

Sutherland went on to explain the bias that comes from using data primarily from the police and prosecutors to explain criminal behavior:

> The criminologists have used the case histories and criminal statistics from these agencies of criminal justice as their principal data. From them, they have derived general theories of criminal behavior. These theories are that, since crime is concentrated in the lower class, it is caused by poverty or by personal and social characteristics believed to be associated statistically with poverty. (p. 47)

Sutherland (1973) pointed out that these theories do not include the criminal behaviors of persons not in the lower class such as business and professional persons. Crimes committed by business identified by Sutherland include misrepresentation in financial statements by corporations, manipulation in the stock exchange, bribery of public officials to secure favorable contracts and legislation, misrepresentation in advertising, embezzlement, short weights, and tax frauds. Crimes by the medical profession consist of illegal sale of alcohol and narcotics, illegal services to underworld criminals, fraudulent reports and testimony in accident cases, fake specialists, restriction of competition, and fee splitting (p. 48).

Not only are these behaviors real crime, according to Sutherland (1973), but they are "convictable" (p. 53), and the losses from these crimes are both financial and social:

> The financial loss from white collar crime, great as it is, is less important than the damage to social relations. White collar crimes violate trust and therefore create distrust, which lowers social morale and produces social disorganization on a large scale. Other crimes have relatively little effect on social institutions or social organization.
>
> White collar crime is real crime. It is not ordinarily called crime, and calling it by this name does not make it worse, just as not calling it crime does not make it better. It is called crime here because it is in violation of the criminal law and belongs within the scope of criminology. (p. 52)

Sutherland concluded this article by asserting that "a theory of criminal behavior which will explain both white collar crime and lower class criminality is needed" (p. 61). Throughout the article, he claimed that differential association theory is a general theory and is applicable to all criminal behavior including white collar crime.

Sutherland published a second article on white collar crime in the *American Sociological Review* 5 years later (Sutherland, 1945). Sutherland (1945) reported,

> In order to secure evidence as to the prevalence of such white collar crimes, an analysis was made of the decisions by courts and commissions against the seventy largest industrial and mercantile corporations in the United States under four types of laws, namely, antitrust; false advertising; National Labor Relations [Law]; and infringements of patents, copyrights, and trademarks. (p. 132)

Among these 70 corporations, Sutherland found that 547 such adverse decisions had been made, for an average of 7.8 decisions per corporation, and that each corporation had at least 1 adverse decision. However, only 49 (or 9%) of these decisions were made in the criminal courts (p. 132). But Sutherland contended that these decisions could be used as a measure of criminal behavior if the other 498 decisions could be shown to be decisions in which the behavior of the corporations was criminal.

Sutherland (1945) used "a combination of two abstract criteria generally regarded by legal scholars as necessary to define crime" (p. 132). These were a legal description of an act as socially injurious and legal provision of a penalty for the act. He argued that these criteria applied to all 547 decisions. In examining the criterion of social injuries, Sutherland found that all of the classes of behavior under which the decisions were made were legally defined as socially injurious. This was determined by words in the statutes such as "crime" and "misdemeanor" in some as well as "unfair," "discrimination," and "infringement" in others. He asserted that the statutes were intended to protect persons engaged in the same occupations as the offenders and the general public as consumers or as constituents of social institutions that were affected by the violations (p. 132).

According to Sutherland (1945), violations of the antitrust laws, laws against false advertisement, and laws against infringements were acts of theft and fraud, whereas violations of the National Labor Relations Law were a form of assault (p. 133). With reference to the Sherman Antitrust Law, Sutherland wrote,

> The Sherman Antitrust Law states explicitly that a violation of the law is a misdemeanor. Three methods of enforcement of this law are provided. First, it may be enforced by the usual criminal prosecution, resulting in the imposition of fine or imprisonment. Second, the attorney general of the United States and the several district attorneys are given the "duty" of "repressing and preventing" violations of the law by petitions for injunctions, and violations of the injunctions are punishable as contempt of court. This method of enforcing a criminal law was an invention and . . . is the key to the interpretation of the differential implementation of the criminal law as applied to white collar criminals. Third, parties who are injured by violations of the law are authorized to sue for damages. . . . All three of these methods of enforcement are based on

decisions that a criminal law was violated and therefore that a crime was committed; the decisions of a civil court or a court of equity as to these violations are as good evidence of criminal behavior as is the decision of a criminal court. (p. 133)

Although Sutherland was attacked by the legal profession for calling "crimes" acts defined in statutes as "torts,"[7] his works had a major impact on criminology at the time. According to Lindesmith (1988), "A survey of 1940-1950 publications selected Sutherland's study as the most important one of the decade" (p. xii).

Assumptions About People and Society

Conflict/radical/Marxist theorists do not speak with one single voice. Yet, their research methods and their basic assumptions about people and society are quite similar. Most theorists within this perspective use historical documents to support their assertions about society. Many examples of this can be cited. Marx, for example, spent his life in the library gathering support for his assertion that the history of all societies is a history of class struggle. Quinney used U.S. government documents of the President's Crime Commission and the National Advisory Commission of Civil Disorders to support his contention that members of these commissions were from the power elite and that their purpose was the control of the lower classes. Similar methodologies were used by Chambliss and Reiman as well as by numerous other conflict theorists.

Conflict theorists also are in general agreement about their assumptions about people and society. Like the functionalists discussed in Chapter 4, conflict theorists view the world from a macro level of analysis. That is, they consistently examine the social structure of the total society in their analyses. Throughout the works of Marx and Bonger, for example, these theorists stressed the evils of a capitalist economic system in societies. Du Bois emphasized the impact of slavery on the United States, Pennsylvania, and Philadelphia as related to crime.

In contrast to the functionalists, who stressed that society is based on consensus, the conflict theorists argue that society is based on coercion and exploitation. Du Bois's major point throughout his works on crime was that the coercion and exploitation of the system of slavery explained much of the crimes of African Americans in America. Chambliss argued that the origin of laws, such as the vagrancy laws of England during the 14th century, emerged as a way in which to coerce the poor into working for low wages. Thus, society was seen by these theorists as fluid and unstable. In fact, many of these theorists, such as Marx and Quinney, were advocating revolutionary change. In his more radical stage, Quinney called for the collapse of the capitalist system in America.

Like the interactionists discussed in Chapter 7, conflict theorists also argued that definitions of crime were created arbitrarily. The conflict theorists take this a step further and argue that crime and deviance are defined by those with economic and political power and are imposed on the poor and powerless. Quinney's (1970b) *The Social*

Reality of Crime presented this perspective in six propositions in the first chapter. Thus, conflict theorists maintain that phenomena are generated by the powerful and are imposed on the powerless passive agents in society. Slaves in Du Bois's writings and the "surplus population" in Quinney's works provide examples of this. Criminal behavior, then, is not a result of the free will of individuals but rather is determined by society.

Finally, the social phenomena examined by these theorists are both objective overt behavior and subjective covert behavior. Lynching (as discussed by Du Bois) and murder (as discussed by Reiman) both are objective overt behavior that can be seen and measured. But the carnival mirror of crime introduced by Reiman and the power mentioned frequently by Quinney are subjective covert behavior. Discrimination, prejudice, and bias are central parts of many of the works discussed in this chapter. These attitudes are subjective and covert.

Earl Richard Quinney (1934-)

Although Richard Quinney had brief interests in photography, forestry, and hospital administration, his education was primarily in sociology (Martin, Mutchnick, and Austin, 1990, pp. 381-382). In his graduate work at Northwestern University and the University of Wisconsin, Quinney studied with mainstream sociologists such as Kimball Young, Howard Becker,[8] and Marshall Clinard. Like other sociologists discussed in previous chapters such as Ruth Shonle Cavan and Émile Durkheim, Quinney had an early interest in religion that became a continuous theme in many of his writings. In fact, as the biographical inset on Quinney (Inset 8.2) points out, he originally planned to write his dissertation on religion. After Becker died, Quinney selected a new dissertation chair and a new topic, *Retail Pharmacy as a Marginal Occupation*. According to Martin and colleagues (1990), "Quinney used Sutherland's work on differential social organization as well as Merton's work on strain theory as the basis for his dissertation" (p. 386). Although his earliest publications from his dissertation (Quinney, 1963, 1964a, 1965b) were on more mainstream topics, the seeds of conflict theory were there.

In 1966, De Fleur and Quinney published an article in which they used math models to rewrite Sutherland's nine propositions of differential association to test the internal logic of the theory (De Fleur and Quinney, 1966). In 1967, Quinney co-authored, with his doctoral dissertation chair, Marshall Clinard, a book titled *Criminal Behavioral Systems* (Clinard, Quinney, and Wildeman, 1994). In this work, which has undergone several revisions, Clinard and Quinney created a typology of nine behavioral systems. Sutherland's white collar crime theory had been criticized for ignoring the individual behavior in corporations. The authors created a new typology, occupational criminal behavior, that separates it from Sutherland's original corporate criminal behavior. Quinney's works related to Sutherland's differential as-

---

INSET 8.2

Earl Richard Quinney (1934-)

Richard Quinney was born on May 16, 1934, in Sugar Creek, Wisconsin. He is the son of Floyd and Alice Quinney (Martin, Mutchnick, and Austin, 1990). Quinney spent much of his early schooling in a now defunct one-room school. After leaving the one-room school, Quinney attended Delevan High School. In 1952, Quinney completed high school and enrolled at Carroll College, where he studied biology and sociology. He graduated in 1956 and headed to Northwestern University, where he initially intended to study hospital administration (Martin et al., 1990, p. 382). However, he changed his mind and switched over to sociology.

Following the completion of his master's degree, Quinney became interested in pursuing his Ph.D. He selected the University of Wisconsin–Madison, where he was awarded a research assistantship. While at that university, he selected Howard Becker as his dissertation chair. Quinney originally selected religion as his dissertation topic, but after Becker died unexpectedly, Quinney left the university and later selected Marshall Clinard to direct his dissertation. In 1962, Quinney completed his dissertation, *Retail Pharmacy as a Marginal Occupation*.

Since receiving his first academic appointment at the University of Kentucky, Quinney has held numerous academic appointments at institutions such as New York University, the University of North Carolina at Chapel Hill, Brooklyn College, Brown University, and Northern Illinois University. He retired from Northern Illinois in 1998 as a professor emeritus. Beginning in 1963, Quinney published numerous articles and books on crime in America and on theoretical issues in criminology. Most notable were *The Social Reality of Crime* (Quinney, 1970b) and *The Problem of Crime* (Quinney, 1970a), which sparked much discussion in the discipline after their publication. (His most recent contributions to peacemaking are discussed in Chapter 10 of the present book.) His writings have earned him several prestigious awards including the Sutherland Award from the American Society of Criminology.

—Shaun L. Gabbidon
Pennsylvania State University at Harrisburg

SOURCE: Excerpted from the writings of Shaun L. Gabbidon.

---

sociation and white collar crime were rewarded by the American Society of Criminology in 1984, when Quinney was the recipient of the prestigious Sutherland Award.[9]

Quinney quickly moved from his early positivist mainstream position to the conflict/radical perspective. This change began in 1970 with his publication of *The Social Reality of Crime* (Quinney, 1970b). By the mid-1970s, his works had taken a more Marxist tone with the publication of *Critique of the Legal Order* (Quinney, 1974) and *Class, State, and Crime* (Quinney, 1977).[10] By the 1980s, he had made a return to his religious interests with the publication of *Providence* (Quinney, 1980b). His major interests turned to criminology as peacemaking during the late 1980s and 1990s (see Chapter 10).[11]

Conflict Theory

Quinney's most important contribution to conflict theory was his 1970 publication of *The Social Reality of Crime* (Quinney, 1970b). The six propositions contained in the opening chapter presented a clear and precise definition of conflict theory that seemed to serve as the springboard for launching this perspective as a prominent criminological theory during the 1970s and 1980s.[12] These propositions also made Quinney one of the few criminology theorists to come close to meeting Homans' (1964) social science definition of a theory.

Quinney (1970b) opened his book with the following discussion of theory construction and the purpose of theory:

> Much of criminological theory, based on positivistic assumptions, has sought to explain the "causes" of crime. . . . Causal explanation need not be the sole interest of criminologists. The objective of any science is not to formulate and verify theories of causation but [rather] to construct an order among observables. . . .
>
> A statement of causation does not necessarily state the nature of reality but [rather] is a *methodological construction* of the observer: "Causes certainly are connected by effects, but this is because our theories connect them, not because the world is held together by cosmic glue." The scientist who defines a causal relationship has to see that it is a construct imposed by himself in order to give meaning to a significant problem. . . .
>
> What is required in the explanation of crime, *if* a causative explanation is formulated, is a conception of causation that is attuned to the nature of social phenomena. . . . Therefore, the social scientist's constructs have to be founded upon the *social reality* created by man. (pp. 5-6)

In the preceding quotations, Quinney distinguished conflict theory from functionalist and mainstream criminology in both theory construction and research methods. Whereas Homans, as discussed in Chapter 1, suggested that a theory must consist of propositions that state relationships and form a deductive system, Quinney argued that "propositions must be consistent with one another and must be integrated into a system" (p. 7). With reference to his own theoretical propositions, Quinney asserted,

> With the theory that I am constructing are several propositions that are consistent and integrated into a theoretical system. One or more specific statements express in probability form the relationships within the proposition. Further, the propositions are arranged according to *a system of proposition units*. The propositions express relationships that are both coexistent and sequential. The theory thus assumes that patterns of phenomena develop over a period of time. Each proposition unit within the theoretical model requires explanation, and each unit relates to the others. Ultimately, the theoretical system provides the basis for an integrated theory of crime. (pp. 7-8)

After discussing the basic concepts of conflict theory such as process, conflict, power, and social action, Quinney (1970b) turned to the six propositions:

> The theory contains six propositions and a number of statements within the propositions. With the first proposition, I define crime. The next four are the explanatory

units. In the final proposition, the other five are collected to form a composite describing the social reality of crime. (p. 15)

Proposition 1: Definition of crime. Crime is a definition of human conduct that is created by authorized agents in a politically organized society (Quinney, 1970b, p. 15). For Quinney, this is the essential point of the theory. Crime is a definition of behavior that is conferred on some persons by others. Legislatures, police, prosecutors, and judges are representatives of the criminal justice system and are responsible for formulating and administering criminal law.[13] Persons and behaviors, therefore, become criminal because of the *formulation and application* of criminal definitions. Thus, *crime is created* (p. 15). Quinney (1970b) further stated that "crime is not inherent in behavior" (p. 16). In this statement, Quinney distinguished his theory from that of the Positivist School discussed in Chapter 3. Finally, Quinney claimed, "It follows, then, that *the greater the number of criminal definitions formulated and applied, the greater the amount of crime*" (p. 16).

Proposition 2: Formulation of criminal definitions. Criminal definitions describe behaviors that conflict with the interests of the segments of society that have the power to shape public policy (Quinney, 1970b, p. 16). Quinney explained that not only is crime defined by political agents of society, but criminal definitions are formulated according to the interests of those *segments* of society that have the *power* to translate their interests into public policy. That is, those segments of society with power protect their vested interests through the definition and application of criminal law. Because criminal definitions exist due to conflict between segments of society, Quinney (1970b) noted, "The greater the conflict in interests between the segments of society, the greater the probability that the power segments will formulate criminal definitions" (p. 17).

Proposition 3: Application of criminal definitions. Criminal definitions are applied by the segments of society that have the power to shape the enforcement and administration of criminal law (Quinney, 1970b, p. 18). Quinney (1970b) asserted in this proposition that the "powerful interests intervene in all stages in which criminal definitions are created" and that the interests of the powerful also operate in *applying* criminal definitions. The probability of the application of a criminal definition "*varies according to the extent to which the behaviors of the powerless conflict with the interests of the power segments*" (p. 18).

Proposition 4: Development of behavior patterns in relation to criminal definitions. Behavior patterns are structured in segmentally organized society in relation to criminal definitions, and within this context persons engage in actions that have relative probabilities of being defined as criminal (Quinney, 1970b, p. 20). Quinney (1970b) asserted, "Although behavior varies, all behaviors are similar in that they represent the *behavior patterns* of segments of society" (p. 20). Consequently, "*persons in the segments of society whose behavior patterns are not represented in formulating and applying criminal definitions are more likely to act in* ways that will be defined as criminal than [are] those in the segments that formulate and apply criminal definitions" (p. 21).

In Propositions 2 to 4, Quinney was stating that those with economic and political power define the behaviors of the powerless as criminal, especially if these behaviors conflict with the vested interests of the powerful. He also asserted that the behaviors within a given segment of society are similar. Thus, specific segments of society are more likely to have their behaviors defined as criminal. In addition, even when the powerful might commit acts defined as crimes, they are less apt to have the enforcement of criminal laws applied to them than are the poor and powerless.

Proposition 5: Construction of criminal conceptions. Conceptions of crime are constructed and diffused in the segments of society by various means of communication (Quinney, 1970b, p. 22). Thus, Quinney argued that the powerful ruling class creates an ideology of crime that serves its interests. These images of crime and the criminal are portrayed through the mass media and diffused throughout society. Although these ideologies of crime are created by the powerful, they are sold to the masses as the "real" universal reality of crime. This is a very Marxian idea. Marx asserted that the ideology of the powerful is presented to the society as a consensus of the values of the total society. Reiman (1995) illustrated this in his conception of the "carnival mirror of crime" that falsely presents street crime as the most dangerous one-on-one crime (p. 51). Reiman, who is discussed later in this chapter, concurred with Quinney that the purpose of constructing this conception of street crime as the most dangerous is to take the attention of the masses away from the crimes of the powerful.

Proposition 6: The social reality of crime. The social reality of crime is constructed by the formulation and application of criminal definitions, the development of behavior patterns related to criminal definitions, and the construction of criminal conceptions (Quinney, 1970b, p. 23). Thus, in the sixth proposition, Quinney collected the first five propositions into a composite summary. The social reality of crime was constructed in all of the preceding propositions. Quinney insisted that the ruling class benefits from the legal system and that *crime control is, in reality, class control.*

Quinney (1970b), then, contended,

The theory as I have formulated it is inspired by a change currently altering our view of the world. This change, found at all levels of society, has to do with the world that we all construct and, at the same time, pretend to separate ourselves from in assessing our experiences. . . .

For the study of crime, a revision in thought is directing attention to the process by which criminal definitions are formulated and applied. In the theory of the social reality of crime, I have attempted to show how a theory of crime can be consistent with some revisionist assumptions about theoretical explanation and about man and society. The theory is cumulative in that the framework incorporates the diverse findings from criminology. (pp. 24-25)

Marxist Theory

Quinney (1977) took a more Marxist stance when he attacked capitalism and asserted that the existing social order is based on class struggle:

> The struggle between classes, central to developing capitalism, is regulated by capitalist justice. Justice in capitalist society, today as always, is an ideological and practical instrument in class struggle. . . . The immediate fact is that capitalist justice secures the capitalist system. In an understanding of capitalist justice, especially in relation to crime, we can demystify our history and current experiences and move to a theory and practice that will realize a socialist state. (p. 2)

The capitalist notion of justice, as presented by Quinney (1977), was most explicitly represented in the problem of crime. He asserted, "Since the middle 1960s, with the increasing crisis of capitalism, official and public attention has focused on rising crime and its control" (p. 6). As a result of this crisis, the war on crime was launched by President Johnson. In 1965, Congress enacted the Omnibus Crime Control and Safe Streets Act. The act opened with the following statement:

> Congress finds that the high incidence of crime in the United States threatens the peace, security, and general welfare of the nation and its citizens. To prevent crime and to insure the greater safety of the people, law enforcement efforts must be better coordinated, intensified, and made effective at all levels of government. (pp. 6-7)

Quinney (1973) argued that a new form of crime control was established in capitalist society. That is, "the ruling class formulates criminal policy for the preservation of domestic order, an order that assures the social and economic hegemony of the capitalist system" (p. 59). (It also ensures that makers of criminal policy are members of, or representatives of, big business and finance.)

The war on crime included legislation, presidential commissions, and policy research by liberal academicians. Quinney (1973) examined the composition of some of these commissions to support his point that criminal justice had become capitalist justice aimed at control of the masses of poor citizens and that "public interest" actually was the interest of the dominant economic class (p. 61). For example, of the 19 members of the President's Crime Commission in 1967, 15 were lawyers and 1 of the non-lawyers was the San Francisco chief of police. Other members were heads of the League of Women Voters and National Urban League. Most of the members had wealthy connections and were of the "law and order mentality" (pp. 61-66). Quinney did a similar analysis of the National Advisory Commission on Civil Disorders and found that 11 of these members were appointed to the Riot Commission and 13 were appointed to the Violence Commission. These commissions were composed of state governors and government officials, U.S. and state representatives and senators, university presidents, heads of businesses and industries, and the president of the United Steel Workers of America (pp. 71-73). Although Quinney did not make this point, most of the members of the three commissions were white males and only 4 were women. He did point out that the members represented the established elements of political and economic life in the United States. Thus, those who were the subjects of the commissions—those who rioted, committed crimes, and engaged in acts of violence—found no voice on these commissions. Quinney concluded that this represented still "another victory for the corporate economy and the capitalist state" (p. 73).

Quinney (1973) also scrutinized student scholarships and research grants received by academicians. He argued that independent scholarship is a myth because the research of scholars is supported by government agencies and, therefore, is influenced by the interests of the politic authorities.

> Social scientists have conducted research, supported by government grants, which provides information for manipulating and controlling the rest of the population. This information has come either from research sponsored for the explicit purpose of obtaining information or from studies that supposedly were independent of applied interests.... Then there are the programs developed to train government agents (for example, policemen, parole officers, and prison guards) within the curriculum of universities. (p. 33)[14]

The purpose of all the commissions, graduate fellowships, research grants, and criminal laws, according to Quinney (1977), is crime control as a means of checking threats to existing social and economic order (p. 45). Quinney further asserted that capitalism systematically creates an unemployed sector of the working class that he called the "surplus population." These people are dependent on fluctuations in the economy and/or technology making their skills obsolete. Thus, pressures build for the growth of a welfare system that results in the political control of the surplus population (p. 48). Quinney explained,

> Thus, the relative surplus population, in the reserve army, takes a variety of forms under advanced capitalist production. The reserve army includes "the unemployed; the sporadically employed; the part-time employed; the mass of women who, as houseworkers, form a reserve for the 'female occupations'[15]; the armies of migrant labor, both agricultural and industrial; the black population with its extraordinarily high rates of unemployment; and the foreign reserves of labor." (p. 70)

Quinney further noted that most of the crime identified and processed through the criminal justice system is the predatory crime by this surplus population. The criminal justice system controls the crime of the surplus population by what Quinney called the "repressive workers" (p. 116) who engage in the actual or threatened use of physical force and legal punishment.

The criminal justice system, therefore, secures the capitalist order so that the capitalist class can continue to accumulate capital. Quinney (1980a) predicted that as capitalistic development reaches its final stage, there will be a crisis in capitalism and a crisis in criminal justice as even criminal justice fails to control the population. He stated, "The final development of capitalism is also the initial development of socialism" (pp. 166-167). This will bring changes to criminal justice. "Instead of a justice based on the needs of the capitalist class, to the oppression of everyone else, a social justice develops under socialism that serves the needs of all people." Quinney's (1973) Marxist criminological theory can best be summarized in his own words:

1. American society is based on an advanced capitalist economy.

2. The state is organized to serve the interests of the dominant economic class, the capitalist ruling class.

3. Criminal law is an instrument of the state and ruling class to maintain and perpetuate the existing social and economic order.

4. Crime control in capitalist society is accomplished through a variety of institutions and agencies established and administered by a governmental elite, representing ruling class interests, for the purpose of establishing domestic order.

5. The contradictions of advanced capitalism—the disjunction between existence and essence—require the subordinate classes [to] remain oppressed by whatever means necessary, especially through the coercion and violence of the legal system.

6. Only with the collapse of capitalist society and the creation of a new society, based on socialist principles, will there be a solution to the crime problem. (p. 16)

In the preceding statements, Quinney was advocating not only a change from capitalism to socialism but also a change in criminal justice policy. Chapter 10 examines Quinney's contributions to peacemaking and his contention that we need to replace punishment, oppression, and control with love, compassion, and community.

Critique of Quinney

The preceding discussion did not include all of Quinney's works on conflict/Marxist theory. However, it did make the point that he made many outstanding contributions to this area of criminological theory. Because there are so many similarities in the writings of Turk, Chambliss, and Quinney, it sometimes is difficult to distinguish the criticisms of Quinney from the general reviews of conflict/radical/Marxist theory. But as Lilly, Cullen, and Ball (1995) suggested, "Quinney was to become not only the most prolific of the criminological conflict theorists but also the most controversial" (p. 156). As we have seen in this chapter, and as will be seen when we examine peacemaking in Chapter 10, Quinney had many transitions in his scholarship.

I have moved through the various epistemologies and ontologies in the social sciences. After applying one, I have found that another is necessary for incorporating what was excluded from the former, and so on. Also, I have tried to keep my work informed by the latest developments in the philosophy of science. In addition, I have always been a part of the progressive movements of my time. My work is thus an integral part of the social and intellectual changes that are taking place in the larger society, outside of criminology and sociology. One other fact has affected my work in recent years: the search for meaning in my life and in the world. (Bartollas, 1985, p. 230)

Many criminologists see this ability as the mark of a scholar, but others (e.g., Toby, 1979[16]) see Quinney's theoretical works as "old sentimentality." Klockars (1979) criticized Quinney's theory as "abstract mystification" because he contended that it violates the crucial social science concept of "objective interest" (p. 492).

Quinney's theoretical works have been criticized because they do not fit the mainstream positivist paradigm in criminology for testability. Instead of quantitative "empirical" analysis of his theories, Quinney and other conflict/radical/Marxist theorists have used historical documentation to support their theories. In discussing Quinney, Akers (1979) stated,

> A theory is judged primarily by comparison with other theories and by empirical evidence on its validity. A philosophy is judged primarily by comparison with other philosophies and how it has worked in practice. I have written elsewhere on this issue and have analyzed Marxist theory within the context of other theories and empirical evidence.... Those readers who know of my work will not be surprised to learn that I find little empirical support for Marxist theory in criminology. (pp. 527-528)

Akers also criticized Quinney for the focus of his theory:

> Quinney is mainly interested in explaining the behavior of criminologists, both those applied criminologists working in the criminal justice system and academic criminologists. He does so in the same way [as] he explains all aspects of the law formation and enforcement system—criminologists behave as they do "to control anything that threatens the capitalist system." (p. 530)

Quinney has come under attack for his call to abolish capitalism and establish a socialist society. Quinney (1980a) argued,

> The only lasting solution to the crisis of capitalism is socialism. Under late advanced capitalism, socialism will be achieved in the struggle of all people who are oppressed by the capitalist mode of production, namely, the workers and all elements of the surplus population. . . .
>
> The objective of our analysis is to promote a further questioning of the capitalist system, leading to a deeper understanding of the consequences of capitalist development. The *essential meaning* of crime in the development of capitalism is the need for a socialist society. (pp. 67-68)

Akers (1979) stated, "I think Quinney's assertions about the need to bring about a socialist society that would be nonrepressive are utopian" (p. 528). He contended,

> Quinney makes assertions about the impact of capitalism, the truth of which cannot be assessed without comparisons with historical and contemporary noncapitalist systems. . . . Quinney is proposing that there is no criminology studied or practiced in socialist societies. Perhaps in some future utopian socialist society, there will be no crime, . . . but in the real world, criminology is not a product only [of] capitalist systems. (p. 533)

Klockars (1979) also challenged Quinney's claims that "predatory crimes" are the product of capitalism:

> What can one say of an explanation of predatory crimes that finds it to be the "reproduction of capitalism" or an interpretation of rape as the social psychological effect of the contradictions of capitalism? Stalin's purge of the thirties is not, after all, today. Are the Gulags . . . close enough? Does the rape and carnage described in chapter eight of *Gulag Archipelago Two*, "Women in Camp," somehow not matter? (p. 499)

These critics argued that Quinney not only failed to make adequate comparisons between crime in capitalist and socialist societies but also failed to provide a clear policy statement for changing capitalist societies to socialism. For example, Lilly, Cullen, and Ball (1989) criticized Quinney and Marxist theorists for their "inability or unwillingness . . . to provide blueprints for policy" (p. 178).

Whereas feminist theorists, such as Leonard (1982) and Naffine (1987), have criticized Quinney for failing to include women in his analysis of powerless groups, positivist mainstream criminologists often have simply ignored Quinney's works. For example, Wilbanks (1987) made a claim that racism in the criminal justice system is a myth but totally ignored Quinney's (1970b) *The Social Reality of Crime*, which contended that those with power define crimes based on their vested interests. Despite extensive criticisms of Quinney, there is evidence that scholars recognize his importance to criminological theory. Quinney was chosen by Martin and colleagues (1990) as one of 15 "pioneers" in criminology who are "representative of the significant writers and thinkers in criminology" (p. viii). Each pioneer was given a chapter, and Quinney was the only theorist of the conflict perspective included in the book.

One of Quinney's major critics, Akers (1979), had this to say:

> Richard Quinney was my major professor and dissertation director, my mentor, [and a] professional role model, and [he] is my friend. Much of my sociological and criminological interests were formed under his tutelage. It is a tribute to his intellectual and educational philosophy that he inspired me to be interested in the same problems as he, without indoctrinating me to take the same approach with the same answers as he. (p. 529)

As mentioned in the biographical inset on Quinney (Inset 8.2), he has received many awards and honors in recognition of his contributions to criminology and theory. Most important, Quinney continues to be a groundbreaker in criminological theory and thought. His current impact on theory is examined in detail in Chapter 10.

William Joseph Chambliss (1933-)

William Chambliss was born in Buffalo, New York, but was quite mobile throughout his life. He attended high school in East Los Angeles and in Virginia (Chambliss, 1987, pp. 1, 5). Like Robert Merton (see Chapter 4), Chambliss's fam-

INSET 8.3   **William Joseph Chambliss (1933-)**

William Chambliss was born on December 12, 1933, in Buffalo, New York. He is the youngest of six children born to Joseph H. and Jean Chambliss. Chambliss (1987) told the story of how he accidentally discovered criminology. After completing his junior year of high school, he and a friend decided to hitchhike to Seattle, Washington, en route to Alaska. With only $20, they were intent on working their way to Alaska. Unfortunately, when they got to Seattle, a longshoremen's strike stopped them from making it to Alaska.

After diminishing their funds, they headed east in search of work. They found employment, first, picking strawberries and, second, working in the pea fields of southeastern Washington (Chambliss, 1987, p. 1). In this second job, Chambliss began to work among inmates from the Washington State Penitentiary. Chambliss soon became friends with some of the inmates and concluded three things from his interaction with them: "(1) All the cons to whom I talked were planning new capers as soon as they were released from prison; (2) their friendship with me had sexual overtones; [and] (3) the white and black inmates were openly at war with one another" (Chambliss, 1987, p. 5).

After his stint in Washington state, Chambliss headed to the East Coast. He ended up in Virginia, where his father resided. In Virginia, Chambliss met his stepbrother, who introduced him to "penology." Chambliss enrolled at the University of Virginia, majoring in psychology. Funding problems forced him to return to California, where college was free. Chambliss enrolled at the University of California, Los Angeles, majoring in psychology and English. During his junior year, he took a sociology course titled "Social Disorganization." Chambliss (1987) noted, "I was very lucky to have a superb teacher: Donald Cressey" (p. 5). But Cressey informed Chambliss that criminology was studied in sociology, not psychology. Because Chambliss already was well into his program, he completed his B.A. degree in 1955.

ily was working class, and Chambliss was a member of a gang, the "Solons." Chambliss explained his membership in the gang as follows:

> My junior year of high school found me going to school in East Los Angeles. To even get into the school building you had to walk a gauntlet of people from different gangs sitting beside the entrance staring at each person who entered. . . . I was luckier than most, however. My best friend, Billy Hummel, had a "rep" and was fullback on the football team. Also, I was a member of the "Solons," a gang that made headlines in the [Los Angeles Times] when we gathered in a schoolyard late one night to witness a fight between a member of the Solons and another gang. The fight was broken up by the police, but the L.A. Times headlines portrayed a scene of gang warfare with chains and tire irons. It was an early experience in the power of the press and police to create a major crime out of a trivial incident. Being Billy Hummel's friend and a member of the Solons made me appear [to be] a whole lot tougher than I was. (p. 1)

As indicated in the biographical inset on Chambliss (Inset 8.3), he attended the University of Virginia and then the University of California, Los Angeles, using

Chambliss soon was drafted into the army to fight in Korea. He served in the Counter Intelligence Corps (CIC). This experience led Chambliss to gain hands-on criminology experience. This experience came in the form of "criminality of the soldiers in Korea." As Chambliss (1987) pointed out, "American and Korean soldiers raped, stole, assaulted, intimidated, and generally terrorized the Koreans" (p. 5). After seeing further injustices, Chambliss went to one of his commanders and told him that he wanted no part of this activity. This stance, surprisingly, did not backfire, and Chambliss did not take part in any inappropriate behavior.

On returning to the United States, Chambliss had the dream of becoming a warden. At the recommendation of Cressey, Chambliss enrolled in the Department of Sociology at Indiana University in 1958. He received his M.A. in sociology in 1960 and his PhD in sociology with a minor in law in 1962. After completing his degree, he joined the faculty at the University of Washington. It was during an American Sociological Association meeting that Chambliss was asked about his Marxist analysis of law in a recent article Chambliss had written. Because he was unfamiliar with Marx, he was intent on learning more about Marx's writings. After his first year at the University of Washington, Chambliss associated himself with a recently appointed Marxist scholar. This, along with other writings, began a long and continuing productive career. Chambliss has served as a visiting scholar throughout the world and has taught at numerous universities. He has received numerous awards including a Fulbright research fellowship and the Bruce Smith Award for contributions to criminology and criminal justice in 1986. In 1999, Chambliss was awarded an honorary doctorate of law degree from the University of Guelph in Ontario. He also served as president of the American Society of Criminology during the 1989-1990 period. Chambliss currently is chair of the Department of Sociology at George Washington University in Washington, D.C.

—*Shaun L. Gabbidon*
Pennsylvania State University at Harrisburg

SOURCE: Excerpted from the writings of Shaun L. Gabbidon.

money "I could beg, borrow, and earn working, shooting pool, and playing poker" (Chambliss, 1987, p. 5). During his undergraduate days, he decided on a career as a prison warden. But throughout his life, he was plagued with the question, "What are prisons for?"

Chambliss (1987) suggested that he learned a lot about crime when he was drafted into the army in 1955 and sent to Korea with the Counter Intelligence Corps (CIC). He noted that "crime was part and parcel of what it meant to be a CIC agent in Korea" (p. 5). Interrogations consisted of beatings, threats, administering shocks with electrical wires, and other forms of torture.

> Korea was a military dictatorship where corruption of U.S. and Korean military and law enforcement agencies was rampant. Of course, the crimes of the military and the government went undetected and unpunished. Korean civilians, however, were arrested for crimes, tried, and sent to prison. Their problem was not that they committed crime[s] while others did not; their problem was that they did not do so from a position of power. The people being sent to prison were not the thieves and terrorists of the U.S.

or Korean military, they were the people in the villages who stole to survive. I wondered again: What are prisons for? (p. 6)

Chambliss had many other professional experiences that informed his scholarship and research. These included a research study of vice and corruption in Seattle, Washington, where he discovered that "certain kinds of highly profitable crimes flourished *not* in opposition to law enforcement agencies but [rather] in tandem with them" (Chambliss, 1987, p. 7); a visiting professorship in Nigeria, where he found government corruption again; and a year in England spent reading old manuscripts on piracy in the British Museum (pp. 7, 9). After a short visiting professorship in Oslo, Norway, he returned to the University of Delaware and finally to George Washington University in Washington, D.C., where he continued to study state organized crime. All of these experiences provided the resources for a variety of research projects. In "The Saints and the Roughnecks," Chambliss (1973) examined class and delinquency. His major examination of government and bureaucratic involvement in crime came in two other journal articles. Chambliss's (1964) classic study of the "Sociological Analysis of the Law of Vagrancy" is perhaps his most well-known work in criminology.

Class and Delinquency/Crime

Chambliss's theoretical perspective can be found in the introductions to his several edited books. In the introduction to *Crime and the Legal Process* (Chambliss, 1969), for example, he stressed the power of interest groups to influence the legal system. Legal norms were seen simply as a device by which persons in positions of power maintain and enhance their advantaged positions by using state power to coerce the mass of people into doing what is consistent with the power elite (p. 8). Chambliss and Seidman (1971) argued, "The more economically stratified a society becomes, the more it becomes necessary for the dominant groups in the society to enforce through coercion the norms of conduct which guarantee their supremacy" (p. 33). Chambliss illustrated the differential enforcement of societal norms in his study of the Saints and the Roughnecks.

The Saints. Based on his observations for 2 years of two gangs of boys at Hanibal High School,[17] Chambliss (1973) suggested that selective perception, bias, and the processing and punishing of some types of criminality and not others "means that visible, poor, nonmobile, outspoken, undiplomatic 'tough' kids will be noticed, whether their actions are seriously delinquent or not" (p. 31).

The Saints consisted of "eight promising young men—children of good, stable, white upper middle class families, active in school affairs, good pre-college students" (Chambliss, 1973, p. 24). Although Chambliss (1973) stated that they "were some of the most delinquent boys at Hanibal High School," the community residents and parents were totally unaware that "sowing wild oats" completely occupied the daily routine of these young men. The Saints, according to Chambliss, were constantly occupied with truancy, drinking, wild driving, petty theft, and vandalism. Yet, Chambliss reported that none of the boys ever was officially arrested during his 2 years of observation. The Roughnecks, however, consisted of six lower class white boys who were students at Hanibal High School (p. 24). This gang of boys was constantly in trouble with the police and community, even though their rate of delinquency was about equal to that of the Saints.

The Saints' principal daily concern was with getting out of school. Chambliss (1973) described the elaborate process used by the boys as follows:

> The most common procedure was for one boy to obtain the release of another by fabricating a meeting of some committee, program, or organized club. Charles might raise his hand in his 9:00 chemistry class and ask to be excused—a euphemism for going to the bathroom. Charles would go to Ed's math class and inform the teacher that Ed was needed for a 9:30 rehearsal of the drama club play. The math teacher would recognize Ed and Charles as "good students" involved in numerous school activities and would permit Ed to leave at 9:30. Charles would return to his class and Ed would go to Tom's English class to obtain his release. Tom would engineer Charles' escape. The strategy would continue until as many of the Saints as possible were freed. After a stealthy trip to the car (which had been parked in a strategic spot), the boys were off for a day of fun. . . . This pattern was repeated nearly every day. (p. 24)

Their technique for covering truancy was so successful that teachers did not even realize that the boys were absent from school much of the time. Cheating on examinations was rampant. Because none of the boys studied, they were primarily dependent on one another. Teachers contributed to their deception by giving the boys the benefit of the doubt (Chambliss, 1973, p. 26). It is surprising, however, that they were so highly successful in school. The average grade for the group was "B." Nearly all of these boys were popular, and some of them held offices in the school. Six of the boys played on athletic teams.

The local police also saw the Saints as good boys who were among the leaders of the youths in the community. On rare occasions when they might be stopped for speeding or for running a stop sign, they always were polite, were contrite, and pleaded for mercy. None ever received a ticket or was taken into the precinct by the local police (p. 26).

Every Friday and Saturday night, most of the Saints would meet between 8:00 and 8:30 and go into Big Town. Big Town activities included drinking heavily in taverns or nightclubs, driving drunkenly through the streets, committing acts of vandalism, and playing pranks (Chambliss, 1973, p. 25). Chambliss (1973) described some of these pranks as follows:

> Construction sites and road repair areas were the special province of the Saints' mischief. A soon-to-be-repaired hole inevitably invited the Saints to remove the lanterns and wooden barricades and put them in the car, leaving the hole unprotected. The boys would find a safe vantage point and wait for an unsuspecting motorist to drive into the hole. Often, though not always, the boys would go up to the motorist and commiserate with him about the dreadful way the city protected its citizenry.

Leaving the scene of the open hole and the motorist, the boys would then go searching for an appropriate place to erect the stolen barricade. An "appropriate place" was often a spot on a highway near a curve in the road where the barricade would not be seen by an oncoming motorist. (p. 25)

Chambliss (1973) reported that only twice in 2 years were the boys stopped by a Big City[18] policeman (p. 26). The first stop was for speeding. Chambliss reported that the boys drove over the speed limit every time they drove, whether they were drunk or sober. In this instance, the driver managed to convince the policeman that it was simply an error. The second stop occurred when they were leaving a nightclub. They were walking through an alley, one of the boys stopped to urinate, and they were making obscene comments. A foot patrolman came into the alley, lectured the boys, and sent them home. Before they got to the car, one of the boys began talking in a loud voice again and was arrested for disturbing the peace. After paying a $5 fine at the police station, and with the assurance that there would be no permanent record of the arrest, the boy was released (p. 26).

The boys did not consider any of their activities as "delinquency"; they simply viewed themselves as having a little fun. Likewise, Hanibal townspeople never perceived the Saints as delinquents. The Saints were good boys who just went in for an occasional prank (Chambliss, 1973, p. 27). After all, they were well dressed, were well mannered, and had nice cars.

The Roughnecks. The members of the two gangs were approximately the same age, and both groups engaged in an equal amount of sowing wild oats. The Roughnecks, however, were "not so well-dressed [and] not so well-mannered" as the rich boys (Chambliss, 1973, p. 27). Still, the Roughnecks were not particularly disruptive in school.

During school hours, they did not all hang around together but tended instead to spend most of their time with one or two other members of the gang who were their special buddies. Although every member of the gang attempted to avoid school as much as possible, they were not particularly successful, and most of them attended school with surprising regularity. . . .

The group of boys had a grade point average [of] slightly above "C." No one in the group failed either grade, and no one had better than a "C" average. They were very consistent in their achievement, or at least the teachers were consistent in their perception of the boys' achievement. (p. 28)

The Roughnecks engaged mainly in three types of delinquency: theft, drinking, and fighting (Chambliss, 1973, p. 27). Chambliss (1973) explained their stealing as follows:

Petty stealing was a frequent event for the Roughnecks. Sometimes they stole as a group and coordinated their efforts; other times they stole in pairs. Rarely did they steal alone.

> The thefts ranged from very small things like paperback books, comics, and ball-point pens to expensive items like watches. . . .
>
> Ron committed the most serious of the group's offenses. With an unidentified associate, the boy attempted to burglarize a gasoline station. Although this station had been robbed twice previously in the same month, Ron denied any involvement in either of the other thefts. When Ron and his associate approached the station, the owner was hiding in the bushes beside the station. He fired both barrels of a double-barreled shotgun at the boys. Ron was severely injured; the other boy ran away and was never caught. Though he remained in critical condition for several months, Ron finally recovered and served six months of the following year in reform school. (p. 27)

With reference to the gangs' fighting activities, Chambliss (1973) noted that this was apparent to everyone. At least once a month, the boys got into some type of fight.

> Most fights were scraps between members of the group or involved only one member of the group and some peripheral hanger-on. Only three times in the period of observation did the group fight together: once against a gang from across town, once against two blacks, and once against a group of boys from another school. (p. 27)

Drinking actually was limited among the Roughnecks. This was partially because the boys did not have ready access to liquor. Because they usually did not have cars available, they could not travel very far. Most of the boys had little money, and the bars in town would not serve them. Their major source of alcohol was a local drunk who would buy them a fifth in exchange for some extra money to buy liquor for himself (Chambliss, 1973, p. 28). Chambliss noted, however, that drinking was their most obvious form of delinquency because it would be easy to see when one of the boys hanging out on the street corner was high.

Whereas the Saints had limited contact with the police, the Roughnecks were perceived by the community to be "constantly involved with the police." People said, "Too bad that these boys couldn't behave like the other kids in town, stay out of trouble, be polite to adults, and look to their future" (Chambliss, 1973, p. 27). There was a high level of mutual distrust and dislike between the Roughnecks and the police. The boys believed very strongly that the police were unfair and corrupt (p. 28). Chambliss (1973) pointed out that the sporadic harassment of the group by the police for hanging out on the street corner made no sense to the boys because the "police would come to the corner occasionally and threaten them with arrest for loitering when the night before the boys had been out siphoning gasoline from cars and the police had been nowhere in sight" (p. 28). Chambliss reported that during his observation, each member of the Roughneck gang was arrested at least once. Several of the boys were arrested a number of times and spent at least 1 night in jail. In addition, two of the boys were sentenced to 6 months' incarceration in schools for boys (p. 28).

Chambliss (1973) concluded by arguing that the Roughnecks actually were truant and delinquent less frequently than the Saints. However, because of the economic standing of their families, they were more visible. Through necessity, the Roughnecks congregated in a crowded area where everyone in the community passed frequently including teachers and law enforcement officers. Because the Saints left Hanibal and traveled by cars to Big City, their escapades were relatively invisible. They also had mobility, roaming the city and rarely going to the same area twice (p. 29). Although the Saints rarely fought as the Roughnecks did, the Saints frequently endangered their own and other people's lives with their pranks and by driving after they had been drinking. Community members, according to Chambliss, were not aware of the transgressions of the Saints. Even if the Saints had been less discreet, their delinquencies would have been perceived as less serious than those of the Roughnecks. Chambliss concluded,

> The answer lies in the class structure of American society and the control of legal institutions by those at the top of the class structure. Obviously, no representative of the upper class drew up the operations chart for the police which led them to look in the ghettoes and on street corners—which led them to see the demeanor of lower class youth[s] as troublesome and that of upper middle class youth[s] as tolerable. Rather, the procedures simply developed from experience—experience with irate and influential upper middle class parents insisting that their son's vandalism was simply a prank and his drunkenness only a momentary "sowing of wild oats"—experience with cooperative or indifferent, powerless, lower class parents who acquiesced to the laws' definition of their son's behavior. (p. 30)

Bureaucratic and Governmental Crime

In examining the government's political and economic role in crime, Chambliss (1971, 1989b) contended that traditional research by social scientists distorts the descriptions of crime. By using traditional data sources[19] such as police and court data, Chambliss (1971) asserted that researchers overemphasize street crimes and deemphasize "corruption as an institutionalized component of America's legal-political system" (p. 1150). He further argued that this approach obscures perceptions to the extent that America's law and politics creates and perpetuates organized crime in the major cities. In a similar argument, Chambliss (1989b) claimed that policies of state governments perpetuate criminal behavior of governmental officials on national and international levels. Areas of government corruption and involvement in crime discussed by Chambliss in these two articles included organized crime (Chambliss, 1971), piracy, narcotic and arms smuggling, and assassinations and murder (Chambliss, 1989b).

Organized crime. Although most people view organized crime as something that exists outside law and government, Chambliss (1971) indicated that organized crime is a creation of law and government. He also stated that organized crime is a "hidden but nonetheless integral part of the governmental structure" (p. 1151). He gave the place he studied a pseudonym of Rainfall West and described its focus as follows:

> The relationship between vice and the political and economic system dramatically illustrates the interdependency. The cabal that manages the vices is composed of important businessmen, law enforcement officers, political leaders, and a member of a major trade union. Working for, and with, this cabal of respectable community members is a staff which coordinates the daily activities of prostitution, gambling, bookmaking, the sale and distribution of drugs, and other vices. (p. 1151)

Chambliss further pointed out that there is a lack of consensus regarding the laws prohibiting gambling, prostitution, pornography, drug use, and high interest rates on personal loans. Even persons who agree that such behavior is improper disagree on the appropriate legal response. A major reason for this disagreement is the demand for these services by members of the respectable community. In Rainfall West, prostitutes work out of apartments on the fringes of the lower class area of the city and are proud to report that *all* of their clients are "very important people" (p. 1153). Pornographic films shown in the back rooms of restaurants and game rooms provide more evidence that the principal users of vice in Rainfall West are middle and upper class clientele. Bookmakers also report that the bulk of the "real business" comes from "doctors, lawyers, and dentists" in the city.

> It's the big boys—your professionals—who do the betting down here. Of course, they don't come down themselves; they either send someone or they call up. Most of them call up 'cause I know them or they know Mr. _____ [one of the key figures in the gambling operation]. (p. 1153)

It is no surprise that not all of the businesses and professionals in Rainfall West participate in the vices. Some of the leading citizens sincerely oppose the presence of vice in their city. Members of law enforcement are placed in the middle of the two conflicting demands. On the one hand, they must enforce the law; on the other, there is disagreement over whether or not some acts should be subject to legal sanctions. The officers are placed in a difficult situation when some influential persons in the community insist that the laws be rigorously enforced while others demand that some laws not be enforced, at least against them. Faced with this dilemma, the officers follow the line of least resistance. They use the discretionary power given them as law enforcers. Typically, this means that law enforcers adopt a tolerance policy toward the vices, selectively enforcing these laws only when it is to their advantage to do so (Chambliss, 1971, p. 1154). Chambliss (1971) asserted that the law enforcement system maximizes its visible effectiveness by creating and supporting a show government that manages the vices. Whatever the particulars, the ultimate result is the same.

> A syndicate emerges—composed of politicians, law enforcers, and citizens—capable of supplying and controlling the vices in the city. The most efficient cabal is invariably one that contains representatives of all the leading centers of power. Businessmen must be involved because of their political influence and their ability to control the mass media. . . . The cabal must also have the cooperation of businessmen in procuring the

loans which enable them, individually and collectively, to purchase legitimate businesses as well as to expand the vice enterprises. (p. 1155)

Chambliss reported that in Rainfall West, the goal of maintaining a smooth-functioning organization takes precedence over all other institutional goals (p. 1157). Where conflict arises between the long-range goals of the law and the short-range goal of sustaining the organization, the former lose out, even at the expense of undermining the socially agreed-on purposes for which the organization presumably exists. Chambliss pointed to the links between the elites and the crime cabal. He noted that the most obvious nexus is manifested by the campaign contributions from the economic elite to the political and legal elites. After providing several pages of examples detailing the corruption in Rainfall West, Chambliss asserted, "There is abundant data indicating that what is true in Rainfall West is true in virtually every city in the United States and has been true since at least the early 1900s" (p. 1169). Finally, he declared,

> The study of organized crime is thus a misnomer; the study should consider corruption, bureaucracy, and power. By relying on governmental agencies for their information on vice and the rackets, social scientists and lawyers have inadvertently conibuted to the miscasting of the issue in terms that are descriptively biased and theoretically sterile. . . . As a consequence, the real significance of the existence of syndicates has been overlooked, for instead of seeing these social entities as intimately tied to, and in symbiosis with, the legal and political bureaucracies of the state, they have emphasized the criminality of only a portion of those involved. Such a view contributes little to our knowledge of crime and even less to attempts at crime control. (p. 1173)

Piracy. Chambliss (1989b) cited piracy during the 16th and 17th centuries as an example of state-supported crime. He began his historical analysis of piracy by examining the treatment of the Native American population when explorers from Spain and Portugal came to the "New World" at the close of the 15th century:

> A large, poorly armed Native American population made the creation of a slave labor force for mining and transporting the precious metals an easy task for the better armed Spanish and Portuguese settlers willing to sacrifice human life for wealth. Buttressed by the unflagging belief that they were not only enriching their motherland and themselves but also converting the heathens to Christianity, Spanish and Portuguese colonists seized the opportunity to denude the newly found lands of their wealth and their people. (p. 184)

Chambliss (1989b) asserted that by the 16th and 17th centuries, the European nation-states were involved in intense competition for control of territory and resources. Military power was the basis for expansion and the means by which nation-states protected their borders. One alternative to war for accomplishing this expansion was to enter into an alliance with pirates. France, England, and Holland chose this less risky course (p. 185). Chambliss explained the emergence of piracy as follows:

> A ship laden with gold and silver could not travel fast and was easy prey for marauders. . . . To complicate matters, ships were forced by the prevailing winds and currents to travel in a predictable direction. These conditions provided an open invitation for pirates to exploit the weaknesses of the transporting ships to their advantage. Poverty and a lack of alternatives drove many young men to sea in search of a better life. (p. 185) . . .
>
> [The French government] saw in piracy a source of wealth and a way of neutralizing some of the power of Spain and Portugal. (p. 186)

Chambliss noted that England and Holland were quick to join the French. Piracy remained a crime punishable by death, but some pirates were given license to murder, rape, plunder, destroy, and steal. With the emergence of capitalism during the 1600-1900 period, the essential determinant of a nation's ability to industrialize and to protect its borders was the accumulation of capital. Piracy helped to equalize the balance and reduce the tendency toward the monopolization of capital accumulation (p. 188).

Arms and narcotics smuggling. According to Chambliss (1989b), "Smuggling occurs when a government has successfully cornered the market on some commodity or when it seeks to keep a commodity of another nation from crossing its borders" (p. 188). He contended that these smuggling activities are some of the most important forms of state-organized crime today. Much of the U.S. involvement in narcotics smuggling can be understood as a means of funding the purchase of military weapons for nations and insurgent groups that could not be funded legally through congressional allocations or for which U.S. law prohibited support. For example, Chambliss reported,

> In violation of U.S. law, members of the National Security Council . . ., the Department of Defense, and the CIA [Central Intelligence Agency] carried out a plan to sell millions of dollars worth of arms to Iran and use profits from those sales to support the Contras in Nicaragua. . . . The Boland Amendment, effective in 1985, prohibited any U.S. official from directly or indirectly assisting the Contras. To circumvent the law, a group of intelligence and military officials established a "secret team" of U.S. operatives, including Lt. Colonel Oliver North, Theodore Shackley, Thomas Clines, and Maj. General Richard Secord, among others. . . .
>
> Whether President Reagan or then Vice President Bush were aware of the operations is yet to be established. What cannot be doubted in the face of overwhelming evidence in testimony before the Senate and from court documents is that this group of officials of the state oversaw and coordinated the distribution and sale of weapons to Iran and to the Contras in Nicaragua. These acts were in direct violation of the Illegal Arms Export Control Act, which made the sale of arms to Iran unlawful, and the Boland Amendment, which made it a criminal act to supply the Contras with arms or funds. (p. 192)

Chambliss (1989b) further noted that in 1986, the Reagan administration admitted that Adolfo Chamorro's Contra group, which was supported by the CIA, was helping a Colombian drug trafficker to transport drugs into the United States. Chamorro was arrested for his involvement, and testimony during his trials revealed innumerable instances in which drugs were flown from Central America into the United States with the cooperation of military and CIA personnel (p. 193).

Chambliss (1989b) also provided the following evidence of U.S. participation in the support and transportation of opium during the Vietnam War:

> The French were defeated in Vietnam and withdrew, only to be replaced by the United States. The United States inherited the dependence on opium profits and the cooperation of the hill tribes, who in turn depended on being allowed to continue growing and shipping opium. The CIA went a step further than the French and provided the opium-growing feudal lords in the mountains of Vietnam, Laos, Cambodia, and Thailand with transportation for their opium via Air America, the CIA airline in Vietnam. (p. 189)

State-organized assassinations and murder. Although assassination plots and political murders usually are associated with military dictatorships and European monarchies, Chambliss (1989b) demonstrated that the practice of assassinations has become a tool of international politics that involves modern nation-states of many different types:

> In 1953, the CIA organized and supervised a coup d'état in Iran that overthrew the democratically elected government of Mohammed Mossadegh, who had become unpopular with the United States when he nationalized foreign-owned oil companies. The CIA's coup replaced Mossadegh with Reza Shah Pahlevi, who denationalized the oil companies and, with CIA guidance, established one of the most vicious secret intelligence organizations in the world: SAVAK. In the years to follow, the shah and CIA-trained agents of SAVAK murdered thousands of Iranian citizens. . . .
>
> In 1970, the CIA repeated the practice of overthrowing democratically elected governments that were not completely favorable to U.S. investments. When Salvador Allende was elected president of Chile, the CIA organized a coup that overthrew Allende, during which he was murdered along with the head of the military, General Rene Schneider. Following Allende's overthrow, the CIA trained agents for the Chilean secret service (DINA). DINA set up a team of assassins who could "travel anywhere in the world . . . to carry out sanctions including assassinations." (p. 198)

Chambliss (1989b) also provided more recent examples of U.S. government involvement in foreign assassinations including plots to assassinate Muammar Qaddafi and Fidel Castro (p. 200). Another example of state involvement in murder concerns the environmental organization Greenpeace. When France was planning nuclear testing in the Pacific in 1985, Greenpeace sent its flagship to New Zealand with instructions to sail into the area where the atomic testing was scheduled to occur. The French secret service located the ship before it arrived at the scene and blew up the ship, killing one of the crew members (p. 200). Chambliss suggested that the most flagrant violation of civil rights by U.S. federal agencies is the Federal Bureau of Investigation's (FBI) counterintelligence program COINTELPRO, which was designed to disrupt, harass, and discredit groups that the FBI decided were in some way "un-American." According to the 1976 Church Committee, such groups included the American Civil Liberties Union, antiwar movements, and civil rights organizations. When COINTELPRO was exposed, it disbanded, but illegal surveillance of U.S. citizens continues today (p. 201).

Theoretical analysis of state-organized crime. The starting point for Chambliss's (1989b) theory is the assumption that in every era, political, social, and economic relations contain certain inherent contradictions that produce conflicts and dilemmas for people (p. 201). As is true for much of the work of radical criminologists, Chambliss contended that this conflict centers on the law:

> Law is a two-edged sword; it creates one set of conflicts while it attempts to resolve another. The passage of a particular law or set of laws may resolve conflicts and enhance state control, but it also limits the legal activities of the state.... There is a contradiction, then, between the legal prescriptions and the agreed goals of state agencies. (pp. 201-202) ...
>
> The law is a fundamental cornerstone in creating legitimacy and an illusion (at least) of social order. It claims universal principles that demand some behaviors and prohibit others. (p. 196)

Chambliss (1989b) further contended that the most important characteristics of state-organized crime in the modern world are at one with characteristics of state-organized crime during the early stages of capitalism. The contradictions that are the force behind state-organized crime today are the same as those that were the impetus for piracy in 16th-century Europe. The accumulation of capital determines a nation's power, wealth, and survival today, just as it did 300 years ago (p. 202).

The Law of Vagrancy

In the study of vagrancy laws, Chambliss (1964) explored the relationship between particular laws and the social setting in which these laws emerge and take form. He also attempted to provide an analysis of the law of vagrancy in Anglo-American law. He asserted that the first full-fledged vagrancy statute was passed in England in 1349. This statute stated,

> Because that many valiant beggars, as long as they may live of begging, do refuse to labor, giving themselves to idleness and vice, and sometimes to theft and other abominations; it is ordained, that none, upon pain of imprisonment shall, under the colour of pity or alms, give anything to such which may labour or presume to favour them towards their desires; so that thereby they may be compelled to labour of their necessary living. ...
>
> Every man and woman, of what condition he be, free or bond, able in body, and within the age of threescore years, not living in merchandize nor exercising any craft,

nor having of his own whereon to live, nor proper land whereon to occupy himself . . ., shall be bounded to serve him, which shall him require. . . . And if any refuse, he shall on conviction by two true men . . . be committed to gaol til he find surety to serve.

And if any workman or servant, of what estate or condition he be, retained in any man's service, do depart from the said service without reasonable cause or license before the term agreed on, he shall have pain of imprisonment. (p. 68)

In 1351, this statute was strengthened by the stipulation that "none shall go out of the town where he dwelled in winter, to serve the summer, if he may serve in the same town" (Chambliss, 1964, p. 68). By 1360, the punishment for these acts became imprisonment for 15 days. Chambliss (1964) declared that changes in the vagrancy statutes were a result of changes in the social structure and were designed to force laborers to accept employment at a low wage so as to ensure landowners an adequate supply of labor at a price they could afford. He further explained that the vagrancy statutes represented an attempted substitute for serfdom (p. 70). He argued specifically that the Black Death, which struck England around 1348, was the major impetus for these laws. Because at least 50% of the population of England died during this plague, it decimated the labor force. At that time, the economy in England was dependent on cheap labor. Other changes in the social structure resulted from the crusades and various wars that made money necessary for the landowners. As a result, the lords frequently sold the serfs their freedom (p. 69). The serfs wanted their freedom because the larger towns were becoming more industrialized and could offer both greater personal freedom and a higher standard of living.

The vagrancy statutes have remained in effect since 1349, and the substance of the statutes has changed very little for some time after the first ones that took effect during 1349 to 1351. In 1495, for example, the statute was changed only to make the punishment more severe as follows:

Here it is provided that vagrants shall be "set in stocks, there to remain by the space of three days and three nights, and there to have none other sustenance but bread and water and after the said three days and nights, to be had out and set at large, and then to be commanded to avoid the town. (Chambliss, 1964, p. 70)

Chambliss (1964) also found that the vagrancy laws actually had a period of dormancy during which the statutes were neither applied nor altered. The processes of social change in the culture, and the trend away from serfdom and into a "free" economy, deterred the usefulness of these statutes (p. 71). By the 16th century, there was a shift of focus in the vagrancy laws from the earlier concern with laborers to a concern with criminal activities. The first statute (in 1530) to actually focus on criteria for adjudging someone a vagrant and also to increase the punishment for vagrancy stated,

If any person, being whole and mighty in body, and able to labour, be taken in begging, or be vagrant and can give no reckoning how he lawfully gets his living . . ., and all other idle persons going about, some of them using divers and subtle crafty and unlawful games and plays, and some of them feigning themselves to have knowledge of . . . crafty sciences . . ., shall be punished as provided. . . . The offender shall be had to the

next market town, or other place where they (the constables) shall think most conve-
nient, and there to be tied to the end of a cart naked, and to be beaten with whips
throughout the same market town or other place, till his body be bloody by reason of
such whipping. (p. 71) . . .

But, for those who use "divers and subtil crafty and unlawful games and plays,"
etc., the punishment is ". . . whipping at two days together in manner aforesaid." . . .
For the second offense, such persons are: . . . scourged two days, and the third day to be
put upon the pillory from nine of the clock till eleven before noon of the same day and
to have one of his ears cut off.

And if he offend the third time: ". . . to have like punishment with whipping, standing on the pillory, and to have his other ear cut off." (p. 72)

Chambliss reported that just 5 years later, the statute for the first time made a person
who repeated the crime of vagrancy a felon, and the punishment of death was applied
to the crime of vagrancy. According to Chambliss, the statutory changes were a direct
response to changes in England's social structure during this period. With an increased emphasis on commerce and industry in England at the turn of the 16th century came considerable traffic bearing valuable items that needed protection. This situation not only called for the enforcement of existing laws but also called for the
creation of new laws that would facilitate the control of persons preying on merchants transporting goods. The vagrancy laws, therefore, were revived to fulfill this
purpose (p. 72). The new focal concern resulted in the statute of 1547, which stated,

Whoever man or woman, being not lame, impotent, or so aged or diseased that he or
she cannot work, not having whereon to live, shall be lurking in any house, or loitering
or idle wandering by the highway side, or in the streets, cities, towns, or villages, not
applying themselves to some honest labour, and so continuing for three days; or running away from their work; every such person shall be taken for a vagabond. And . . .
upon conviction of two witnesses . . ., the same loiterer [shall] be marked with a hot
iron in the breast with the letter V, and adjudged him to the person bringing him, to be
his slave for two years. (p. 73)

Chambliss asserted that the major emphasis in all the statutes always was on the "refusal to labor" or "begging." The "criminalistic" aspect of such persons was relatively unimportant (p. 75).

Finally, Chambliss (1989b) turned to the vagrancy laws in the United States and
noted that the 18th-century vagrancy laws in England were adopted by the United
States. There were some exceptions, for example, Maryland's statutes restricting vagrancy laws to "free" Negroes. For all states, according to Chambliss, vagrancy laws
were even more concerned with the control of criminals and undesirables than had
been the case in England (p. 75). The vagrancy laws in the United States have been
used principally as a mechanism for clearing the streets of the derelicts who inhabit
the skid rows of large urban areas. They also have been applied to prostitutes and
other persons deemed by the police and courts to be either actively or peripherally involved in criminal activities. Chambliss further suggested that the laws are used to arrest and confine the "down-and-outers" who inhabit certain sections of our larger

cities. The laws also were used to control the movement of workers during the Depression years and in California to restrict the admission of migrants from other states (p. 76).

Chambliss (1989b) concluded this study by asserting that the functioning of the police and courts and the creation and application of procedural and substantive laws are significantly related to the cultural needs of a specific time and place. The vagrancy laws further demonstrate the importance of vested interest groups in the emergence and/or alteration of laws (p. 77). Chambliss's analysis of the vagrancy laws, therefore, is inconsistent with the perception of many mainstream criminological theorists that the law is simply a reflection of public opinion.

Critique of Chambliss

Although this has not been an exhaustive coverage of the works of Chambliss, it demonstrated his many significant contributions to our understanding of crime. However, Chambliss has received only limited coverage in current theoretical texts (Akers, 1997; Lilly et al., 1995; Martin et al., 1990). The most interesting and controversial discussions of his works have been published in the journal *Criminology*. Most of the criticisms have centered around his work on the vagrancy laws. Klockars (1979) referred to Chambliss's original 1964 article as a "little classic" (p. 487). Adler (1989a) suggested, "The debate over the history of vagrancy began more than two decades ago when William Chambliss (1964) published a seminal article on vagrancy statutes and the evolution of criminal law" (p. 210). Adler went on to state that the seminal article has been "long considered one of the most persuasive statements of the Marxist position" (p. 210). Support for this is found in the fact that the article was included in all of Chambliss's edited works as well as numerous other edited publications.

Probably the weakest challenge to Chambliss's works was made by Klockars (1979), who attacked Chambliss on technical grounds (pp. 488-489). Chambliss (1969, 1975) published reprints of the article in his edited works in 1969 and 1975. However, in 1975, he made minor revisions in his theoretical interpretations of the vagrancy laws and simply stated "by permission of the author and the publisher." Akers (1979), writing in the same issue of *Criminology* as did Klockars, noted the following:

> I have known Bill Chambliss, a theorist prominently featured in the paper by Carl Klockars, for some thirteen years. He was one of my closest colleagues during the beginning period of my professional career, and I learned nearly as much from him as I did from Quinney. . . . I have been greatly influenced by all of these men not only by reading what they have written (which in each case has been influential and prolific) but also by my personal contacts with them over the years. Each is a recognized leading figure in the discipline, and I count each as a friend. (p. 529) . . .
>
> Moreover, I am not sure what is proven by detailing the change or by showing that Chambliss, who has moved less in that direction, changed some sentences in his vagrancy article in its latest reprint. Certainly change is allowable, and I don't believe

that Chambliss made the changes to correspond with his latest stance to mislead the reader. More to the point, this says nothing about the validity or value of the new stance. The question is, did the change take place because of new evidence or lack of empirical validity of the old perspective? (p. 539)

Adler (1989a) began his article by recognizing the influence of Chambliss's article:

> For Chambliss (1964, 1984), the "vested economic concerns of a ruling elite defined class interests. In part, his article, which continues to be cited as an authoritative source, has been so influential because his research extended far beyond theoretical formulations. Rather, he supported his model by examining the relationship between class concerns and vagrancy law since the fourteenth century. Thus, his argument seemed to be solidly grounded in historical fact. (p. 210)

Adler then proceeded to challenge Chambliss's work by using recent historical scholarship. He argued that medieval historians have discovered that serfdom was waning well before the Black Death. He claimed that most medieval historians have found that serfdom was in sharp decline by the late 13th century and that the works of these historians undercut Chambliss's argument (p. 211). It is interesting, as pointed out by Chambliss (1989a, p. 231) in his response to Adler, that Adler never examined the original vagrancy statutes himself but rather relied on other historians to criticize Chambliss's interpretation of the statutes. One of Adler's (1989a) major criticisms was that Chambliss analyzed the social context of vagrancy laws in one-dimensional terms—economics/class (p. 223). Adler claimed that Chambliss's argument was flawed and that continued dependence on this flawed argument to support class-based analyses challenges the authority of Marxist criminological theory (p. 223).

In his response to Adler, Chambliss (1989a) stated throughout that Adler not only misinterpreted his work but also misrepresented much of the Marxist perspective. In addition, Chambliss suggested that the vagrancy article was the first in a series of articles he had published on lawmaking and that if Adler had read further,

> [Adler] would have discovered that the theory of law creation which I am developing, but which was not articulated at the time I wrote the vagrancy article, argues that the emergence of vagrancy law, in common with other laws, is the result of a process in which lawmakers attempt to deal with the contradictions, conflicts, and dilemmas inherent in the political, economic, and social relations of a particular historical period. (p. 233)

Finally, in a rejoinder to Chambliss's response, Adler (1989b) accused Chambliss of choosing to "disregard the findings of the 81 historical studies to which I referred" (p. 239). In reading the two essays, one gets the impression that the two authors are not communicating. Adler failed to respond to Chambliss's criticism that Adler relied on secondary historical sources without reading the original vagrancy statutes, and Chambliss did not acknowledge the historical sources used by Adler in his first article. As pointed out in the biographical inset on Chambliss (Inset 8.3), he has received significant recognition for his scholarship during recent years. Chambliss received a

Fulbright research fellowship, received the 1986 Bruce Smith Award (of the Academy of Criminal Justice) for contributions to criminology and criminal justice, and served as president of the American Society of Criminology during the 1989-1990 period.

Jeffrey H. Reiman (1942-)

Jeffrey Reiman was born in Brooklyn, New York, in 1942. Although Reiman's (1995) book, *The Rich Get Richer and the Poor Get Prison* (originally published in 1979), has been widely used in criminology/criminal justice classes and is now in its fifth edition, Reiman is primarily a philosopher. He received his B.A. in philosophy from Queens College in 1963 and his Ph.D. in philosophy from Pennsylvania State University in 1968. He currently is William Fraser McDowell Professor of Philosophy at the American University in Washington, D.C. (p. 221). He was a Fulbright scholar in India before joining the Center for the Administration of Justice at the American University in 1970. After several years of holding a joint appointment in the Justice Program and the Department of Philosophy and Religion, he joined the philosophy and religion faculty full-time in 1988. His major publication in criminology has been *The Rich Get Richer and the Poor Get Prison*. Excerpts from this book have appeared in numerous edited books. In addition, he has authored or co-authored several articles of importance to criminological theory.

A Radical Perspective on Crime

Throughout his writings on the criminal justice system, Reiman asserted that the ideology of criminal justice places the emphasis on the individual and the poor to divert attention away from the real dangers of society. Reiman (1993) claimed that when the justice system concentrates on the individual wrongdoers,

> it diverts our attention away from our institutions, away from consideration of whether our institutions themselves are wrong or unjust or indeed "criminal." ... The criminal law is put forth as politically neutral, as the minimum requirements of any society, as the minimum obligations that any member owes his fellows to make social life of any decent sort possible. ...
>
> By virtue of its focus on *individual* criminals, it diverts us from the evils of the social order. By virtue of its presumed neutrality, it transforms the established social (and economic) order from being merely *one* form of society open to critical comparison with others into the conditions of any social order and thus immune from criticism. (p. 141)

Reiman further argued that this approach brands the individual who attacks the established institutions as one who has declared war on organized society and who must, therefore, be met with the weapons of war. He further stated that to look only at the individual responsibility is to look away from social responsibility to the individual. He contended that "justice is a two-way street—but criminal justice is a one-way street" (Reiman, 1993, p. 142; 1995, p. 156). This means that when a system holds an individual responsible for a crime, it is implicitly conveying the message that the social conditions in which the crime occurred are not responsible for the crime, and "it literally acquits the society of criminality or injustice" (Reiman, 1993, p. 142).

Reiman (1993) further contended that in a competitive industrialized society such as ours, the assumption that economic success is potentially available to all actually produces crime:

> But by holding individuals responsible for this crime, those who enjoy that high standard of living can . . . reap the benefits of the competition for success and escape the responsibility of paying for the costs of that competition. By holding the poor crook legally and morally guilty, the rest of society not only passes the costs of competition on to the poor, but they effectively deny that they (the affluent) are the beneficiaries of an economic system that exacts such a high toll in frustration and suffering. (p. 145)

Reiman and Headlee (1981) also differentiated between radical criminology and Marxist criminology as follows:

> Briefly put, radical criminology is the view that class societies, like capitalism, rest disproportionately greater power in the hands of some ruling group, who then use that power to shape criminal laws and criminal justice policy to serve their own aims while putting this forth as the public interest. Radical criminology studies, in short, the abuse of power by the powerful. . . .
>
> Marxism studies society, capitalism in particular, as a structure of production which itself determines what aims and intentions individual agents in that structure will have and what they will perceive as in the public interest. (p. 26) . . .
>
> Marxism is a theory of how societies function, how they reproduce themselves, and how they are transformed. Its central proposition is that these things can be best understood by looking at the way in which society is organized for the production of material life. (p. 27)

Reiman and Headlee, then, suggested that in the current economic crisis, radical/Marxist theories explain the existing criminal justice policy. They contended that during times of economic crisis, the crimes of the poor are continuous, with acts done at all levels of society. They observed that during such a crisis, people at all levels of society are grabbing for the declining surplus but that those with power are able to use the law and its institutions to do their grabbing and to protect the resources they have (p. 41). Most of Reiman's work in criminology was a critique of the failures of the criminal justice system to solve the crime problem. Part of this failure, he argued, is the result of criminal justice policies that discriminate against the poor. In his detailed examination of the justice system, he provided data to support this point.

The Criminal Justice System

In describing the failures of the criminal justice system, Reiman uses the terms "pyrrhic defeat theory" and the "carnival mirror of crime." Both concepts point to the bias of the criminal justice system against the poor and against individuals.

The pyrrhic defeat theory. Reiman (1995) suggested, "On the whole, most of the system's practices make more sense if we look at them as ingredients in an attempt to maintain rather than to reduce crime" (p. 4). He further argued that the criminal justice system fails to reduce crime while making it appear as though crime is the work of the poor. He called this approach to crime the pyrrhic defeat theory. A pyrrhic victory is a military victory purchased at such a cost in troops and treasure that it amounts to a defeat (p. 4). He further asserted that the pyrrhic defeat theory explains the current shape of our failing criminal justice policy as follows:

> This failure is really *three* failures that work together. First, there is the failure to implement policies that stand a good chance of reducing crime and the harm it causes. . . . Second, there is the failure to identify as crimes the harmful acts of the rich and powerful. . . . Third, there is the failure to eliminate economic bias in the criminal justice system, so that the poor continue to have a substantially greater chance than better off people of being arrested, charged, convicted, and penalized for committing the acts that are treated as crimes. (pp. 149-150)

Reiman argued that the effect of the current criminal justice policy is to narrow the public's conception of dangerous crime to the acts of the poor. He also presented several proposals for a justice system that would maintain and encourage a stable and visible class of criminals as follows:

> *First.* It would be helpful to have laws on the books against drug use or prostitution or gambling—laws that prohibit acts that have no unwilling victims. . . .
> *Second.* It would be good to give police, prosecutors, and judges broad discretion to decide who got arrested, who got charged, and who got sentenced to prison. . . .
> *Third.* The prison experience should be not only painful but also demeaning. The pain of loss of liberty might deter future crime. But demeaning and emasculating prisoners by placing them in an enforced childhood characterized by no privacy and no control over their time and actions, as well as by the constant threat of rape or assault, is sure to overcome any deterrent effect. . . . Indeed, by humiliating and brutalizing prisoners, we can be sure to increase their potential for aggressive violence.
> *Fourth.* It goes almost without saying that prisoners should neither be trained in a marketable skill nor provided with a job after release. Of course, their prison records should stand as a perpetual stigma to discourage employers from hiring them. . . .
> *Fifth.* The ex-offenders' sense that they will always be different from "decent citizens," that they can never finally settle their debt to society, should be reinforced by the following means. They should be deprived for the rest of their lives of rights such as the right to vote. They should be harassed by police as "likely suspects" and be subject to the whims of parole officers. . . .

> In short, *asked to design a system that would maintain and encourage the exis-*
> *tence of a stable and visible "class of criminals," we "constructed" the American crim-*
> *inal justice system!* (pp. 2-3)

Thus, Reiman suggested that the cost in human lives of the justice system policies results in a pyrrhic defeat approach to crime.[20]

The carnival mirror of crime. In his analogy of the carnival mirror of crime, Reiman
suggested that crime is created by the decisions made throughout the criminal justice system, beginning with the criminal law, police, courts, and corrections. He
was not stating that the criminal law creates crime but rather that it simply "mir-
rors" real dangers that threaten us. Reiman pointed out that this does not mean
that the officials in the criminal justice system create criminals but rather that they
react to real dangers in society. The criminal justice system is just a mirror of the
real dangers in our midst—"*or so we are told*" (Reiman, 1990, p. 40; 1995, p. 51).

Reiman, however, questioned the accuracy of this mirror. The more misshapen a
mirror is, the more the distorted image it shows is created by the mirror, not by the reality reflected. It is in this sense that Reiman contended that crime is created. The
faces that appear in this mirror are poor, young, urban, disproportionately black
males who appear in the arrest statistics of the FBI's Uniform Crime Reports as well
as court and corrections data. These people make up the official core of the enemy
forces in the war against crime. Reiman (1990) explained this distorted mirror of
crime as follows:

> It is not my view that this reality is created out of nothing. The mugger, the rapist, the
> murderer, the burglar, [and] the robber all pose a definite threat to our well-being, and
> they ought to be dealt with in ways that effectively reduce that threat.... Of central im-
> portance, however, is that the threat posed by the typical criminal is not the greatest
> threat to which we are exposed.... We have a greater chance ... of being killed or dis-
> abled, for example, by an occupational injury or disease, by unnecessary surgery, or by
> shoddy emergency medical services than by aggravated assault or even homicide! Yet
> even though these threats to our well-being are graver than that posed by our poor,
> young, urban black males, they do not show up in the FBI's index of serious crimes....
> *They never become part of the reality reflected in the criminal justice mirror.* ...
>
> Similarly, the general public loses more money *by far* ... from price-fixing and mo-
> nopolistic practices and from consumer deception and embezzlement than from all the
> property crimes in the FBI's index combined. Yet these far more costly acts are either
> not criminal, or if technically criminal, [then] not prosecuted, or if prosecuted, [then]
> not punished, or if punished, [then punished] only mildly.... *Their faces rarely appear*
> *in the criminal justice mirror, although the danger they pose is at least as great [as,] and*
> *often greater than, those who do.* (pp. 44-45)

When Reiman stated that crime is created, he meant not just that the label "crime" is
applied but also that it is applied inappropriately. By referring to crime as created, he
pointed to human actors, rather than to objective dangers, as determining the shape
of the reality of crime in society. He further asserted that emphasizing the "one-on-

one" crimes of the typical criminal diverts attention away from the mine disasters and other occupational injuries caused by violations of safety regulations. Deaths from unsafe working conditions are called "accidents," not murders.

The absentee killer. Reiman (1990) used the mine disaster as an example of an absentee killer. He suggested that what keeps a mine disaster from being identified as a mass murder is the fact that it is not "one-on-one harm." According to Reiman, a mine executive does not want his or her employees to be harmed (p. 51). What the executive wants is "maximum profits at minimum costs." If 26 workers die because the executive cut corners on safety, then the executive is not a killer but rather is just doing his or her job. The executive is, at most, responsible for an "indirect harm." Reiman distinguished the "one-on-one murderer" from the "absentee killer" as follows:

> The one who kills in a heated argument kills from passion. . . . The one he killed was someone he knew, a specific person who at the time seemed to him to be the embodiment of that [which] frustrates him, someone whose very existence makes life unbearable. I do not mean to suggest that this is true of all killers, although there is reason to believe it is true of many. . . . What it does do, however, is suggest that the killer's action, arising out of passion, does not show general disdain for the lives of his fellows. Here is where he is different from the doer of *indirect harm.* Our absentee killer intended harm to no one in particular, but he *knew his acts were likely to harm someone.* . . . Nor can our absentee killer claim that "he was not himself." His act is done not out of passion but [rather] out of cool reckoning. . . . In his willingness to jeopardize the lives of unspecified others who pose him no real or imaginary threat in order to make a few dollars, he shows his general disdain for all his fellow human beings. In this light, it is surely absurd to hold that he is less evil than one who kills from passion. (p. 54)

In addition, Reiman pointed to diseases such as black lung disease among coal miners and acute byssinosis or brown lung disease among American cotton textile workers. He also pointed to workers installing insulation who die from exposure to asbestos fibers. Still others die from cancer and occupationally related skin disease (p. 62). All of these could be avoided, or at least minimized, by implementing better safety regulations. The more general population is exposed to diseases and death resulting from various forms of air pollution, cigarette smoking, and food additives (p. 68).[21]

The rich get richer and the poor get prison. After establishing the economic bias in the creation of crime, Reiman (1995) turned to the criminal justice system processing of those who have violated the law. He contended that the "weeding out of the wealthy" starts at the very entrance to the criminal justice system.

> Not only are the poor arrested and charged out of proportion to their numbers for the kinds of crimes poor people generally commit—burglary, robbery, assault, and so forth—but when we reach the kinds of crimes poor people almost never have the opportunity to commit, such as antitrust violations, industrial safety violations, embezzlement, and serious tax evasion, the criminal justice system shows an increasingly be-

nign and merciful face. The more likely that a crime is the type committed by middle and upper class people, the less likely that it will be treated as a criminal offense. (p. 109)

Reiman proceeded to trace the bias in the criminal justice system in the conviction and sentencing[22] of legal offenders. Again, he contended that this bias against the poor has an important "bonus" for the rich. The identification of crime with poverty paints the picture that the threat to decent middle Americans comes from those below them on the economic ladder, not from those above them. For this to happen, the system not only must identify crime and poverty but also *must fail to reduce crime so that it remains a real threat* (p. 161).

To "rehabilitate" criminal justice and protect American society, Reiman (1995) made some very controversial policy recommendations:

We must put an end to the crime-producing poverty in our midst.

Let the crime fit the harm and the punishment fit the crime.

We must legalize the production and sale of "illicit drugs" and treat addiction as a medical problem.

We must develop correctional programs that promote rather than undermine personal responsibility, and we must offer ex-offenders real preparation and a real opportunity to make it as law-abiding citizens.

We must enact and vigorously enforce stringent gun controls.

We must narrow the range in which police officers, prosecutors, and judges exercise discretion, and we must develop procedures to hold them accountable to the public for the fairness and reasonableness of their decisions.

We must transform the equal right to counsel into the right to equal counsel as far as it is possible.

We must establish a more just distribution of wealth and income and make equal opportunity a reality for all Americans. (pp. 183-193)

Critique of Reiman

Reiman (1995) provided a substantial amount of data in his book, *The Rich Get Richer and the Poor Get Prison,* to support his contention that the criminal justice system has an economic bias against the poor. He also presented a convincing argument that the criminal justice system has failed to reduce crime. Yet, like other scholars such as Cavan, Frazier, and Du Bois, Reiman's works have received little, if any, attention from current theorists (Akers, 1997; Curran and Renzetti, 1994; Lilly et al., 1995; Williams and McShane, 1994). Perhaps this is because his book has been used primarily as an undergraduate text and, therefore, would not stimulate much research interest. In addition, most undergraduate criminology majors align themselves personally and politically with the most conservative aspects of criminal justice

Table 8.1 Conflict/Radical/Marxist Theory

Karl Marx (1818-1883)	Willem Bonger (1876-1940)	W. E. B. Du Bois (1868-1963)	Edwin Sutherland (1883-1950)
Richard Quinney (1934-)	William Chambliss (1933-)		Jeffrey Reiman (1942-)
Feminist Theory (1980s-2000s)		Peacemaking (1990s-2000s)	

policy (Wilson and Moyer, 1992, p. 281). Therefore, these undergraduate students tend to resist Reiman's radical perspective of crime and criminal justice.

Finally, the fact that Reiman is a philosopher by training, and most of his writing has been published in philosophy, might account for the failure of his works to receive more recognition among criminologists. His accomplishments within philosophy, however, would suggest that his works are highly regarded in philosophy. It is time for criminologists to acknowledge the important contributions that Reiman has made to criminological theory and justice policy.

Summary

This is not an exhaustive presentation of the conflict/radical/Marxist perspective on criminological theory. As a group, the theorists included in this chapter provide a solid knowledge and understanding of the current conflict perspective. The historical development and the contributions of this perspective to current and future theories are illustrated in Table 8.1. They have analyzed the crime problem with an emphasis on economics and race as a major determinant of how crime is defined. This chapter also provided insight into the policies implemented within the criminal justice system. Unlike the Chicago School with its diversity of methodologies, the conflict theorists as a whole rely primarily on historical documents to support their theoretical arguments. Thus, they are subject to criticism by mainstream criminologists that conflict theories cannot be validated using the social science definitions of theories by scholars such as Homans (1964) and Merton (1968b).

Among the authors included in this chapter, Sutherland, Quinney, and Chambliss have received the most criticism and the greatest recognition for their scholarship. Critics have pointed to these authors' lack of empirical evidence and their emphasis on class as a major explanation for how crime is created and laws are enforced. In addition, feminists have been concerned with these authors' failure to include women in their analyses. Whereas there were many factors that led to the emergence of feminist criminological theory, the criticisms of conflict theory certainly were a major force in the development of feminist theory. These issues are presented in Chapter 9.

Notes

1. In this article, Bohm (1982) discussed the similarities and differences among radical (critical), conflict, Marxist, socialist, and "new" criminology. In this chapter, however, the discussion is limited to radical (critical), conflict, and Marxist criminology.

2. Mehring (1951) presented a somewhat different explanation for this conversion. He noted that the adoption of Christianity by Heinrich Marx for himself and his family in 1824 must be understood as an act of "civilized progress for the freer spirits of Judaism" (p. 3). He further stated, "There can be no doubt that Heinrich Marx had attained that humanistic culture which freed him entirely from all Jewish prejudices" (p. 4).

3. Because the 1932 Uniform Crime Reports in the United States did not include data on race and crime, Bonger used prison and police statistics.

4. This idea was later developed by Sutherland in his study of white collar crime and by Cressey (1953) in his book, *Other People's Money*.

5. Additional details on Du Bois and his works may be found in Gabbidon (1996).

6. Details of Sutherland's differential association theory and the professional thief were included in Chapter 3. His white collar crime works are presented here as groundwork for later conflict theory.

7. For details on these criticisms, see Tappan (1947).

8. This Howard Becker should not be confused with Howard S. Becker, the interactionist and graduate of the University of Chicago who was discussed in Chapter 7.

9. At the plenary session of 1984 American Society of Criminology (ASC) meeting in Cincinnati, Ohio, where Quinney received the Sutherland Award, Quinney gave a nontraditional speech titled *Myth and Art of Criminology*. This speech began with the playing of Willie Nelson's song, "On the Road Again." Quinney's speech was built around this theme, with only an occasional mention of crime or criminology. Although the ASC opted to print only excerpts from the speech, the speech was published in its entirety in *Legal Studies Forum* (Quinney, 1985).

10. Quinney described this transition in his article, "There's a Lot of Folks Grateful to the Lone Ranger," published in *The Insurgent Sociologist* (Quinney, 1973). Again, this was an unusual and nontraditional piece. However, he described his change in perspective in this article as follows: "But the bad guys in my criminology have changed of late. Earlier, I was in pursuit of the criminal. As a life's work, like the Lone Ranger, I chose to fight the bad guys, *turning the blinding light of justice on criminals. . . .* The criminal consisted of anyone who violated the law—that is, anyone who violated laws that preserved the American way of life. Someplace along the way, however, it occurred to me that there were others who were violating criminal laws such as businessmen and politicians. But this was only a transition period, for soon I realized that the really bad guys were those who make laws to protect their own selfish interests, those who oppress others" (p. 60).

11. In a 1983 presentation before the faculty at Northern Illinois University, Quinney stated, "Everything that I am writing today builds on my previous work." This suggests that Quinney had a theoretical and research agenda with a purpose and that he is a scholar who continues to grow intellectually.

12. Some criminologists credit Austin Turk with establishing a theory that set the course of criminological theory during the 1970s and 1980s. Certainly, Turk and Chambliss entered criminology from graduate school at about the same time, and Quinney, Turk, and

Chambliss shared many similar ideas on criminological theory. For a more detailed discussion of Turk's works, see Lilly, Cullen, and Ball (1995, pp. 142-149).

13. Most flowcharts for the criminal justice system found in introductory texts begin with crimes known to the police. Quinney was pointing out that the first step in the creation of a criminal act is the legislation of a law defining an act as a crime. This first proposition is very similar to Becker's assertion in Chapter 7 that society creates deviance by defining an act as deviant and applying the label.

14. For a detailed listing of topics for graduate student fellowships and research grants for faculty, see Quinney's (1974) *Critique of the Legal Order* (pp. 34-42). These topics emphasize crime control and law and order.

15. This reference to women as houseworkers is one of the few times that Quinney mentioned women in his writings prior to the 1990s.

16. For a more thorough discussion of the criticisms of Quinney and of radical criminology, see the 1979 issue of *Criminology,* Vol. 16, No. 4. This entire issue was devoted to radical criminology.

17. Unfortunately, Chambliss provided no details regarding the methods he used during these 2 years of observation.

18. Chambliss used "Big Town" and "Big City" interchangeably in this article in discussing the Saints' weekend activities.

19. In the publication of government corruption and organized crime, Chambliss (1971) gathered data over a period of 7 years, from 1962 to 1969. "Most came from interviews with persons who were members of either the vice syndicate, law enforcement agencies, or both. The interviews ranged in intensity from casual conversations to extended interviewing, complete with tape-recording, at frequent intervals over the full seven years of the study. In addition, I participated in many, though not all, of the vices that comprise the cornerstone upon which corruption of the law enforcement agencies is laid" (p. 1151). Chambliss continued this line of research and broadened it to the international level (Chambliss, 1989b). This quest led him to research in Sweden, Nigeria, Thailand, and the Americas. With reference to his methods, he wrote, "My methods were adapted to meet the demands of the various situations I encountered. Interviews with people at all levels of criminal, political, and law enforcement agencies provided the primary database, but they were supplemented always with data from official records, government reports, congressional hearings, newspaper accounts (when they could be checked for accuracy), archives, and special reports" (p. 183).

20. After publishing the first edition, Reiman stated clearly in the later editions that "I am not maintaining that the rich and powerful intentionally make the system fail to gather up the resulting benefits" (Reiman, 1990, p. 6; 1995, p. 6). Instead, Reiman (1990) stated, "A closer approximation is this: The criminal justice system we have is characterized by beliefs about what is criminal and about what to do about crime that predate[s] industrial society. Rather than being anyone's conscious plan, the system reflects attitudes so deeply embedded in tradition as to appear natural" (p. 6). Reiman (1995) stated, "My view is rather that the system has grown up piecemeal over time and usually with the best of intentions. The unplanned and unintended overall result is a system that not only fails to reduce crime but does so in a way that serves the interests of the rich and powerful. One consequence of this fact is that those who could change the system feel no need to do so. And thus it keeps on rolling along" (p. 6).

21. Reiman provided extensive data analysis to support his contentions that the "crimes" of the rich do as much or more harm as do the one-on-one crimes of the young, poor, urban, mostly black males (see, e.g., Reiman, 1995, p. 80, Table 3a).

22. Evidence for this bias in sentencing was provided by Reiman (1995, p. 125, Table 5; pp. 128- 131, Tables 6-7).

DISCUSSION QUESTIONS

1. What are the distinctions among the ideas and concepts of radical, conflict, and Marxist perspectives of crime and society as discussed by Bohm? What is the significance of these differences?

2. Who had the greater impact on current conflict/radical theorists, Marx or Bonger? Support your answer by explaining the contributions of each and the specific ideas of later theorists that demonstrate the contributions.

3. How much influence do you think the personal biographies of Bonger and Du Bois had on their writings about race and crime? Explain the differences in their biographies and their writings. What can we learn from these two scholars about our own perspectives of crime and criminals?

4. Based on the theories presented in this chapter, how would you explain the overwhelming numbers of poor and racial/ethnic minorities within our prison populations today? How does this explanation differ from a functionalist and/or a Classical School perspective?

5. Sutherland's study of white collar crime was a pioneer work in conflict theory. What do you think was his influence on later conflict theorists? Be specific and support your answer.

6. What was Quinney's most significant contribution to conflict and/or Marxist theory? Explain the contribution and justify your answer.

7. Chambliss made some very strong criticisms of those in governmental and bureaucratic power. Describe and evaluate some of these criticisms.

8. In light of evidence in Chambliss's writings regarding the government's involvement in smuggling drugs and arms, evaluate claims made by some organizations that the U.S. government encouraged the infiltration of drugs into this country to raise money for the smuggling of arms not authorized by Congress.

9. Feminists have criticized conflict theorists for ignoring women. How would a feminist perspective change the writings of Reiman or Quinney? Be specific.

9 CHAPTER

Feminist Criminology

Feminist scholars (Daly and Chesney-Lind, 1988; Moyer, 1985b, 1992; Naffine, 1996; Simpson, 1989; Wilson and Rigsby, 1975) have noted the "androcentric"[1] nature of criminology. That is, the study of crime and the justice process is shaped by male experiences and understandings of the social world (Simpson, 1989, p. 605). Studies based on male perspectives form the core of "general" theories of crime/deviance without taking female experience as crime participant or victim into account. The inadequacies of criminological theories based on biased research that ignores women has been well documented by Leonard (1982) and Naffine (1987). Furthermore, Simpson (1989) indicated that when research has included female offenders and victims of crime, all too often the studies have fallen prey to sexism or, in its extreme form, misogyny.

In a recent work, the Australian feminist scholar Ngaire Naffine challenged the male empiricist's commitment to a traditional research ideal of objectivity (Naffine, 1996). She further questioned the male empiricist's assumption that it is possible for the researcher to get himself or herself out of the field of vision—out of the line of inquiry—when studying an object. A related assumption that Naffine disputed is that criminologists studying crime are interchangeable because they absorb, assimilate, and constitute knowledge in essentially similar ways (p. 22). That is, "the particular identity of the person doing the particular processing is less critical as the laws of the mind are universal" (p. 23). The ideal of the neutral scientific inquirer, according to Naffine, has led to sloppiness (p. 27). Instead of considering the characteristics of the inquirer and how he or she might entail a certain worldview, the inquirer has simply been expunged, having been deemed to be neutral.

Naffine (1996) also criticized the male criminologist for his choice of subjects to study:

> He conveys the impression that somehow it is rational, and perhaps even more scientifically controlled, to look at one sex only, but then he makes little of either the limitations or the interesting specificity of his research. Studying men, it seems, is just what criminologists do. My objection . . . is therefore to bad science on (conventional) science's own terms. (p. 26)

Daly and Chesney-Lind (1988) also noted,

> One consequence of male-centered (or androcentric) systems of knowledge is inaccurate readings of human history, evolution, and behavior, although these are presented as objective and authoritative depictions of the human condition. The central problem is that men's experiences are taken as the norm and are generalized to the population. (pp. 499-500)

Yet, Daly and Chesney-Lind asserted that when feminists analyze women's situation and the ways in which gender relations structure social life, they are accused by male criminologists of having a "narrow focus on women." Although feminists might displace men as the central (or sole) actors and might give more attention to women, they do not ignore men and masculinity.

> This approach spawns a perception by men that they are being neglected, misunderstood, or cast as the ignominious "other," a reaction akin to that of white people toward critical analyses of race or ethnic relations. Both perceptions express a sense of entitlement about *whose* social reality is worthy of description and explanation, and *who* can be trusted to get it right. (p. 500) . . .
>
> The irony is that feminist scholarship is characterized as being only about women or as hopelessly biased toward women when in fact the project is to describe and change both men's and women's lives. By contrast, nonfeminist scholarship is more narrow, focusing as it does on the lives and concerns of men without problematizing gender relations or men as a social group. (p. 501)

In addition to being responsible for biased research that has led to inadequate theories of crime and warped criminal justice policies, male criminologists also have managed to control the academic curriculum and publications. This "malestream" perspective of research, theories, academic curriculum, and criminal justice policies has been sustained by male gatekeepers (Moyer, 1985a, 1986). There has been an abundance of feminist scholarship (Eigenberg and Baro, 1992; Wilson, 1991; Wilson and Moyer, 1992; Wright, 1987) providing evidence of gatekeeping practices that have maintained this male dominance in the academic curriculum and publications.

The Historical Background

The biased research and gatekeeping described heretofore is not unique to criminology, although criminology is one of the most male-dominated academic disciplines. This section examines both the history of feminism and the historical development of feminist criminology.

The Feminist Movement

Some feminist scholars, such as Daly and Chesney-Lind[2] (1988, p. 497) and Smart (1995, p. 165), have referred to a "second-wave" feminism as occurring during the 1960s, and other feminists on occasion have referred to second-wave feminism as occurring among the young during the 1990s.[3] However, this presents a distorted image of the history of feminism. In fact, one can find traces of feminism throughout history. For the purposes of this chapter, the history of the feminist movement reviewed is primarily that in the United States.

History of Feminism in America

Abigail Adams (1744-1818) was among the first women in this country to speak for women's rights. In a letter dated March 31, 1776, Adams wrote to her husband, John Adams, as he was writing the *Declaration of Independence*:

> Remember the ladies . . . and be more generous and favorable to them than your ancestors. Do not put such unlimited power into the hands of husbands. Remember all men would be tyrants if they could. . . . If particular care and attention is not paid to the ladies, we are determined to foment a rebellion and will not hold ourselves bound by any laws in which we have not voice or representation. (Rossi, 1988, p. 10-11; Spender, 1983, pp. 113-114)

But her husband replied as follows on April 14, 1776:

> As to your extraordinary code of laws, I cannot but laugh. . . . We have only the names of masters . . . and rather than give up this, which would completely subject us to despotism of the petticoat, I hope General Washington and all our brave heroes would fight. (Rossi, 1988, p. 11; Spender, 1983, p. 114)

Even though John Adams did not heed the words of his wife for equality, other women continued the cause. The first women's rights convention in the United States was held at Seneca Falls, New York, in 1848. Among the women who worked for women's equality were Susan B. Anthony (1820-1906) and Elizabeth Cady Stanton (1815-1902), who formed a "partnership that existed for almost fifty years" (Spender, 1983, p. 258). Stanton stated,

> We were at once fast friends, in thought and sympathy we were one, and in the division of labor we exactly complemented each other. In writing, we did better work together than either did alone. While she is slow and analytical in composition, I am rapid and synthetic. I am the better writer, she the better critic. She supplied the facts and statistics and I the philosophy and rhetoric, and together we have made arguments that have stood unshaken by the storms of thirty long years: arguments that no man has answered. (Spender, 1983, p. 259)

Some of the most important work of the women's movement was done when Anthony and Stanton combined in common goals with Frederick Douglass (1818-1895), Sojourner Truth (born Isabella Bomefree, 1797-1883), and Harriet Tubman (1821-1913) of the anti-slavery movement. Of particular importance was the voice of Truth at the 1851 women's rights convention in Akron, Ohio, where she declared,

That man over there says women need to be helped into carriages, and lifted over ditches, and to have the best place everywhere. Nobody ever helps me into carriages, or over mud-puddles, or gives me any best place! And ain't I a woman? Look at me! Look at my arm! I have [plowed], and planted, and gathered into barns, and no man could head me! And ain't I a woman? I could work as much and eat as much as a man —when I could get it—and bear the lash as well! And ain't I a woman? I have borne thirteen children, and seen them most all sold off to slavery, and when I cried out with my mother's grief, none but Jesus heard me! And ain't I a woman? (Collins, 1990, p. 14)

Tubman, who was defined as a criminal for escaping from slavery and leading hundreds of slaves to freedom through the Underground Railroad, also was active in women's organizations after the war (Giddings, 1984, p. 94).

In addition to the women's suffragists and anti-slavery activists, other feminists included the anti-lynching journalist and women's rights activist, Ida Wells-Barnett (1862-1931); Margaret Sanger (1879-1966), whose reproductive rights work provided women with knowledge of birth control; and Alice Paul (1885-1997), author of the Equal Rights Amendment (Duster, 1970; Rossi, 1988).

Although the feminist movement of the 1960s was predominantly a white middle class women's movement, researchers such as Rice (1990) and Simpson (1991) have noted that criminological research and theories based on only these women are involved in a "triple oppression of race, class, and gender" (Rice, 1990, p. 57). Jaggar and Rothenberg (1984, pp. 82-90) and Walby (1990, pp. 3-5) identified several feminist frameworks—including liberal feminism, traditional Marxism, radical feminism, socialist feminism, feminism and women of color—that are used to explain the roots of oppression for women. Whereas most of the works of feminist criminologists have not fallen within the socialist feminist framework, the other frameworks have been used frequently by feminist criminologists. It is essential, therefore, that criminologists understand that feminists do not speak with one voice. For the sake of illustration, the various feminist theories are discussed in one of the specific categories designated by Jaggar and Rothenberg (1984) and Walby (1990). However, many of these theorists could be placed in more than one category.

Assumptions About People and Society

Feminist criminologists do not speak with one voice; neither do they use a single methodology. For example, Adler (1975) used case studies or qualitative data, but Simon (1975) used secondary data for a quantitative analysis of trends or changes in women's crime. Stanko (1990) used primarily qualitative data that she collected through 51 interviews to explore how men and women experience safety and danger. She used quotes from these individual case studies for a micro level of analysis. Mann (1996) conducted a quantitative analysis of a larger sample of women arrested for homicide in six cities. Thus, she used secondary data on large groups of people for a macro level of analysis. Many feminist theorists use both qualitative and quantitative methods, depending on the research questions they are studying.

Whereas liberal feminists argue that inequality is not structural, most other feminist criminologists state that women's inequality is a result of the capitalist and/or patriarchal structure that allows men to oppress and control women. These feminists would see society as based on coercion and conflict, not on consensus. For example, Wilson (1993) claimed that in a patriarchal society, men seek to control and exploit women's sexuality in much the same way as a "masculinist science" dreams of conquering and exploiting the wilderness (p. 53).

Some of the social phenomena discussed in feminist theories are objective overt behaviors, whereas others are subjective covert behaviors. Rape as researched by Rafter and Natalizia (1981) and Stanko (1985), homicide as studied by Mann (1996), and lynchings as discussed by Davis (1983) clearly are objective overt behaviors that one can see happening. By contrast, the oppression, sexism, and chivalry within the works of Moulds (1978); the misogyny among the Puritans (Wilson, 1993); and the stereotypes, misconceptions, and myths about black women cited by Young (1986) all are subjective covert attitudes and behaviors that cannot actually be seen. It probably is safe to say that all theories contain both objective overt phenomena and subjective covert phenomena.

Most of the theorists mentioned heretofore, therefore, seem to see phenomena as imposed on passive agents such as Young's (1986) stereotypes of the black woman as the "black Amazon" or the "sinister Sapphire" and the racist, sexist, and classist type-scripts imposed by juvenile justice officials in making arrest decisions (Sealock and Simpson, 1998). Implicit in these arguments is the perception of those in power trying to maintain the stability of society or the status quo. But feminist criminologists also have suggested that the imposition of these strategies to control and oppress women, the poor, and the racial/ethnic minorities has resulted in active resistance. Davis (1975) posed that the police brutality in California during the 1960s intended to control blacks and keep them as passive agents instead generated black activism. In a similar way, Stanko (1985) suggested that male violence against women intended to coerce and oppress women resulted in women generating strategies to negotiate their safety. Thus, efforts by the powerful males, whites, and rich to oppress and control the "powerless" helped to generate active agents that produced a more fluid society.

History of Feminist Criminology

As indicated previously, the study of criminology historically has been based on male experiences and perspectives. Overall, women offenders and victims have been ignored. On the rare occasions when women offenders have been mentioned, such as Lombroso's (1958) late 19th-century study of *The Female Offender* discussed in

Chapter 3, the theory was sexist and represented an extreme form of misogyny. Lombroso accounted for female crime in terms of inherent biological characteristics that he asserted are worse than those of any man. Pollak (1950) used women's biology to explain the low crime rates among women. He argued that a woman's body makes it easy for her to practice deceit and conceal her crimes.

> But whether or not [a] woman's body still does force her to concealment, it should be noted that it does actually make it much easier for her to practice deceit than does the body of [a] man. Not enough attention has been paid to the physiological fact that man must achieve an erection in order to perform the sex act and will not be able to hide his failure. His lack of positive emotion in the sexual sphere must become overt to the partner, and pretense of sexual response is impossible for him, if it is lacking. [A] woman's body, however, permits such pretense to a certain degree, and lack of orgasm does not prevent her ability to participate in the sex act. (p. 10)

Even though the early studies of women's prisons (Giallombardo, 1966; Heffernan, 1972; Moyer, 1980; Ward and Kassebaum, 1965) were primarily stimulated by and patterned after the classic studies of men's prisons by Clemmer (1940) and Sykes (1958), they were important efforts to study a neglected topic in the sociology of corrections. It was not until the 1970s that the roots of feminist research and theory began to originate in criminology. Thus, feminist criminological theory is not yet fully developed and does not meet the classical social science definition of theory as stated by Homans (1964), Turner (1978), and Merton (1968b). Nevertheless, these theories make important contributions as feminist criminological orientations and as interpretations of data. Except for the various quantitative studies by feminists such as Simon, Simpson, and Mann, much of feminist theory is similar to conflict theory in philosophy and structure.

Liberal Feminists

According to Jaggar and Rothenberg (1984), early liberal theorists postulated the fundamental equality of all men (p. 83). The new social ideals were liberty and equality. Thus, the liberal feminists advocate equality of opportunities and freedom of choice for women. Walby (1990) noted that liberal feminists are concerned with the denial of equal rights to women in education and employment that is based on prejudice and sexist attitudes (p. 4). Liberal feminists further contend that discrimination is not systematic and that equality can be achieved through affirmative action and the Equal Rights Amendment.

Freda Adler and Rita Simon. This perspective emerged in criminology through the pioneer works of Freda Adler and Rita Simon (Adler, 1975; Simon, 1975). The opportunity theory proposed by these two scholars suggested that as the women's movement opened educational and occupational doors to women, women's participation in criminal activities also would increase. Adler (1975) described this emancipation process as follows:

Women are no longer indentured to the kitchens, baby carriages, or bedrooms of America. The skein of myths about women is unraveling, the chains have been pried loose, and there will be no turning back to the days when women found it necessary to justify their existence by producing babies or cleaning houses. Allowed their freedom for the first time, women—by the tens of thousands—have chosen to desert those kitchens and plunge exuberantly into the formerly all-male quarters of the working world. (p. 12) . . .

In the same way that women are demanding equal opportunity in fields of legitimate endeavor, a similar number of determined women are forcing their way into the world of major crime. (p. 13)

Adler also contended that the increase in women's crime would occur in traditional male crimes of aggression and violence. She used numerous anecdotes of women criminals to support her theory of the masculinization of women's crime.

Marge is forty-three years old, with brown hair headed for gray and muscular legs somewhat the worse for the wear. . . . Since her husband disappeared one day eighteen years ago, she has worked a total of fifteen years either as a waitress or a barmaid.

It was as a barmaid in a small restaurant . . . [that] she gave her first serious thought to being a prostitute—like a fellow barmaid. . . .

But soon, Marge gave up the idea of prostitution—partly because of her figure, which she didn't feel was suited for the trade, and partly because of her "strong Catholic upbringing."

In place of prostitution, Marge found a more acceptable degree of reprehensibility in shoplifting. . . . At first, she began by putting small items, like watches, into her pocket. Later, she progressed to more sophisticated methods.

Five years ago, Marge robbed her first bank. The planning took her some months. "It was something that came to me all of a sudden. . . . I guess maybe I got the idea from watching TV or something. . . . I first thought of it seriously and thought, 'No, I couldn't do that. . . . I'm a woman,' you know? But when I thought more about it, what the hell, it didn't seem so bad.

I remember that first job. It was like a cheap high afterward. I went home and turned on the radio to see what they would say about me on the news."

To her disappointment, after that first heist, police described her to the news media as a "male dressed in women's clothing." That upset Marge a bit. "Well, I mean, I know I'm no beauty queen, but I didn't think I was that bad." (pp. 6-7)

The importance of Adler's pioneer work was blurred during the 1970s as her research was sensationalized by the mass media, politicians, and some male criminologists who enjoyed the idea that feminism might have a negative impact on women by increasing their participation in crime. However, Adler's scholarship during recent years has brought her both national and international recognition. She is a distinguished professor at Rutgers University. In appreciation for her scholarship and service, the American Society of Criminology honored Adler as a fellow, conferred on her the Herbert Bloch Award, and elected her as its president in 1994.

Simon (1975), who analyzed data from the Federal Bureau of Investigation's Uniform Crime Reports for a project funded by the National Institute of Mental Health, also adhered to the opportunity or emancipation theory to explain increases in women's crime. Unlike Adler, however, Simon indicated that increases in women's crime would come in the crimes traditionally committed by women.

> Contrary to impressions that might have been gleaned from the mass media, the proportion of females arrested for violent crimes has changed hardly at all over the past two decades. Female arrest rates for homicide, for example, have been the most stable of all violent offenses. Further probing of female arrest rates in the Type II offenses revealed that the offenses that showed the greatest increases were embezzlement and fraud and forgery and counterfeiting. (p. 46)

Simon went on to predict the following trends in women's crime:

> If present trends in these crimes persist, approximately equal numbers of men and women will be arrested for fraud and embezzlement by the 1990s, and for forgery and counterfeiting the proportions should be equal by the 2010s. (The prediction made for embezzlement and fraud can be extended to larceny as well.) On the other hand, if trends from 1958 to 1972 continue, fewer women will be arrested for criminal homicide and aggravated assault. (p. 41)

Simon explained this decrease in future arrests for homicide and aggravated assault as related to the increase in opportunities for employment outside the home. Simon further explained that women's commissions of these acts typically are the result of frustration, subservience, and dependency that have characterized the traditional female role. She claimed that as "women's employment and educational opportunities expand, their feelings of being victimized and exploited will decrease and their motivation to kill [will] become muted" (p. 4).

The research predictions of Adler (1975) and Simon (1975) that the criminal activities of women will become, and are becoming, more like those of men in kind and/or degree have been challenged by several scholars such as Steffensmeier (1978) and Feinman (1980).

Darrell J. Steffensmeier and Clarice Feinman. A more sophisticated analysis by Darrell Steffensmeier used data from both the Uniform Crime Reports and the U.S. Bureau of the Census (Steffensmeier, 1978, pp. 568-569). Although Steffensmeier agreed that levels of female property crime have increased substantially since 1960, most of the increase has occurred in larceny/theft. The high percentages of increase noted by some researchers are the result of the relatively low size of the initial base rate for female arrests. With reference to the narrowing of the gap, Steffensmeier (1978) stated,

> Comparison of male and female levels of property crime revealed that, with the exception of stolen property, the relative gap between the sexes has been narrowing since 1960. This closing of the gap, however, does not necessarily mean that females are catching up with males in propensities to commit property crimes. While females have made relative gains, absolute differences are still large and have generally increased so

that female property crime levels continue to lag far behind those of males. Catching up appears to be the case only for the offenses of larceny and fraud/embezzlement. Nonetheless, even if current trends for these offenses continue, female rates will not match male rates in the foreseeable future. (pp. 577-578)

Using the actual numbers of arrests reported in the Uniform Crime Reports, according to Clarice Feinman, indicates that "the increase is not as great as one might be led to believe" (Feinman, 1980, p. 14). Thus, Feinman concurred with Steffensmeier (1978) that the gap between men's and women's crimes is not closing. In addition, Feinman (1980) noted,

The property crimes that have produced the largest increase in women's arrests are larceny/theft and fraud, both of which represent petty unsophisticated crimes of low reward. Larceny, as a category in the Uniform Crime Reports, includes shoplifting, pickpocketing, purse snatching, and thefts without use of force. Studies done in the 1970s report that the overwhelming number of women arrested for larceny were [accused of] shoplifting. Fraud includes welfare fraud, passing bad checks, and credit card fraud. (p. 19)

Feinman (1980) and Steffensmeier (1978) also challenged the assumptions by Adler (1975) and Simon (1975) that the alleged changes in women's crime are the result of the women's movement. Steffensmeier (1978) appeared not to understand the purpose of the women's movement, as evidenced by the following statement: "The image, however, is a highly dubious inference from existing arrest data and to some extent appears to reflect wishful thinking that women are indeed making inroads into traditional male dominated white collar and corporate criminal endeavors" (p. 579). Steffensmeier also seemed to assume that the women's movement began during the 1960s (p. 579), whereas Feinman (1980, p. 18) and Simon (1975, p. 11) indicated that the women's movement in America can be traced to time preceding the Civil War. Both Feinman and Steffensmeier questioned Simon's assertion that the economic opportunities provided for women by the women's movement accounted for the increase in women's property crime. All of these scholars—Adler, Feinman, Simon, and Steffensmeier—were quite successful in bringing the issue of women's crime to the attention of criminologists and have made tremendous contributions to our understanding of women's crime. As indicated earlier, not all feminists agree with the liberal feminists.

Marxist Feminists

Marxists reject the liberals' belief that it is possible for people to have genuine equality of opportunity while they remain within a class society where many produce the wealth but the wealth and power remain in the hands of a few (Jaggar and Rothenberg, 1984, p. 85). In fact, traditional Marxists see women's oppression as originating with the introduction of private property. Private ownership of the means of production by relatively few persons—and those persons all male—instituted a class system. Jaggar and Rothenberg (1984, p. 85) and Walby (1990, p. 4) asserted that in the view of Marxist feminists, women are oppressed primarily by capitalism, and men's domination over women is a by-product of capital's domination over labor. Gender inequality is a result of capitalism.

Elizabeth Moulds, Nicole Rafter, and Eleena Natalizia. Marxist feminism developed in criminology in association with the controversy that arose during the 1970s regarding the claim that women were receiving preferential treatment within the criminal justice system. Elizabeth Moulds was among the first to address this issue by using the concepts of chivalry and paternalism to explain differential sentencing within the criminal courts. Moulds (1978) contended that the subordinate and oppressed positions of women are the result of chivalry, which is a concept that emerged during the Middle Ages as

> an institution of service rendered by the crusading orders to the feudal lords, to the divine sovereign, and to womankind. "Ladies" were special beneficiaries of the practice of chivalry—knights were sworn to protect their female weakness against dragons and devils. (p. 417)

Moulds asserted that this focus on the benefits that women presumably derive from the practice of chivalry has diverted attention from the oppression of women due to the power relationship of male domination (p. 418). She further stated that the power relationship is more accurately described by the term "paternalism" defined as follows: "The derivation of the term 'paternalism' from a Latin-English kinship term suggests its root meanings: a type of behavior by a superior toward an inferior resembling that of a male parent to his child" (p. 418). Moulds further claimed that women have paid a high price for this alleged chivalry and preferential treatment. Because men dominate the criminal justice system, the policies are based on a view of women as less able than men. One example is the sexual double standard of treatment for female and male juveniles.

The Marxist feminist position was more clearly presented by Nicole Rafter and Eleena Natalizia, who stated,

> Capitalism and sexism are intimately related, and it is this relationship that accounts for the inferior status traditionally given to women by the American criminal justice system. Sexism is not merely the prejudice of individuals; it is embedded in the very economic, legal, and social framework of life in the United States. The criminal justice system, as one part of that institutional framework, reflects the same sexist underpinning that is evidenced throughout the capitalist society. (Rafter and Natalizia, 1981, p. 81)

Rafter and Natalizia (1981) continued to explain that capitalism exists through the traditional structure of monogamy and the nuclear family. The division of labor essential for a capitalist system cuts off those who produce from control over the means of production. It also dictates that men shall be the chief producers for public distribution of goods, whereas women shall function as nurturers and produce for family consumption in the home. Thus, men became the heads of all major institutions in society including the family and the criminal justice system. "Women are properly chattel of the dominant men in their lives (husbands, fathers, lovers, pimps), and women's work is defined as unworthy of significant remuneration" (p. 83).

Rafter and Natalizia (1981) argued that because the entire justice system has been dominated by men,

> our legal framework "has been codified by male legislators, enforced by male police officers, and interpreted by male judges." . . . Even more significant to the class analysis presented here, these legal functionaries as representatives of the dominant bourgeois ideology serve as conduits through which bourgeois morality becomes codified in our legal structures. (p. 83)

Thus, Moulds (1978) and Rafter and Natalizia (1981) both argued that the criminal justice system has failed to meet the needs of women. However, Rafter and Natalizia provided a more definitive analysis of why and how this occurs. Both Moulds (1978) and Rafter and Natalizia (1981) suggested that the discriminatory treatment of juvenile girls who are involved in status offenses is a major result of the capitalistic system that gives control to men. Rafter and Natalizia also maintained that the legal system oppresses women through its almost total failure to respond to issues that concern women such as wife abuse, incest, rape, production of unsafe methods of birth control, and forced sterilization. Because these problems have the greatest significance for poor and working class women, class is at least as critical as sex in the struggle to obtain legal equality for women. This failure not only is the result of male legislators and justice officials but also is due to the traditional concept of women as property of men. With reference to rape, Rafter and Natalizia stated, "Traditionally, when a woman is raped, it has been regarded as a property crime, an offense whose victim is the man whose property (i.e., wife or daughter) has been defiled" (p. 88).

Rafter and Natalizia (1981) went on to point out that the legal system, when applied to assault or murder within the home, is based on the premise of the sanctity of the family home and that a man's home is his castle (p. 89). Thus, our patriarchal society, by keeping women dependent on their husbands and failing to provide adequate legal protection to abused wives, continues to perpetuate the victimization of women. Rafter and Natalizia also declared that chivalrousness is a tool for the preservation of patriarchy rather than an effort to treat women with special kindness (p. 92).

Radical Feminists

According to Jaggar and Rothenberg (1984), liberal feminists and Marxist feminists draw on philosophical traditions, whereas radical feminism, by contrast, is a very recent political theory that still is in the process of development (p. 86). They insisted that the oppression of women is fundamental. Jaggar and Rothenberg (1984, p. 87) and Walby (1990, p. 3) indicated that the basis of this oppression is the appropriation and/or control of women's sex and bodies. Radical feminists also claim that the oppression of the sexual bodies of women provides the conceptual model for understanding forms of oppression such as racism and class society. Radical feminists in criminology most frequently have been concerned with the victimization of women and male violence. In so doing, they have expanded feminist criminological theory to include both offenders and victims.

Elizabeth A. Stanko. Elizabeth Stanko[4] has been one of the strongest advocates for this perspective (Stanko, 1985, 1987, 1990, 1992). It is important to begin by exploring the path that Stanko (1992) indicated is chosen by crime prevention advisers. Stanko (1987) pointed out that based on official victimization studies, "young, single, black, Hispanic or Asian poor men who live in urban areas" have the greatest risk of interpersonal violence and are more apt to sustain injury as a consequence of victimization (p. 125). Yet, according to Stanko (1992), men of all ages report less "fear of crime" (which may be taken to represent individuals' diffuse sense of danger about being physically harmed by criminal violence) than do women, who have lower officially reported victimization rates (p. 118). Using rape as an example, Stanko suggested,

> What is generally agreed by conventional criminologists is that women *feel* at greater risk of rape but that this concern is not founded in *actual* experience. Crime against women, most criminologists now agree, is seriously underreported and underrecorded. ... Despite the shortcomings of crime surveys for capturing "family" crime, the crime survey frames the contemporary debate about violence and the fear of violence in a way that fails to take into account what women themselves say about the dangers they face throughout their lives and in particular the danger associated with violence within the home. (p. 121)

Stanko (1985) claimed, however, that "to be a woman is to be potentially sexually and/or physically assaulted by men" (p. 17). Stanko (1985, 1990) noted that violence is an ordinary experience for women. She explained this as follows:

> Our everyday behavior reflects our precautions, the measures we take to protect ourselves. We are wary of going out at night, even in our neighborhoods. We are warned by men and other women not to trust strangers. But somehow they forget to warn us about men we know: our fathers, our acquaintances, our co-workers, our lovers, our teachers. (Stanko, 1985, p. 9)

Stanko asserted that it is women's inability to predict when male aggression will occur that makes women feel vulnerable and powerless and that forces women to negotiate their safety on a daily basis. It is not that women think that every man is violent but rather women's inability to predict which men are violent and when the violence may occur that makes men intimidating to women.

Stanko (1985) further argued that women's vulnerability to violent and intimidating behavior is due to their social position, not to their biological position. That physical and/or sexual violence can happen without interference, and sometimes with encouragement from others, is evidence of women's powerlessness. That is, gender inequality is the root of male violence (p. 71). Stanko stated,

The physical and/or sexual abuse of women is a manifestation of male domination it-self; so often characterized as typical, it has been seen to be a natural right of men. Fa-thers have the right to use their daughters as they please; husbands, their wives; bosses, their female employees; even men unknown to us act as if they have the right to com-ment or abuse any woman's body. (p. 71)

When Stanko (1985) discussed sexual harassment in the workplace, she declared that it is a form of men's threatening, intimidating, or coercive sexual behavior and is a form of discriminatory treatment at work including the following:

Looks, comments, pats, pinches, propositions—actions that men say are "apprecia-tive" of women as women in the workplace (as opposed to an appreciation of women as workers)—are experienced by women as harassing, as abhorrent, and as an abusive working condition. (p. 133)

If women report the harassment, it often is trivialized as an office romance, as just a sexual (but unthreatening) game, or as a conscious manipulation on the part of the woman to gain benefits (p. 35). This last explanation may even be an effort to show the woman as the office temptress or seductress seeking job promotions by some gull-ible male.

Because of these ordinary experiences of sexual and physical violence, Stanko (1990) argued that women develop strategies to negotiate their safety. She asserted that what women basically do is manage danger as a continuing and conscious pro-cess that eventually may become routine (p. 7). Her analysis of these strategies is based on research interviews that she conducted between 1985 and 1989 in London and in the New England area of the United States. The population interviewed in-cluded men and women; blacks, whites, Hispanics, and Asians; rich and poor; het-erosexual and homosexual; 16 to 72 years of age, who were willing to share their ex-periences, precautions, worries, and fears about personal danger posed by their fellow citizens (pp. 4, 10).

Stanko (1990) explored experiences with strategies for safety on the street, at work, and at home. Among traditional strategies for street safety used by women, she found the following: "I always have my keys in my hands . . ., and I have a whistle and I always have my arms free" (p. 16). An American man stated, "I carry a gun, and if that doesn't do it, just my strength [will protect me]. I'm protected" (p. 24).

A male electrician's apprentice in central Massachusetts reported his concern for safety at work that stemmed from colleagues. His concerns were based on an incident in which "I almost got thrown down a flight of stairs by a guy about twice my size. . . . He was angry over the fact that he was making only 25 cents more an hour than me" (p. 26). Because no one came to his rescue, the man's strategy was simply to watch his back and check and double-check his safety. A London worker described how she manages danger as follows:

On a regular basis, I do a couple of things which I have come to do in the last few years. I tend to move my car late at night. My job is 9 to 5, but I certainly don't leave my office at 5. What I do is around 5, when most of the people are leaving the city, I will go and get the car and move it to the front of my office. (p. 27)

Stanko (1990) quoted a Hispanic man in Massachusetts who thought that danger could arise without warning in his home and has developed safeguards to protect himself and his family:

> I'm always expecting the unexpected. . . . I always make sure that the house is secure and also the family. I tell the children never to open the door without asking who it is. When I have to go out for a couple of minutes, I tell them to say I'm in the bathroom, to leave a name and phone number and say I will call them back in five minutes. Never to say they are alone. (p. 30)

A woman who was raped by an unknown man who had crawled into her first-story bedroom described how she fortified her present home in central Massachusetts:

> We built this house because I had been raped. We really built it. I think everybody thinks we're crazy. I've got locks, you know. Our doors are really good. We have grates on the basement windows. . . . Very small windows at the top. [The house is set up] high enough so that somebody can't look in. I keep the windows locked [and] lock the door at all times. . . . So I feel apprehensive in general, but somewhat more safe within this house. (p. 32)

Stanko pointed out, however, that no matter how secure a home might be against intruders, a woman who lives with someone who is physically and/or sexually violent has the potential for experiencing violence locked in the home with her. The typical targets of this type of violence are women and children. One child reported,

> My dad would beat up my mom, and me or one of my sisters would call the police if it got really bad. . . . I was really scared, for her and for me, because it was really obvious that if he was going to hurt her, he would hurt us too. (p. 31)

Although this child was pretty helpless to deal with the danger, Stanko pointed out that part of monitoring danger might lie in carefully observing the behavior of the threatening person. One male interviewed by Stanko reported the physical abuse he experienced after his father died when he was 4 years of age, leaving a widow with four children:

> I had a difficult time. There was a real cycle of violence. I was the oldest boy, and my mother would hit me and I would hit them and she would hit me. She used to have a 2[-by-]4 [large stick] on top of the refrigerator which she would use or threaten to use when I wouldn't listen. Seeing my brothers crying and in the corner or getting hit was probably the most upsetting thing in the long run. And that went on until I was 13 or so, when I left for the seminary. (p. 56)

Stanko cited many other cases of victimization and strategies for dealing with crime and fear of crime. In sum, Stanko (1992) argued,

> The case of fearful women demands that we ask questions about crime and criminality from a radical feminist perspective. It is not enough to allow a discipline to separate the inquiry about women from the inquiry about men, thereby marginalizing or silencing women's realities. Why does the criminal law continue to miss much of what affects women's safety, anxiety, and experiences of danger? Women's lives are, after all, still invisible within the wider conventional discipline of criminology. (p. 132)

Nanci Koser Wilson. Another one of the early pioneer feminist scholars (Adler, 1997, pp. 3-5),[5] Nanci Koser Wilson argued that the societal response to both the victimization of women and their criminal offenses is shaped by our need of their work. That is, the pattern of societal response to women is determined by what feminine work is functional for a patriarchal industrial society. Wilson (1985) further noted that women's jobs are extensions of their roles as housewives:

> At the same time, jobs in the commercial labor market continue to be largely sex segregated, with the female jobs receiving much lower pay than the "male" jobs. . . . And not only are female jobs lower paid, but they involve significantly different kinds of work. Many female jobs are extensions of the housewife role—"secretary as 'office wife'," e.g., and nursing, teaching, and other service or human relations jobs are typical. Further, female jobs involve less mobility, which has important impacts on the types of crime women commit. (p. 3)

Wilson continued this line of reasoning by noting that society protects victims who are valuable and ignores those who are not. She further suggested that we protect people from depredations harmful to the social fabric, not necessarily from victimizations that are painful to them as persons. She identified three "women-only" victimizations as rape, wife battering, and sexual harassment and explained patriarchal response to these acts as related to women's work. Because traditionally, women have been defined as sexual property, rape is both a crime of violence and a crime of theft (p. 4). Wilson further noted,

> Most arguments between husband and wife leading to battering center around child care, food needs, housekeeping, sex, and money. . . . A battering is seen by the man (and the woman so long as she stays) as an assertion of power within the relationship. (p. 5)

Wilson concluded the following regarding sexual harassment cases:

> The male employer uses his labor market power (to hire, fire, promote, [and] demote) to gain sexual access to his employee. . . . Women's work in the commercial labor market is housework. They nurse, teach small children, provide food, [and] assist men at tasks. . . . Because the commercial labor market is so sexually segregated, with women

frequently playing housewife roles to male bosses, it is quite natural that the male boss seeks sexual access as well as the "domestic" duties of the *bonne femme*. (p. 5)

Wilson, however, did assert that women's greater work role in the commercial labor market has given them a little more public power. She used prostitution as an example of how the response to women's crime is based on the sexual function that women serve for the patriarchal society.

> Prostitutes serve the function of providing casual uncommitted sex to men who are transient, who are living temporarily without their wives, and to those who desire "kinky" sex. . . . The demand itself . . . is a direct outcome of a patriarchal system which caters to male sexual "need" and at the same time offers few alternatives to the pay [that] a young woman could make in the trade of prostitution. (p. 9)

In addition to claiming that men seek to control women's sexuality, Wilson (1993) asserted that a "masculinist science" embodies a dream of conquering the wilderness (p. 53). What counts in this dream, according to Wilson, is not so much more and more productivity but rather human control of natural productivity. Many feminist scholars contend that control over women and their labor was the first form of exploitation that men invented. Ecofeminists further state that the exploitation of women and nature developed coterminously, nourishing one another (p. 53). Wilson (1985, 1993) used the crime of witchcraft among the Puritans as an example of the patriarchal effort to control the wild nature of women and the natural wilderness:

> The universe was seen as a Great Chain of Being, "composed of an immense . . . number of links ranging in hierarchical order from the meagerest kind of existence, which barely escape nonexistence, through 'every possible' grade up to . . . the Absolute Being."
>   For Puritans, each link in the chain fulfilled its nature and purpose partly by obeying the next highest link in the chain. Among human beings, a similar hierarchy had been ordained with "husbands superior to wives, parents to children, masters to servants, ministers to congregants, and magistrates to subjects. . . . In each of these relations, inferiors served God by serving their superiors." (Wilson, 1993, p. 55)

Wilson further explained that the Puritans were steeped in a tradition whose theology, in direct contrast to animistic, nature-centered rival religions, inherited a linear hierarchical monotheism. During times of stress, the fear of heresy arose with new vigor within the patriarchal Puritan religion. What came to be called witchcraft included some elements of pagan belief systems. The witch persecutions were useful for validating the new patriarchal religion as well as validating an increasingly centralized secular and male hierarchy in medicine, politics, and agriculture. The specter of possible resistance to the taming of all nature resulted in intense witch fears that culminated in the deaths of perhaps 9 million persons (p. 57). The witch beliefs of the Puritans were strongly marked fears of disruption of the "Chain of Being," particularly of rebellion among women and damage caused to domesticated nature.

Witches were also seen as dissatisfied with their place in the natural hierarchy. This made them angry and vengeful. Specific sorts of crimes were likely to be performed by witches. . . . They could cause men to be impotent, [and] they could prevent conceptions and procure abortions in women. They also might kill newborns . . . [and attempt] to dominate their husbands, which was a "natural vice" in women.

Theologically and legally, the crime of witchcraft consisted in making a pact with the devil, whose supernatural power he lent to humans. With this power, a person could perform *maleficium,* that is, harm various parts of the natural order. She could cause disease, injury, or even death among humans and other animals. She could interfere with domestic processes like dairying, brewing beer, and making cloth. . . . [She] could create droughts and storms at sea. . . . Maleficium could be performed by look, by touch, and specifically *by curse.* (p. 58)

There was a high concentration of women among the accused, which may suggest misogyny and the desire to control women. Women were viewed as a part of wild nature that needed taming. Their natural role was to nurture. Wilson (1993) interpreted this as patriarchal Puritans' fear of the vengeance of dissatisfied women. Thus, at the heart of the witches' crime was rebellion against hierarchical order and allegiance to an alternative force whose main purpose and power appeared to be the creation of chaos. Thus, fertility in women and in nature would be subjected to strict masculine design and control—and, where it went wild, it would be criminally punished. Wilson made the following suggestions about the current criminal justice response to "contemporary witchcraft":

The fear of wild nature and the intense desire to tame it for man's benefit . . . is still strong. A "neutral" scientific technology informs our actions. Nature now tends toward no other end than to be molded by men in power to their current benefit. . . . The tendency toward diversity and fullness is seen to arise from the bottom of the hierarchy, spontaneously rather than as a deliberate plan from the top; its danger to women and nature is not lessened but perhaps increased. (p. 70) . . .

For the patriarchal mind, wild women and wild nature still pose a significant threat to orderly, male-controlled production and reproduction. (p. 71)

In this chapter, we see that Wilson has combined her radical feminist analysis with her research on environmental crime. Thus, the works of Stanko and Wilson serve quite well as examples of radical feminist criminology.

Feminism and Women of Color

All of the liberal, Marxist, and radical feminists whose works were discussed in the previous sections are white scholars. In fact, the issues identified previously by the feminist movement during the 20th century were primarily the concerns of white middle class or professional women. Jaggar and Rothenberg (1984) pointed out, "Although women of color do not utilize any single theoretical framework, their writings invariably reflect a concern that the complexities of race and gender (and often class as well) be explored simultaneously" (p. 89).

Walby (1990) contended that the neglect of ethnic difference and inequality in many white feminist and nonfeminist writings has come under intense scrutiny (p. 13). It was further noted by Jaggar and Rothenberg (1984) that "women of color must deal with the realities that they are both female and nonwhite in a society defined by patriarchy and white supremacy" (p. 89). Walby (1990) argued,

> Ethnic variation and racism mean that the chief sites of oppression of women of color may be different from those of white women. This is not simply a statement that women of color face racism which white women do not but also a suggestion that this may change the basis of gender inequality itself. . . .
>
> The intersection of ethnicity and gender may alter ethnic and gender relations. Not only is there the question of recognizing ethnic inequality and the different sites of oppression for women of different ethnicities, but the particular ways in which ethnic and gender relations have interacted historically change the forms of ethnic and gender relations. (p. 14)

Although both groups (white women and ethnic women) are oppressed by the patriarchy, white women continue to experience the privileges of their race. The core theme of black women, then, is the struggle against racism and sexism.

Collins (1990) suggested, "Black feminist thought consists of specialized knowledge created by African American women which clarifies a standpoint of and for black women" (p. 22). She asserts that an Afrocentric feminist consciousness requires both an Afrocentric worldview and a feminist sensibility (p. 28). Collins contended that we should shift statements from "I am a feminist" to "I advocate feminism" so as to provide women who are concerned about both feminism and other political movements with an avenue to express the support without giving primacy to one particular group (p. 35). This background provides a framework for examining the criminological works of African American feminists.

Vernetta D. Young. Feminist African American scholars in criminology have been interested in a variety of topics. Vernetta Young has challenged the assumptions and stereotypes that have prevailed regarding black females as offenders and victims (Young, 1980, 1986). Young (1980, p. 27) used the 1972-1975 National Crime Survey victimization data to examine Adler's (1975) assertions regarding the pattern of crime for blacks and whites with a focus on female criminality. Young (1980) indicated,

> Adler (1975) speculates that the current pattern of black female crime is indicative of the future pattern for white female criminals. She proposes that, since slavery, "sex-role convergence" has occurred among black males and black females to a far greater degree than among white males and white females. This has led, according to Adler, to a similarity not only in criminal behavior patterns of black males and black females but also in the patterns for black females and white males. Furthermore, with the emergence of the women's liberation movement, Adler suggests that there will be the same sex-role convergence among white males and white females resulting in similar patterns of behavior. (pp. 26-27)

Young (1980) reported that her data analysis indicates that the phenomenon of female crime and race is one of considerable complexity. She disputed Adler's contention that black female criminality can be explained by the fact that during the slave era, there was sex role reversal among black males and black females. Therefore, "the pattern of black female criminality differs from that of the white female . . ., and the pattern for black females is closer to the pattern of white males than it is to the pattern for white females" (p. 33). Young asserted that these explanations are not supported by the data.

Young (1986) further contended that characterizations presented by early theorists were based on an image of the "ideal" woman that was specific to upper class white women. She noted that black females were not characterized as good women and bad women, as white women were. Thus, she challenged the stereotypes, misconceptions, and myths about the black woman. One of these myths is the myth of the black matriarchy. Young explained that the characterization of the black female as matriarch has resulted in two images (pp. 307-308). First, the image of the black Amazon focuses on the strong role of women in black families and asserts that the black female gained dominance through her economic support of the family. This assumes a role reversal of the black male and black female that can be traced to the slave era. Again, Young claimed that this myth explains Adler's (1975) assertions that Young refuted in her 1980 article discussed previously. As a result of this stereotype of the black Amazon, the black woman has been pictured as masculine, domineering, strong, tough, assertive, and able to endure hardships.

The second image of the black matriarch that Young (1986) discussed is the "sinister Sapphire." This characterization indicates that the strong role of the black matriarch in the family has undermined the natural leadership of the black male. In turn, the black male, to assert his masculinity, had to subjugate the black females. Thus, the black male and black female were to blame for their lack of progress. The black woman, therefore, has been stereotyped as nagging, shrewish, castrating, dangerous, and "treacherous toward and contemptuous of black men" (p. 308).

Another image of the black woman that Young (1986) discussed is that of mammy, in which she has a role as mother for her own children and as a domestic and substitute mother in the homes of whites. In this role, she was characterized as "patient, wise beyond all wisdom, long suffering, religious, and nurturing" (p. 309). Finally, the myth of the black matriarch has produced an image of the black female as a seductress who is loose, immoral, and sexually deprived. According to Young, not only did the gender role expectations of black females presented by early theorists differ from those for good white females, but for black females even the positive characterization of the mammy had negative implications.

Young (1986) summarized her points as follows:

Black women in American society have been victimized by their double status as blacks and as women. Discussions of blacks have focused on the black man, whereas discussions of females have focused on the white female. Information about black females has been based on their position relative to black males and white females. Consequently, black women have not been perceived as a group worthy of study. Knowledge about these women is based on images that are distorted and falsified. In turn, these images have influenced the way in which black female victims and offenders have been treated by the criminal justice system. (p. 322)

In a later article, Young and Greene (1995) suggested that these misconceptions could be changed if the university criminology/criminal justice curriculum were expanded to include African American scholars whose research has challenged the mainstream research and theories. Young (1989) noted that most discussions of black crime merely note that African Americans are arrested disproportionately compared to whites, but there seems to be no effort to develop theoretical and etiological explanations of black crime. Young and Greene (1995) asserted,

> Although the study of crime in America was undertaken at the same time by African American and white scholars, most works by the former remain unknown. The historical marginalization of those works is tied inextricably to issues of race. (p. 87)

Young and Greene argued that for the issues of African Americans and crime to be clarified, the works excluded until now must be integrated into the criminology/criminal justice curriculum. They divided the African American scholars into three time periods. The earliest group of African American scholars were dominated by the works of W. E. B. Du Bois (1868-1963), who was discussed in Chapter 8, and Monroe Work (1866-1945). These two scholars did not attribute the criminality of blacks to any biologically inherent inadequacy but recognized the differential effects of slavery and emancipation on various segments of the black population. Young and Greene further cited Du Bois as follows:

> Negro crime was caused by the "violent economic and social changes . . . [and] the sad social history that preceded [emancipation]." . . . The faults of Negroes included both individual personality factors, such as unreliability and lack of proper self-respect, and structural factors, such as poverty and low wages. . . . The faults of whites were related primarily to the administration of the criminal justice system. (p. 92)

Young and Greene (1995) then introduced a second group of scholars who wrote after the development of the Chicago School (1930s) and during the civil rights era (1950s and 1960s). They named a representative group of African American scholars who "made significant contributions to understanding African Americans and crime: John T. Blue, Lee P. Brown, E. Franklin Frazier, Mozell Hill, Earl R. Moses, and Gwynne Peirson" (p. 93). Frazier, who completed his Ph.D. in sociology at the University of Chicago in 1931, was discussed in Chapter 5. Finally, Young and Greene presented the writings of contemporary (1970s and 1980s) African American scholars and suggested that this group contains an unprecedented number who began to study criminology/criminal justice as a direct result of increased educational opportunities. These scholars dealt with more specific crime issues including violence, internal colonialism, homicide, crime in the black community, institutionalized racism, and gender and crime. Although there is emerging a large body of scholarship by contemporary African American criminologists, Young and Greene correctly noted that these scholars still are being ignored in the criminology/criminal justice curricula.

Many criminology texts are being written without recognizing the contributions of any African American scholars mentioned in the three periods just described. Likewise, they also are ignored in the college and university curricula.

Young and Greene (1995) concluded with a plea for pedagogical reconstruction that requires strategies for including African American perspectives in the criminology/criminal justice curriculum. Finally, they stated,

> It is important to view this paper as a work in progress that provides material for future research and dialogue. We have presented only a sample of available writings. Our intent is to continue the dialogue begun in earlier works by acknowledging African Americans' contributions to the study of [criminology/criminal justice]. It should be clear that (1) African Americans' works have a history that parallels mainstream works; (2) along with perspectives that support mainstream criminology, these works include those that differ from the mainstream; and (3) there is no monolithic "African American perspective." (pp. 100-101)

Angela Y. Davis. As a feminist black activist, Angela Davis was actively involved in the "Black Power" movement of the 1960s and 1970s. She studied French literature at Brandeis University and received a scholarship to study philosophy at Goethe University in Frankfurt, Germany (Davis, 1975). She returned to the United States and studied for her doctorate in philosophy with Herbert Marcuse at California State University, San Diego. During this time, she joined the Communist Party (p. 188) and became a leader in the political protest activities of the Black Power movement in California. Davis gave many accounts of police brutality to black activists. The following is an example:

> They gave us the gory details of the police slaying of eighteen-year-old Gregory Clark not too far from our office. . . .
>
> On a warm afternoon in February, Gregory Clark and a friend were cruising down Washington Boulevard in a late-model Mustang. They were drinking soda pop, the cans covered by brown paper bags. When they reached Vineyard, they were motioned over to the curb by an LAPD [Los Angeles Police Department] cop who, according to the brother who survived, told them they didn't look like they "fit" the car. Then, seeing the brown bags and without a shred of proof, he accused them of drinking beer while driving. (p. 169) . . .
>
> The two brothers protested, the witnesses said. They had the registration to prove that they hadn't stolen the car, and the cans themselves were proof of what they were drinking. But the cop, Warren B. Carleson, refused to hear their explanation. . . . Ordering them out of their car, he prepared to handcuff them. . . . In any case, there was a brief scuffle before Carleson locked the manacles around his wrists. The victim was caught, but Carleson did not stop there. According to those watching the encounter, he knocked Gregory Clark to the sidewalk, and while he lay face down, his hands cuffed behind him, Carleson shot Gregory in the back of the head with a .38 revolver. (Davis, 1975, p. 170)

Davis (1975) then related her involvement in protests of police brutality during the trial, but the officer won the case on the grounds of self-defense. Davis's political activities increased, and she became involved in the campaign to free the Soledad brothers, who were black political prisoners. During a revolt involving members involved in the movement to free the prisoners, a trial judge was killed (p. 278). A warrant was issued for Davis's arrest on charges of conspiracy to commit murder and kidnapping. She went underground, and her name was entered on the FBI's 10 most-wanted criminals list (p. 15). In October 1970, Davis was arrested in New York City. After 16 months in jail as a political prisoner (p. 375), Davis was acquitted of all counts against her (pp. 394-395). It is from these experiences in jail that she could provide a perspective of the jails and prisons in America at this time in history. Many of her observations were supported by researchers studying prisons at that time. Davis[6] stated,

> Jails and prisons are designed to break human beings, to convert the population into specimens in a zoo—obedient to our keepers but dangerous to each other. In response, imprisoned men and women will invent and continually invoke various and sundry defenses. Consequently, two layers of existence can be encountered within almost every jail or prison. The first layer consists of the routines and behavior prescribed by the governing penal hierarchy. The second layer is the prisoner culture itself: the rules and standards of behavior that come from and are defined by the captives in order to shield themselves from the open or covert terror designed to break their spirits. (p. 53)

During her time in prison, Davis (1975) made the following observations[7]:

> A woman a few cells down gave me a fascinating description of a whole system through which the women could adopt their jail friends as relatives. I was bewildered and awed by the way in which the vast majority of the jail population had neatly organized itself into generations of families: mothers/wives, fathers/husbands, sons and daughters, even aunts and uncles, grandmothers and grandfathers. The family system served as a defense against the fact of being no more than a number. It humanized the environment and allowed an identification with others within a familiar framework. (p. 54)

Davis also noted that homosexuality was at the core of the family system but that the family structure was not closed to "straight" women (p. 55).[8] She further explained,

> Since the majority of the prisoners seemed to be at least casually involved in the family structure, there had to be a great number of lesbians throughout the jail. Homosexuality is bound to occur on a relatively large scale in any place of sexually segregated confinement. I knew this before I was arrested. I was not prepared, however, for the shock of seeing it so thoroughly entrenched in jail life. (p. 55)

Once acquitted and released from jail, Davis continued to live in California and to teach black philosophy and aesthetics as well as courses in women's studies (Davis, 1983). She also continues to be active in the struggle to fight racism and repression in an organized united manner. She serves as a national board member of the National Political Congress of Black Women and of the National Black Women's Health Project (Davis, 1985).

In discussing the continued oppression of black people after the emancipation of the slaves, Davis (1983) suggested that the sharecroppers were no better off than the outright peons. Those who "rented" the land immediately after emancipation rarely possessed the money for rent payments or to purchase the necessities to harvest their first crop (p. 88). Many of the emancipated blacks ended up in prison for alleged crimes and became part of the convict lease system.

> Through the convict lease system, black people were forced to play the same old roles carved out for them by slavery. Men and women alike were arrested and imprisoned at the slightest pretext—in order to be leased out by authorities as convict laborers. Whereas the slaveholders had recognized limits to the cruelty with which they exploited their "valuable" human property, no such cautions were necessary for the postwar planters who rented black convicts for relatively short terms. "In many cases, sick convicts are made to toil until they drop dead in their tracks." (p. 89)

Davis (1983) further asserted that during the post-slavery period, most black women who did not toil in the fields were to become domestic servants. She declared, "In the eyes of the former slaveholders, 'domestic service' must have been a courteous term for a contemptible occupation not a half-step away from slavery" (p. 90). Davis stated,

> From Reconstruction to the present, black women household workers have considered sexual abuse perpetrated by the "man of the house" as one of their major occupational hazards. Time after time, they have been victims of extortion on the job, compelled to choose between sexual submission and absolute poverty for themselves and their families. (p. 91) . . .

> Since slavery, the vulnerable condition of the household worker has continued to nourish many of the lingering myths about the "immorality" of black women. In this classic "catch-22" situation, household work is considered degrading because it has been disproportionately performed by black women, who in turn are viewed as "inept" and "promiscuous." (pp. 92-93)

In a later publication, Davis (1985) discussed the anti-rape movement of the early 1970s that challenged many of the myths regarding rape. One myth that was refuted in this effort is the myth that the rape victim has control over whether or not her body is violated during the rape act, that is, that the victim is morally responsible for the crime committed against her (p. 5). She also refuted the widespread myth that if a woman does not resist, then she is implicitly inviting violation of her body.

Although there is a pervasive fear among most women of being raped, at the same time, many women believe that it cannot really happen to them. However, Davis (1985) noted,

Rape happens anytime, anywhere, to females of all ages—from infants of four months to women over ninety years old, although the single largest group of rape survivors is composed of adolescent girls between the ages of 16 and 18. Rape happens to women of all races and all classes, regardless of sexual orientation. (p. 6)

Davis further declared that rape is not an act of lust committed by strangers who cannot control their sexual desires. She stated that, instead, men's motives for rape arise from their need to exercise power and control over women through violence.

Most rapists indeed are not psychopaths, as we are led to believe by typical media portrayals of men who commit crimes of sexual violence. To the contrary, the overwhelming majority of rapists would be considered "normal" according to prevailing social standards of male normality. (p. 6)

Davis then suggested that the "most insidious myth about rape is that it is most likely to be committed by a black man" (p. 6). According to Davis (1983), the myth of the black rapist of white women is the twin of the myth of the bad black woman. She further explained that these myths have their roots in slavery.

Slavery relied as much on routine sexual abuse as it relied on the whip and the lash. Excessive sex urges, whether they existed among individual white men or not, had nothing to do with this virtual institutionalization of rape. Sexual coercion was, rather, an essential dimension of the social relations between slavemaster and slave. . . . The license to rape emanated from and facilitated the ruthless economic domination that was the gruesome hallmark of slavery. (p. 175)

Davis (1983) then addressed the myth of the black rapist as a distinctly political and racist invention:

As Frederick Douglass points out, black men were not indiscriminately labeled as rapists during slavery. Throughout the entire Civil War, in fact, not a single black man was publicly accused of raping a white woman. If black men possessed an animalistic urge to rape, argued Douglass, this alleged rape instinct would have certainly been activated when white women were left unprotected by their men who were fighting in the Confederate Army. (p. 184)

The menacing specter of the black rapist did not appear on the historical scene immediately after the Civil War. During the period of emancipation, when the black man tried to claim his rights to work and independence, the myth of the black rapist appeared to justify lynchings of "uppity niggers." Lynching now was explained and rationalized as a method to avenge black men's assaults on white southern womanhood (Davis, 1983, p. 186). Davis (1983) then commented that both Douglass and Ida B. Wells pointed out in their analyses of lynching that the cry of rape became a legitimate excuse for lynching and that former white proponents of black equality became increasingly afraid to associate themselves with the black people's struggle for liberation (p. 188).

Davis (1985) suggested that because of this history of lynching, the mythical black rapist, and much of the early activism of the 1970s that was focused on delivering rapists into the hands of the judicial system, "many Afro-American women were understandably reluctant to become involved with a movement which might well lead to further repressive assaults on their families and communities" (p. 6). She further asserted that many of the early feminist theories about rape "tended to bolster and legitimize anti-male anger by defining rape as an inevitable product of masculine nature" (p. 8) and that they failed to take into account the class and racial components of many rapes suffered by working class women and women of color. She also noted that rape frequently is a component of torture inflicted on women political prisoners. She argued that, in contrast to these early feminist theories, "rape bears a direct relationship to all of the existing power structures in a given society" (p. 9). Furthermore, this involves complex structures reflecting the complex interconnectedness of race, gender, and class oppression. In presenting her own feminist theory for the causes and elimination of rape, Davis argued,

> The very same social conditions which spawn racist violence—the same social conditions which encourage attacks on workers, and the political posture which justifies U.S. intervention in Central America and aid to the apartheid government in South Africa—are the same forces which encourage sexual violence. Thus, sexual violence can never be completely eradicated until we have succeeded in effecting a whole range of radical social transformations in our country. (p. 11) . . .
>
> And the systematic oppression of women in our society cannot be accurately evaluated except as it is connected to racism and class exploitation at home and imperialist aggression and the potential nuclear holocaust which menace the entire globe. (p. 12)

Davis, however, suggested that recognizing the larger sociopolitical context of sexist violence does not require that feminists ignore the specific and concrete necessity for an ongoing campaign against rape.

So far, this chapter has presented the history and diversity of feminist thought on crimes by women and victimization of women. The works of several feminist scholars were used as examples of each of the major theoretical approaches among feminists in criminology. The next part of the chapter concentrates more fully on the biographical sketches and theoretical contributions of two feminist criminologists.

Coramae Richey Mann (1931-)

Coramae Richey Mann, a feminist scholar, began her education and work in clinical psychology in Chicago. As indicated in the biographical inset on Mann (Inset 9.1), her early work involved her with social programs in Cook County. After earning her Ph.D. in sociology (criminology) at the University of Illinois in 1976, she began another successful career in academia. As a criminologist, her research has been directed toward those oppressed by the juvenile and criminal justice system—

INSET 9.1

Coramae Richey Mann (1931-)

Coramae Richey Mann was born in 1931 in the only "colored hospital" in Chicago, Provident Hospital, while her mother was home visiting her own mother. After the birth, her mother returned with Coramae to Dayton, Ohio, where Coramae's father was a high school teacher and coach of the football, baseball, and basketball teams. Her mother was a classical pianist who had gone to the Chicago Conservatory of Music. After her maternal grandfather died, Coramae's family returned to Chicago. Instead of sending her to Chicago public schools, her parents sent her to Palmer Memorial Institute, a "colored boarding school" in North Carolina, and later to Minneapolis, Minnesota, to live with relatives and attend high school.

Mann, who now is a professor emeritus in the Department of Criminal Justice at Indiana University and in the School of Criminology at Florida State University, received her B.A. and M.A. degrees in clinical psychology from Roosevelt University in Chicago. After earning her M.A. in 1961, she worked as a research psychologist for the Chicago Board of Health, as research project coordinator and administrative director for the Planned Parenthood Association in Chicago, and as research project coordinator/consulting psychologist for the Chicago Board of Education and Northeastern University.

In 1976, Mann received her Ph.D. in sociology/criminology from the University of Illinois at Chicago. While doing her doctoral work, she was awarded the American Sociological Association Minority Fellowship. After this, she launched a successful career in teaching, research, and service at Florida State University and Indiana University. Beyond her university teaching and service, Mann has achieved national recognition for her research and publications and for her service to professional organizations such as the American Society of Criminology (ASC) and the Academy of Criminal Justice Sciences. In 1994, she was appointed to the National Criminal Justice Commission with the goal of producing an independent critical assessment of the U.S. justice system. Also, as a member of the ASC's Policy Task Force, she advised Attorney General Janet Reno on drugs and the community. Mann has published four books—*Images of Color, Images of Crime* (Mann and Zatz, 1998b), *When Women Kill* (Mann, 1996), *Unequal Justice* (Mann, 1993c), and *Female Crime and Delinquency* (Mann, 1984)—as well as approximately 30 book chapters and articles in professional journals.

Mann's many accomplishments and contributions to the discipline have not gone unrewarded. She was the recipient of both the Bruce Smith Award of the Academy of Criminal Justice Sciences and the Distinguished Scholar Award of the ASC's Women and Crime division in 1995. She also was named a fellow of the Academy of Criminal Justice Sciences in 1996 and a fellow of the ASC in 1999. In 1999, Mann also received the Distinguished Scholar Award from the ASC's People of Color and Crime division.

SOURCE: Coramae Richey Mann vita, American Society of Criminology, *People of Color and Crime* division newsletter, Spring 2000, Vol. 1, pp. 1-2.

youths, women, and racial/ethnic minorities. She has received several national fellowships and grants for educational and research purposes as well as several honors and awards.

Conceptions of Race and Ethnicity

Mann's works on race and ethnic minorities have made significant contributions to our understanding of crime and justice. After providing traditional definitions of race and ethnicity (Mann, 1998b, p. 3), she argued with Zatz that race is a social construction (Mann and Zatz, 1998a, 1998b). According to Zatz and Mann (1998),

> This means that (1) race is not a fixed identity—it is socially decided rather than biologically determined; (2) racial categories and the meanings attached to race make sense only in their historical contexts and in light of specific social relations (e.g., slave-master, maid-employer, doctor-patient); and (3) racial dynamics are flexible, fluid, and *always* political. (p. 2)

Zatz and Mann further stated that a consequence of racism found in this society is the deep schisms between American citizens that result from racial segregation in housing and jobs.

> The proliferation of African American rural and inner-city ghettos, Latino barrios, and Chinatowns, and the shameful theft of land from Indians that left them on small isolated reservations, reflect the imposed segregation that is "more entrenched in American cities today than ever imagined." (pp. 4-5)

Zatz and Mann (1998) went on to explain that race, gender, and class are interlocking systems of domination and oppression of our social structure. They continued by pointing out that the domination and oppression lend themselves to stereotypes such as

> the African American welfare queens, drunken American Indian men, and Latino drug-dealing gang-bangers. Consider, too, Aunt Jemima of pancake and syrup fame; the evil Fu Manchu and the sexy Susie Wong; and Pocahontas and her Mexican counterpart, la Maliche. . . . Gender is very much a part of each of the racist depictions. (p. 7)

Zatz and Mann (1998) further argued that the power of these stereotypes lead to five faces of oppression. First is the exploitation of workers such as slavery and the use of garment workers in the Third World. Second, marginalization applies to people whom the system of labor cannot or will not use including old people, young African Americans and Latinos, single mothers, the physically disabled, and American Indians living on reservations. Third is the powerlessness of those who have little or no control over making decisions in the workplace such as food servers at fast-food places and factory assembly line workers. Fourth is the systemic violence exemplified by unprovoked attacks including church burning, gay bashing, and looting of Korean grocery stores. Fifth, cultural imperialism occurs when the dominant group's experiences, values, goals, and achievements are taken as normal, that is, as the way things should be; stereotyping, they contend, is an important part of cultural imperialism (e.g., everyone knows that gay people are promiscuous and that Indians are alcoholics) (pp. 7-8).[9]

Racism and the Criminal Justice System: The Controversy

Throughout these works (Mann, 1987, 1993a, 1993b; Mann and Zatz, 1998a, 1998b; Zatz and Mann, 1998), Mann suggested that racial/ethnic stereotypes and racial oppression are the foundation for a racist justice system. In fact, the controversial issue of racism in the criminal justice system became prominent after Wilbanks (1987) published his book, *The Myth of a Racist Criminal Justice System*. At that time, Mann was in the process of writing her book on race and unequal justice, which was published in 1993 (Mann, 1987, p. 1; Mann, 1993c). At least two debates between Mann and Wilbanks occurred at professional criminology meetings. In these debates, Wilbanks basically stated the position in his book, and Mann challenged and refuted Wilbanks' claims.

The two sides of this controversy were published in 1987. Although Wilbanks (1987) used the term "racist" in the title of his book, Mann (1987) pointed out,

> Wilbanks quickly and inexplicably abandons the term racism and substitutes racial prejudice and racial discrimination in its stead. It is my contention that all terms are applicable when the plight of minorities in the criminal justice system is examined. . . . More in accord with our urbane times, racial prejudice has not declined but [rather] has simply "gone underground" and become more subtle. That is, it has become institutionalized—the process that "institutionalized racism" connotes. (p. 2)

Wilbanks (1987) stated, "The book was undertaken to explain why blacks in the U.S. are 8 times more likely, on a per capita basis, to be in prison than are whites" (p. 3). He contended that this is because blacks are eight times more likely to offend and not the result of racial selectivity by the police and courts. Mann (1987) challenged the validity of Wilbanks' methodology as follows:

> After repeatedly stating that the research is "sparse," Wilbanks is chagrined that with or without controls, "a sizable race effect" cannot be demonstrated at decision points throughout the criminal justice system. Aside from not defining "sizable," "substantial," or even "race effect," Wilbanks uses his aggregate study in two states (California and Pennsylvania) for one year (1980) as the exemplar. . . . Unfortunately, the value of this effort is diminished since Wilbanks did not use any controls in the study. (p. 3)

Mann criticized Wilbanks not only for the narrowness of his quantitative data but also for his neglect of the qualitative research data as a rich source of information.

> Clearly, one method is insufficient to explore such a sensitive issue as racism in the criminal justice system. As Wilbanks suggests, future research on this question should concentrate on individual decision makers. . . . This cannot be fully accomplished without qualitative methods such as observation, interviews, biographical analyses, testing, card sorts, and similar techniques. (p. 5)

Finally, Mann questioned Wilbanks' exclusive concern with the black-white gap in both arrests and incarcerations. She suggested that, based on the Uniform Crime Reports for the 1979-1985 period, there also were overrepresentations of arrests of Hispanic Americans, Asian Americans, and Native Americans disproportionate to their numbers in the population (p. 3).

Mann (1993c) carefully employed the minority experiences of the major racial/ethnic groups to explain the racism, the history of exploitation, the law and its enforcement, and the unequal justice for minorities as the justice system responds to the "minority crime problem." In this work, she examined African Americans as well as black West Indians, Hispanic Americans (which commonly include people of Mexican, Puerto Rican, Cuban, and other Latin American descent), Asian Americans (Chinese Americans, Japanese Americans, Koreans, Filipinos, and Southeast Asians), and Native Americans (pp. 5-21). In support of her conceptualization of racial prejudice and stereotypes as well as institutionalized racism, she recounted the history of discrimination and exploitation of each minority group. The following is an example:

> The first African slaves arrived in Virginia in 1619 . . ., a fact that illustrates two salient points: (1) African Americans were the only racial or ethnic group brought here against their will and (2) African Americans are among the oldest Americans with a history and cultural heritage largely formed in this country. (p. 6) . . .
>
> In the forging of the new Constitution, the slaves could not be counted as people but only as property or "three-fifths of a man." (p. 7)

Hispanic Americans illustrate the exploitation of the land originally belonging to Mexico and the discrimination and prejudice they continue to experience by those of European descent. Mann stated,

> Mexican Americans have the distinction of being among the oldest and the newest Americans, since many settlements of people in the Southwest came from Mexico and were here long before the Anglo-Americans arrived. However, most Mexican Americans came to this country in the twentieth century. . . . The war against Mexico (1845) resulted in the acquisition of vast areas that are now California, Nevada, Arizona, Utah, New Mexico, and parts of Colorado, Kansas, Oklahoma, and Wyoming. . . . Suddenly the Mexicans, who originally had a country larger than the United States, became the minority in the new states. (p. 8)[10]

Among the Asian Americans, the "ultimate demonstration of racism" was the executive order by President Roosevelt in 1942 that led to the internment of 110,000 men, women, and children—citizens and aliens alike—nearly the entire Japanese American population (Mann, 1993c, p. 15). They were rounded up on the West Coast and placed in concentration camps in the desert, the Rocky Mountains, and Arkansas—"places where nobody had lived before and no one has lived since." Although this part of the chapter has looked at only three of the racial/ethnic groups that she discussed in that chapter, Mann (1993c) used this "minority view" to make the following point:

Any effort to understand the plight of racial minorities in the American criminal justice system must include the historical and experiential background of each of the
groups and the evolutionary circumstances that helped to determine how they are defined and how these definitions have led to their contemporary status in that system.
(p. 21)

Mann (1993c) devoted a chapter to explanations of minority crime and challenged the heavy emphasis of most theories of race and crime as being primarily concerned with African Americans and violent crime (p. 70). She further suggested that
the literature is replete with theories that include biogenic, psychogenic, and
sociogenic factors to explain African American (and occasionally other minority) homicide and other forms of violent crime. Mann credited much of the emphasis on violent crime to the historical tradition of violence in this country. She noted the violence
of the lynch mobs associated with the Ku Klux Klan that emerged in the backcountry
of South Carolina in 1767. Furthermore, "lynching is not an obsolete phenomenon;
today there are isolated lynchings of minorities reported across the country" (p. 104).
Other indicators of a violent tradition in this country suggested by Mann are the wars
that raged between whites and American Indians from 1607 to 1890, the ongoing
blood feuds between families in the mountains of the Southeast, and the government's use of deadly force such as the National Guard's killing of Colorado strikers in
1912 and their killing of unarmed Kent State University students in 1970. In addition
to the stereotypes of minorities as violent, Mann examined the bias and discrimination in the laws and law enforcement to support her contention that the criminal justice system is racist. The following is an example:

The west coast Chinese were damaged economically by such racially discriminatory
laws as the 1857 statutes in Oregon that required every Chinese miner to pay a
monthly tax to the local sheriff for property protection. If it was not paid, the result
was seizure and sale of all property within the hour. Other laws prohibited Chinese immigrants from owning real estate.... California ordinances ... structured the occupational choices of the Chinese: business and occupational licenses were denied to "any
alien ineligible for citizenship." (p. 125)

Mann (1993c) examined other laws and court decisions that discriminated
against racial/ethnic minorities. She pointed to the *Plessy v. Ferguson* (1896) court
decision that upheld a Louisiana railroad law requiring "separate but equal" accom-
modations for African Americans and Euro-Americans that provided a constitutional basis for segregationist state laws (p. 124). For more than 50 years, it was lawful to deny blacks equal protection of the laws by compelling racial segregation.

In the 1830 decision in *Cherokee Nation v. Georgia,* the U.S. Supreme Court rejected the plea of the Cherokee for the court to intervene and protect their lands. Like
other tribes, they were ousted from their lands and escorted west. They were stripped
of their lands and segregated on reservations, and their sovereignty was removed by
the elimination of their abilities to make treaties. The final blow came in 1886, when
the court ruled that the Indians were wards of the federal government for their own
protection (p. 124).

Mann (1993c) went on to document police prejudice and discrimination in their interactions with various racial/ethnic minority groups. Studies of police discretion cited by Mann (pp. 133-138) provide support for racial prejudice and discrimination by officers who make street decisions based on stereotypes that they have learned through training and experiences. For example, Police Chief Daryl Gates blamed deaths that occurred as a result of choke holds on Africa Americans by Los Angeles police officers on the victims "for not having veins in their necks 'like normal people' " (p. 152).

In examining unequal justice, Mann (1993c) dealt with pretrial experiences of minorities, such as bail and detention, as well as court personnel including judges, selection of juries, prosecutors, and public defenders. For example, she cited an earlier observational court study (Mann, 1984) that found that the type of representation (private attorney or public defender) made a significant difference in sentencing outcomes for women felons (Mann, 1993c, p. 178). Controlling for race, the study revealed that African American women with public defenders were not likely to receive prison sentences, whereas African American women who engaged private attorneys were likely to receive prison sentences. White women, by contrast, were not likely to receive prison sentences whatever type of attorney represented them.

One of the most controversial court sentences is the death penalty. Mann (1993c) explored the vast body of literature that indicates that there is racial bias in the application of capital punishment (p. 203). Although the bias starts with the prosecutor's decision to charge the offender with a capital offense, the majority of African Americans and other minorities on death row have killed white persons.

Finally, Mann (1993c) pointed to the numerous studies of prison populations documenting the fact that "the extended reach of the criminal justice system has been far from uniform. . . . The criminal justice system disproportionately engages minorities and the poor" (p. 220). This heavy increase in prison populations in general and the overrepresentation of minorities result in the "minority correctional warehousing." In addition, cultural differences between minorities (e.g., Native American and Muslim religious traditions and practices) and their white prison guards and staff result in documented discrimination demonstrated in racial slurs, harassment, brutality, and violation of minority prisoners' rights.

Thus, Mann (1993c) provided substantial evidence to support her claims of unequal justice in the processing of offenders at various stages of the criminal justice system. She noted that this evidence leaves "little doubt that there are racial differences and that such differential treatment is generally detrimental to minority defendants" (p. 210).

In addition to examining the unequal justice of minorities, Mann (1989) turned to the racial discrimination and prejudice against women offenders (black, Hispanic, and Native American) by officials in the criminal justice system. She noted that they experience "double discrimination" by the justice system because of their gender and their race/ethnicity (p. 95). She further argued,

An analysis of grand larceny and felonious assault cases sampled from criminal cases in all 50 states isolated a *disadvantaged pattern of discrimination* which resulted in adverse treatment of black women at virtually all stages of the criminal process. (p. 98)

To support this claim of a disadvantaged pattern of discrimination, Mann reviewed the data from official statistics and research studies and found that black women are most frequently arrested for criminal homicides and are more likely to be arrested for prostitution. In fact, Mann (1995) later noted that in 1986, the last year that the Uniform Crime Reports included Hispanic arrests, "African Americans and Hispanics were the only persons of color arrested for prostitution and commercialized vice in proportions higher than their population percentages" (p. 119). She indicated that public order offenses, such as drunkenness and driving under the influence, dominate arrests for Native American women, whereas property crimes are the most frequent arrest offenses for Asian American women (p. 124). This would seem to lend credence to the influence of racial stereotyping presented by Mann and Zatz (1998a, 1998b).

Mann (1989) suggested that there is a "black shift phenomenon," especially in prison populations (p. 99). That is, "As compared to whites, African [American] women seem underdefended and oversentenced. . . . They may have been over-arrested and overindicted as well" (Mann, 1995, p. 125).

Mann (1989) proposed a "devaluation hypothesis" to explain the shift in prison populations to blacks and other racial/ethnic minority women (p. 100). She defined the devaluation hypothesis as the idea that the criminal justice system values white lives and devalues black and minority lives in the imposition of harsher sentences if the victims are white rather than black or other minorities. This devaluation could be seen particularly in an interracial crime (p. 111, note 7).

Women Who Kill

For this exploratory study, Mann (1988, pp. 34-35; 1990a, pp. 177, 180; 1990b, pp. 93-94; 1993a, pp. 231-232; 1993b, p. 200; 1996, pp. 32-35) collected a random sample of cleared female homicide cases in Chicago, Houston, Los Angeles, and New York as well as all of the female cases in Atlanta and Baltimore[11] for the years 1979 and 1983. These six cities were chosen because they had homicide rates equal to or higher than the national rates for both years and because they provide modest regional representations of homicides for the years selected.

Characteristics of homicide offenders. Although Mann (1990a) reported a decrease of black female homicide arrests from 1979 to 1983, the subgroup of 230 black women who committed homicide comprised 77.7% of the sample of 296 cases (12.8% were white and 9.5% were Hispanic) (pp. 179-180). However, Mann (1996) stated,

> But a comparison in terms of race/ethnicity for the most part reveals that racial/ethnic status is not a distinguishing characteristic of women who kill or of those whom they kill. Regardless of race or ethnicity, female homicide offenders tend to be under thirty years of age, in some form of marital status, unemployed, mothers, and with better than a junior high school education. Hispanic women are the most likely to have been in a once-married status. (p. 120) . . .

A single significant difference was found as regards the race/ethnicity of the victims. Although the majority of murders committed by women tended to be intraracial, among the interracial homicides it was discovered that white women are more likely to kill African Americans ... than African American women are to kill whites. (p. 122)

Mann (1990a) asserted that the present research is consistent with previous research in findings that women most often kill men of their own race, that is, that female homicide is intersexual and intraracial (p. 184). Mann (1996) also found that murder occurred more frequently in residences but less often for African American and Hispanic offenders than for white offenders. Women of color were more likely than white women to commit murder in the street, in a tavern, or in other places outside the home (p. 122). She further reported that white female homicide women were more likely to have prior arrest records than were women of color and that prior arrests of white women were in the misdemeanor category, whereas non-whites were more apt to have violent arrest histories (pp. 140, 142). The data also indicated that non-white female murderers were more likely than white women to be charged with the more serious murder/manslaughter category. Among women of color, African Americans received more serious charges than did Hispanic women. Hispanic women were more apt to be sent to prison than were either African American or white women, but Hispanic women's sentences were for shorter prison terms. Mann concluded, "The more serious charges brought initially against non-white defendants and sustained throughout the later stages of the process effectively labeled them as persons to be maintained in the system" (p. 143). Finally, she noted that these findings do not support the "devaluation theory," which suggests that the criminal justice system does not value the lives of African Americans as much as those of whites.

Domestic homicides. These homicides involve "interpersonal relationships" that are intimate. Most frequently, the affiliation between the domestic homicide offender and her victim was common-law marriage, followed by a relationship as lovers and then marriage (Mann, 1988, p. 38; 1996, pp. 79, 85). "In most cases, despite the lack of legal marital status, the victim and the offender shared or had once shared an intimate sexual and personal existence" (Mann, 1988, p. 35). Mann (1988) found that women who killed in nondomestic situations were predominantly single, in contrast to those who killed in domestic situations. In the latter, most of the victims were male, which supports the previous studies' findings that domestic violence is intersexual (p. 43).[12] This study also found that African American women clearly were the dominant killers of males, who also were African Americans. This supports other studies that reported that domestic homicides are intraracial (Mann, 1988, p. 78; 1996, p. 79).

In examining domestic violence, Mann (1996) noted that most homicides took place in the shared residence of the offender and victim or in the yard of a residence (p. 86). Unlike several previous studies that found the most frequent rooms to be the kitchen or bedroom, Mann reported that the living room, family room, or den was the most frequent location for homicides, followed by the bedroom and then the kitchen. Mann's data also indicated that the gun had replaced the knife as the most frequent weapon used by women (p. 87).

One of Mann's most controversial findings among feminists was her claim that the homicides within these domestic cases did not support the concepts of the battered women's syndrome and learned helplessness. With regard to this, Mann (1996) explained,

> The battered woman syndrome is frequently employed in homicide cases as a rationale for self-defense and implies that the murder was "reasonable and necessary" because the offender "reasonably believed she was in imminent danger of serious bodily harm or death and that the force she used was necessary to avoid danger." . . . Several of the findings in this study are contrary to such a defense. The finding of premeditation in more than half of the cases challenges both the idea of "reasonableness" and the "objective immediacy standard." . . . Finally, the fact that almost half of the domestic homicide offenders had prior arrest histories, including 30 percent who had previously been arrested for violent crimes, belies a suggestion that they were either helpless or afraid of their victims. (p. 171)

Mann (1996) also found that a substantial proportion of domestic homicide victims had previous arrest records, especially prior violent arrest records (p. 82). They also were more likely to have been drinking before their deaths, suggesting "victim precipitation" in these homicides. Mann provided the following case as typical of a victim-provoked domestic homicide:

> Case 2130: Ida's husband of eleven years came home about 8:30 p.m. after a "Thank God It's Friday" drinking spree to find his sisters-in-law in the house. Willie was very angry because the women were there, and a number of insults were exchanged during the ensuing domestic quarrel. Enraged, Ida, thirty-five, removed a .22 pistol from her purse and shot Willie, thirty-eight, one time in the chest. After he was shot, Willie was able to unload and break the gun down. In an effort to protect her mother, their thirteen-year-old daughter claimed that she had shot her father. An autopsy revealed that Willie had a .16 blood alcohol level. The district attorney entered a no bill in the case. (p. 82)

Female intragender homicide. Although Mann (1993b, 1996) observed that most intragender homicide occurs outside the home and usually between acquaintances, lesbian homicides are the exception. Mann (1996) reported finding five lesbian cases, all of which were intraracial: three African American couples, one white couple, and one Hispanic couple (p. 91). Lesbian domestic homicides occurred in the home on weekends or during evening hours. Mann illustrated a lesbian domestic homicide as follows:

> Case 5208: Jackie, age twenty-eight, and her lover, Karla, forty-seven, had lived together for thirteen years and shared the bedroom in the house they rented. Both had been drinking since noon on a Friday and were drunk when the homicide took place the following Saturday morning at 10:15. . . . The lovers got into an argument. . . . In

the course of the argument, Karla spat the food she was eating at Jackie. In angry response, Jackie stabbed Karla in the stomach and the left side. Jackie, who claimed the murder was an accident, stated, "I didn't mean to do it." (p. 92)

Most of the intragender offenders denied responsibility for the homicides, claiming self-defense (i.e., that the homicides were accidents) or that they were innocent. Presumably, the courts believed them (Mann, 1993b, p. 205). Applying Mann's devaluation hypothesis to gender of the victim, her data did not provide significant differences in the ways in which the criminal justice system dealt with the cases with female victims and those with male victims (Mann, 1993, p. 217; 1996, p. 139). Mann (1996) indicated that the women homicide offenders more frequently were charged with murder or manslaughter when they killed other females, but after this, the system tended to favor male victims. That is, the differences are not significant. The data do suggest that when a female murders a male, she is slightly more likely to receive harsher treatment from the criminal justice system than when her victim is another female (p. 139). This provides some support, albeit not very strong support, for the devaluation hypothesis regarding women victims.

Female homicide child victims. The final subgroup to be discussed in Mann's (1993a) study involved 25 women (10 in 1979 and 15 in 1983) who killed 41 children under 18 years of age (p. 232). The majority of the victims were less than 1 year of age, and 3 of those were newborns. Two of the unmarried mothers appeared to experience shame and frustration, as illustrated by the following case:

> Case #N8320: At the time of the filicide, this 21-year-old black student had one child, aged two, by a former boyfriend. The putative father had broken off with the offender and allegedly threatened her life and the life of the unborn child. As a result, according to one witness, the mother-to-be was very depressed. The baby was born in the bathroom and since the offender lived with her mother, she tried to hide the baby in a plastic bag. When her mother yelled at her to get out of the bathroom, the offender claims that in a state of shock she threw the baby out of the sixth-floor window. (p. 233)

By contrast, Mann (1996) described the following case as senseless:

> Case 5221: The twenty-four-year-old mother claimed that she did not know that she was "that pregnant" when, as she used the commode, the baby came out head first into the toilet. Neither the offender, her mother, nor her brother would remove the newborn, stating that they were "afraid to pick up the baby." The female infant apparently was in the commode for fifteen to twenty minutes and was still breathing when the police arrived. She died on the way to the hospital. . . . The mother, who was a known prostitute with a number of misdemeanor arrests, was sentenced to a six-month jail term and five years of probation for the infanticide. (p. 72)

Mann (1993a) explained that data suggest that a female child has less value than a male child (p. 234). The majority of filicides under 1 year of age and among 2- to 5-year-olds were females. Although most of the mothers and filicides were intraracial, Mann (1996) indicated that there were occasional cases that were interracial (p. 74). Mann (1993a) further indicated that most of the offenders with victims in the 2- to 5-year-old category had child abuse histories (p. 237). Mann argued that the early identification of these women as child abusers and the use of some type of intervention therapy might have prevented these deaths. The following case suggests how therapeutic intervention might have saved a 3-year-old's life:

> Case #L8316 concerns a 29-year-old Mexican American mother who had given birth to eight children, two of whom died at her hands. The offender was acquitted of the murder of her eight-month-old, who died from choking after being force fed, but was required to serve three months in jail and was still on five years probation for child abuse. The court social worker described events leading to the last murder as typical of "battered child syndrome": The 3-year-old female victim showed signs of neglect [and] had pneumonia, emphysema, scars, cuts, bruises, burns, and fractures. According to reports, the mother had abused all of her children.... Even her husband was allegedly afraid of the offender. (p. 237)

Women who killed newborns and babies under 1 year of age were more apt to get probation or short jail terms. Those who killed children in the 2- to 5-year-old group were more apt to get prison sentences. Mann (1993a) posed that deaths of the older children might have been more brutal and involved histories of child abuse and neglect, thereby resulting in harsher treatment by the courts (pp. 238-239). Overall, Mann found little in their backgrounds to distinguish women who kill their children from other women who kill (p. 242).

Critique of Mann

Mann has been one of the most productive feminist scholars examining issues of crime and criminal justice for women, racial/ethnic minorities, and youths. A major strength of her works is the inclusion of African Americans, Hispanic Americans, Native Americans, and Asian Americans in her analysis of racism in the criminal justice system in *Unequal Justice* (Mann, 1987, 1993c) and in *Images of Color, Images of Crime* (Zatz and Mann, 1998). The issue of racism in the criminal justice system is quite controversial, and reviews of *Unequal Justice* have reflected the continuation of the debate.

Wilbanks (1993), who argued that racism in the criminal justice system is a myth, suggested that Mann's book "contains the best argument for the discrimination thesis" (p. 54). He further stated that most readers, including those seeking a statement supporting evidence for the "minority perspective," will find Mann's thesis to be too radical (p. 53). Some might suggest that Wilbanks' review lacks "rigorous scholarship" because he criticized her work without providing substantive material from *Unequal Justice* to support his claims. In light of this, it is surprising that Wilbanks closed his emotional and negative review by stating that Mann "is not in the habit of rigorous thinking" (p. 54).

Green (1994) acknowledged that many criminologists, as well as most criminal justice practitioners and the general public, may disagree with the conclusions that Mann makes (p. 421). Zingraff (1993) also criticized Mann for her sweeping claims but cautioned that the value of her work should not be neglected:

> Readers looking for a compendium of evidence on racism as a component of law and social control in the U.S. will find it here. What will agitate some is Mann's disappointing tendency to insert sweeping categorical claims about the conditions she describes or the bigotry she discerns. The system of unequal justice this book explains merits much anger and resentment, but the polemics can distract readers from the legitimacy of its scholarship.... The powerful data summarized here [are] worthy of intensive review and should be widely available. (p. 227)

Similarly, Green (1994) stated in his review,

> Therefore, many who hear about this book ... will dismiss it as merely another by some liberal academician to sell a Marxian view of crime. This response will be unfortunate.... Granted, the book presents little new evidence.... What is new about Mann's work is her "minority view." Actually, throughout the book, but specifically at the conclusion of each chapter, Mann summarizes the major problems in the definition and measurement of minority crime ... from the perspective of minority criminologists and criminal justice practitioners. The most thought-provoking ideas of her book are in these sections. (p. 421)

Green further noted that Mann's argument that the misconceptions and myths about minority crime come from mainstream criminologists' almost exclusive reliance on quantitative methods of crime data analysis is unsettling to many mainstream criminologists. Furthermore, Mann's thesis that minority crime is rooted in the historic oppression of people of color and that, therefore, such research should be undertaken primarily by minority researchers is offensive to some criminologists. Green concluded his review as follows:

> Mann also begins the important task of relating the literature on minority crime to the broader historical, social, and economic experiences of various minority groups in the United States.... Much more work needs to be done on other decision-making points in the criminal justice system from this perspective (particularly on law and enforcement practices), but her lively work on the relationship between skin color and criminal justice outcomes offers compelling ideas for theory and research. (p. 421)

Even though the review by Zingraff (1993) was quite brief, he and Green (1994) presented a much needed objective scholarly assessment of Mann's "minority view" of racial/ethnic crime and the criminal justice system.

Whereas the reviews of *Unequal Justice* (Mann, 1993c) did not appear in major criminology professional journals, Block's (1998) review of *When Women Kill* (Mann, 1996) appeared in *Justice Quarterly*. Block (1998) noted that Mann's methodology, which involves a random sample of women arrested for homicide in six

U.S. cities for 1979 and 1983, "is painstaking and straightforward." She further explained,

> Mann's work provides the kind of building block called for in the 1991 "agenda for the future of homicide research" presented at the charter meeting of the Homicide Research Working Group. . . . It addresses three of the items on that agenda: research on vulnerable but understudied groups (women), studies of the risk of becoming an offender as well as the risk of becoming a victim, and the comparison of homicide patterns and trends across cities. (p. 362)

Block also indicated that Mann's study included all women arrested for homicide, regardless of the criminal justice outcome. This differentiates Mann's research from other studies of female homicide patterns that limited the population to women who had been tried, convicted, and sentenced to prison.

Block suggested that "not only the data set but also the menu of variables is innovative" (p. 363). In addition to typical pieces of information, the *When Women Kill* data set contains intriguing variables that seldom are reported. Despite the vast amount of interesting information offered, Block noted that the straightforward way in which facts are presented leaves most of the interpretation to the reader. This organization is difficult to follow and leaves the reader searching for material to illuminate a theoretical or practical intervention problem (p. 364). Block proposed, however, that *When Women Kill* is a gold mine of information for those who are willing to dig. Block concluded her review by stating,

> With this study, Coramae Richey Mann provides a touchstone of facts in a subject that is often emotionally charged. She finds no support for a "profile of monstrous female killers." . . . The development of theories that meet the test of reality, and of effective programs and policies, must rest on focused descriptions such as these. *When Women Kill* undoubtedly will become one of the most-used and best-thumbed references on the shelf of anyone interested in violence or violence prevention, whether they deal in theory or in practice. (p. 365)

Even though these reviews provided criticisms of Mann's research methods and presentation, they also recognized her excellent contributions and provided evidence that her research will stimulate innovative approaches by future researchers, theorists, and practitioners in criminology. Mann's works may be defined as criminological orientations or criminological interpretations of data given that they do not meet the classic social science definition of theory. Some theorists may argue that the concepts, such as institutionalized racism and the devaluation hypothesis, would make Mann's work fit in as one of the "special theories" that Merton asserted are necessary for the development of theories of the middle range. Most definitely, Mann's emphasis on unequal justice and her research analysis of women who kill provide important policy implications for the criminal justice system to consider. As indicated in the biographical inset on Mann (Inset 9.1), her numerous contributions have been rewarded by honors that she has received from various professional associations and by universities and government agencies.

Sally S. Simpson (1954-)

Sally Simpson was born in Pendleton, Oregon, where she received her early education including her B.S. in sociology with honors in 1976. As indicated in the biographical inset on Simpson (Inset 9.2), she received her M.A. in sociology in 1978 and her Ph.D. in sociology with distinction in 1985. She had a variety of teaching experiences before joining the faculty at the University of Maryland at College Park in 1989. She has conducted research on a variety of topics in criminology, but her publications have been predominantly on feminist theory and corporate crime. During the past 10 years, she has increasingly received recognition for her excellent scholarship and for her service to professional associations.

Conflict and Female Correctional Officers in Male Prisons

One of Simpson's earliest research interests emerged during her studies at Washington State University when she wrote her thesis on women correctional officers in male prisons. Simpson and White[13] (1985) reported a study that examined sources of conflict among male and female correctional officers in three all-male federal prisons. The data were from a larger study of the organizational contexts of correctional officer work (p. 285). The authors created and administered an attitude scale to measure respondent liberality regarding the appropriateness of women for correctional positions (p. 284). The research examined both demographic variables of officers and the organizational and cultural structures of the prisons to understand the attitudes toward women correctional officers.

Simpson and White (1985) argued that conflicts between male and female correctional officers are a function of differences in the gender role culture of the formerly all-male correctional officer role and that this gender role culture is embedded in the organization of the prison itself (p. 295). In conclusion, they stated,

> Clearly, our data support the interpretation that these attitudes are embedded in the organizational structure of the prison. However, we must exercise caution not to overinterpret these findings. . . .
>
> If our interpretations are correct, we can anticipate that while gender role biased attitudes may derive from the larger culture, those measured by our scale reflect the fact that the correctional officer position has historically been an all-male one in the all-male prison. These attitudes and beliefs, then, are part of the organizational structure of the prison. Changes are not likely to occur easily. (p. 295)

The Feminist Perspective in Crime and Justice

Simpson's works in feminist criminology came more than a decade after the works of the early pioneer feminists such as Adler, Simon, and Wilson discussed earlier. Yet, her feminist theory (Simpson, 1989, 1991; Simpson and Elis, 1995) makes a

INSET 9.2

Sally S. Simpson (1954-)

Sally Simpson was born September 15, 1954, in Pendleton, Oregon. Her parents owned and operated a wheat ranch. Her father died when she was an infant, and her mother took over the operation of the ranch. After graduation from high school, Simpson attended Oregon State University, where she received a B.S. in sociology with honors in 1976. She received her M.A. in sociology in 1978 from Washington State University. One of her mentors, Gerald Garrett, was a visiting professor at Washington State. Garrett influenced Simpson to take a position at Troy State University at the Torrejon Air Force Base near Madrid, Spain. After returning to the United States, she enrolled in the doctoral program in sociology at the University of Massachusetts at Amherst. Her dissertation project was a pooled cross-sectional analysis of archival and secondary data that examined the anti-competitive behavior of 52 survivor corporations. These corporations were spread across 55 years of business activity. Simpson received her Ph.D. with distinction in 1985.

Simpson taught at College of the Holy Cross in Worcester, Massachusetts, from 1983 to 1985 while completing her dissertation. She was a visiting assistant professor at Smith College in Northampton, Massachusetts, during the 1985-1986 period. She returned to Oregon, where she taught at the University of Oregon from 1986 to 1989. While teaching at that university, Simpson received two small grants to conduct research on women, class, and crime. She also received a Post-Doctoral Research Fellow at the Harvard Business School to work with Amitai Etzioni and Rosabeth Moss Kanter during the 1988-1989 period. The research fellowship at Harvard involved construction of an interview schedule and in-depth interviews with 79 corporate executives at three U.S. firms.

Simpson joined the faculty of the Institute of Criminal Justice and Criminology at the University of Maryland at College Park in 1989. She is an associate professor as well as director of the graduate program at that university. In addition to her teaching and administrative and committee work, Simpson continues to conduct research and receive grants to study women offenders and corporate crime. She has an impressive publication record including articles in top professional journals, book chapters, an edited book on criminological theory, and a book on corporate crime that is in process.

At the national level, Simpson serves on numerous editorial boards of professional journals. She was elected and served as chair of the Section on Crime, Law, and Deviance of the American Sociological Association during the 1995-1996 period. She also served as executive secretary of the American Society of Criminology (ASC) during the 1995-1998 period. She received the ASC's Herbert Bloch Award in 1999.

In addition to her very active professional life, Simpson and her husband, Stas Wronka, are the parents of a son, Gabriel Ian Wronka, born September 18, 1997.

SOURCE: Sally S. Simpson vita and personal conversations and professional interactions at conferences.

critical contribution to the development and expansion of feminist criminology. This is partially because of the clarity with which she writes. Her works also are valuable because of her ability to challenge previous directions without attacking other scholars.

Simpson (1989) argued,

Feminism is best understood as both a worldview and a social movement. . . . As such, feminism is both analytical and empirical. In its incipient form, feminist research almost exclusively focused on women—as a way of placing women at the center of inquiry and building a base of knowledge. As it has matured, feminism has become more encompassing, taking into account the gendered understanding of all aspects of human culture and relationships. (p. 606)

Simpson made it clear that feminist theory is not a single perspective but rather a cacophony of comment and criticism that offers insights from a woman's perspective. Feminists also are concerned with "demystifying masculine knowledge as objective knowledge" (p. 608).

Race, Class, and Gender

Simpson (1989, 1991; see also Simpson and Elis, 1995) has been among the first feminist criminologists to note the importance of the complex interplay of gender, class, and race oppression as it relates to crimes by women and victimization of women. Simpson and Elis (1995) cautioned feminists not to practice the essentialism for which they have criticized male criminologists:

Despite their important contributions to criminological study, feminist scholars often fall into their own brand of reductionism by assuming that the experiences of women . . . are universal and distinct from those of men. This type of thinking is defined as *essentialism,* and critics claim that this form of reductionism subsumes all female experiences into one common experience, most typically that of middle class whites. (p. 47)

Simpson (1989) claimed that feminist criminologists are guilty of the "add race and stir" shortsightedness that pervades feminist thinking (p. 619). She asserted that there is enormous risk in ignoring the race-crime relationship, which has been justified by "poorly conceived offender self-report surveys" (p. 617). Reliance on quantitative data also provides a foundation to dichotomize race into white and black (or non-white). Accordingly, Simpson stated that more quantitative research is needed on minority groups other than blacks—such as Chicanos and other Hispanics, Asians, and Native Americans—to establish a better knowledge base. Qualitative research also needs to be done that probes culture and subjective differences between women of color and whites (p. 619). This qualitative approach will add detail to how crime and justice are gendered and will lead to richer theory and better criminology (p. 622).

Simpson (1991) applied race and class to explore female violent crime. In this work, she proposed that black females appear to respond differently to conditions of poverty, racism, and patriarchy compared to their class, gender, and racial counterparts. That is, "black females, especially those in the 'underclass,' engage in what might be considered anomalous behavior for their gender . . . but not for their race" (p. 116). According to Simpson, violent crime among underclass black females is taken as illustrative of vertical (power) and horizontal (affiliative) differences between blacks and whites, between males and females, and between social classes.

Simpson (1991) asserted that most theories of crime are class sensitive but not race and gender sensitive (p. 121). Therefore, she assessed three theories for their ability to account for gender, class, and racial differences in violent offending. Simpson cited Colvin and Pauly's (1983) effort to relate delinquency of youths to the type of employment (e.g., skilled worker/monopoly capitalist vs. unskilled worker/competitive capitalist) of their parents:

> Parents who experience alienative bonding to authority in coercive work situations re-produce those relations with their children. . . . Therefore, children whose parents are least skilled and subject to coercive discipline at work are more likely to act out in criminally violent ways. (Simpson, 1991, p. 121)

Simpson (1991) asserted that Colvin and Pauly's theory adds conceptually to the class-violent delinquency relations but fails to account for gender and race differences among juveniles whose parents are similarly located in the class structure (p. 122).

The second perspective, Hagan, Simpson, and Gillis's (1987) power-control theory, includes gender but only under certain class and familial structures. Power-control theory builds on the idea that workplace-family power relations affect how parental discipline operates (mother or father as instrument of control) as well as which child is most apt to be disciplined by which parent (male or female as object of control). Simpson (1991) suggested, "Appropriate modifications of the theory should focus on how violence is related to freedom to deviate, an absence of controls, and/or socialized risk preferences" (p. 123). With reference to power-control theory, Simpson criticized the theory for its failure to address how patriarchy varies across racial groups and class lines. With reference to Messerschmidt's (1986) socialist-feminist approach to crime, Simpson (1991) credits this approach with at least being concerned with its failure to link race and racism systematically with class and patriarchy. According to this perspective, patriarchal capitalism creates two distinct groups: the powerful (males and capitalists) and the powerless (females and the working class) (pp. 124-125). Opportunities to commit crime vary according to one's structural position. Simpson closed her discussion of the socialist-feminist theory as follows:

> As noted earlier, one of the flaws of socialist-feminism is its neglect of how racial oppression and racism interact with other forms of oppression to produce distinct patterns of criminal offending. A related problem is its insensitivity to intragender variations in violent offending. To suggest that males are violent and females are not ignores the empirical reality of black female crime. (p. 125)

After analyzing these theories, Simpson concluded,

> A review of the empirical literature on violence reveals the confounding effects of gender, race, and class. Although their combined influences are difficult to tease out, a firm understanding of how they interact is fundamental for a more inclusive and elegant criminological theory. (p. 129)

Simpson then conducted several crime and victim studies to examine the interrelationships among gender, race, and class.

Courtship Violence and Social Control

Miller and Simpson (1991) examined the previous research on perceptions of formal and informal controls as effective deterrence of violence (p. 336). Most of the research suggests that the perceived certainty and perceived severity of formal sanctions are not important determinants in the process of deterrence. It is, instead, the informal controls that are influential in facilitating conformity. These studies also reported that women express a greater fear of rule breaking and higher perceptions of risk of sanction threats, both formal and informal, than do males. The studies concerned specifically with physical abuse in intimate relationships reported the following:

> First, males perceive informal sanctions to be more likely than legal sanctions as a reaction to abuse. Moreover, they perceive social condemnation and self-stigma as the most costly consequences of arrest. Second, of the various possible informal consequences associated with battering, men assume that the loss of their partner[s] is least likely. (p. 337)

Research suggests, however, that women in physically abusive relationships often do terminate such ties, although a woman might experience a series of separations and reconciliations prior to a permanent breakup. Several determinants indicate when a woman is apt to leave an abuser. These include the length of time the intimates have been together, the strength of the commitment of the relationship, and whether the offender and victim are married (p. 338). A woman who leaves is more likely to have endured less severe violence, less likely to have initiated criminal proceedings against her partner, and more likely to be more economically independent compared to women who stay in such relationships.

In their research, Miller and Simpson (1991) compared females who seek formal intervention to those who either use informal coping strategies or choose to terminate their relationships (p. 339). They also contrasted female responses with male responses to violence. Contrary to most research of intimates that focus on couples who are married or living together, Miller and Simpson examined intimate violence dating and courtship (p. 341). They administered a questionnaire to 640 college students in eight university classes.[14]

Focusing on formal sanction severity first, Miller and Simpson (1991) reported that for all respondents, only race and serious dating are significant predictors. "Whites and Asians are more apt than blacks and Hispanics to perceive police intervention, court time, and jail as a big problem in their lives" (p. 344). With reference to gender, they stated,

> Gender has no effect on perceptions of formal severity.... Some key differences in perceptions of formal sanction severity do, however, emerge when male and female

subsamples are analyzed separately. Among male respondents, seriously violent offenders are less likely than other males to perceive arrest, sentencing, and jail to be severe. . . . The race and serious dating effects are exclusively female. White and Asian females perceive greater sanction severity than their black and Hispanic counterparts, as
do females who are dating. Perceptions of sanction severity are stronger among
women involved in serious relationships. (p. 345)

Miller and Simpson further reported a strong inverse relationship between formal
sanction certainty and mild violence. Gender effects are strong. Women are much less
likely than men to think that courtship violence will result in a formal justice response. Male perceptions of sanction risk, unlike female perceptions, are affected by
participation in mild violence (p. 346). Furthermore, both black and Hispanic males
are significantly less likely than white and Asian males to perceive the criminal justice
process as certain. Among women, those who have experienced intimate violence
doubt sanction certainty, as do those more knowledgeable about the problem of
courtship violence. Knowledge and experience seem to create cynicism among
women about the criminal justice process. Miller and Simpson summarized these
findings as follows:

In sum, we find strong support for our hypotheses that perceptions of sanction certainty and severity are gendered. In four of six equations in which variables are mod-
eled for the whole sample, gender strongly affects perceptual deterrence. Consistently
important variables, although not necessarily so for both males and females, include
(1) race, (2) experience with violence in past dating relationships, (3) beliefs that others excuse and rationalize intimate violence, and (4) dating status. (p. 349)

Bias in Juvenile Offender
Arrest Decisions and Type-Scripts

Sealock and Simpson (1998) noted that, theoretically, race and class discrepancies
in police decisions to arrest are commonly explained as reflecting power differentials
between the advantaged and the disadvantaged (p. 428). They asserted, however,
that these types of explanations do not apply when gender is considered as an extrale-
gal factor predicting arrest. If power dictates arrest probabilities, then females should
be at greater risk for arrest than males. Data do not support this prediction. Sealock
and Simpson (p. 429) "attempt both to explain the societal origins of individuals' decision-making heuristics and to extend the operation of these heuristics to police arrest decisions.

Type-scripts. Sealock and Simpson (1998) used the concept of type-scripts based
on Harris's (1977) earlier work on the development and consequences of normative type-scripts. Sealock and Simpson (1998) explained this concept as follows:

Commonly identified types in criminological research include gender, race, and socio-economic status. Each "type" entails a certain socially approved "script" of behaviors that all similarly defined persons are expected to follow. . . .

In sum, according to type-scripts theory, society supports shared expectations [that] the different types of individuals will choose different classes of behavior; an individual acting as expected from his or her type is simply following a type-script. (p. 430)

Sealock and Simpson continued by suggesting that society supports whatever type-scripts are most useful in maintaining the current power structure. In modern societies, for example, patriarchy dictates that white males retain economic, political, and sexual power while females maintain primary domestic roles. Women who do not conform and are deviant disrupt male dominance and societal scripts. Those who go against their expected type-scripts are considered "countertypes" (p. 431).

Sealock and Simpson (1998) applied the functional theory of deviant type-scripts to focus on the arrest stage and the operation of heuristics based on type-scripts in police officers' decisions regarding juvenile offenders:

In this research, we provide a further empirical test of the predicted outcomes by examining not only the gender differences but also differences in race and socioeconomic status in the immediate outcome of a crime's commission, as manifested by the arrest decision. (p. 434)

Data and methods. For this study, Sealock and Simpson (1998) used the juvenile offense portion of the data for the 1958 Philadelphia birth cohort compiled by Wolfgang, Figlio, and Sellin (1972). Their research consisted of police contact information for all persons who were born in Philadelphia in 1958 and lived in that city at least from their 10th to their 18th birthdays. For their study, Sealock and Simpson analyzed contacts with police that occurred between 1968 and 1975 for juveniles from 10 to 17 years of age (pp. 436-437). The data are based on official police records. The authors examined the relationship between arrest and type-scripts/countertypes by coding offenses according to whether they were male-typed, neutral, or female-typed. According to Sealock and Simpson, the data show a disproportionate representation of males, blacks, and low socioeconomic status across crime types in this sample (p. 442). Of the 15,662 police contacts examined in this study, 51% were classified as male-typed (e.g., robbery), 31% as female-typed (e.g., shoplifting), and 17% as neutral (e.g., drug possession). They also reported that males were less likely to be arrested when they committed female-typed offenses than when they committed neutral or male-typed offenses. Although female suspects were most likely to commit female-typed offenses, they were arrested most frequently for offenses classified as neutral or male-typed.

As part of their analysis, Sealock and Simpson (1998) asserted,

According to type-scripts theory, it is not in the interest of middle class white males to have white females arrested and potentially incarcerated. On the other hand, black males are generally expected to fit the script of serious street crime. . . . It would appear, then, that the gender-typing variable subsumes a large portion of the effect of gender alone on whether a youth is arrested. . . . The gender-typing variable itself remains significant, however, as do the other demographic and contact-related suspect variables: Youths committing female-typed offenses, whites, and youths of above-average SES [socioeconomic status] are less likely to be arrested. (p. 443)

Sealock and Simpson also examined status offenses and type-scripts (p. 449). They reported that there were no gender differences in likelihood of arrest for status offenses witnessed by the police. Among those status offenses that came to the officers' attention through other means, females were significantly more apt to be arrested than were males. The authors further noted that non-white females were significantly more likely to be arrested at their first status offense contacts than were white females. Although their findings "support Harris's type-scripts argument," the authors contended that it is possible to explain these differences "as evidence of paternalistic attitudes toward female offenders" (p. 550).

Finally, Sealock and Simpson (1998) suggested that the gender-typing scheme used in the study might have failed to convey the essence of typing and countertyping. They illustrated this point by observing that white females experienced more police contacts for female-typed offenses than for male-typed or neutral offenses. However, most female-typed offenses still were linked to black males and females of low socioeconomic status (p. 454). It is conceivable, they stated, that the offenses classified here as female-typed actually were connected more closely to economic factors than to gender-related factors.

Corporate Victimization of Women

Simpson and Elis (1996) applied a feminist theoretical perspective to examine the corporate[15] victimization of women. Although there has been much research on corporate or white collar crime, they pointed out that researchers have not been concerned with the gendered nature of white collar crime and victimization. They argued that the victims of corporate crime are ubiquitous including rich and poor, urban and rural, male and female, young and old, and members of all racial and ethnic groups (p. 33). Simpson and Elis acknowledged that women have been excluded from most full-time employment in the labor force. Thus, male workers are more likely to be exposed to unsafe working conditions that increases male risk of corporate victimization. Little is known about women's occupational risk when they are in these high-risk occupations because women have been excluded from most occupational health research. Female employment tends to be concentrated in clerical, sales, and service jobs, especially among non-white and unmarried women, who tend to live in poverty.

Although some might claim that "unemployed" women have the luxury of being in their safe homes, Simpson and Elis (1996) argued that women in dual roles as homemakers and mothers not only produce unpaid work but also have an increased vulnerability to certain types of corporate victimization:

The National Safety Council proclaims that one is more apt to be injured in the home than at work. For women, this translates into injuries from (1) household cleaning products that contain chemicals and can cause burns, systemic poisoning, and skin and eye irritations and (2) tasks like cooking, moving furniture, cleaning windows, and so forth.... Responsibility for maintaining a safe household is deferred from manufacturers (who provide very little information about product safety) to wives and mothers....

Women have become increasingly vulnerable to corporate crime victimization from pharmaceutical companies, which have developed, in conjunction with physicians, drugs and devices that prevent reproduction. (pp. 34-35)

Among these harmful drugs and medical devices for women are intrauterine devices for insertion into the uterus, tampons, and silicone gel breast implants. These are used ostensibly to enhance women's well-being. Simpson and Elis also pointed to sexist advertising that encourages women to buy products such as cosmetics that might be harmful to them.

Marketeers' conception and rendering of female beauty is also directly related to women's attempts physically to alter the way they look. Thanks to the medical profession, invasive surgeries are offered to women....: techniques that can trim fat from the body, remove lines from the face, and plump up breasts thought to be too small or sagging.... Others include hysterectomies, forced sterilization for minority women, and cesarean sections. (p. 36)

Simpson and Elis (1996) contended that not only is corporate crime victimization differentiated by gender, but the law and access to it also reflect gender bias. They further suggested that feminists offer insight into this differentiation (p. 38). As noted earlier in this chapter and by Simpson (1989), there is no single feminist theory but rather several perspectives or orientations. Each one differs in its explanations of the historical development and source of gendered social organization, who benefits from such social organization and how, and tactics for change (Simpson and Elis, 1996, p. 39). Simpson and Elis applied these various feminist perspectives to explain their different approaches to corporate victimization of women. For example, to the extent that males and females are treated differently as victims or plaintiffs, liberal feminists advocate adopting gender-neutral legislation for equal protection under the law. Liberals assert that better integration of women into positions of power within corporations will offer more protection and support for female victims of crime (pp. 39-40). Radical feminists, on the other hand, look to male subordination of women and control of women's sexuality to understand the ways in which women are victimized by corporations. From the socialist-feminist viewpoint, corporate victimization of women represents the power of capitalist males to expropriate women's labor and reproductive power for males' benefit (pp. 40-41). With reference to race, the authors suggested,

A modified version of socialist-feminist criminology, one that is sensitive to micro processes and intragender diversity, would better account for the ways in which all women, including minorities, are victimized by corporations and the extent to which access to redress is structured not just by gender but also by race. (p. 42)

After providing three qualitative case studies,[16] Simpson and Elis concluded,

> Drawing on empirical evidence, we have applied a modified socialist-feminist theory to account for gendered corporate victimization and gender bias inhibiting access to institutional redress (legal and otherwise). This theory explains victimizations that occur within both public and private spheres. It also explains the manner in which women's victimization and access to institutional means of redress vary by race and social class. (p. 50)

Critique of Simpson

Simpson's professional career has been developing rapidly since she received her doctorate in 1985. She has established an impressive publication record that demonstrates both productivity and superb scholarship. Because she is a relatively young scholar, there is little that has been written about her career and scholarship. However, she has made unique and major contributions to feminist criminological theory. Perhaps the most important of these has been her emphasis on the interconnections of gender, race, and class as they relate to offenders and victims of crime. Simpson (1989, 1991; see also Simpson and Elis, 1995) has pointed out the necessity for feminist criminologists to follow this approach. In her own research (Miller and Simpson, 1991; Sealock and Simpson, 1998; Simpson and Elis, 1996), she has examined the relationship of gender, race, and class to issues of victimization and the impact of type-scripts on decisions to arrest alleged offenders.

There has been significant recognition of the quality of Simpson's works in terms of fellowships, honors, frequent citations, and reprints. Simpson's (1989) article "Feminist Theory, Crime, and Justice" has been reprinted in two different edited books. Simpson's (1991) article "Caste, Class, and Violent Crime" has also been reprinted in two different edited theory books.

Finally, as a somewhat younger scholar, she has been given leadership opportunities at the university and national levels (see biographical inset [Inset 9.2] for details). All of this speaks to her integrity as well as to her outstanding scholarship.

Summary

This chapter has presented a history of the feminist movement and a discussion of the various types of feminists, with selected criminology scholars to represent each of the feminist theoretical perspectives. The chapter closed by highlighting the biographies and works of two outstanding feminist criminological theorists who have made unique contributions. Obviously, there are other scholars who could have been included. It was my intent to select those who most clearly illustrate the diversity in and development of feminist criminological theory. The flowchart depicted in Table 9.1 illustrates the development of feminist criminological theory.

TABLE 9.1 Feminist Theory

Abigail Adams (1744-1818)	Sojourner Truth (1797-1883)	Elizabeth Cady Stanton (1815-1902)	Susan B. Anthony (1820-1906)	Harriet Tubman (1821-1913)	Ida Wells Barnett (1862-1931)	Margaret Sanger (1879-1966)

Liberal Feminist	Marxist Feminist	Radical Feminist	Feminism and Women of Color
Freda Adler	Elizabeth Moulds	Elizabeth Stanko	Vernetta Young
Rita Simon	Nicole Rafter	Nanci Koser Wilson	Angela Davis
Clarice Feinman	Eleena Natalizia		
Darrell Steffensmeier			

Coramae Richey Mann (1931-)	Sally S. Simpson (1954-)

Even though feminist theory does not meet all of the specifications for a classical social science theory, it has made significant contributions to theory, research, and justice policy. Because many of these theorists are critical of the patriarchal nature of most mainstream theories of crime and justice, it seems obvious that, in many ways, these theorists are challenging the "old paradigm" (Kuhn, 1970). The feminist perspective continues to be discussed in Chapter 10 as part of the peacemaking perspective of criminological theory.

Notes

1. Rice (1990) used the term "machocentric" criminology to describe a discourse that is male-centered (p. 57). She pointed out that this frequently is used with reference to black men and black street crime.

2. Daly and Chesney-Lind (1988) also pointed out in a footnote that the concepts of "second-wave" and "third-wave" feminism ignore the "first-wave" feminism that had its beginnings during the 19th century in the United States and in some European countries (p. 498). Yet, this ignores the earlier feminists in this country and throughout the world.

3. The use of the concept of "third-wave" feminists has happened most frequently at National Women's Studies Conferences and other gatherings where there are a lot of young feminists just approaching or entering adulthood.

4. Stanko is a nationally and internationally recognized radical feminist scholar in criminology. Stanko, who received her degrees from the City University of New York, taught for more than a decade at Clark University in Massachusetts. She now is a faculty member in the Department of Law at Brunel University as well as a senior research fellow in the Institute of Criminology at the University of Cambridge. She also has traveled internationally, conducting research and participating in professional conferences.

5. Adler (1997) documented, in a history of the Women and Crime division of the American Society of Criminology, that Wilson participated in one of the earliest panels on feminist criminology in 1975, where she presented a paper on "Styles of Doing Time in a Co-Ed Prison" (p. 3). Wilson also was a cofounder of the Women and Crime division, was elected as the vice chair in 1982 and 1984 (p. 4), and served as the first editor of the division's newsletter from 1982 to 1986 (p. 5). She is recognized on the national level for her pioneer work in feminist criminology and environmental crime. She teaches classes in both of these areas in the Department of Criminology at Indiana University of Pennsylvania.

6. This description of prison life by Davis (1975), based on her experiences in prison, is similar to Goffman's (1961) theoretical analysis of total institutions in *Asylums* based on his research. See Chapter 7 for details.

7. Again, these observations by Davis (1975), based on her experiences in prison, are similar to the theoretical concepts of Giallombardo (1966) based on her research.

8. This finding of homosexuality at the core of the family structure also is supported by Giallombardo's (1966) work. It should be noted, however, that because Davis was kept in solitary confinement most of the time (reportedly "for her own safety"), she was not a participant in this family structure.

9. This edited volume (Mann and Zatz, 1998b) contains articles written by scholars concerning history, stereotyping and marginalization, crime, law enforcement, and justice as they relate to American Indians, African Americans, Latinos and Hispanics, Asian Americans, Euro-Americans, and "white privilege."

10. Mann also noted that those who have come across the borders during recent decades are referred to as illegal emigrants. By the 1960s, the close and friendly borders had disappeared, and there has been a hardening against Mexican immigrants and contract laborers. This has intensified as we enter the 21st century.

11. During the summer of 1985, data-collection trips were made to Chicago, Houston, and Atlanta; and in the spring and summer of 1986, additional trip destinations included Los Angeles, New York, and Baltimore (Mann, 1993a, p. 231). Faculty research grants for travel funds were awarded to Mann by Florida State University (p. 243, note 2). For additional details of this study, see Mann (1988, 1990a, 1990b, 1993a, 1993b, 1996).

12. When Mann (1988, 1993b, 1996) explored the homicides involving female offenders and female victims, she reported finding a few homicides involving either current or former lesbian lovers.

13. Simpson credited a number of professors as mentors who guided her through her student days and into her successful career. Among these are Mike Creighton (Oregon State University), Mervin White and Gerald Garrett (Washington State University, where Garrett was a visiting professor from the University of Massachusetts), and Anthony Harris and Roland Chilton (University of Massachusetts, Amherst). She also acknowledged Vicki Swigert, a colleague at Holy Cross College, who mentored Simpson during her early teaching experiences. In addition to acknowledging the importance of these people to the development of her career, Simpson has mentored a number of graduate students. Among the students she has worked and published with at the University of Maryland are Susan Miller, Lori Elis, Denise Herz, and Christopher Koper.

14. For more details of the methodology for this study, see Miller and Simpson (1991, pp. 341-3422).

15. Simpson has authored several papers and publications on the topic of corporate crime. This one is most pertinent for this chapter because of its feminist perspective.

16. The first case involved a fire at an Imperial Food Products poultry processing plant in Hamlet, North Carolina, that killed 25 workers and injured 56 others. Although the cause of the fire was accidental, the deaths and injuries were linked to violations of Occupational Safety and Health Administration (OSHA) safety violations. The workforce consisted primarily of impoverished black females who had to cope with excessive heat in a room with no fans or windows. As assembly line workers that required repetitive hand movements, many of them developed carpal tunnel syndrome as well as other diseases. In the second case, a 36-year-old black woman, who had been hired as an industrial nurse, reportedly was subjected to sexual and racial harassment by the human resources manager of Regal Tube Company. After repeated requests to the general manager and letters written to the Equal Employment Opportunity Commission seeking to have the harassment stopped, the male supervisors at Regal did not support the woman's efforts to deal with the matter. After 16 months, during an incident in which the human resources manager reportedly threatened to kill her, the woman fell down a flight of stairs. She received 2 months' disability compensation and then resigned. The third case involved Ortho Pharmaceutical Company and concerned a product liability lawsuit. A woman who had purchased an Ortho All-Flex diaphragm was taken to the emergency room and diagnosed with toxic shock syndrome. She remained in the hospital for 41 days, periodically comatose and near death.

DISCUSSION QUESTIONS

1. Assume that you had no knowledge of feminism prior to reading this chapter. Answer the question, "What is a feminist?" Support your answer with material from this chapter.

2. How does a feminist perspective of history, crime, and law differ from the "androcentric" view of history, crime, and law? How is it similar? Use the ideas of specific feminist theorists such as Naffine and Simpson.

3. Abigail Adams was among the first Americans to speak for women's rights. What were the most important rights that feminists have sought over the decades until the present? Which feminists have made the greatest contributions in advancing women in American society? Be sure to name these feminists and their contributions. Why were the rights or contributions important, and why are the feminists you name worthy of special recognition?

4. Feminists during the early to mid-20th century (1920s to 1960s) were predominantly white middle class women. Scholars such as Rice, Young, and Simpson have criticized feminists for "essentialism." What are these feminists advocating? Why is this important or not important?

5. The works of Wilson and Stanko have been used to illustrate a radical feminist perspective of criminology. Using specific material from their publications, explain why they fit *or do not fit* into the radical feminist perspective. If you ar-

gue that they *do not* fit, then indicate what other feminist approach they fit. Justify your answer by using material in the chapter.

6. Under feminism and women of color, the chapter discusses the works of Young and Davis. Discuss the contributions of these two scholars, and compare and contrast each of their works with those of Mann.

7. Considering the works of all the feminist scholars presented in this chapter, what is unique about the contributions made by Mann and by Simpson? Why are these important?

8. Considering all of the feminists (1960s to 1990s) whose works have been discussed in this chapter, which one would you deem most valuable in the advancement of feminist criminological theory? Explain why you selected this feminist theory.

9. Assume that the president of the United States has recognized you for your knowledge of feminist theory and has assigned you to a special commission to develop criminal justice policy and to suggest specific programs to remedy the inequities presented in this chapter. What policy and programs would you suggest? The president is not familiar with feminist criminological theory, so you need to justify your proposed policies and programs using the details of theories from this chapter.

10 CHAPTER

Peacemaking in Criminology

The works of both feminists and critical theorists are important to the peacemaking perspective that is explained in this chapter. Emerging perspectives such as peacemaking, environmental crime, and left realism have in common a reaction against the claim of traditional criminologists that their research, theory, and policy are objective, rational, and scientific. Along with the appearance of these perspectives, the 1990s also have brought the evolution of postmodernism to criminology. This is examined briefly in this chapter.

Postmodernist Criminology

Although postmodernism can be traced beyond the past decade, it was not until the 1990s that it began its entrance into criminological theory. As noted by Schwartz and Friedrichs (1994), there was a great deal of diversity among criminologists as they examined postmodern theory. For example, they suggested that "much of what has been published is only a pretentious intellectual fad" and that much of what has been written under the name of poststructuralism/postmodernism is "a kind of academic word playing with no possible link to anything but a kind of pseudo-intellectualized ghettoes" of the university or "*crap*" (p. 227). Among criminologists who have applied this theoretical perspective to the study of crime and criminal justice are Lippens (1998); Milovanovic (1996); Quinney and Wildeman (1991); Schwartz and Friedrichs (1994); Vold, Bernard, and Snipes (1998); Williams and McShane (1999); and Wonders (1996).[1] These various scholars have used a variety of terms for the perspective and applied it to a diversity of issues.

Wonders (1996) used the concept of "deconstruction" in applying feminist and postmodern theory to challenge determinate sentences (p. 612). She further asserted that the emergence of both feminist and postmodern theory has influenced the works of many disciplines. Schwartz and Friedrichs (1994) also claimed that critical criminology has been an umbrella for the evolution of a series of emerging perspectives such as feminism, left realism, and peacemaking (p. 222). They argued, however, that postmodern thought is perhaps the least developed and least understood of the various perspectives to emerge in critical criminology. It is likely that both explanations have some validity.

Vold and colleagues (1998) suggested that most criminology is modernistic or "naturalistic" in the sense that science is viewed as an objective process directed toward predicting and controlling the world (p. 269). One of the most important aspects of postmodernism in criminology and other social sciences is an attack on all aspects of positivism (Schwartz and Friedrichs, 1994, p. 225). Thus, postmodernism challenges this paradigm and argues that it is impossible to separate values from the research agenda. According to Vold and colleagues (1998),

> At the same time, postmodernists tend to seek out the disparaged points of view to make them more explicit and legitimate. The goal is not simply to tear down and replace it with the other but rather to come to a situation in which different grammars can be simultaneously held as legitimate, so there is a sense of diversity of points of view without assuming that one is superior and the others are inferior. (p. 270)

In another approach, Milovanovic (1996) used the concept of "affirmative postmodern criminology" (p. 567). He declared that it emerged as a paradigm for deconstructing oppressive forms and for affirmatively reconstructing the new order.

> Rather than privileging linear effects and homeostasis (order), postmodern analysis is more likely to assume nonlinear effects and far-from-equilibrium conditions (orderly disorder). . . . Postmodern criminology is faced with the dilemma of how to better model or map complex dynamics, those which predominantly exhibit nonlinearity (complexity) over time. (p. 568)

Finally, Milovanovic acknowledged the affirmative postmodernists' desire for a more humanistic world that allows a diversity of desires and discourses (p. 606).

Peacemaking

The peacemaking perspective in criminology was introduced with the publication of Pepinsky and Quinney's (1991) edited book, *Criminology as Peacemaking*. They emphasized three peacemaking traditions: religious and humanistic, feminist, and critical.[2] Since then, there has emerged an expanding body of literature written by other scholars in criminology and related disciplines. These scholars see our society as dominated by a culture of competition and oppression along with a criminal justice system that returns violence with a violent punishment such as capital punishment for those who kill. Pepinsky (1993) stated, "The criminal justice enterprise in which we find ourselves feeds us on collective fear and hope" (p. 391). Part of the process of establishing a fear of crime is the use of the language of violence and obedience (Pepinsky, 1998). Our criminal justice system has replaced treatment and rehabilitation for addicts and other criminals with a "war on drugs" or a "war on crime," which has failed as evidenced by the growing prison population and the renewal of the war each decade. This language of war and violence permeates our culture and society, often introducing this perspective to our children. Gibbs (1996) used the kindergarten report card of his daughter, Sarah, to show how the vocabulary of war has permeated our educational institutions:

> Students are introduced to the war model of learning very early in their academic careers. A few years ago, our daughter Sarah brought home her report card from kindergarten. One of the dimensions on which she was graded was "attacks simple problems." Mrs. Curry, her teacher, assigned her a G for good, the highest of the three ratings, so as a parent I had reason to rejoice. Then, it dawned on me that this was pretty aggressive language to assess how kindergartners approach problem-solving.
>
> Besides the "attacks simple problems" that appeared on Sarah's report card, other war phrases of evaluation include "conquers material," "masters problems," "aggressively pursues objectives," "tackles problems," and "hits the books." These embody the war model of learning. As in all war, they imply separation; something out there differs from you and poses a threat or challenge that you must conquer or control. (p. 577)

Gibbs further noted that in the war model, it does not matter how one plays; instead, what matters is whether one wins or loses. In this model, the process of learning gets lost and creates distance and self-centeredness. By contrast, the peace model requires openness, trust, and cooperative learning.

Cultural and Historical Background for Peacemaking in Criminology

Even though peacemaking has appeared only recently in academia and the justice system as an alternative to war and violence, several scholars/activists from the 19th and early 20th centuries have emphasized spiritualism, human rights, and nonviolence. The lives and contributions of Mahatma Gandhi, Jane Addams, and Martin Luther King, Jr., are discussed in this part of the chapter.

Mahatma Gandhi (1869-1948)

On October 2, 1869, Putlibai Gandhi, the fourth wife[3] of Karamchand Gandhi, gave birth to Mohandas Karamchand Gandhi (later known as Mahatma Gandhi). Thus, he was born into the *Bania* (trader) caste in Porbandar, India, where members of his family had been appointed as *Diwan* or chief minister beginning in the 18th century (Nanda, 1981, chap. 1). At 7 years of age, Gandhi moved with his parents to

Rajkot, where he attended primary school. During his adolescence he experimented with eating meat and smoking, which was a violation of community and family rules.

At 13 years of age, and in accordance with the Hindu custom of child marriage, Gandhi was married to Kasturbai, who was the daughter of a merchant, Gokuldas Makanji. He continued his education and struggled to be a fond husband, a dutiful son, and a good student. Although early marriage had not been his choice, later in his life, Gandhi wrote in his autobiography that "everything on that day seemed to me right and proper and pleasing." Nanda (1981, chap. 10) discussed Gandhi's feelings as follows:

> He was passionately fond of his child wife. . . . Thoughts of her haunted him in the classroom, [and] at night he kept her awake with his "idle talk."
>
> Early marriage had by no means been his choice, and if precocity is one aspect of his sex life, its evanescence is another and perhaps a more important one. As a child, he had read a *Gujerati* pamphlet advising lifelong fidelity to the wife; the monogamous ideal was henceforth indelibly imprinted on him: "No other woman had any attraction for me in the same sense she [Kasturbai] had. I was too loyal a husband and too loyal to the vow taken before my mother to be slave to any other woman."

In 1888, Gandhi sailed to England to study law. It was during that period in London that he decided to live on a vegetarian diet and eventually joined the Vegetarian Society. He also studied books on simple living as well as various religious books including the Hindu book of moral discourse, *Gita,* which he read for the first time (Chronology of Events, 1999a). While in London, he also read and studied law books in preparation for the law examinations. He sailed to India in 1891 to practice law. When he landed in Bombay, he was shocked to learn that his mother had died. In Bombay, he was advised that he should study Indian law to gain experience of the High Court and to secure what briefs he could.

After 2 years in Bombay, Gandhi left India for South Africa to do legal work for a Muslim firm. As he traveled across South Africa by train, he experienced for the first time the discrimination against Indians. The following is an account of this experience:

> His brief stay at Durban had given him disconcerting evidence of color prejudice. He was taken by Abdulla to see the Durban court. The European magistrate ordered him to take off his turban. Gandhi refused and left the courtroom and wrote a letter of protest in the local press. . . . He had never before encountered blatant racial prejudice.
>
> The experience in Durban, however, was nothing compared with what befell him in the course of his journey from Durban to Pretoria. When his train reached Maritzburg late in the evening, he was ordered to shift to the van compartment. He refused but was unceremoniously turned out of the first-class carriage. It was a bitterly cold night as he crept into the unlit waiting room of Maritzburg station and brooded over what had happened. . . . Determined to face whatever happened, he resumed his journey. (Nanda, 1981, chap. 4)

The trip from Durban to Pretoria dramatized for Gandhi the condition of Indian immigrants in South Africa. Gandhi became the first Indian enrolled as advocate of the Supreme Court of Natal and founded the Natal Indian Congress.

For approximately two decades, Gandhi worked to end the discriminatory laws against Indians in South Africa. In 1896, he returned to India and then came back to South Africa with his wife and children. Over the years in South Africa, his wife sometimes joined Gandhi in his efforts to gain equality for Indians. During this period, Gandhi organized a hospital in Johannesburg following the outbreak of a plague. He led Indians in taking the oath of passive resistance[4] against the newly amended legal ordinance that required all Indians to register. In 1908, Gandhi reached a compromise with the government to allow voluntary compliance by Indians to the Registration Act, but he was almost killed by some who considered this a betrayal. Gandhi continued nonviolent protests for a variety of causes including the invalidation of Indian marriages in South Africa and the miners' strike in protest of a tax. Gandhi and his wife both were arrested in the protest march against a law that invalidated Indian marriages. Gandhi endured a series of arrests, releases, imprisonments, and (in one instance) deportation. In 1914, the Indian Relief Act was passed, and Gandhi returned to India to continue his protest work confronting the policies of the English (Chronology of Events, 1999b).

After traveling in India and gathering evidence of Indian oppression, he took up the cause of the textile workers and the peasants as an experiment in *Satyagraha,* which means "truth force." Gandhi first took up the textile workers' cause.

> The morale of the workers was not to be boosted by working up their passions. There was to be no violence. . . . There was no room for bitterness [or] for fabrication of grievances, exaggeration of claims, or competition in invective. The strikers' enforced idleness was to be utilized in constructive activities; alternative trades were to be learn[ed], houses were to be repaired, and roads in workers' colonies were to be swept. (Nanda, 1981, chap. 20)

After the first few days, the morale began to sag. It was not possible for most of these people to exist without work and wages. Gandhi was filled with anguish and decided to undertake a fast. The object of the fast was to rally the workers, but it also put pressure on the mill owners. Thus, Gandhi accepted a compromise, and the strikers went back to work. Gandhi inaugurated the first regular union of workers, which blossomed into the Ahmedadab Textile Labour Association.

The textile workers' labor dispute was scarcely settled when Gandhi was drawn into a conflict between peasants of the Kheda district and the local administration on the remission of land revenue. Gandhi called on the peasants to "fight unto death against such a spirit of vindictiveness and tyranny" and to refuse to pay the land revenue. Again, Gandhi led the peasants in peaceful resistance until the dispute was settled. This was the first agrarian Satyagraha that Gandhi organized in India.

Swadeshi, or the use of homemade goods, was another plank in the noncooperation movement that Gandhi had been preaching since his return from South Africa. He led a campaign to boycott foreign cloth and advocated the use of the spinning wheel to make hand-spun and hand-woven cloth. In 1921, as part of his campaign for the boycott of foreign cloth, he lit a "monster bonfire" of foreign cloth in Bombay. He was arrested and sentenced to 6 years of imprisonment. After 2 years in prison, he was operated on for appendicitis and released. In 1925, Gandhi founded the All India Spinners Association. He had an emotional attachment to the spinning wheel and to seeing it as a means of economic survival for farmers, laborers, and helpless widows in the village.

> The spinning wheel gradually became the center of rural uplift in the Gandhian scheme of Indian economics; [around] it were to be built up anti-malaria campaigns, improvements in sanitation, [and] settlement of village disputes. . . . The economics of the spinning wheel were thus the economics of a new village economy. . . . There is no doubt that the spinning wheel symbolized Gandhi's protest against industrialism and materialism. (Nanda, 1981, chap. 30)

Beginning in 1928, Gandhi led the effort to seek complete independence for India. The first step he took was to call for the celebration of "Independence Day" on January 26, 1930. He advocated a campaign of civil disobedience and nonpayment of taxes. The Salt Tax, although relatively light, hit the poorest in the land. Gandhi announced that he would lead a group of Satyagrahis to the seashore for the breach of the Salt Laws. At the end of this protest march, Gandhi and some 60,000 Indians were imprisoned. Gandhi's arrest stimulated, rather than slackened, resistance to the government (Nanda, 1981, chap. 33).

As in South Africa, Gandhi led a number of protests and was arrested, imprisoned, released, and so forth. He also continued to conduct numerous fasts. While in prison in 1933, Gandhi arranged for the publication of a weekly newspaper called *Harijan*, which means "children of God." It was Gandhi's name for the untouchables. During one of the arrests when both Gandhi and his wife were interned in Aga Khan's Palace at Poona, his wife died. The following is an account of her death:

> On February 22, 1944, she passed away in the lap of her husband. "I am going now," she said to him. "We have known many joys and many sorrows." One of her last wishes was that she should be cremated in a sari made from yarn spun by him.
>
> "We were," wrote Gandhi in reply to a letter of condolence, . . . "a couple outside the ordinary." The sixty-two years of their married life had been a period of continual growth. In spite of the immense intellectual gap between them, he had learn[ed] to respect her opinions and to let her make her own decisions. (Nanda, 1981, chap. 49)

After the death of his beloved wife, Gandhi's health began to cause concern for the government. He was released on May 6, 1944. Gandhi was not pleased with his release. He felt ashamed that he fell ill while imprisoned. It turned out that he was suffering from the aftereffects of malaria as well as hookworm and amoebic infections that had resulted in acute anemia (Nanda, 1981, chap. 49). He continued his propaganda to end the discrimination against the untouchables, and he intensified his efforts to establish the independence of India. In 1945, he stated that "peace is impossible without equality and freedom of India" (Chronology of Events, 1999c). Gandhi's quest for independence for all of India became difficult when the Muslims of India began to riot seeking a petitioning of India.

> The Muslim League observed August 16, 1946, as the "Direct Action Day." On that day, Calcutta witnessed a communal riot. . . . For four days, bands of hooligans armed with sticks, spears, hatchets, and even firearms roamed the town, robbing and killing at will. The "Great Calcutta killing" . . . took a toll of more than five thousand lives. . . .
>
> The non-Muslim[s] of Calcutta reeled under the initial impact, but then, taking advantage of their numerical superiority, hit back savagely. . . . Two months later, reprisals followed in the Muslim-majority district of Noakhali in East Bengal. . . . Local hooligans burn[ed] the Hindus' property, [looted] their crops, and desecrated their temples. (web.mahatma.org.in/books/bchap51.htm)

Gandhi was in Delhi when the news from East Bengal arrived. Although he was in poor health and his friends tried to dissuade him, he canceled his plans and decided to leave for East Bengal. He set out to restore the confidence between the two communities. His presence acted as a soothing balm on the villages. When the Independence of India Bill was passed in 1947, Gandhi objected to the partition of India and Pakistan. Gandhi was mobbed in the Calcutta house and conducted another fast for peace. In January 1948, doctors warned that the fast must be ended, and the Central Peace Committee decided on a Peace Pledge. Gandhi broke his fast and decided to continue his activities. However, this was not to be. The first warning came on January 20, when a bomb exploded a few feet from where he was addressing his prayer meeting. He took no notice of the explosion. He was assassinated on January 30. The following is an account of this event:

> On the evening of January 30th, he left his room in Birla House for the prayer ground. It was only a two-minute walk, but he was a little late that day. . . . With his forearms on the shoulders of his grandnieces, Ava and Manu (walking sticks, as he called them), he walked briskly. As he approached the prayer ground, the congregation of five hundred made a passage for him; many rose, [and] some bowed low in reverence. He said he was sorry for being late, lifted his hands, and joined them in a namaskar (salutation). Just at that moment, Godse edged forward through the crowd, bent low as if to prostrate himself at the Mahatma's feet, whipped out his pistol, and fired three shots in quick succession. Gandhi fell instantly with the words "He Rama" (Oh, God). (Nanda, 1981, chap. 52)

The impact of Gandhi's life and nonviolent protests on peacemaking in criminology becomes evident later in this chapter. Next, the life and works of Addams are examined.

Jane Addams (1860-1935)

Born on September 6, 1860, in Cedarville, Illinois, Jane Addams was one of the younger members of a large wealthy family. Her mother died when she was 2 years of age, and the major influence on her life was her father,[5] John H. Addams, who was a

Quaker, state senator, and mill owner (Deegan, 1991, p. 37). As a child, she admired her father's physical stature and was very sensitive about her own physical limitations. Addams (1960) expressed this in the following quote, originally published in 1910:

> My father taught the large Bible class in the lefthand corner of the church next to the pulpit, and to my eyes at least, [he] was a most imposing figure in his Sunday frock coat, his fine head rising high above all the others. I imagined that the strangers were filled with admiration for this dignified person, and I prayed with all my heart that the ugly, pigeon-toed little girl, whose crooked back obliged her to walk with her head held very much upon one side, would never be pointed out to these visitors as the daughter of this fine man. (p. 23)

Although Addams did have physical maladies throughout her lifetime, she stated that these sentiments were "the manifestations of a child's adoring affection, so emotional, so irrational, so tangled with the affairs of the imagination" (p. 24).

As a child and later as an adult, Addams was sensitive to poverty and inequalities. At 7 years of age, she had her first exposure to poverty when she visited a mill with her father. This mill was located near the poorest quarter of a neighboring town. Addams was appalled at the shabby streets and the horrid little houses so close together in which people lived. Addams (1960) declared, "When I grew up, I should, of course, have a large house, but it would not be built among the other large houses but [rather] right in the midst of horrid little houses like these" (p. 21). And, of course, she did this in 1889, when she and Ellen Gates Starr established Hull House in Chicago.

Addams entered the Rockford Female Seminary in Rockford, Illinois, in 1879 and graduated in 1881. Her father died in August of that year, and she was left confused, depressed, and in despair (Deegan, 1991, p. 37). After a year as a student at the Women's Medical College in Philadelphia, she dropped out and returned home to regain her health. After drifting at home for a year, she and a college friend, Starr, traveled to Europe. While in Europe, they visited a social settlement house, Toynbee Hall in London's East End. This settlement house provided Addams and Starr with a new direction in their lives in that Toynbee Hall was designed to work with the poor and provide leadership to a district populated by the exploited working classes (p. 38). The two women returned to Chicago and began the process of political activism that led to the establishment of Hull House.

The purpose of the settlement house was to help the underprivileged. Because many of the poor immigrants lived in the vicinity of Halstead and Harrison Streets, Hull House was selected as the location for the settlement house (Deegan, 1991, pp. 77-78). Among the early programs established after Addams and Starr moved into the Hull House were a kindergarten class, a day nursery (p. 84), and a public kitchen (p. 101). These eventually were expanded as volunteers increased and as needs were identified.[6] For example, Addams (1970) stated that "a frame cottage of six rooms across our yard has been fitted up as a creche" that served between 30 and 40 children daily (p. 47). She further explained,

> This site for a settlement was selected . . . because of its diversity and the variety of activit[ies] for which it presented an opportunity. It has been the aim of the residents to respond to all sides of the neighborhood life, not to the poor people alone, nor to the well-to-do, nor to the young in contradistinction to the old, but [rather] to the neighborhood as a whole, "men, women, and children taken in families as the Lord mixes them." The activities of Hull House divide themselves into four [or] possibly more lines. . . . They might be designated as the social, educational, and humanitarian. I have added civic—if indeed a settlement of women can be said to perform civic duties. (pp. 32-33)

Sometimes, services provided were both humanitarian and social, or both educational and humanitarian, and so forth. Among the other services provided by the Hull House were a relief fund, five bathrooms in the rear of the settlement open to the neighborhood, a coffee house, an information and interpretation bureau, industrial education, college extension classes, and a large number of clubs for specific groups of immigrants and other groups in need of social and humanitarian assistance (pp. 35-40, 44-49).

Addams and other residents of Hull House were active in the city of Chicago as well as in Hull House. Addams was a strong advocate for several social justice issues including opposition to child labor, support for compulsory education, and working for the establishment of a juvenile court.

Addams and others at Hull House were concerned about the employment of children in stores and factories. Kelley and Stevens (1895) argued that the 19th ward of Chicago was the best district in all of Illinois for a study of child labor (p. 54). This ward contained many factories in which children were employed and had a large body of "cash children." The authors illustrated this with the Christmas experience of one girl:

> A little girl, thirteen years of age, saw in an evening paper of [last] December 23 . . . an advertisement for six girls to work in one of the best-known candy stores, candidate[s] to apply at seven o'clock the next morning. . . . To reach the place in time, she spent five cents of her lunch money for car fare. Arriving, she found other children, while but one was wanted. She was engaged as the brightest of the group and sent to a downtown branch. . . . This time she walked, then worked, then worked til midnight, paying for her dinner and going without supper. She was paid fifty cents and discharged with the explanation that she was only required for one day. No cars were running at that hour, and the little girl walked across the worst district of Chicago to reach her home and her terrified mother at one o'clock on Christmas morning. (pp. 55-56)

It also was claimed that children were found in the greatest number where conditions of labor were most at risk for health, mutilation, and death (pp. 58, 65). Addams (1907) argued that child labor also has a demoralizing effect on parent-child relations:

> You will hear a child say, "My mother can't say nothing to me. I pay the rent," or "I can do what I please because I bring home the biggest wages." All this tends to break down the normal relation of parent and child. (p. 162)

Addams further noted that the United States, compared to the most advanced European nations, is deficient in protective legislation and suggested that this is the result of the emphasis placed on personal liberty at the first constitutional conventions (p. 151). This country, she argued, assumes that regulation of industry is unnecessary and that the protection of children from premature participation in the labor industry is not the concern of the government (p. 156). Addams perceived a connection between uniform child labor legislation and enforcement and uniform compulsory education laws, and she argued that both were important factors in securing educated producers for the nation (p. 168).

Addams (1895) suggested that problems of economics and cultural differences often bring these children into the justice system. She noted that "four fifths of the children brought into the Juvenile Court in Chicago are the children of foreigners" (p. 181). According to Addams, many of these child offenders are arrested for trifling acts that are due to the harsh demands of parents who are accustomed to the patriarchal authority in the household (p. 179). Thus, the parents hold their children in a "stern bondage" that requires the surrender of all of their wages and allows no time or money for pleasures. Addams provided the following illustration of how this can lead to delinquency:

> A Polish boy of seventeen came to Hull House one day to ask a contribution of fifty cents "toward a flower piece for the funeral of an old Hull House club boy." A few questions made it clear that the object was fictitious, whereupon the boy broke down and half-defiantly stated that he wanted to buy two twenty-five cent [tickets], one for his girl and one for himself, to a dance . . . [and] that he hadn't a penny of his own, although he had worked in a brass foundry for three years and had been advanced twice, because he always had to give his pay envelope unopened to his father; "just look at the clothes he buys me" was his concluding remark. (p. 179)

Addams also pointed out that many younger children are constantly arrested for petty thieving because they are too eager to take home food or fuel that will relieve the distress and need that they hear discussed so constantly. Many other children have defiantly thrown off parental control and had their premature flings in city life, bringing them into contact with local authorities.

> Boys of ten and twelve will refuse to sleep at home, preferring the freedom of an old brewery fault or an empty warehouse to the obedience required by their parents, and for days these boys will live on the milk and bread which they steal from the back porches after the early morning delivery. Such children complain that there is "no fun" at home. (p. 181)

Thus, Addams was especially concerned about juvenile offenders and their harsh and repressive treatment by the courts. She suggested that juvenile courts should perform functions of nurturing and protecting young criminals. Instead of the repressive response to juveniles such as prison, Addams (1907) argued that the kindly concern for the young by probation officers was a better solution (p. 81). It was the job of the probation officer to care for the wayward child and to provide assistance to keep the child permanently away from police, courts, and penal institutions. Addams was praised as a "saint" for her work at Hull House and in working for changes in education, labor, and court legislation and enforcement for the poor, immigrants, women, children, and workers. This work is similar to the changes advocated by Gandhi in South Africa and India. Also, many current adherents to the peacemaking perspective in criminology seem to have built on the ideas of Gandhi and Addams.

In addition to dedicating her life to caring for the underprivileged and helping to implement useful reforms as a social worker, Addams was a cultural feminist and a pacifist. She opposed militarism found in city government. Addams (1907) argued that municipal administrations "depended upon penalties, coercion, compulsion, [and] remnants of military codes to hold the community together" (p. 34). She became a strong pacifist activist at the beginning of World War I. She argued that a friendly and cooperative relationship among all peoples was becoming more possible. Expressing her strong resistance to the coercion of war, Addams (1922) stated,

> We revolted not only against the cruelty and barbarity of war but even more against the reversal of relationships which war implied. We protested against the "curbed intelligence" and the "thwarted goodwill," when both a free mind and unfettered kindliness are so sadly needed in human affairs.... But we also believed that justice between men or between nations can be achieved only through understanding and fellowship and that a finely tempered sense of justice, which alone is of any service in modern civilization, cannot possibly be secured in the storm and stress of war. (p. 4)

In the preceding quote, Addams was speaking for the International League for Peace and Freedom, which was made up of a number of the leading organizations of women. Addams was the first president of this organization, later known as the Women's Peace Party (p. 130), and she made herself available to speak at many women's organizations. She noted, "After the United States entered the war, the press throughout the country systematically undertook to misrepresent and malign pacifists" (p. 134). Deegan (1991) explained,

> As a pacifist before World War I, Addams was lauded as a "good woman." However, with the building of patriotic feeling from 1913 until America's entry into the war in 1917, she became the target of animosity and personal attack. By 1917, she was socially and publicly ostracized. She went from being a saint to being a villain. Booed off speaking platforms and abandoned by her friends, colleagues, and, most notably here, other sociologists, Addams was a social pariah. (p. 40)

After the war ended, Addams gradually resumed leadership in American thought. However, Deegan (1991) asserted that it was primarily the impact of the Depression that restored her to the forefront of American leadership. Addams was the cowinner of the Nobel Peace Prize in 1931 (Addams, 1960), and she again became the spokesperson for many values and policies such as the establishment of social security. Deegan (1991) stated, "Dying in 1935, she was mourned worldwide as a great leader and interpreter of American thought" (p. 40).

Martin Luther King, Jr. (1929-1968)

Martin Luther King, Jr., was born on January 15, 1929, in Atlanta, Georgia. He was the second child and first son of Martin Luther King, Sr., who was pastor of the Ebenezer Baptist Church. Other children born to the Kings were Christine and Alfred Daniel Williams King. King's grandfather, James Albert King, had a "plantation style, field hand status" as a sharecropper (King, 1969, p. 75; Williams, 1970, p. 149). Williams (1970) explained that King's father

left his father's farm for the streets of Atlanta, where he did the best he could in that urban setting. In short order, he was preaching in two small Baptist churches before he had "paper one." Martin, Sr., had not yet graduated from high school. But by taking evening classes, he did get his diploma and went on to take classes at Morehouse College.

Adam Daniel Williams had been cut from the same tough cloth before King, Sr., came down the pike. He, too, had taken courses at Morehouse and, more importantly, put Ebenezer Baptist Church back in the black through his judicious administration. King, Sr., married Williams' daughter Alberta. She had gone to [the] Hampton Institute. . . . She also attended Spelman College in Atlanta and worked briefly as a teacher. (p. 150)

Williams (1970) further suggested that the King family valued education and that Martin, Jr., was a very good student (p. 165). "He was extremely self-possessed, and his abilities as a speaker were unquestioned" (p. 25). He advanced to Morehouse at 15 years of age. King was growing a strong social consciousness at Morehouse and wanted to learn firsthand what life was like for really underprivileged people. He took summer jobs doing hard manual labor (King, 1969, pp. 84-85). He graduated from Morehouse in 1948 and secured a B.D. degree at Crozer Theological Seminary in Boston in 1951. He was ordained by his father at the Ebenezer Baptist Church in 1948 at 18 years of age and became assistant pastor there (p. 87). King also attended lectures on philosophy at the University of Pennsylvania and at Harvard University (Williams, 1970, p. 27). He also received a Ph.D. in systematic theology from Boston University in 1955.

It was during his student days in Boston that King met Coretta Scott, who was studying at the New England Conservatory of Music (King, 1969, p. 89; Williams, 1970, p. 26). Scott was born in a modest house on her paternal grandfather's farm near Marion, Alabama, to Obadiah ("Obie") and Bernice McMurry Scott. Coretta noted,

My grandfather Jeff Scott . . . and my grandmother, Cora Scott, worked long hours in the field and sold pine timber in order to get together enough money to acquire the farm they both longed for. The struggle drove Cora Scott to an early grave, but by the time I knew my grandfather, he owned three hundred acres of land and was an important man in that rural black community. (King, 1969, p. 21)

Coretta's maternal grandfather, Martin McMurry, was part American Indian and was born just before the Emancipation Proclamation. She stated that "both of my grandfathers were leading men in the community" (King, 1969, p. 23). Her father worked in a lumber mill and worked extra jobs so that he could buy land, buy his own sawmill, and educate his children (Edythe, Coretta, and Obie). After graduating from high school, Coretta attended and graduated from Antioch College in Ohio in 1951. Edythe and Coretta were the first blacks to enter Antioch (p. 39). It was at Antioch that Coretta became active in civil rights, the National Association for the Advancement of Colored People (NAACP), a race relations committee, and a civil liberties committee. It also was at Antioch that she seriously began to study music.

King and Scott courted for about a year and were married by "Daddy King" on the lawn of her parents' home on June 18, 1953 (King, 1969, p. 71). They returned to Boston for a year where he completed his Ph.D. and she completed her music studies at the New England Conservatory (p. 89). His wife shared King's commitment to the civil rights movement. Among the many ways in which she became active was to use her musical skills to give benefit concerts for the movement.

In September 1954, the couple moved to Montgomery, Alabama, where King became the pastor of the Dexter Avenue Baptist Church.[7] Their first child, Yolanda Denise ("Yoki"), was born in Montgomery on November 17, 1955. Williams (1970) suggested, "It is somehow both fitting and paradoxical that Montgomery forged the cradle of the Confederacy as well as the cradle of the contemporary civil rights movement" (p. 155). Rosa Parks, a seamstress, is credited for the action that sparked the civil rights movement when she refused to give up her seat on a Montgomery bus. Coretta King described the incident:

> On December 1, 1955, Mrs. Rosa Parks, a forty-two-year-old seamstress whom my husband aptly described as "a charming person with a radiant personality," boarded a bus to go home after a long day working and shopping. The bus was crowded, and Mrs. Parks found a seat at the beginning of the Negro section. At the next stop, more whites got on. The driver ordered Mrs. Parks to give her seat to a white man who boarded; this meant that she would have to stand all the way home. Rosa Parks was not in a revolutionary frame of mind. She had not planned to do what she did. . . . As she said later, "I was just plain tired, and my feet hurt." (King, 1969, p. 113)

After a meeting at the Dexter Avenue Church of black ministers and civic leaders, it was decided to have a bus boycott on Monday, December 5. It made the front page of all the newspapers, and the boycott was a great success. Later, Martin wrote, "From this moment on, I conceived of our movement as an act of massive noncooperation. From then on, I rarely used the word 'boycott' " (cited in King, 1969, p. 115). The Montgomery Improvement Association was formed, and King was elected president. In a speech to a group of 5,000, he said,

> We are here this evening to say to those who have mistreated us so long that we are tired. Tired of being segregated and humiliated [as well as] tired of being kicked about by the brutal feet of oppression. . . . We have no alternative but to protest. We have

been amazingly patient . . ., [but] we come here tonight to be saved from that patience. (cited in King, 1969, p. 118)

A motor pool of volunteer drivers was organized, and pick-up stations were selected throughout the city with dispatchers to match passengers and destinations. By now, King was consciously emulating the Gandhian technique of passive resistance (p. 121). Thus, noncooperation became nonviolence and later became Gandhi's doctrine of Satyagraha (Williams, 1970, p. 174). Reactions to Gandhi and to King were similar. Both received threats on their lives and on the lives of their families, both were imprisoned for their activities, and both experienced attempts on their lives and eventually were assassinated. Coretta King described the harassment as follows:

At any hour, day or night, the phone would ring and some man or woman would pour out a string of obscene epithets, of which "nigger son of a bitch" was the mildest. Often the women callers raved on about sex, accusing Martin and me of incredible degeneracies. Frequently the call ended with a threat to kill us if we didn't get out of town. (King, 1969, p. 123)

On January 30, 1956, at about 9:30 p.m., one of the threats became a reality. A bomb was thrown onto the front porch of the Kings' house. Coretta and the baby, Yoki, were at home, and Martin was speaking at a mass meeting. He rushed home and found his family safe because they had moved to the back of the house before the bomb exploded (King, 1969, p. 127). He spoke to the crowd of angry people outside his house:

My wife and my baby are all right. I want you to go home and put down your weapons. We cannot solve this problem through retaliatory violence. We must meet violence with nonviolence. . . . Remember, if I am stopped, this movement will not stop because God is with this movement. Go home with this glowing faith and this radiant assurance. (pp. 129-130)

On November 13, 1956, the U.S. Supreme Court affirmed a decision by a U.S. court declaring Alabama's state and local laws requiring segregation on buses unconstitutional. Although it would be a month or more before desegregation would occur, there was a celebration. When 40 or 50 carloads of the Ku Klux Klan rode through the Negro section of Montgomery that night, people did not empty the streets and turn off the lights as they had done in the past. All the lights were on, and blacks walked along the streets or stood in groups chatting casually. Because they had marched together and achieved their first triumph, they no longer were afraid (p. 143).

After the Montgomery victory of the buses, other movements inspired by Montgomery started up in places such as Mobile, Alabama; Tallahassee, Florida; and Atlanta, Georgia. King became involved in coordinating these movements. While organizing a mass meeting in Atlanta, he received word of bombing and violence in Montgomery. Coretta King wrote that Ralph Abernathy and Martin "decided that they must rush back immediately to calm our people and comfort them. Martin asked me to represent him in Atlanta" (King, 1969, p. 151). On February 14, 1957, a large meeting was held in New Orleans, Louisiana, to form a permanent organization to fight segregation and achieve civil rights. It was called the Southern Christian Leadership Conference (SCLC), and King was elected president. That spring, he moved to put pressure on the Eisenhower administration for dragging its heels in the matter of black voting rights. On May 17, 1957, 37,000 marchers assembled in front of the Lincoln Memorial. In his speech, King said,

> Give us the ballot, and we will no longer plead—we will write the proper laws on the books.
> Give us the ballot, and we will fill the legislatures with men of goodwill.
> Give us the ballot, and we will get the people judges who love mercy.
>
> (cited in King, 1969, p. 160)

That fall, a son, Martin Luther King, III, was born (King, 1969, p. 161). As King's national reputation grew, there were increased demands on his travel schedule to make speeches and to organize the movement throughout the South and into northern cities such as Detroit, Chicago, and Washington. His travels included a pilgrimage to India with members of his family in March 1959[8] (p. 173). Coretta King stated, "Martin returned from India more devoted than ever to Gandhian ideals of nonviolence and simplicity of living" (p. 178). For 3 years after the founding of SCLC headquarters in Atlanta, King had been commuting between Montgomery and Atlanta. Because he believed that he had to give more time to the civil rights struggle, he resigned from the Dexter church in Montgomery, effective January 1960, and moved to Atlanta (p. 183).

In Atlanta, King became copastor with his father at the Ebenezer Baptist Church. During that same year, student sit-ins to desegregate lunch counters and restaurants began in Greensboro, North Carolina, and the Student Nonviolent Coordinating Committee (SNCC) was formed (King, 1969, p. 188). The next year, the Freedom Riders began protests designed to desegregate interstate buses and bus terminals in the South. Although these efforts to desegregate accomplished a great deal, many people were arrested and some lost their lives. In the midst of all this, the Kings' third child, Dexter ("named for our beloved church in Montgomery"), was born (p. 205). Their fourth child, Bernice Albertine ("Bunny"), was born on March 28, 1964 (p. 220).

In the spring of 1963, the Birmingham movement began to help desegregate the lunch counters. King went to Birmingham to lead the protests and to try to get the merchants and Birmingham officials to agree on four moderate points: desegregation of store facilities, upgrading and hiring of Negroes on a nondiscriminatory basis, dropping of charges against the imprisoned protesters, and creation of a biracial committee to work out a timetable for further desegregation of Birmingham (King, 1969, p. 221; Williams, 1970, p. 180). The businessmen were willing to negotiate, but city officials were not and obtained an injunction against the demonstrators. King and Abernathy decided to lead a march in violation of the injunction. Both were arrested and sent to the Birmingham jail. They were denied their rights to consult with their lawyers and to communicate by phone with the outside.[9] Coretta King tried to contact President Kennedy, and when she finally heard from the president, he told her that the Federal Bureau of Investigation had been sent to Birmingham and that her husband, who was all right, would be calling her. While in prison, King sent a letter to the Birmingham clergy in response to their criticisms of the movement and their calling the activities "unwise and untimely" and "outsiders coming in." This was a very lengthy letter, but following are some excerpts from this now famous letter:

> In any nonviolent campaign, there are four basic steps: (1) collection of the facts to determine whether injustices are alive, (2) negotiation, (3) self-purification, and (4) direct action. We have gone through all of these steps in Birmingham. There can be no gainsaying of the fact that racial injustice engulfs this community.
>
> Then came the opportunity last September to talk with some of the leaders of the economic community. In these negotiating sessions . . ., promises were made by the merchants such as the promise to remove the humiliating racial signs from the stores. . . . The signs remained. . . . So we had no alternative except that of preparing for direct action, whereby we would present our very bodies as a means of laying our case before the conscience of the local and national community.
>
> Nonviolent direct action seeks to create such a crisis and establish such creative tension that a community that has constantly refused to negotiate is forced to confront the issue. . . . There comes a time when the cup of endurance runs over and men are no longer willing to be plunged into an abyss of despair.
>
> But before closing, I am impelled to mention one other point in your statement. . . . You warmly commended the Birmingham police force for keeping "order" and "preventing violence." I don't believe you would have so warmly commended the police force if you had seen its angry violent dogs literally biting six unarmed, nonviolent Negroes . . . [and] if you would observe their ugly and inhuman treatment of Negroes here in the city jail. (King, 1963a)

On May 10, 1963, an agreement was announced. It was almost word for word an acceptance of the original demands of the movement. "The stores were to be desegregated, hiring of Negroes upgraded, charges dropped, and the Senior Citizens Committee or the Chamber of Commerce would meet regularly with black leaders to reconcile their differences" (King, 1969, p. 231).

The "March on Washington" of an estimated 250,000 people occurred on August 28, 1963 (King, 1969, p. 237). On this day, King delivered his famous "I Have a Dream" speech on the steps at the Lincoln Memorial. He proclaimed,

> I say to you today even though we face difficulties of today and tomorrow, I still have a dream. . . . I have a dream that one day this nation will rise up, live out the true meaning of its creed: We hold these truths to be self-evident, that all men are created equal.
>
> I have a dream that one day on the red hills of Georgia, the sons of former slaves and the sons of former slaveowners will be able to sit down together at the table of brotherhood. I have a dream that one day even the state of Mississippi, a state sweltering with the heat of oppression, will be transformed into an oasis of freedom and justice.

I have a dream that my four little children one day will live in a nation where they will not be judged by the color of their skin but by the content of their character. . . . This will be the day when all of God's children will be able to sing with new meaning, "Let freedom ring." . . . When we allow freedom to ring from every town and every hamlet, from every state and every city, we will be able to speed up that day when all of God's children, black men and white men, Jews and Gentiles, Protestants and Catholics, will be able to join hands and sing in the words of the old Negro spiritual, "Free at last! Free at last! Great God A-mighty, we are free at last!" (cited in King, 1969, pp. 239-240; see also King, 1963b)

King continued the struggle for freedom for the rest of his life. He led the demonstrations in Selma to Montgomery for voting rights; he went to Los Angeles to calm the violence in Watts; and his desegregation campaign took him north into cities such as Chicago, Philadelphia, New York, Cleveland, and Detroit. During the summer of 1966, the King family rented and lived in a slum apartment in the Chicago ghetto to call national attention to the conditions and to bring some comfort to the people who lived there (King, 1969, pp. 276-280). It was decided to concentrate the Chicago movement on open housing (p. 288). There was a rally at Soldier Field in Chicago and a march including the King family and 50,000 people on July 10, 1966 (p. 282). To grapple with Chicago's problem of poverty and unemployment, Operation Breadbasket was organized by the SCLC and led by Jesse Jackson. Because the movement now was involved in the economic struggle of the poor, the Poor People's Campaign was organized throughout the country. Although King encouraged his wife to become internationally active in the peace effort, he was concerned about spending his limited time and effort with the movement for black freedom. During the final year of his life, however, King took his most explicit and outspoken steps in opposing the war in Vietnam. He argued,

The promises of the Great Society have been shot down on the battlefields of Vietnam. The pursuit of this widened war has narrowed domestic welfare programs, making the poor, white and Negro, bear the heaviest burdens. . . . It is estimated that we spend $322,000 for each enemy we kill, while we spend in the so-called war on poverty in America only about $53 for each person classified as poor. . . . We must combine the fervor of the civil rights movement with the peace movement. (cited in King, 1969, p. 292) . . .

I want you to know that this is a moral commitment with me. . . . For a long time, I encouraged my wife to be active in the peace movement. Finally, I could no longer stand silently by. I have spoken my convictions that this is the most evil and unjust war in the history of our country. (p. 296)

In April 1968, King went to Memphis, Tennessee, to make final preparations for a nonviolent march he was scheduled to lead. There were threats and rumors of an attack on him. He told an audience in Memphis,

We've got some difficult days ahead. But it really doesn't matter to me now because I've been to the mountaintop.

> Like anybody else, I would like to live a long life. I just want to do God's will. And He's allowed me to go to the mountain. And I've looked over, and I've seen the Promised Land. I may not get there with you, but I want you to know tonight [that] we as a people will get to the Promised Land. (cited in King, 1969, p. 316)

The next day, April 4, 1968, as King was leaving the Negro-owned and -operated Lorraine Motel to go out to dinner, he was shot and killed. Benjamin E. Mays gave the following eulogy at the funeral:

> We have assembled here from every section of this great nation . . . to give thanks to God that He gave to America, at this moment in history, Martin Luther King, Jr. . . . God called the grandson of a slave on his father's side and said to him: "Martin Luther, speak to America about war and peace, about social justice and racial discrimination, about its obligation to the poor, and about nonviolence as a way of perfecting social change in a world of brutality and war." (p. 353) . . .
>
> As Mahatma Gandhi challenged the British Empire without a sword and won, Martin Luther King, Jr., challenged the interracial wrongs of his country without a gun. And he had the faith to believe that he would win the battle for social justice. . . . It took more courage for King to practice nonviolence than it took his assassin to fire the fatal shot. (p. 355)

It also should be acknowledged that King received numerous honors during his lifetime. He was awarded honorary doctorate degrees from more than a dozen American colleges and universities as well as from several foreign countries. In 1963, a *Newsweek* poll named King as the nation's undisputed "Negro Leader" (Williams, 1970, p. 65). In January 1964, King also was honored as *Time* Magazine's "Man of the Year" for 1963 (pp. 68, 168). He also was given the Nobel Peace Prize in 1964 (King, 1969, p. 2; Williams, 1970, pp. 73-75). The prize in 1964 was worth $54,000, all of which King donated to civil rights causes and nonviolent studies (Williams, 1970, p. 75). In accepting the award in Oslo, Norway, King stated,

> I am mindful that only yesterday in Birmingham, Alabama, our children, crying out for brotherhood, were answered with fire hoses, snarling dogs, and even death. I am mindful that only yesterday in Philadelphia, Mississippi, young people seeking to secure the right to vote were brutalized and murdered.
>
> Therefore, I must ask why this prize is awarded to a movement which is beleaguered and committed to unrelenting struggle; to a movement which has not won the very peace and brotherhood which is the essence of the Nobel Prize. After contemplation, I conclude that this award, which I receive on behalf of the movement, is a profound recognition that nonviolence is the answer to the crucial political and racial questions of our time—the need for man to overcome oppression without resorting to violence. (cited in King, 1969, pp. 12-13)

Gandhi has been cited frequently in the peacemaking literature for his nonviolent protest, especially by Richard Quinney. Although King[10] has been mentioned occasionally, Addams never has received recognition for her early work for social justice and peace. It must be recognized that all three of these people, who dedicated their lives to improving the civil rights and economic lives of their people, were laying the foundation for the peacemaking theorists in criminology.

Assumptions About People and Society

In Chapters 8 and 9 (on conflict/radical and feminist theories, respectively), it was noted that there was a diversion from the traditional mainstream approach to research and theory as well as a variety of perspectives and approaches by the theorists. This also is true in the present peacemaking chapter. Like conflict/radical and feminist theories, peacemaking uses a predominantly qualitative methodology as opposed to the more mainstream emphasis on the quantitative method. For peacemaking, there is some reliance on history (and spiritualism) such as Quinney's (1991) inclusion of Gandhi and Buddhism in "The Way of Peace" and Tifft and Markham's (1991) comparison of the battering of women and the battering of Central Americans by the United States during the 1980s. Galliher (1991) used the Willie Horton case to point to the use of racism in politics. Some authors such as Milovanovic (1991), who cited the works of Hegel, Nietzsche, and others in his discussion of the peacemaking community, were much more philosophical. Pepinsky (1988) used the Norwegian and American responses to crime to illustrate the need for a change from punishment of crime to a peacemaking approach to crime in the United States. Those from the critical perspective, such as Scimecca (1991) and Elias (1991), as well as some feminists, such as Knopp (1991) and Harris (1991), further emphasize the need for policy reform in our "justice" system.

Like other perspectives discussed in this book, the peacemaking perspective examines both an individual (micro) level and a collective/societal (macro) level in analyzing crime or criminal behavior. Quinney (1993) used a micro level when he stated, "If we want to reduce crime—and yes, even eliminate crime—we need first to live personal lives of loving kindness, of loving others, including our neighbors in crime" (p. 4). Those "peacemakers" who examine crime from the feminist tradition, such as Harris (1991) and Rucker (1991), advocate reforms of the criminal justice system, and programs in prisons use a macro level of analysis. Because most of the theorists in this chapter emphasize that peacemaking in criminology must begin with each individual, the micro level of analysis tends to dominate this chapter.

The majority of peacemaking criminologists also emphasize subjective covert phenomena as opposed to objective overt phenomena. For example, Brock-Utne (1989) differentiated between negative peace and positive peace, and Quinney (1991) stated that "crime is suffering" and that "peace and harmony come from the awareness of the oneness of all things." He also used concepts of "peace and justice" and "compassion." Pepinsky (1988, 1993, 1998) discussed "remorse and empathy," "unresponsiveness/responsiveness," and "fear and hope." These all are values and feelings that are both subjective and covert. However, behaviors such as Gandhi's famous Salt March of the 1930s are objective and overt phenomena. Barak's (1991) reporting of how Aurora, Illinois, responded to homelessness is both objective overt and subjective covert. It is objective in that the behavior of the homeless made this phenomenon obvious, as did the services established by the religious groups and social agencies. The subjective aspect of this program is that the housing, food pantries, and the like were the result of *hesed*, the Hebrew word meaning "mercy," "steadfast and enduring love," or "interhuman compassion" (p. 58) instead of the fear and hostility toward the homeless that so often brings law enforcement in to punish the poor and homeless (objective and covert behavior).

For peace and justice to occur, there must be a change from the current criminal justice system in which people are seen as passive agents to be controlled by a society that imposes prison and punishment on people who are alleged to have violated definitions of crime imposed by those with economic and political power (Fuller, 1998; Knopp, 1991; Pepinsky, 1988). Those who advocate peacemaking in criminology argue that for peace and social justice to be achieved, people must be allowed to be active, free-willed agents who are permitted to generate their own values and behavior. For example, Sanzen (1991) suggested,

> Crime control is too narrow a focus on criminal justice's role in making peace. Peace means reducing the power that is based on control, domination, [and] exploitation . . ., which produce segregation. Peace means increasing people's power to do things *with* others rather than *to* others. (pp. 239-240)

Pepinsky (1998) noted,

> We put a premium on obedience. We do so to our peril. . . . It is poisonous pedagogy . . . to make a child feel or do something for his or her own good. . . . You learn to please the parents you . . . love and want to please, to say nothing of to avoid pain and rejection. . . . You learn, in other words, to lie.
>
> I suffer watching defendants plead guilty in local courts. It is such a humiliating experience, assuring the judge count by count. (p. 145)

Pepinsky further argued that active, free-willed, self-functioning citizens develop through empathy and responsiveness to them and by listening and paying attention to what they say.

Finally, peacemakers view society as based on conflict and coercion and as imposed so as to maintain a stable society or the status quo. But those criminologists who adhere to the peacemaking perspective propose a fluid society based on consensus that allows equality and integration of all citizens.

Current Peacemaking in Criminology

Peacemaking in criminology that has emerged during the 1990s rejects mainstream traditional criminological theory and policy as based on a hierarchical military model that seeks to return violence with violence. By contrast, the peacemaking perspective seeks to understand the suffering that causes crime and to extend compassion, harmony, and social justice to the persons who have been identified as deviants or criminals.

Some of those writing from the peacemaking perspective predominantly emphasize the spiritual and religious tradition. Others write from the feminist tradition. Of these feminists, some deal with crime and justice, and a few raise issues regarding education and world peace. Finally, the critical tradition is composed of a large group of criminologists who object to the vindictive nature of the criminal justice system, which practices punishments that return violence with violence. Instead of imprisonment, the death penalty, and wars on crime and/or drugs, they seek reconciliation and rehabilitation. Although it is difficult to fit each author into one of these categories, this chapter places each into the category that seems the best fit. The reader should recognize that other theorists might disagree with some choices or that these theorists could be placed in more than one category. Pepinsky is a good example of a theorist whose works could easily fit several categories.

Spiritual and Religious Traditions

Richard Quinney

Richard Quinney[11] has been instrumental in much of the change that has occurred in criminological theory for several decades. His early publications were more mainstream, and then he moved into conflict/Marxist theory. Over the past decade or so, his publications have been spiritual in theme, and during more recent years he has extended the spiritual to include peacemaking in criminology. Quinney (1991) led the way in pointing to the failure of our public policies to bring us closer to understanding and solving the problem of crime. He presented the following observations to explain his position:

> (1) Thought of the Western rational mode is conditional, limiting knowledge to what is already known. (2) The truth of reality is emptiness; all that is real is beyond human conception. (3) Each life is a spiritual journey into the unknown and unknowable. . . . (4) Human existence is characterized by suffering; crime is suffering. . . . (5) Through love and compassion, beyond the egocentric self, we can end suffering and live in peace, personally and collectively. (6) The ending of suffering can be attained in a quieting of the mind and an opening of the mind. . . . (7) Crime can be ended only with the ending of suffering, only when there is peace. . . . (8) Understanding, service, [and] justices . . . flow naturally from love and compassion. . . . (9) *A criminology of peacemaking,* the nonviolent criminology of compassion and service, seeks to end suffering and thereby eliminate crime. (pp. 3-4)

A Tibetan Buddhist master was quoted by Quinney and Wildeman (1991) as saying that the suffering we experience in the world "is caused by the six afflictions—ignorance, desire, pride, anger, jealousy, and greed" (p. 115). The most hopeful way in which to attain world peace and to end global suffering, he added, is by developing within ourselves compassion and loving kindness toward others. Quinney (1993) also challenged criminologists to reexamine their personal and professional agendas with reference to public policy. He stated, "Criminology may easily join economics as a dismal science. If not a dismal science, certainly much of criminology is a science for a mean-spirited time" (p. 3). He quoted from *The Dhammapada,* an ancient text of Buddhism: "All that we are is a result of what we have thought" (p. 4). Quinney suggested that "hatred begets hatred; love makes us loving" (p. 4). He further introduced Gandhi's philosophy of Satyagraha. This is the idea that social action comes out of an informed human heart and a clear and enlightened mind that fully understands its own suffering and, therefore, the suffering of others (Quinney, 1991, p. 10). Quinney (1991) stated,

> All of this is to say, to us as criminologists, that crime is suffering and that the end of crime is possible only with the ending of suffering. And the ending of suffering and of crime, which is the establishing of justice, can come only out of peace, out of a peace that is spiritually grounded in our very being. . . . We as human beings must *be* peace if we are to live in a world free of crime, in a world of peace. (p. 11)

According to Quinney (1993),

> What is required, in our work as criminologists, is not only an academic literature and a professional organization but [also] ways of thinking, speaking, and writing that foster peace. This is a compassionate criminology, a criminology of peacemaking.
>
> When we engage in a mean-minded criminology—a criminology of prejudice and punishment—we become the lives we lead. . . . Such a criminology—as a daily diet— can make us uncaring and unloving, just as it helps to maintain a social ethos of hate, selfishness, and violence. (p. 4)

In an early publication, Quinney (1985) asserted that "crime is one of the predominant myths of our contemporary society" (p. 295). As criminologists, we are part of the myth. Quinney claimed,

> There are those who are the subject of the myth: the public and the large part of the public that is defined as criminal at any time. There is the apparatus—the reifying structure—of the myth: the police, the courts, the prisons, and all the functionaries of these institutions. And, not least are the storytellers: the newspaper reporters, the social critics, the preachers, and the criminologists. As high priests of the myth, we criminologists tell the story in detail and make it appropriate for the time and place. (p. 295)

Quinney (1993) further exhorted us that the objective of criminology is quite simple—to be kind to one another, to break down the barriers that separate us from one another, to live moment to moment our connection to all that is, and to have compassion (p. 6). Using compassion, wisdom, and understanding, we practice a criminology of nonviolence. And in the practice, we become more compassionate, more wise, and more understanding in our own daily lives. We are what we think and practice (p. 7). Quinney quoted the words of the Dalai Lama of Tibet before the latter received the Nobel Peace Prize, "What is required is a kind heart and a sense of community which I call universal responsibility," as a guide for criminologists (p. 8). Quinney and Wildeman (1991) contended that peace can come only out of peace. "There is no way to peace. . . . Peace is the way." In other words, "without *inner* peace in each of us . . . , there can be no *social* peace between people and no peace in societies, [in] nations, and in the world" (pp. 116-117).

Finally, after emphasizing the need for inner peace in each individual before there can be peace in the world and an end to crime, Quinney (1998) turned to his own life by keeping a journal. He referred to the process of writing in his journal as attending to the wonder of his daily life. He suggested that these journal entries now are a thread woven into a tapestry of his life. And he admitted, "I am witness to an experience that, in my telling, others can learn from. As the leaf nourishes a tree" (p. 61).

As a university professor in his 60s, Quinney (1998) confronted life and wrote,

> Every day is a perfect day, a day of holiness, when no distinctions are made. It is the distinction between life and death I seek to erase in my daily living of late. The mind has created the distinction between life and death, a distinction that I now realize is a false one. Life is constant, fixed, [and] ever-present. We are born out of life, and we die into life. . . . Death is but a part of the continuity of life. (p. 25) . . .
>
> I watch, and action comes out of my awareness in the here and now. In the words of Zen Master Linji of an earlier century, "If you attain real true perception and understanding, birth and death don't affect you—you are free to go or stay." The future takes care of itself. (p. 13)

In the closing chapter of his journal, Quinney declared, "I write as a way of mourning. . . . I mourn, and I celebrate, this life and this death" (p. 181). Although some criminologists might doubt that this work is a contribution to the field of criminology, Gibbs (1999), in his review of *For The Time Being* (Quinney, 1998), noted that the "subject of the book is at the same time both broader and narrower than criminal justice and criminology." Gibbs further argued that Quinney has had a central role in shaping the discipline and has been a "creative and provocative force" in criminology for more than three decades.

John J. Gibbs

John J. Gibbs,[12] professor of criminology at Indiana University of Pennsylvania, also claimed that the path to peace must involve a change of consciousness at the individual level (Gibbs, 1995). He suggested that to achieve peace in criminology, this individual approach must be "spiritually based and ideologically free" (p. 449). Like other authors of the peacemaking in criminology perspective, Gibbs (1995) endorsed Buddhism as a peaceful philosophy of life and spiritual practice. This is in contrast to our current society, which is dominated by the economic institution that is based on the principle of competitive self-interest, hierarchy, and social control of the underclass. Gibbs also asserted that class boundaries are maintained and described in military terms as follows:

The United States, for example, has waged wars against poverty, crime, drugs, and other social problems. Police are conceptualized as crime fighters. Wars require enemies who must be characterized as subhuman to motivate the troops. The more unredeemable the enemy can be established in the public mind . . ., the more the oppressive force of social control agents can be justified. (p. 449)

Gibbs (1995) concurred with other peacemaking criminologists that how we frame events and problems has everything to do with what we do about them. Buddhism provides a very different approach to crime and criminal justice. It proclaims that life is suffering, and at its most basic level, human life seems to consist of alternating states of pain and pleasure as well as need and fulfillment. Gibbs further stated that "eliminating the causes of suffering requires a radical personal transformation" (p. 452). He declared, "We cannot expect that a worldview that evolves from self-centered and group-centered reactions to existential anxiety will promote peace and harmony among people" (p. 451). Instead, from the Buddhist perspective, all things are empty and exist only in the context of all other things. Gibbs stated, "Buddha's central insight, variously known as interbeing, dependent co-arising, and dependent origination, concerns the transactions that shape everything and particularly human consciousness" (p. 451). Putting personal transformation first helps us to better understand the forces shaping our social institutions and how they shape us (p. 453). Understanding this reality and achieving peace will occur one person and one action at a time.

An emphasis on the personal and spiritual does not mean that we disregard what we've learned about social action or about systemic change. Nor does it reject empirical methods for acquiring such knowledge. We should merely beware how our rational processes can dominate and how ego enhancement might become our implicit objective. (p. 455)

As stated earlier in this chapter, Gibbs (1996) rejected the war model for education and promoted the peacemaking model.[13] Gibbs contended that the war model emphasizes how to do things, which is a person-task distinction model, as opposed to the peacemaking model, which stresses the person-task process or transaction model (p. 578). He further argued that the war model promotes "separation and dominance," whereas the peace model creates "unity and harmony." He stated that the process-centered approach to schoolwork also creates understanding and is the "key to real learning." Gibbs pointed out that this process-oriented approach "constitutes the Zen way of learning" (p. 579).

Buddhists also advocate that we focus on the here and now rather than on expectations or objectives. Gibbs cited Thich Nhat Hanh as stating, "When we are able to take one step peacefully and happily, we are working for the cause of peace and happiness for the whole of humanity" (Hanh, 1991, cited in Gibbs, 1995, p. 453). Gibbs (1995) also emphasized the importance of spirituality, which captures our connection to the whole. Spirituality includes everything and nothing. It transcends description but not experience. It forces us to drop conceptual schemes that distance the observer and the observed, and it asks us simply to be in the situation in its totality (p. 454). The spiritual approach promotes continual inquiry.

Finally, Gibbs (1995) suggested that adopting a peacemaking perspective in criminal justice or other systems incurs the risk of turning it into an ideology—a set of ideas, concepts, or values that provides a framework for events (p. 454). The danger comes when ideologies substitute for inquiry and we accept the conclusions uncritically. When ideologies clash, they destroy the prospects of peace and mutual understanding.

J. Peter Cordella

J. Peter Cordella posed that it is our social contract model of community and the corresponding assumption of the self-interested nature of people that involves the alienation and exclusion of some that results in conflict and crime (Cordella, 1991, p. 30). Instead of the rational modern society based on fear and punishment, Cordella (1991) advised the return to a mutualist model of community. This type of community allows us to care for one another, as opposed to the rational society in which we care only for ourselves and in which "we have become associates, not friends" (p. 33). He further noted that "mutual affection, common life, and reconciliation" (p. 34) are common themes found in communitarian religious sects. According to Cordella, "Theologically, each of the mutualist communities equates the subordination of self-will with human freedom" (p. 40). The subordination of self-will must be a "matter of spontaneous self-expression in action" that leads to freedom and is the basis of morality. He argued that the following situation exists among the mutualist religious communities:

> The Hutterites are the best example of the subordination of organic relations to the mutualist intention. Central to the Hutterite way of life is a "community of goods." Private ownership, according to the Hutterites, is against the nature and will of God. When one seeks permanent membership as an adult, one must make a vow that involves making peace with God, the community, and the desire to own property. . . . "Whoever cannot give up his private property as well as his own self-will cannot become a disciple or follower of Christ." . . . There are no distinctions between rich and poor, nor are there many distinctions according to occupations. . . . People never worry about food, clothing, or housing, regardless of their physical or mental capabilities or their age. (p. 40)

The Mennonite theology argues that the coercion of formal rules, which are the lifeblood of bureaucratic structures, does not allow for community. "*Gemeinde,* the Mennonite version of community, is guided by only one law, the law of *agape*" (Cordella, 1991, p. 36). The law is based on Matthew 22:39b, which states that "you shall love your neighbor as yourself." This must be done voluntarily and, ideally, is internalized and is a symbol of commitment to the Mennonite community. Cordella noted that one of the most profound commitments of a community is the provision of a context that encourages people to trust and depend on each other (p. 37).

Gregg Barak

Gregg Barak suggested that the suppression of the human potential of those who are homeless and the perpetuation of their misery are a "product of a society characterized by gross structural inequality and social injustice" (Barak, 1991, p. 48). Among the 3 million homeless in the United States are

> men, women, [and] children of all racial and ethnic backgrounds; urban and rural workers; displaced and deinstitutionalized persons; alcoholics, drug addicts, AIDS victims, [and] the mentally ill; physically abused mothers and their babies; sexually abused teenagers and preadolescents; neglected elderly; and migrants, refugees, and veterans. (pp. 47-48)

These people, Barak argued, are the product of the economic policies of the 1980s that benefited the top two thirds of society while expanding the poverty of the lower one third of society. In addition, the homeless experience the impersonal forces of alienation and detachment as well as victimization by other homeless people and by traditional street crimes. In many cities, the homeless are objects of law enforcement and subjects for criminalization (p. 54). The city of Tucson, Arizona, is an example. Few shelter beds or soup kitchens were available to homeless people, but the unofficial policies of the city were to run the homeless out of town. Homeless people also had been known to be verbally harassed and physically abused by police. They often were handcuffed, arrested, and charged with criminal trespass, squatting, or loitering.

In contrast to the experience of the homeless in Tucson, Barak (1991) presented the nonviolent alternative response to the homeless in Aurora, Illinois (p. 55). He explained that many in Aurora had been dependent on blue collar industrial jobs prior to the 1970s and 1980s. With the transformation of the nation's economy into a service/information-oriented economy, many in Aurora were affected by the economic slump, and increasing numbers slipped into poverty and homelessness. In response to this, Aurora organized a "unique model of ecumenical interchurch and interagency cooperation." Among the agencies/organizations organized to deal with the problem of a depressed economy were the Aurora Area Interfaith Food Pantry (established in 1981), the Aurora Soup Kitchen and Clothes Closet (both began in 1982), the Public Action Deliver Shelter (PADS) (started in 1983), and PADS A.M. (opened in 1985) (p. 56). Barak noted that PADS, both organizationally and politically, was the driving force of advocacy for the homeless in Aurora. PADS argued that all people should be entitled to food and shelter including alcoholics, fire victims, drug abusers, the mentally ill, and the unemployed (p. 56). All of these services eventually became legally incorporated as the Hesed House. "This community-based initiative created a private nonprofit-public partnership" (p. 58).

The ideology/philosophy adhered to in support of the Hesed House is from the Hebrew scriptures. According to Barak (1991),

> From the Hebrew scriptures, *hesed* is translated sometimes to mean "mercy," other times to mean "pity," but more often to mean "steadfast and enduring love." And Jose

Miranda, the liberation theologian, has translated *hesed* as "interhuman compassion." . . . "All of our English translations lack the dimension of action that the Hebrew word implies. The Hebrew talks of *doing hesed* with someone. . . . It implies liberating self and others. . . . The person doing *hesed* is also engaging in the "ministry of hospitality"—in the provision of caring humane encounters. (p. 58)

The concept of *hesed* also may be interpreted as "love-justice," calling for action on behalf of the poor and oppressed and calling on people to "practice what they preach."

In sum, the Hesed House is a place for the operation of a multiversity of human services provided for those people who need them most when they need them most. However, Barak (1991) concluded that this is not a long-term solution. He argued that criminologists and others need to act as human agents in the formation of public policy. He further asserted that the interaction among "class struggle and the discursive language on homelessness, the homeless, victimization, criminalization, punishment, justice, and the *crime and control* talk" helps to maintain the existing social order (p. 61).

The Feminist Tradition

As indicated in Chapter 9, feminists do not speak with one voice. Also, since feminist theory in criminology became established during the 1990s, feminist scholarship has made major contributions on new topics and theoretical perspectives that have developed such as peacemaking. The feminists examined in this chapter have defined peace, examined world peace, pointed to the conceptual similarities between the feminist and peacemaking perspectives, and proposed changes in the criminal justice system based on both feminism and peacemaking.

Birgit Brock-Utne

Birgit Brock-Utne,[14] a native of Norway, used a feminist perspective to explore peace and peace education (Brock-Utne, 1985). She began by defining peace as both the absence of direct violence (e.g., war) and the absence of indirect or structural violence (p. 1). Indirect violence can be used to describe the relationship among industrialized countries. It also can be used to characterize the state within a specific country where society is structured to sustain inequalities among people. Brock-Utne (1985) included UNESCO's plan for peace adopted at the General Conference in Paris in 1982 to stress the importance of human rights and respect as central to peace. According to Brock-Utne, the UNESCO document states,

There can be no genuine peace when the most elementary human rights are violated or while situations of injustice continue to exist; conversely, human rights for all cannot take root and achieve full growth while latent or open conflicts are rife.

Peace is incompatible with malnutrition, extreme poverty, and the refusal of the rights of peoples to self-determination. Disregard for the rights of individuals and peoples, the persistence of inequitable international economic structures, interference in the internal affairs of other states, foreign occupation, and apartheid are always real or potential sources of armed conflict and international crisis. The only lasting peace is a just peace based on respect for human rights. (p. 3)

Brock-Utne (1985) explained the connection between the feminist movement and the "work of peace" (p. 131). She suggested that as women who fight for their own rights become more politically concerned, they see that most institutions are built by men and need to be changed. She contended that feminist women do not want equality on men's premises and do not want to copy men or copy men's ways. By contrast, Brock-Utne stated,

> We are trying to cooperate and break down competition. We use assertiveness training so that women become self-assertive, independent, [and] critical, but at the same time we want to keep the caring aspects of our education and to teach men to also care about living beings, children and grown-ups, plants and animals, [and] Mother Earth. (p. 32)

Brock-Utne noted that women have to fight against their own oppression to help others.

Brock-Utne (1991) posed that women who are part of the new feminist ideology naturally will think differently about defense questions than will most men (p. 134). These women will be skeptical of military institutions, which are the incarnation of masculinity. These feminists refuse to accept concepts such as "security" and "defense." This feminist perspective would be a contribution to both the peace movement and peace studies. Furthermore, Brock-Utne stated, "All-women peace groups have been initiators of large and successful peace marches and festivals" (p. 132). In conclusion, she declared that not only can feminists teach other women about security and defense, but they also can teach men. Feminists can teach about the oppressive structures of patriarchy and about creating a new and peaceful society based on equality.

Karen J. Warren and Duane L. Cady

Similar ideas were expressed by Karen J. Warren and Duane L. Cady when they stated, "The most obvious connection between feminism and peace is that both are structured around the concept and logic of domination" (Warren and Cady, 1996, pp. 1-3). They suggested that any feminist movement to end the oppression of women also must include efforts to end the multiple oppressions of racism, classism, ageism, heterosexism, ethnocentrism, anti-Semitism, and imperialism. Genuine peace, they argued, is not merely the absence of war with order imposed from outside but also a process in which life-affirming, self-determined, environmentally friendly ends are sought and accomplished through cooperation, interaction, and equality. Feminism and peace share a commitment to the elimination of coercive power and systems of privilege and domination.

M. Joan McDermott

M. Joan McDermott[15] explored the concerns of criminology as peacemaking and those of feminist ethics (McDermott, 1994). She suggested that the feminist perspectives that are most consistent with scholarship in feminist ethics are the peacemaking and nonviolent responses (p. 22). McDermott (1994) further suggested that feminist ethics has grown out of a commitment to two basic feminist assumptions: that women and their values are of profound moral significance and that social institutions and practices have encouraged discrimination against women and the suppression of women's moral values (p. 23). McDermott approached her analysis based on the idea that there are differences in ethical concerns and priorities between men and women and that feminist ethics assumes that moral orientations are related to the conditions of people's lives (p. 28).

McDermott (1994) pointed to the work of Carol Gilligan, who distinguished between a rights/justice moral orientation that includes rules, autonomy, and a hierarchy of values and power and a care/response moral orientation that assumes interdependence and is nonhierarchical (pp. 28-29). Although most people use both modes of moral reasoning, one mode tends to dominate. It is argued that feminists and peacemaking criminologists tend to use the care/response predominantly. McDermott also contended that feminist ethics require caring individuals to be responsive to others' points of view. To make moral judgments, one must be aware of the needs and points of view of others because human relationships and interdependencies create responsibilities (p. 31). We exist in a web of relationships, and the self is defined in relationships. McDermott also asserted that many feminists extend the web of ethical relationships to a consideration of a connection to the environment.

Moral behavior and justice, according to McDermott (1994), flow from caring and responsiveness. She claimed that there is a universal ethic contained in feminism that "it is wrong to hurt anyone and it is right to sustain human relationships" (p. 32). Women's moral thinking is contextual in that it responds to actual people in actual situations. Bonds to each other provide the context of ethical commitments (p. 33). Another important concept of feminist ethics is equality. Responsiveness requires equality and human connectedness as well as a nonhierarchical structure. When one person has power or wants power over another, there cannot be a stable relationship. Finally, McDermott indicated that emotions and feelings are as important as intellect and reason for feminist moral judgments (p. 33).

Turning to the ethic of nonviolence found in the literature on peacemaking in criminology, McDermott (1994) identified the emphases, concerns, and priorities of that perspective (p. 24). The first priority of peacemaking is that we cannot achieve justice and peace without loving and compassionate people.

> The connection of the inner peace to the outer peace is the connection between individuals who behave morally and a morally responsible society. . . . Responsive persons or groups work on problems by changing themselves. . . . For criminology as peacemaking, the inner peace–outer peace, personal change–social change connection is the framework for additional concerns and priorities. Connectedness (as opposed to au-

tonomy) is another emphasis of peacemaking. An individual's actions have consequences for others. Because of these connections, "violence begets violence." (p. 25)

Peacemaking priorities also include a nonviolent ethic that compassion, forgive-
ness, and love lead to understanding, service, and justice (McDermott, 1994, p. 26).
Responsiveness also expresses both accountability and connectedness. Peacemaking
contends that individuals are responsive because they understand and appreciate the
implications of ties to the social and natural world. Again, responsiveness requires
equality because responsiveness requires mutual respect, not pity or condescension.
Inequality supports and sustains violence (p. 27). The peacemaking view is that oppression, domination, and superiority breed violence.

Thus, both peacemaking and feminist ethics have in common many underlying
concerns and priorities. Although this does not mean that they agree on all issues and
interpretations, McDermott (1994) stated that there are points of convergence:

> Both rely on natural (not criminal law) definitions of crime and injustice. Both per-
> spectives see the individual as tied to other individuals and the environment in such a
> way that caring and responsiveness flow from relationships with specific others. Both
> views contend that it is wrong to hurt anyone and it is right to sustain human relation-
> ships. In both views, moral actors treat others with respect, for a just society cannot
> recognize inferior classes. Both peacemaking criminologists and feminist ethicists rec-
> ognize the importance of emotion as a source of knowledge and a motivator for action.
> (p. 34)

In conclusion, McDermott (1994) noted that criminology as peacemaking presents a nonviolent alternative for a criminal justice system that contrasts with the
mainstream emphasis on force and violence. For many practitioners and theorists,
the nonviolent ideas of peacemaking are "wildly idealist, romantic, impractical, and
unworkable" (pp. 40-41). Feminists envision a system that recognizes women's victimization and suffering and that restores peace to the community. Feminist justice
involves a humanistic vision that rejects all forms of discrimination.

M. Kay Harris

M. Kay Harris[16] began her book chapter with a comparison of the conventional
systems improvement orientation with the crime prevention/social reform orientation to criminal justice (Harris, 1991). The former orientation takes for granted existing political, economic, and social institutional structures, and its proposals are for
more effective or more rigorous enforcement of the law. The latter orientation emphasizes the social and economic underpinnings of crime and the need to address
them through policies and programs focused on families, neighborhoods, schools,
and other institutions (pp. 83-84). By contrast, Harris (1991) explained that feminism offers a set of values, beliefs, and experiences (p. 87). Feminism is a way of looking at the world and has a broader vision than simply seeking the rights of women.
She presented the core values that transcend the differences among feminists as fol-

lows: "Among the key tenets of feminism are three simple beliefs—that all people have equal value as human beings, that harmony and felicity are more important than power and possession, and that the personal is the political" (p. 88). Harris suggested that felicity and harmony are viewed as the highest values by feminists. All people are viewed by feminists as part of a network that stresses the themes of caring, sharing, nurturing, and loving (p. 88). She stated that "empathy, compassion, and the loving, healthy, person-oriented values" must be applied in both the private and personal realms of home and family and in the public worlds of politics and power where public policy making and diplomacy are practiced.

Like other peacemakers, Harris (1991) contended that the war on crime is the domestic equivalent of the international war system (pp. 90-91). Budget hearings for increased appropriations illustrate the similarities in rationales and rhetoric used in seeking money for war efforts, whether labeled as in defense of criminals, Communists, or other enemies. They both contain ideologies of deterrence, retaliation, and hierarchical military structures. They also include a sense of urgency and willingness to sacrifice other important interests to attain greater weaponry, technology, and fighting forces. Harris concluded, "People concerned with international peace need to recognize that supporting the 'war on crime' is supporting the very establishment, ideology, structures, and morality against which they have been struggling" (p. 92).

Harris (1991) challenged the entire basis of our criminal punishment system and called for the abandonment of imprisonment, at least as we know it today (p. 94). She declared,

> Feminist values suggest that we should move toward conceiving restriction of liberty as having less to do with buildings, structures, and walls and more to do with human contacts and relations. Few, if any, creatures are dangerous to all other creatures at all times, especially to those with whom they are directly and closely connected on an ongoing basis. . . . A range of compassionate, constructive, and caring arrangements needs to be created. (p. 95)

Our energies, Harris concluded, must be focused on the full panoply of global peace and social justice issues.

Fay Honey Knopp

Fay Honey Knopp[17] identified herself as a Quaker feminist and prison abolitionist who has struggled for 50 years of her adult life to be a self-determined human (Knopp, 1991, p. 181). Her struggle has been against the oppressive institutions of patriarchy and the oppressive institutions of punishment. She stated emphatically that "prisons *do not work*" because they are based on the "*war model*" discussed by several other authors in this chapter. Knopp (1991) claimed that the reasons why the war model responses fail is because they neglect victims/survivors and because offenders' needs for restoration, resocialization, and reeducation rarely are considered in the sentencing process (p. 182). She stated that one task of prison abolitionists is consciousness raising or the perceived need of a new system of restorative justice with respect for all victims and victimizers. This would involve a new system rooted in the concept of a caring community (p. 183). Other tasks or strategies for prison abolitionists are decarceration, or a moratorium on prisons, and excarceration that involves moving away from the notion of imprisonment and providing appropriate and workable alternatives such as restitution, community service work, and dispute and mediation processes (p. 185). The attrition model involves the restraint of the few and addresses the concerns of feminists and abolitionists more than do the other strategies.

One approach to the caring community is the Safer Society Program founded by Knopp (1991). It is a place where "power and equality of all social primary goods—liberty, opportunity, income, wealth, and the bases of self-respect—are institutionally structured and distributed to all members of society and where the spirit of reconciliation prevails" (p. 184). The primary message is that the sources of antisocial behavior are rooted in the social, political, cultural, and economic structures of society and that solutions must be found there. According to Knopp (1991),

> The Safer Society Program prefers a social justice prevention model based on community responsibility for one another's safety and on respect for all persons involved in the sexual assault. Thus, we suggest the formation of three coordinated task forces or components for communities that wish to control and reduce sexual assaults: a perpetrator prevention/education proponent, a victim/survivor prevention component, and an offender restoration component. (p. 188)

Finally, Knopp (1991) contended that the Safer Society Program must keep a sharp eye on whether programs are retraining offenders into traditional role behavior between men and women or encouraging new nonpatriarchal roles (p. 192). She concluded by stating that the message must be clear. The male victimizer must take responsibility for his sexual crimes. But the community also must examine its responsibility to uncover the societal roots of sexual violence and find ways in which to reduce the potential for such violence to occur.

The Critical Tradition

Like the feminist tradition, the critical tradition sees social control as based on power and domination. However, feminists see the patriarchy and male domination as the causes of inequality and suppression, whereas critical theorists see social class, race, sex, and age as problematic (Fuller, 1998, p. 46). According to Fuller (1998),

> The critical tradition has special significance for the peace perspective because the war perspective is so entrenched in our society. . . . The critical tradition holds that many obvious truths are simply the successful implementation of dominant power structures into our ways of thinking and perceiving. (p. 47)

Harold Eugene Pepinsky (1945-)

As indicated in the biographical inset on Harold Pepinsky (Inset 10.1), he was born into an academic family. He has studied in Norway and also has studied Chinese

INSET 10.1

Harold Eugene Pepinsky (1945-)

Harold Pepinsky was born on January 18, 1945, the only child of academic parents who both had Ph.D.s in counseling psychology. All four of his grandparents also were academic/professional people, making Pepinsky a third-generation professor. His wife, Jill Bystydzienski, also is an academic professor. During the early 1960s, Pepinsky's parents took him to Trondheim, Norway, where he finished high school. On returning to the United States, he studied Chinese language and literature at the University of Michigan, where he received a B.A. with distinction in 1965. Pepinsky earned a J.D. cum laude from Harvard Law School in 1968 and was admitted to the Ohio bar that year. He was a Harvard voluntary defender at Harvard Law School for 2 years. It was during law school that he began to search for an answer to the question, "What is crime?" He credits teachers and colleagues, such as Lloyd Ohlin, Leslie Wilkins, and Paul Jesilow, as influential in challenging his thinking on this issue (Pepinsky, 1991a, pp. 1-7). He then left the legal profession and pursued a Ph.D. in sociology at the University of Pennsylvania, studying under Marvin Wolfgang. Before receiving his Ph.D. in 1972, Pepinsky was a visiting assistant professor at the University of Minnesota.

Pepinsky taught for 2 years at the State University of New York at Albany before moving to Indiana University in 1976. He continues to teach criminal justice at Indiana, although he currently is on leave as a visiting professor at Iowa State University. Pepinsky also taught East Asian languages and culture at Indiana from 1977 to 1996. In the spring of 1983, he was a visiting research associate at the Centre for Criminological and Socio-Legal Studies at the University of Sheffield. In the spring of 1986, he received a Fulbright and was a visiting scholar in the Department of Criminology and Criminal Law at the University of Oslo Faculty of Law. During this period, he was able to study "peaceful societies" and developed some of his conceptual theory for peacemaking while translating his ideas into Norwegian in preparation for invited lectures. Those who read Pepinsky's works will note the influence of Norwegian scholars and friends such as Nils Christie and Birgit Brock-Utne. Finally, in the spring of 1990, Pepinsky was a visiting professor in law at the University of Dar es Salaam.

In addition to the publications cited in this chapter, Pepinsky has published *The Geometry of Violence and Democracy* (Pepinsky, 1991a), *Myths That Cause Crime* (Pepinsky and Jesilow, 1984), and *Crime Control Strategies* (Pepinsky, 1980). Pepinsky and Jesilow received the Outstanding Book Award of the Academy of Criminal Justice Sciences in 1986. Also, Pepinsky has published a vast number of articles in professional journals and book chapters on topics such as police patrol and decision making (based on his dissertation), Chinese justice and law, abolishing prisons, and peacemaking. He has an outstanding record of invited lectures and of conference presentations that are both interdisciplinary and international. In addition to conference and colloquia papers presented throughout the United States, Pepinsky has made presentations in Japan, Poland, Norway, China, Denmark, the United Kingdom, and Portugal from 1971 to the present.

SOURCE: Personal and professional vita provided by Pepinsky.

law and languages. Although he has a law degree and was admitted to the Ohio bar in 1968, Pepinsky left the legal career to study sociology at the University of Pennsylvania under Marvin Wolfgang. Pepinsky is a professor of criminal justice at Indiana University and was a visiting professor of sociology at Iowa State University for the 1999-2000 academic year.

Pepinsky and Quinney (1991) had a major impact on criminology with their edited book, *Criminology as Peacemaking*. In the closing chapter of that book, Pepinsky (1991b) pointed out that there is a collective ignorance in this society regarding the connection between crime and punishment and war (p. 300). As has been stated by other peacemaking theorists, Pepinsky declared, "Crime is violence. So is punishment, and so is war" (p. 301). He further stated that it is necessary to strip away the mask of peace from U.S. criminal justice so that it can be seen for what it actually is. It is more important still to offer people safety and security in place of war. Pepinsky concluded, "The most important message in this work, to me at least, is that peacemaking exists, is well researched and understood, and is quite prevalent even in as violent a place as the United States" (p. 325). In response to criminologists of the right, who claim that crime is a personal failing of the poor, and criminologists of the left, who claim that it is a mark of extreme social disadvantage, Pepinsky (1988) argued that "power over others is the major cause of crime and violence" (p. 539). He further claimed that the distinction between crime and punishment is political—a matter of who has the power to define the situation (p. 540). Pepinsky (1993) argued, "The only morally justifiable collective action for securing peace in the wake of crime rests on evidence that your peace does not connote crime to me" (p. 391). Pepinsky (1988) also advised that criminologists ought to develop a theory of violence that presupposes that the only way in which to reduce the level of crime or punishment in any person or any group is to reduce violence generally (p. 542).

In addition to studying in Norway as a young man, Pepinsky (1988) received a Fulbright research grant in the spring of 1986 that enabled him to study and develop a theory of peacemaking as "unresponsiveness." He stated that while he was in Oslo, "I came to see crime and punishment as synonymous forms of domination" (p. 541).[18] The result, he explained, "is a theory of violence as 'unresponsiveness' and a counterpart theory of peacemaking as a matter of organizing 'responsiveness' " (p. 541). Pepinsky was stating that American law and government favor larger corporations, where the law limits the liability of investors. Thus, limiting the liability of corporate owners to what they invested in the corporation permitted corporations to become large enough and reckless enough to monopolize markets and to ignore the welfare of consumers (p. 545). Pepinsky explained the importance of this as follows:

> "Liability" translates into Norwegian as *ansvar*, usually translated back into English as "responsibility." While working in Norwegian, I found myself . . . contrasting what legal practice does most often and most secretly to young men of the underclass by "holding them responsible" for social disorder with the corresponding legal practice of "limiting responsibility" of the corporate elite. . . . American governments characteristically limit the responsibility of more powerful people for social disorder; when disorder threatens, they propose to restore order by holding weaker persons responsible. (p. 545)

Pepinsky defined responsiveness to mean that what one expects to achieve by one's actions (or, legally, one's intent) is modified continually to accommodate the experience and feelings of those affected by one's actions (p. 546). Pepinsky (1998) later observed,

> While violence and the fear and pain it engenders came from people pursuing their own independent agendas and objectives regardless of how others were affected, responsiveness was interaction in which actors' personal agendas shifted constantly to accommodate others' feelings and needs. (p. 142)

Pepinsky described this responsiveness as "participatory democracy."

The other part of Pepinsky's theory is that violence is unresponsiveness. Pepinsky (1988) asserted that violence results from depersonalization, as when people in bureaucratic positions do things to others without responding to their experience and their feelings (p. 549). It entails a willful disregard for one's effect on others. The passing on of violence or unresponsiveness through law suggests that violence grows by reproduction; that is, unresponsiveness begets unresponsiveness, and violence begets violence (p. 548). Thus, violence and responsiveness operate from the same principles at all levels, from the interpersonal to the international.

> Learning to make peace in place of violence entails not a change in human nature but [rather] a recognition that our nature has a compassionate side as well as recognizing our ability to rechannel energy and investment from our violent side to our peaceful side. (p. 558)

Pepinsky (1998) turned to the "peacemaking courts" of the Navajo Supreme Court to illustrate the basic structural elements and worldview of the Navajo that lead to peace. He described the court function as follows:

> The peacemaker, recognized by community members as "someone who thinks well, speaks well, thinks well, and shows by his or her behavior that the person's conduct is grounded in spirituality," . . . follows a mediation process which culminates in a circle, joined by individuals aggrieved and their clans and individuals who have aggrieved and their clans. The peacemaker begins a conversation about violence which simply moves around the circle, each individual free either to speak or to pass the floor to her or his left. Each time the conversation returns to the peacemaker, s/he summarizes what has been said . . . and in all probability will continue round the circle again and again. . . . To the Navajo, violence is a matter of imbalances of power in interaction. All human interaction is viewed as a conversation. . . . Peace is restored by balancing the conversation. . . . To the Navajo as to me, it is a contradiction in terms to make someone responsible; rather a peacemaking process liberates one's heart to be in tune with others and to continue taking turns in interaction. Participating in a balanced conversation stimulates one's assumption of responsibility. (p. 143)

Pepinsky further suggested that, from a peacemaking point of view, we become safe with others when our relations become empathic (p. 144). By contrast, from a war point of view, safety lies in individuals being perfectly obedient to the commands of those in power. Although we put a premium on obedience, Pepinsky argued, nothing is more fundamental to safe social relations than honesty.

Pepinsky (1998) also saw empathy as essential for peacemaking (pp. 144-150). The traditional war model requires obedience and remorse. For example, the U.S. court system requires a defendant to demonstrate both remorse and obedience by pleading guilty to each offense in open court before a judge. If the defendant refuses to plead guilty and loses in the court trial, then he or she often receives a more severe sentence for failing to show the proper remorse and obedience. Pepinsky also suggested that when parents demand obedience from their children, it teaches the children to lie so as to please the parents and avoid pain. It also teaches them to dissociate from their feelings and inclinations and to reject their own true selves. The children may become dissociated from others as well. Pepinsky suggested, "Violence begins in a state of dissociation or detachment from the feelings, needs, and wishes of the person to be victimized. The dissociation permits violence to begin and to repeat itself" (p. 146).

Pepinsky (1998) indicated that remorse among those perpetrators who commit domestic violence, such as battering and rape, is worthless. He stated, "In the run-of-the-mill cycle of repeated assaults, each assault is followed by a 'honeymoon period' in which the assailant expresses remorse, says he's sorry, [and] tries to do anything to make it up" (p. 147). Of course, this remorse, in most cases, means little because the cycle of violence usually begins anew. Those who work with victims advocate the rule of confidentiality and abiding by the complainant's wishes as crucial. Pepinsky advised that the one who has been victimized suffers a loss of control (p. 154). Resuming control of the victim's social relations is essential for the victimized person to have a sense of personal safety. It is important that the victim's voice be heard and that the one who has been traumatized by the victimization should be the primary guide to what comes next.

> Time and again, I have heard survivors of traumatic violence like incestuous rape say that the most healing, energizing response they received when they first told about the event was from those who sat, listened, said as little as "how terrible; I'm so sorry," and did nothing else to try to take over and fix it. (p. 155)

Pepinsky (1998) claimed that the energy in compassion or empathy lies in learning something new to do by listening to those who will be affected most by what one does next (p. 150). Empathy requires listening. Finally, Pepinsky noted that an attempt to make anyone else empathic or responsible is based on the fallacy of making empathy an act of obedience (p. 156). He argued that empathy and responsibility can be invited only by showing empathy and responsibility.

Susan L. Caulfield

In her book chapter, Susan L. Caulfield[19] argued that the harm-producing theories currently championed by criminologists should be avoided in the future (Caulfield, 1991, p. 229). Specifically, she examined subculture theories along with the ideological role they play and the subsequent perpetuation of violence they promote. Caulfield (1991) contended that the original criminological subculture theories were intended to help find solutions, but the current identification of subculture groups has taken a role far beyond what those early criminologists intended.

> The proliferation of subculture theories by criminologists has resulted in the bastardization of a method for the use of those in positions of power because of an overreliance on the techniques rather than on the implications of using the techniques.
>
> The identification of criminal or deviant subcultures in this society clearly has ideological underpinnings. Groups are labeled as subcultures because such labeling creates the illusion that we are all part of the same group. . . . While it is necessary that such groups be viewed as part of the overall culture, it is also necessary that they be seen as deviant or criminal members in order that the state may take action against them. . . . The behavior is viewed as threatening by those in positions of power. (pp. 230-231)

Caulfield suggested that the identification of national and international subculture groups as deviant allows the U.S. government to exercise control over the behavior of those people.

International subgroups suffering from U.S. policy include El Salvador, Chile, Guatemala, and Vietnam. Caulfield (1991) pointed out, "It is important to understand that the process of identifying subcultures is similar at both domestic and foreign levels and at [both] criminal and noncriminal levels" (p. 232). The identification of groups such as criminals, subversives, and terrorists diverts attention away from what the U.S. government actually is doing. In addition, labeling subgroups as violent creates an atmosphere for violent solutions. That is, the use of the subcultural method harms those who are targeted by the method and supports the state ideology that calls for more social control.

Caulfield (1991) concluded that criminologists need to seek nonviolent ways in which to resolve harm if we really want to reduce harm and promote peace. Finally, she claimed,

> Criminologists are in a position to use peaceful methods within a discipline that both addresses harm and creates harm. . . . In transcending the problem of methodologies and the misuse of methodologies, we should focus our attention on peace—on peace rather than on harm. And ultimately, we should use our knowledge not for harm but [rather] for peace. (p. 236)

Peter L. Sanzen

Peter L. Sanzen[20] began his book chapter by claiming that the criminal justice system was established to contribute to peace (Sanzen, 1991). Instead, it stresses crime control and due process with its emphasis on maintaining order, thereby isolating and segregating people and suppressing the ability of people to have freedom and to mature into the peaceful lives essential for personal and collective safety (p. 239). Sanzen further contended that a shift of focus in education from control and repression to peace is necessary for change in the criminal justice system.

Sanzen (1991) asserted, "From police to prison, the emphasis is on personal submission to the *machinery* of justice" (p. 240). This approach maintains an unjust and coercive system of repression of citizens in both criminal and noncriminal areas.

> The struggle to restore personal order and worth for the ones we call criminal is more difficult because we never refer to them as respected members of society again. They become inmates, prisoners, clients, probationers, parolees, [or] ex-cons, but never a member of a cooperative living arrangement. Their isolation makes transformation to peaceful living more difficult. (p. 241)

An alternative to this repressive situation can take place in education. As a teacher presents a discussion of how criminal justice works, the teacher can explore with students how to attain peace. At the core of teaching peace is an emphasis on the values of justice and dignity. Students also need an understanding of the context for creating a peace value system. "It requires educators to provide a philosophical, sociological, and anthropological examination of the elements that foster cooperative living" (Sanzen, 1991, p. 242). Sanzen (1991) further asserted that the classroom should be the focal point for active decentralized participation by students in the learning process. There also is a need to assist students in breaking down their own values that cause inner conflict for them—such as prejudice, competition, power, and superiority —and to help them realize that we all need each other to be whole.

Joseph A. Scimecca

Joseph A. Scimecca[21] differentiated among conflict resolution, conflict management, and conflict settlement and criticized the alternative dispute resolution (ADR), which he referred to as "the fastest growing phenomen[on] in the legal system today" (Scimecca, 1991, p. 264). He claimed that ADR often is confused with conflict resolution, which is criticized as a new form of social control.

Scimecca (1991) defined conflict resolution as an analytical process that tries to get at the root of the problem and to provide insights into the generic nature of the problem. The goal is to eliminate the sources of conflict and to prevent the return of conflict in the future.

> *Conflict resolution* entails the use of collaborative problem solving in a situation where a neutral third party helps the disputants engage in conciliation, facilitation, and/or mediation. The resolution contributes to the elimination of the sources of the conflict. (p. 265)

Conflict management, according to Scimecca, suggests that conflict is an organizational problem that can be managed by changing conditions within social institutions without any real structural changes in the conditions that produced the conflict (p. 265). It is the conflict experienced by workers that is managed, not the conflict produced by the workplace. Conflict settlement, he explained, fosters an outcome that does not necessarily meet the needs of all concerned but is accepted for the time being because of coercion by a stronger party.[22]

In contrast to conflict management and conflict settlement, Scimecca (1991) contended that conflict resolution is an interdisciplinary process of analysis and intervention that starts from the premise that traditional strategies of bargaining and negotiation settle conflicts but do not resolve them. Scimecca cited the human needs theory of Burton as a theoretical base for conflict resolution (p. 270). The human needs designated by Burton are the need for consistency in response, the need for stimulation, the need for security, the need for recognition, the need for distributive justice, the need to appear rational and develop rationality, the need for meaningful responses, the need for a sense of control, and the need to defend one's role. Burton contended, according to Scimecca, that "unless the human needs of individuals and groups are satisfied, no matter what form or degree of coercion is exercised, there will be no societal stability" (p. 271).

Scimecca (1991) concluded that although conflict resolution still is in its infancy, it offers tremendous potential for peacemaking and the establishment of equality (p. 276). He further expressed the hope that as more comprehensive theoretical frameworks are formulated and more research is accumulated regarding the causes of conflict and the processes of its resolution, the deep-rooted conflicts and social injustices may be altered by the peacemaking possibilities of conflict resolution.

Bo Lozoff and Michael Braswell

Inner Corrections, written by Bo Lozoff and Michael Braswell, is about correctional change from the inside out (Lozoff and Braswell, 1989, pp. xi-xii). It is concerned with one's heart and mind within a spiritual context rather than a specifically religious context. It also stresses empathy and that our positions in life are more alike than they are different. The authors claim that empathy, or "essentially opening ourselves up to our sameness rather than focusing on our differences, is the most powerful way of truly understanding the salient issues of criminal justice" (p. xii). The four cornerstones of this alternative philosophy and approach to corrections are the classic virtues of self-honesty, courage, kindness, and a sense of humor (p. 1). By developing these virtues as part of the rehabilitation process for prisoners, a person can become both happier and more peaceful. Lozoff and Braswell particularly stressed the importance of prisons as centers of kindness. They contended that all of us—prisoners, prison workers, and the general public—must begin, one by one, "to see how crazy it is to attempt rehabilitation or other types of treatment without valuing kindness above all other forms of training, education, or therapy" (p. 193). Lozoff and Braswell also asserted,

> In *Inner Corrections,* the heart of one's rehabilitation always remains one's own heart.
> ... The primary goal is to help build a happier peaceful person right there in the prison, a person whose newfound self-honesty and courage steer him or her to the most appropriate programs and training, a person whose kindness and sense of humor will help him or her to adjust to the biases and shortcomings of a society which does not feel comfortable with ex-offenders. (p. 2)

The purpose of these authors was to encourage all of us to look inward and find the place in ourselves that feels at peace with who we are as we move through life (p. 4). Lazoff and Braswell explained that if we are not at peace with ourselves, then we all are doing time in one type of prison or another (p. 9). They also suggested that "a mind that is open, free of fear, [and] free from unwanted thoughts will be clear and powerful enough to deal with anything" (p. 15).

Lozoff and Braswell (1989) further claimed that true kindness comes from strength and is full of life (pp. 18-19). It is a matter of heartfelt respect for each and every experience of our lives and respect for each person, animal, or anything else we find ourselves dealing with to simply respect the mysteries of life. Kindness, the authors noted, is the opposite of isolation and stems from the power and happiness of inner peace. Returning to the citizens' attitudes toward prisoners, they criticized the negative attitude toward offenders that leads to sense of "us against them" (p. 23). Many people tend to think that offenders should be sent to prison *for* punishment rather than *as* punishment. This mentality is not conducive to inner healing for the offenders or for the individuals who have this attitude. Much of Lazoff and Braswell's book is a presentation of cases and letters from prisoners to Lazoff that provide the reader with challenges of how to respond to these prisoners' situations.

In closing, Lozoff and Braswell (1989) suggested that one of the great ironies in the criminal justice system is that prisons are designed to be narcissistic environments. They noted, "After awhile, it becomes easy for a prisoner to assume the role of always being the needy one, always the one on the receiving end, the assumption being that he or she isn't expected or able to give anything" (pp. 193-194). The authors concluded,

> As the twentieth century dawned, we left the notion of "insane asylums" and gradually acknowledged the need to treat mental illness with compassion, creativity, and hope. Now the twenty-first century is dawning, and it's time for us to take the same step with criminal behavior—leaving behind prisons-as-warehouses and acknowledging the need for truly correctional facilities which surround inmates with kindness, fairness, and encouragement to change their lives for the better. (p. 194)

John R. Fuller

John R. Fuller also looked at peacemaking as an alternative perspective to the war perspective for addressing the problems of crime (Fuller, 1998, p. 41). The peacemaking that is beginning to emerge in both the criminal justice system and academic criminology emphasizes that social justice, conflict resolution, rehabilitation, and cooperation in democratic institutions are necessary to develop meaningful and peaceful communities. The peace perspective is an inclusive policy model to empower all individuals and provide them with an opportunity to control their destinies. Fuller (1998) claimed that the peacemaking perspective has several levels:

1. There is an international/global level which envisions an interconnectedness between all living things. Taking care of the environment and opposing war are concerns . . . at this broad level.

2. At the institutional/societal level, peacemaking looks at systems of government (democracies vs. dictatorships), economic systems (capitalism vs. communism), and religious systems (Christianity, Islam . . .). The peace perspective looks at how our . . . institutions develop and implement rules, policies, and norms which structure the interactions among citizens.

3. At the interpersonal level, the peace perspective looks at how individuals treat each other in resolving conflicts and dispensing power and privilege.

4. Finally, there is an intrapersonal level that considers how we treat ourselves. . . . The peacemaking perspective encourages us to be gentle with ourselves, to forgive our own transgressions and learn to make peace with our souls. (p. 41)

Although the peace perspective often is misunderstood and perceived as being soft on crime, Fuller (1998) argued that instead, it looks to transform both the individual criminal and the institutions that produce this type of person (p. 42). Much of the problem is that our institutions, including the criminal justice system, are patriarchal, are racist, and have a social class bias. Street crime, Fuller explained, is punished more severely than is white collar crime, partially because white collar criminals have the resources for private attorneys to minimize their punishments, whereas poor people do not have such resources. Also, those with power use their influence to maintain the status quo (pp. 57-58). According to the war perspective, people in America can "pull themselves up by their bootstraps" by working hard, deferring gratification, and sacrificing. The peacemaking perspective does not accept this war on crime assumption about opportunity in society. This perspective looks at the offender as a human who has committed unacceptable behavior and advocates dealing with the person in a "kinder and gentler way" (p. 58). The peacemaking theory seeks to help the offender to be able to compete when released from prison by providing job training, literacy classes, drug and alcohol treatment, and interpersonal relations instruction. Fuller further suggested that human worth and dignity should be emphasized in all interactions between and among people (p. 60).

Whereas Fuller contrasted the peacemaking perspective of the criminal justice system with the current war and punishment practices, his most unique contributions have been in the areas of gun control and capital punishment. Gun control is a very controversial topic, even among criminologists. The war model argues that citizens should be allowed to own guns for defensive purposes. The possibility that citizens may have guns presumably deters criminals from mugging or raping citizens or breaking into their homes (Fuller, 1998, p. 196). Opponents of gun control argue that when guns are outlawed, only outlaws will have guns. Or, they argue that guns do not kill people; people kill people (pp. 197-198). From a peacemaking position, guns are part of the crime problem, not part of the solution. Fuller (1998) asserted that for peacemakers, the solution to the problem of violence in the United States is to eliminate guns:

The long history and fascination with guns in the country has prevented many from considering the radical step of disarming the public. Second amendment arguments can be solved by simply amending the Constitution. After all, the founders of the coun-

TABLE 10.1 The Emergence of Peacemaking in Criminology

Mahatma Gandhi (1869-1948)	Jane Addams (1860-1935)	Martin Luther King, Jr. (1929-1968)
Nonviolent protests in South Africa Peaceful resistance in India Satyagraha	Founder of Hull House Child labor laws Mandatory education laws Juvenile court Advocate of world peace Nobel Peace Prize	American civil rights leader Nonviolent protests Baptist pastor Led marches and sit-ins "I Have a Dream" speech Nobel Peace Prize

Spiritual/Religious Tradition	Feminist Tradition	Critical Tradition
Richard Quinney (1934-) John J. Gibbs (1947-) J. Peter Cordella Gregg Barak	Birgit Brock-Utne (1938-) M. Joan McDermott M. Kay Harris Fay Honey Knopp Karen J. Warren and Duane L. Cody	Harold E. Pepinsky (1945-) Susan L. Caulfield Peter L. Sanzen Joseph A. Scimecca Bo Lozoff and Michael Braswell John R. Fuller

Crime is suffering
Spiritually grounded peace
Compassion, wisdom, and understanding
Satyagraha
Criminology of nonviolence
Peace is the way
Buddhism:
  Peaceful philosophy of life
Mutualist model of community
Hutterites and Mennonites
Hesed:
  Mercy and steadfast and enduring love
Ministry of hospitality
	Peace education
	Oppressive patriarchy
	Feminist ethics
	Care/response orientation:
	  Interdependence, nonhierarchical
	Connection to environment
	Human equality
	Human connectedness
	Feminist justice
	Felicity and harmony
	Global peace
	Social justice issues
	Prison abolition
	Safer Society Program
		Violence as unresponsiveness
		Peacemaking as responsiveness
		Participatory democracy
		Empathy requires listening
		Education for peace
		Justice and dignity
		Peace and harmony
		Conflict resolution
		Inner corrections:
		  Self-honesty, courage, and kindness
		Social justice and cooperation
		Democratic and peaceful communities
		Elimination of guns
		Rejects capital punishment

try realized that times would change and made provisions for amendments. The frontier is gone and the reasons for firearms have changed. Hunting for subsistence is no longer required for survival, and the major reason to have a firearm today is because everybody else has one. By taking guns from all citizens, then none of us would need one. (p. 197)

Although many citizens would agree with the peacemaking view that contends that guns do not provide the basis for settling arguments peacefully, the suggestion that we can simply amend the Constitution is controversial.

Fuller (1998) informed us that there are special circumstances when killing another human is condoned (p. 201). The soldier operating under the conventions of war not only is expected to kill the enemy but also may be rewarded for doing so. Self-defense is another type of killing that is allowed. Finally, the law allows the state to take the life of an individual who has been convicted of a capital offense such as murder or treason. Proponents of capital punishment justify the practice as a deterrent and as just desserts. Opponents often ask, "Why do we kill people to teach people that killing people is wrong?" (p. 202). Other arguments against the death penalty are that it is legal homicide, it is unjustified on scientific grounds because its deterrence effects have not been demonstrated by research, there are racial and class biases, and killing a criminal is an act of violence (pp. 211-212). Also, it is a barbaric act, and innocent people have been executed. Fuller concluded that "the peacemaking perspective rejects capital punishment as inconsistent with the objectives of resolving disputes through nonviolent means" (p. 221) and that it is inherently violent and sends the wrong message to society. It also is rejected on the grounds of social justice given that social status, race, and gender all are factors that make it more likely that certain groups of people will receive the death penalty, whereas others equally guilty will be spared. Fuller further argued against capital punishment because of the way in which it dehumanizes both the condemned person and those responsible for doing the killing for the rest of us. Finally, he suggested that capital punishment is a policy that has little relevance to making our society safer.

Critique of Peacemaking in Criminology

The response to the peacemaking perspective in criminology has been largely to ignore it, as was done by Lilly, Cullen, and Ball (1995) and by Vold and colleagues (1998) in their recent editions of texts on criminological theory. Akers (1997) acknowledged peacemaking and devoted three pages to summarizing and criticizing Pepinsky and Quinney's (1991) edited book. Akers (1997) viewed Quinney's definition of crime as a form of suffering as a "spiritual, transcendental, and visionary preaching of nonviolence and a plea to end suffering" (p. 182). Akers contended that this is tautological. He further criticized peacemaking criminology as follows:

> Peacemaking criminology does not offer a theory of crime or of the criminal justice system that can be evaluated empirically.... It may be possible to construct a testable, parsimonious, and valid theory from peacemaking criminology, but at this point it remains a philosophy rather than a theory. It is a utopian vision of society that calls for reforming and restructuring to get away from war, crime, and violence.... This is a highly laudable philosophy of criminal justice, but it does not offer an explanation of why the system operates as it does or why offenders commit crime. It can be evaluated on other grounds but not on empirical validity. (p. 183)

Akers (1997) asserted that there are logical inconsistencies in claiming feminist theory as a foundation for peacemaking in criminology. He challenged Harris's

(1991) use of research suggesting that women are oriented toward nurturing, caring, loving, and peace as not being a "significant part of the feminist tradition" (p. 184). He further asserted that feminists have long rejected the role of "acting like a woman" as a reflection of the patriarchal system of oppression of women. Akers provided no support for this claim. Many feminists would suggest that Akers has a narrow view of feminist theory, needs to read feminist works more broadly, and just does not understand feminist theory. Finally, Akers (1997) claimed that the policies advocated by peacemaking—nonpunitive treatment of offenders, mediation, restitution, offender reintegration, rehabilitation, and so forth—have long been mainstays of the policy recommendations of liberal criminologists and already are common practices in the criminal justice system (p. 185). Akers criticized peacemaking as utopian and lacking empirical evidence but provided no empirical evidence to support this claim.

Williams and McShane (1999) acknowledged peacemaking in criminology in their theory text by presenting a brief summary, and they referred to peacemaking as an "emerging form of criminological theory" (p. 281). This is a reasonably accurate assessment regarding the current state of the peacemaking perspective.

Other criminologists, such as Gibbs (1991) and Moyer (1993), have written more positive book reviews of Pepinsky and Quinney's (1991) *Criminology as Peacemaking*. Both reviews suggested that it requires an open mind to appreciate the perspective. Gibbs (1991) contended that unless one reads the chapters in *Criminology as Peacemaking* with an open mind, some of them will strike the reader as "little more than bromides offered by participants at the Rainbow Festive after a night of heavy dancing to the drums" (p. 263). According to Gibbs, the book is a thoughtful collection of writings by some very genuine and courageous authors, and it deserves a better reading than this. Moyer (1993) concurred with Gibbs and stated that many readers, especially "objective scientists," criminal justice practitioners, and nonreligious criminologists, might view this peacemaking perspective as naive or utopian and might not read beyond the first chapter or so. She argued, however, that "this would be a great loss because this volume provides a challenging proposal for alleviating the violence that currently dominates the American culture" (p. 165). Gibbs (1991) further stated,

> These unabashed expressions of spirituality to an audience of criminologists is a bold move, and one that will draw considerable fire. It should be noted, however, that the brand of religion or spirituality that Pepinsky and Quinney are advocating is not of the fundamentalist, dogmatic, devotional variety. Concepts like Buddhist compassion and loving kindness, Christian agape, and Hebrew hesed represent contemplative traditions, and they are practices or paths that lead to understanding and liberation. (p. 266)

Both reviewers indicated that the concepts and values contained in the Pepinsky and Quinney (1991) volume belong in the education of criminology and criminal justice students. Moyer (1993) recommended the reading of that volume for students, scholars, politicians, and practitioners of criminal justice (p. 168).

The Pepinsky and Quinney (1991) volume stimulated a number of criminologists, such as Gibbs and McDermott, to make important contributions to the peacemaking scholarship. Scholars from other disciplines, such as Brock-Utne, also have contributed to the peacemaking literature. (See Table 10.1 for a chart of the scholars who contributed to the conceptualization and development of peacemaking in criminology.) It is hoped that this emerging theoretical perspective will be more widely read and will lead to positive policy changes in approaches to education and to a more peaceful and compassionate response to individuals who are defined as criminals during the 21st century.

Notes

1. This is not intended to be an exhaustive list of postmodern theorists. The purpose is to illustrate the variety of approaches to this perspective.

2. These three traditions are examined in more detail in a later section of the chapter.

3. The first three wives of Karamchand Gandhi died, and he had two daughters from these marriages.

4. A few months later, Gandhi adopted the word *Satyagraha* in place of passive resistance.

5. By contrast, Gandhi's major influence was his mother. Both Gandhi and Addams had a strong passion for the poor, and both were active in efforts to help the poor and to establish peace.

6. Among the activities of residents of the Hull House was research that examined the distribution of local residents according to ethnicity and income. This study resulted in *Hull House Maps and Papers* (Addams, 1895). Deegan (1991) claimed that this book, drawing on the detailed maps of social life on the South Side of Chicago, established the major substantive interests and methodological technique of the Chicago School of sociology (p. 41). Deegan noted in an earlier publication (Deegan, 1988) that although this book and the maps therein had a monumental influence on Chicago School sociology, this scholarly classic has been erased from the annals of sociology (p. 55).

7. Actually, King had not completed his doctoral dissertation, *A Comparison of God in the Thinking of Paul Tillich and Henry Nelson Wieman* (Williams, 1970, p. 26), and he traveled back and forth between Montgomery and Boston to complete the dissertation (King, 1969, p. 97). Williams (1970) further noted that King had hoped to "satisfy his fondness for scholarship later by turning to the teaching field."

8. King and his wife had previously traveled to Africa and Europe with other black leaders (King, 1969, p. 154 ff.).

9. When King called his wife, she learned that he suddenly was being treated politely and was taken from his cell for exercise and allowed to take a shower. He also had been given a mattress and a pillow (King, 1969, p. 227).

10. Correta King and Kasturbai Gandhi are not usually mentioned in the peacemaking literature, although both played active roles in the movements that their husbands led. Coretta King used her musical talents to raise money to support the protests, and Kasturbai Gandhi died in prison.

11. For details regarding Quinney's biography and other publications, see the biographical inset on Quinney in Chapter 8 (Insert 8.2).

12. John J. Gibbs was born October 10, 1947, in Troy, New York. He has four degrees from the State University of New York at Albany. He earned a B.S. in business in 1969, an M.B.A. in 1975, and an M.A. and a Ph.D. in criminal justice in 1973 and 1978, respectively. He was on the faculty at Rutgers University from 1977 to 1988. During this time period, he also served as associate dean for research. In 1988, he moved to Indiana University of Pennsylvania, where he continues to serve as a professor of criminology. He also was director of the criminology doctoral program from 1994 to 1999. His research interests and publications have been in corrections, fear of crime, theory testing, and peacemaking.

13. For more information on Gibbs's application of Zen to education, read his book, *Dancing With Your Books* (Gibbs, 1990).

14. Birgit Brock-Utne, a social scientist, is a professor at the Institute for Educational Research at the University of Oslo in Norway. She has studied in the United States and received her master's in education at the University of Illinois. Her main academic interests are peace education and research, feminist studies, and educational innovation and action research. Although she has published several books and articles on these issues, they are predominantly in her native Norwegian (Brock-Utne, 1985).

15. M. Joan McDermott is a professor at the Center for the Study of Crime, Delinquency, and Corrections at Southern Illinois University.

16. Prior to joining the faculty in the Department of Criminal Justice at Temple University in 1981, M. Kay Harris served as director of the Washington, D.C., office of the National Council on Crime and Delinquency. Harris has held other positions including those with the Unitarian Universalist Service Committee and the American Bar Association. Within the U.S. Department of Justice, she has held positions with the Office of the Attorney General, the National Institute of Law Enforcement and Criminal Justice, and the National Bureau of Prisons. She frequently is active with citizens' groups, policy makers, and criminal justice practitioners (Pepinsky and Quinney, 1991, p. 330).

17. Fay Honey Knopp is founder and director of the Safer Society Program, a nonprofit research and education center on the prevention of sexual abuse. The center advocates nonrepressive alternatives for victims and offenders. Knopp, a Quaker feminist and prison abolitionist, has been engaged for 35 years in an alternative ministry to imprisoned persons (Pepinsky and Quinney, 1991, p. 331).

18. In explaining his theory of responsiveness, Pepinsky (1988) stated, "My understanding of a nonviolent construct of the world came from translating my previous thinking into Norwegian for a series of invited lectures" (p. 545).

19. Susan L. Caulfield teaches in the Department of Sociology at Western Michigan University. Her work centers on the role of political institutions in the creation and treatment of "criminal" behavior and on the implications of such relationships for crime control and the perpetuation of harm (Pepinsky and Quinney, 1991, p. 329).

20. Peter L. Sanzen teaches criminal justice at Hudson Valley Community College in Troy, New York. His interests include community policing and management and the teaching of justice from a peacemaking perspective.

21. Joseph A. Scimecca is a professor of sociology and conflict resolution at George Mason University. Among his publications are several books and numerous articles in criminology, peace, and conflict resolution journals.

22. Many feminists have objected to traditional mediation for domestic and sexual assaults because the victim/survivor may be coerced into accepting a settlement by a stronger

party. In many of these cases, the perpetrator abides by the settlement for a while, but eventually the abuse and conflict continue.

DISCUSSION QUESTIONS

1. Compare and contrast the mainstream criminological theorists (e.g., Merton, Cohen, Hirschi, Thrasher) and the postmodern and peacemaking theorists discussed in this chapter with regard to their approaches and attitudes toward the social science emphasis as it relates to theory, research, and policy.

2. Review the lives and works of Mahatma Gandhi, Jane Addams, and Martin Luther King, Jr. What were their specific contributions to current peacemaking in criminology? Which one made the greatest contribution to today's peacemaking perspective in criminology? Support your answer.

3. Richard Quinney is considered by many criminologists to be one of the leading theoretical criminologists. As explained in Chapter 8 and this chapter, Quinney has been influential in transforming criminological theory. Although his very early publications are more mainstream, during recent decades he has been a dominant force in the emergence of both conflict/Marxist theory and the peacemaking perspective. Trace and explain the specific contributions he has made to the emergence of these theories.

4. Based on the works of criminologists such as Quinney and Gibbs, analyze the role of spiritualism in the peacemaking perspective.

5. The Norwegian feminist Brock-Utne is not a criminologist, yet her contributions to peacemaking in criminology and education are important. Outline the ways in which her work has influenced criminological theory. Specify in what specific ways her ideas do and/or do not apply to criminology and peacemaking.

6. Feminist criminologists, such as McDermott and Harris, emphasize concepts such as caring, nurturing, and responsiveness. Discuss their essays regarding these and other concepts. Do other peacemaking criminologists also use these concepts? Explain the use of these concepts by McDermott and Harris, and identify and explain the use of these concepts by other criminologists.

7. Pepinsky, along with Quinney, has had a major impact on the emergence of peacemaking in criminology. As indicated in the biographical inset on Pepinsky (Inset 10.1), he has had a unique and diverse educational and professional experience. Because of this and his sensitivity to those without power, he provides new concepts and ideas for developing a nonviolent society. Identify these and explain the influence that these concepts and experiences may have in bringing

peacemaking changes to the criminal justice system and to criminological theory.

8. Scholars (e.g., Knopp, Lozoff and Braswell, Caulfield, Scimecca, Fuller) have emphasized policy changes in the educational and criminal justice systems that should facilitate a change from a coercive and violent war on crime policy to a compassionate nonviolent policy that would lead to individual inner peace, a peaceful society, and a resolution and reduction of crime and violence. Select several of these authors and explain the policy changes that they have proposed. How realistic are these new policies compared to the current law and order policies? Support your answer academically.

9. Is peacemaking in criminology just a utopian dream, as a few critics suggest, or is it a realistic long-term effort to bring peace into the lives of individuals and into society? Or, is it both? Support your answer with scholarly academic evidence.

References

Addams, Jane. (Ed.). (1895). *Hull House Maps and Papers*. New York: Crowell.

Addams, Jane. (1907). *Newer Ideals of Peace*. New York: Mason-Henry Press.

Addams, Jane. (1922). *Peace and Bread: In Time of War*. New York: Macmillan.

Addams, Jane. (1960). *Twenty Years at Hull House*. New York: Macmillan.

Addams, Jane. (1970). The Objective Value of a Social Settlement. In Jane Addams, Bernard Bosanquet, Franklin H. Giddings, J. O. S. Huntington, and Robert A. Woods (Eds.), *Philanthropy and Social Progress: Seven Essays* (pp. 27-56). Montclair, NJ: Patterson Smith.

Adler, Freda. (1975). *Sisters in Crime: The Rise of the New Female Criminal*. New York: McGraw-Hill.

Adler, Freda. (1997). The ASC and Women: One Generation Without, One Generation With. *The Criminologist, 22*, 1, 3-5.

Adler, Jeffery S. (1989a). A Historical Analysis of Vagrancy. *Criminology, 27*, 209-229.

Adler, Jeffrey S. (1989b). Rejoinder to Chambliss. *Criminology, 27*, 239-250.

Agnew, Robert. (1985). A Revised Strain Theory of Delinquency. *Social Forces, 64*, 151-167.

Agnew, Robert. (1992). Foundation for a General Strain Theory of Crime and Delinquency. *Criminology, 30*, 47-87.

Agnew, Robert and Helene Raskin White. (1992). An Empirical Test of General Strain Theory. *Criminology, 30*, 475-499.

Akers, Ronald. (1968). Problems in the Sociology of Deviance: Social Definitions and Behavior. *Social Forces, 46*, 455-465.

Akers, Ronald L. (1979). Theory and Ideology in Marxist Criminology. *Criminology, 16*, 527-544.

Akers, Ronald L. (1994). *Criminological Theories: Introduction and Evaluation*. Los Angeles: Roxbury Publishing.

Akers, Ronald L. (1997). *Criminological Theories: Introduction and Evaluation* (2nd ed.). Los Angeles: Roxbury Publishing.

Akers, Ronald. (2000). *Criminological Theories: Introduction, Evaluation, and Application* (3rd ed.). Los Angeles: Roxbury Publishing.

Anderson, Nels. (1923). *The Hobo*. Chicago: University of Chicago Press.

Anderson Publishing. (1997, Spring). *Anderson's Newsletter for Criminal Justice Educators*. Cincinnati, OH: Anderson Publishing.

Androit, J. L. (Ed.). (1983). *Population Abstract of the United States.* McLean, VA: Androit Associates.

Arneklev, B. J., H. G. Grasmick, C. R. Tittle, and R. J. Bursik, Jr. (1993). Low Self-Control and Imprudent Behavior. *Journal of Quantitative Criminology, 9,* 225-247.

Babbie, Earl. (1989). *Methods of Sociological Research.* Belmont, CA: Wadsworth.

Ball, Richard A. (1983). Development of Basic Norm Violation. *Criminology, 21,* 75-94.

Barak, Gregg. (1991). Homelessness and the Case for Community-Based Initiatives. In Harold E. Pepinsky and Richard Quinney (Eds.), *Criminology as Peacemaking* (pp. 47-68). Bloomington: Indiana University Press.

Barlow, H. D. (1991). Explaining Crimes and Analogous Acts, or the Unrestrained Will Grab at Whatever Pleasure They Can. *Journal of Criminal Law and Criminology, 82,* 229-242.

Bartollas, Clemens. (1985). *Juvenile Delinquency.* New York: John Wiley.

Beccaria, Cesare. (1963). *On Crimes and Punishments* (introduction by Henry Paolucci, Trans.). New York: Macmillan.

Becker, Howard S. (1961). *Boys in White: Student Culture in Medical School.* Chicago: University of Chicago Press.

Becker, Howard S. (1963). *Outsiders: Studies in the Sociology of Deviance.* New York: Macmillan.

Becker, Howard S. (1973). *Outsiders: Studies in the Sociology of Deviance* (rev. ed.). New York: Free Press.

Beirne, Piers. (1979). Empiricism and the Critique of Marxism on Law and Crime. *Social Problems, 26,* 373-385.

Bentham, Jeremy. (1948). *An Introduction to the Principles of Morals and Legislation* (with an introduction by Wilfrid Harrison, Ed.). New York: Macmillan.

Bernard, Thomas J. (1990). Twenty Years of Testing Theories: What Have We Learned and Why? *Journal of Research in Crime and Delinquency, 27,* 324-347.

Binder, Arnold and Gilbert Geis. (1984). Ad Populum Argumentation in Criminology: Juvenile Diversion as Rhetoric. *Crime and Delinquency, 30,* 309-333.

Block, Carolyn Rebecca. (1998). [Review of *When Women Kill,* by Coramae Richey Mann]. *Justice Quarterly, 15,* 361-365.

Bohm, Robert M. (1982). Radical Criminology: An Explication. *Criminology, 19,* 565-589.

Bonger, Willem. (1932). *An Introduction to Criminology.* London: Methuen.

Bonger, Willem. (1969a). *Criminality and Economic Conditions* (with an introduction by Austin Turk). Bloomington: Indiana University Press.

Bonger, Willem. (1969b). *Race and Crime.* Montclair, NJ: Patterson Smith.

Boston, T. D. (1991, May). W. E. B. Du Bois and the Historical School of Economics. *American Economics Association Papers and Proceedings,* pp. 303-307.

Brock-Utne, Birgit. (1985). *Educating for Peace: A Feminist Perspective.* New York: Pergamon.

Brock-Utne, Birgit. (1989). *Feminist Perspectives on Peace and Peace Education.* New York: Pergamon.

Brown, S. E., F. Esbensen, and G. Geis. (1991). *Criminology.* Cincinnati, OH: Anderson.

Bulmer, Martin. (1984). *The Chicago School of Sociology.* Chicago: University of Chicago Press.

Bureau of the Census. (1962). *County and City Data Book.* Washington, DC: Government Printing Office.

Burgess, Ernest W. (1925). The Growth of the City: An Introduction to a Research Project. In Robert E. Park, Ernest W. Burgess, and Roderick D. McKenzie (Eds.), *The City* (pp. 47-62). Chicago: University of Chicago Press.

Burgess, Robert L. and Ronald L. Akers. (1966). A Differential Association-Reinforcement Theory of Criminal Behavior. *Social Problems, 14,* 128-147.

Caulfield, Susan L. (1991). The Perpetuation of Violence Through Criminological Theory: The Ideological Role of Subculture Theory. In Harold E. Pepinsky and Richard Quinney (Eds.), *Criminology as Peacemaking* (pp. 228-244). Bloomington: Indiana University Press.

Cavan, Ruth Shonle. (1928). *Suicide.* Chicago: University of Chicago Press.

Cavan, Ruth Shonle. (1934). *The Adolescent in the Family.* New York: Appleton-Century-Crofts.

Cavan, Ruth Shonle. (1948). *Criminology.* New York: Thomas Y. Crowell.

Cavan, Ruth Shonle. (1961). Concepts of Tolerance and Contraculture as Applied to Delinquency. *Sociological Quarterly, 2,* 243-260.

Cavan, Ruth Shonle. (1964). Underworld, Conventional, and Ideological Crime. *Journal of Criminal Law, Criminology, and Police Science, 55,* 235-240.

Cavan, Ruth Shonle. (1965). Emphasis for the Future: Social Absorption. In Hans W. Mattick (Ed.), *The Future of Imprisonment in a Free Society* (pp. 47-66). Chicago: St. Leonard's House.

Cavan, Ruth Shonle. (1972). *Chicago and I.* Unpublished manuscript, Northern Illinois University.

Cavan, Ruth Shonle. (1986, September). *The Early Chicago School.* Speech delivered at Indiana University of Pennsylvania.

Cavan, Ruth Shonle and Jordan T. Cavan. (1968). *Delinquency and Crime: Cross-Cultural Perspective.* Philadelphia: J. B. Lippincott.

Cavan, Ruth Shonle and Eugene Zemans. (1958). Marital Relationships of Prisoners in Twenty-Eight Countries. *Journal of Criminal Law, Criminology, and Police Science, 49,* 133-139.

Chambliss, William J. (1964). A Sociological Analysis of the Law of Vagrancy. *Social Problems, 12,* 46-67.

Chambliss, William J. (Ed.). (1969). *Crime and the Legal Process.* New York: McGraw-Hill.

Chambliss, William J. (1971). Vice, Corruption, Bureaucracy, and Power. *Wisconsin Law Review,* pp. 1150-1173.

Chambliss, William J. (1973). The Saints and the Roughnecks. *Society, 11,* 24-31.

Chambliss, William J. (Ed.). (1975). *Criminal Law in Action.* New York: John Wiley.

Chambliss, William J. (Ed.). (1984). *Criminal Law in Action* (2nd ed.). New York: John Wiley.

Chambliss, William J. (1987). I Wish I Didn't Know Now What I Didn't Know Then. *The Criminologist, 12,* 1, 5-7, 9.

Chambliss, William J. (1989a). On Trashing Marxist Criminology. *Criminology, 27,* 231-238.

Chambliss, William J. (1989b). State-Organized Crime. *Criminology, 27,* 183-208.

Chambliss, William J. and Robert B. Seidman. (1971). *Law, Order, and Power.* Reading, MA: Addison-Wesley.

Cherokee Nation v. Georgia. (1830). 30 U.S.1 1.

Chronology of Events. (1999a). *1869-1911* [online]. Available: www.mkgandhi-sarvodaya.org/under1.htm

Chronology of Events. (1999b). *1912-1932* [online]. Available: www.mkgandhi-sarvodaya. org/under2.htm

Chronology of Events. (1999c). *1933-1948* [online]. Available: www.mkgandhi-sarvodaya. org/under3.htm

Clemmer, Donald. (1940). *The Prison Community.* New York: Holt, Rinehart & Winston.

Clinard, Marshall B., Richard Quinney, and John Wildeman. (1994). *Criminal Behavior Systems: A Typology.* Cincinnati, OH: Anderson.

Cloward, Richard A. and Lloyd E. Ohlin. (1960). *Delinquency and Opportunity.* New York: Free Press.

Cohen, Albert K. (1955). *Delinquent Boys.* New York: Free Press.

Cohen, Albert K. (1966). *Deviance and Control.* Englewood Cliffs, NJ: Prentice Hall.

Collins, Patricia Hill. (1990). *Black Feminist Thought: Knowledge, Consciousness, and the Politics of Empowerment.* New York: HarperCollins.

Colvin, Mark and John Pauly. (1983). A Critique of Criminology: Toward an Integrated Structural-Marxist Theory of Delinquency Production. *American Journal of Sociology, 89,* 513-551.

Cooley, Charles H. (1902). *Human Nature and Social Order.* New York: Scribner.

Cooley, Charles H. (1909). *Social Organization: A Study of the Larger Mind.* New York: Scribner.

Cooley, Charles H. (1983). *Social Organization.* New Brunswick, NJ: Transaction Books.

Cordella, J. Peter. (1991). Reconciliation and the Mutualist Model of Community. In Harold E. Pepinsky and Richard Quinney (Eds.), *Criminology as Peacemaking* (pp. 30- 46). Bloomington: Indiana University Press.

Coser, Lewis A. (1977). *Masters of Sociological Thought.* New York: Harcourt Brace Jovanovich.

Courtright, Kevin. (1995, March). *An Unrecognized Scholar: An Examination of the Influence of Charles Richmond Henderson Upon the Early Department of Sociology at the University of Chicago.* Paper presented at the meeting of the Academy of Criminal Justice Sciences, Boston.

Cressey, Donald R. (1953). *Other People's Money.* Glencoe, IL: Free Press.

Cullen, Francis T. (1984). *Rethinking Crime and Deviance Theory.* Totowa, NJ: Rowman & Allanheld.

Curran, Daniel J. and Claire M. Renzetti. (1994). *Theories of Crime.* Boston: Allyn & Bacon.

Daly, Kathleen and Meda Chesney-Lind. (1988). Feminism and Criminology. *Justice Quarterly, 5,* 497-538.

Darwin, Charles. (1859). *The Origin of the Species.* New York: D. Appleton.

Darwin, Charles. (1871). *The Descent of Man.* New York: Merrill and Baker.

Davis, Angela. (1975). *With My Mind on Freedom: An Autobiography.* New York: Bantam Books.

Davis, Angela Y. (1983). *Women, Race, and Class.* New York: Vintage.

Davis, Angela Y. (1985). *Violence Against Women and the Ongoing Challenge to Racism.* Latham, NY: Women of Color Press.

Deegan, Mary Jo. (1988). *Jane Addams and the Men of the Chicago School, 1892-1918.* New Brunswick, NJ: Transaction Books.

Deegan, Mary Jo. (1991). *Women in Sociology: A Bio-Bibliographical Sourcebook.* Westport, CT: Greenwood.

De Fleur, Melvin L. and Richard Quinney. (1966). A Reformulation of Sutherland's Differential Association Theory and a Strategy for Empirical Verification. *Journal of Research in Crime and Delinquency, 3,* 1-22.

Delaney, W. P. (1977). The Uses of the Total Institution: A Buddhist Monastic Example. In R. Gordon and B. Williams (Eds.), *Exploring Total Institutions.* Champaign, IL: Stipes.

Dinitz, Simon, Walter C. Reckless, and B. Kay. (1958). A Self-Gradient Among Potential Delinquents. *Journal of Criminal Law, Criminology, and Police Science, 49,* 230-233.

Dinitz, Simon, Frank R. Scarpitti, and Walter C. Reckless. (1962). Delinquency Vulnerability: A Cross-Group and Longitudinal Analysis. *American Sociological Review, 27,* 515-517.

Dodson, D. W. (1962). Obituary: Clifford R. Shaw. *American Sociological Review, 27,* 580-581.

Dubin, Robert. (1959). Deviant Behavior and Social Structure: Continuities in Social Theory. *American Sociological Review, 24,* 147-164.

Du Bois, W. E. B. (1899a). The Negro and Crime. *The Independent, 51,* 1355-1357.

Du Bois, W. E. B. (1899b). *The Philadelphia Negro: A Social Study.* New York: Shocken Books.

Du Bois, W. E. B. (1901). The Spawn of Slavery: The Convict Lease System in the South. *Missionary Review of the World, 14,* 737-745.

Du Bois, W. E. B. (Ed.). (1904). *Some Notes on Negro Crime, Particularly in Georgia.* Atlanta, GA: Atlanta University Press.

Du Bois, W. E. B. (1986). *The Suppression of the Slave Trade to the United States of America, 1638-1870.* New York: Library of America.

Du Bois, W. E. B. and Augustus Granville Dill. (1913). *Moral and Manners Among Negro Americans: Report of a Social Study Made by Atlanta University Under the Patronage of the Trustees of the John F. Slater Fund, With the Proceedings of the 18th Annual Conference for the Study of the Negro Problems.* Atlanta, GA: Atlanta University Press.

Durkheim, Émile. (1897). *Suicide: A Study of Sociology.* New York: Free Press.

Durkheim, Émile. (1933). *The Division of Labor in Society.* New York: Free Press.

Durkheim, Émile. (1938). *The Rules of Sociological Method.* New York: Free Press.

Durkheim, Émile. (1951). *Suicide.* New York: Free Press.

Duster, Alfreda M. (Ed.). (1970). *Crusade for Justice: The Autobiography of Ida B. Wells.* Chicago: University of Chicago Press.

Edwards, G. Franklin. (1974). E. Franklin Frazier. In Morris Janowitz and James Blackwell (Eds.), *Black Sociologists: Historical and Contemporary Perspectives* (pp. 85-117). Chicago: University of Chicago Press.

Eigenberg, Helen and Agnes Baro. (1992). Women and the Publication Process: A Content Analysis of Criminal Justice Journals. *Journal of Criminal Justice Education, 3,* 293-314.

Elias, Robert. (1991). Crime Control as Human Rights Enforcement. In Harold E. Pepinsky and Richard Quinney (Eds.), *Criminology as Peacemaking* (pp. 251-262). Bloomington: Indiana University Press.

Feinman, Clarice. (1980). *Women in the Criminal Justice System.* New York: Praeger.

Ferdinand, Theodore N. (1988). Ruth Shonle Cavan: An Intellectual Portrait. *Sociological Inquiry, 58,* 337-343.

Fitzpatrick, Ellen Frances. (1990). *Endless Crusade: Women Social Scientists and the Progressive Reform.* New York: Oxford University Press.

Frazier, E. Franklin. (1932). *The Negro Family in Chicago.* Chicago: University of Chicago Press.

Frazier, E. Franklin. (1939). *The Negro Family in the United States.* Chicago: University of Chicago Press.

Frazier, E. Franklin. (1949). *The Negro in the United States.* New York: Macmillan.

Freedman, Estelle. (1981). *Their Sisters' Keepers: Women's Prison Reform in America, 1830-1930.* Ann Arbor: University of Michigan Press.

Freud, Sigmund. (1962). *The Ego and the Id* (James Strachey, Ed.). New York: Norton.

Fuller, John R. (1998). *Criminal Justice: A Peacemaking Perspective.* Boston: Allyn & Bacon.

Gabbidon, Shaun L. (1996). An Argument for Including W. E. B. Du Bois in the Criminology/Criminal Justice Literature. *Journal of Criminal Justice Education, 7,* 99-112.

Galliher, John F. (1991). The Willie Horton Fact, Faith, and Commonsense Theory of Crime. In Harold E. Pepinsky and Richard Quinney (Eds.), *Criminology as Peacemaking* (pp. 245-250). Bloomington: Indiana University Press.

Gaylord, Mark and John Galliher. (1988). *The Criminology of Edwin Sutherland.* New Brunswick, NJ: Transaction Books.

Geis, Gilbert. (1972). Jeremy Bentham (1748-1832). In Hermann Mannheim (Ed.), *Pioneers in Criminology* (pp. 51-68). Montclair, NJ: Patterson Smith.

Giallombardo, Rose. (1966). *Society of Women: A Study of a Women's Prison.* New York: John Wiley.

Gibbs, Jack P. (1966). Conceptions of Deviant Behavior: The Old and the New. *Pacific Sociological Review, 14,* 20-37.

Gibbs, John J. (1990). *Dancing With Your Books: The Zen Way of Studying.* New York: Plume Books.

Gibbs, John J. (1991). [Review of *Criminology as Peacemaking,* by Harold Pepinsky and Richard Quinney]. *Criminal Justice Policy Review, 5,* 263-268.

Gibbs, John J. (1995). Peace From Moment to Moment. *Peace Review, 7,* 449-455.

Gibbs, John J. (1996). Making Peace With Books. *Peace Review, 8,* 577-580.

Gibbs, John J. (1999). [Review of *For the Time Being,* by Richard Quinney]. *Criminal Justice Policy Review, 9,* 497-500.

Gibbs, John and Dennis Giever. (1995). Self-Control and Its Manifestations Among University Students: An Empirical Test of Gottfredson and Hirschi's General Theory. *Justice Quarterly, 12,* 231-255.

Giddings, Paula. (1984). *When and Where I Enter: The Impact of Black Women on Race and Sex in America.* New York: Bantam Books.

Gilsinan, James F. (1991). Public Policy and Criminology: An Historical and Philosophical Reassessment. *Justice Quarterly, 8,* 202-216.

Glueck, Sheldon and Eleanor Glueck. (1950). *Unraveling Juvenile Delinquency.* New York: Commonwealth Fund.

Goddard, H. H. (1914). *Feeble-mindedness.* New York: Macmillan.

Goffman, Erving. (1959). *The Presentation of Self in Everyday Life.* Garden City, NY: Doubleday.

Goffman, Erving. (1961). *Asylums: Essays on the Social Situation of Mental Patients and Other Inmates.* Garden City, NY: Anchor.

Goffman, Erving. (1963). *Stigma: Notes on the Management of Spoiled Identity.* Englewood Cliffs, NJ: Prentice Hall.

Goffman, Erving. (1971). *Relations in Public: Microstudies of the Public Order.* New York: Basic Books.

Goffman, Erving. (1983). The Interaction Order. *American Sociological Review, 48,* 1-17.

Goring, Charles. (1913). *The English Conflict: A Statistical Study.* London: His Majesty's Stationary Office.

Gottfredson, Michael R. and Travis Hirschi. (1990). *A General Theory of Crime.* Stanford, CA: Stanford University Press.

Green, Donald E. (1994). [Review of *Unequal Justice: A Question of Color,* by Coramae Richey Mann]. *Contemporary Sociology, 23,* 421.

Hagan, John, John Simpson, and A. R. Gillis. (1987). Class in the Household: A Power-Control Theory of Gender and Delinquency. *American Journal of Sociology, 92,* 788-816.

Hamlin, J. E. (1988). The Misplaced Role of Rational Choice in Neutralization Theory. *Criminology, 26,* 425-438.

Hanh, Thich Nhat. (1991). *Peace Is Every Step: The Path of Mindfulness in Everyday Life.* Berkeley, CA: Parallax.

Harris, Anthony R. (1977). Sex and Theories of Deviance: Toward a Functional Theory of Deviant Type-Scripts. *American Sociological Review, 42,* 3-16.

Harris, M. Kay. (1991). Moving Into the New Millennium: Toward a Feminist Vision of Justice. In Harold E. Pepinsky and Richard Quinney (Eds.), *Criminology as Peacemaking* (pp. 83-97). Bloomington: Indiana University Press.

Hayner, Norman. (1936). *The Sociology of Hotel Life.* Chapel Hill: University of North Carolina Press.

Heffernan, Esther. (1972). *Making It in Prison: The Square, the Cool, and the Life.* New York: John Wiley.

Heidensohn, Frances. (1968). The Deviance of Women: A Critique and an Inquiry. *British Journal of Sociology, 19,* 160-175.

Henderson, Charles R. (1914). *The Cause and Cure of Crime.* Chicago: McClurg.

Herrnstein, Richard J. and Charles Murray. (1994). *The Bell Curve: Intelligence and Class Structure in American Life.* New York: Free Press.

Hirschi, Travis. (1969). *Causes of Delinquency.* Berkeley: University of California Press.

Homans, George C. (1962). *Sentiments and Activities: Essays in Social Science.* New York: Free Press.

Homans, George Caspar. (1964). Contemporary Theory in Sociology. In Robert E. Faris (Ed.), *Handbook of Modern Sociology* (pp. 951-977). Chicago: Rand McNally.

Homans, George C. (1974). *Social Behavior: Its Elementary Forms.* New York: Harcourt Brace Jovanovich.

Hooten, Ernest A. (1939). *The American Criminal.* Cambridge, MA: Harvard University Press.

Huggins, N. (1986). *Du Bois Writings.* New York: Library of America.

Hughes, Everette C. (1945). Dilemmas and Contradictions of Status. *American Journal of Sociology, 50,* 353-359.

Jagger, Allison M. and Paula S. Rothenberg. (1984). *Feminist Frameworks (2nd Ed.).* New York: McGraw-Hill.

Jaques Cattell Press. (1978). *American Men and Women of Science.* New York: R. R. Bowker.

Jeffrey, C. Ray. (1965). Criminal Behavior and Learning Theory. *Journal of Criminal Law, Criminology, and Police Science, 56,* 294-300.

Keane, C., P. S. Maxim, and J. J. Tevan. (1993). Drinking and Driving, Self-Control, and Gender: Testing a General Theory of Crime. *Journal of Research in Crime and Delinquency, 30,* 30-46.

Keller, R. I. (1976). *A Sociological Analysis of the Conflict and Critical Criminologies*. Ph.D. dissertation, University of Montana.

Kelley, Florence and Alzina P. Stevens. (1895). Wage-Earning Children. In Residents of Hull House (Eds.), *Hull House Maps and Papers* (pp. 49-88). New York: Crowell.

Kellor, Frances A. (1900a). Criminal Sociology: The American vs. the Latin School. *The Arena, 24*, 301-307.

Kellor, Frances A. (1900b). Criminal Sociology: II. Criminality Among Women. *The Arena, 24*, 516-524.

Kellor, Frances A. (1900c). My Experiments With the Kymograph. *Harper's Bazaar, 33*, 1755-1760.

Kellor, Frances A. (1900d). Psychological and Environmental Study of Women Criminals: I. *American Journal of Sociology, 5*, 527-543.

Kellor, Frances A. (1901a). The Criminal Negro: I. A Sociological Study. *The Arena, 25*, 59-68.

Kellor, Frances A. (1901b). The Criminal Negro: II. Southern Conditions That Influence Negro Criminality. *The Arena, 25*, 190-197.

Kellor, Frances A. (1901c). The Criminal Negro: III. Some of His Characteristics. *The Arena, 25*, 308-316.

Kellor, Frances A. (1901d). The Criminal Negro: IV. Advantages and Abuse of Southern Penal Systems. *The Arena, 25*, 419-428.

Kellor, Frances A. (1901e). The Criminal Negro: V. Physical Measurements of Females. *The Arena, 25*, 510-520.

Kellor, Frances A. (1901f). The Criminal Negro: VII. Childhood Influences. *The Arena, 25*, 304-310.

Kellor, Frances A. (1901g). The Criminal Negro: VIII. Environmental Influences. *The Arena, 25*, 521-527.

King, Coretta Scott. (1969). *My Life With Martin Luther King, Jr.* New York: Holt, Rinehart & Winston.

King, Martin Luther, Jr. (1963a, April 16). [Letter From Birmingham City Jail addressed to "My Dear Fellow Clergymen"]. New Orleans: Lousiana State University Libraries. Available: www.lib.lsu.edu/lib/chem/display/srs214.html

King, Martin Luther, Jr. (1963b, August 28). ["I Have a Dream" speech delivered in Washington, D.C.]. Available: web66/coled.umn.edu/new/mlk/mlk.html

Klockars, Carl B. (1979). The Contemporary Crises of Marxist Criminology. *Criminology, 16*, 477-515.

Knopp, Fay Honey. (1991). Community Solutions to Sexual Violence: Feminist/Abolitionist Perspectives. In Harold E. Pepinsky and Richard Quinney (Eds.), *Criminology as Peacemaking* (pp. 181-193). Bloomington: Indiana University Press.

Kuhn, Terry. (1987). *Dr. Ruth Shonle Cavan: A Sketch of Her Life in Research and Writing*. Unpublished manuscript, Northern Illinois University.

Kuhn, Thomas S. (1970). *The Structure of Scientific Revolutions* (2nd ed.). Chicago: University of Chicago Press.

Kuper, Adam and Jessica Kuper. (Eds.). (1985). *The Social Science Encyclopedia*. London: Routledge and Kegan Paul.

Lemert, Edwin M. (1951). *Social Pathology: A Systematic Approach to the Theory of Sociopathic Behavior*. New York: McGraw-Hill.

Lemert, Edwin M. (1967). *Human Deviance, Social Problems, and Social Control.* Englewood Cliffs, NJ: Prentice Hall.

Lemert, Edwin M. (1972). *Human Deviance, Social Problems, and Social Control* (2nd ed.). Englewood Cliffs, NJ: Prentice Hall.

Leonard, Eileen B. (1982). *Women, Crime, and Society: A Critique of Criminology Theory.* New York: Longman.

Lewis, D. L. (1993). *W. E. B. Du Bois: Biography of a Race.* New York: Henry Holt.

Liazos, Alexander. (1972). The Poverty of the Sociology of Deviance: Nuts, Sluts, and Perverts. *Social Problems, 20,* 103-120.

Lilly, J. Robert, Francis T. Cullen, and Richard A. Ball. (1989). *Criminological Theory: Context and Consequences.* Newbury Park, CA: Sage.

Lilly, J. Robert, Francis T. Cullen, and Richard A. Ball. (1995). *Criminological Theory: Context and Consequences* (2nd ed.). Thousand Oaks, CA: Sage.

Lindesmith, Alfred R. (1988). Foreword. In Gaylord, Mark S. and John F. Galliher, *The Criminology of Edwin Sutherland* (pp. ix-xiv). New Brunswick, NJ: Transaction Books.

Lindesmith, Alfred R. and John Gagnon. (1964). Anomie and Drug Addiction. In Marshall B. Clinard (Ed.), *Anomie and Deviant Behavior: A Discussion and Critique* (pp. 158-188). New York: Free Press.

Lippens, Ronnie. (1998). Alternatives to What Kind of Suffering? Towards a Bordercrossing Criminology. *Theoretical Criminology, 2,* 311-343.

Lombroso, Cesare. (1863). *The Criminal Man* (5th ed.). Turin, Italy: Fratelli Bocca.

Lombroso, Cesare and William Ferrero. (1895). *The Female Offender.* London: Fisher Unwin.

Lombroso, Cesare and William Ferrero. (1958). *The Female Offender.* New York: Philosophical Library.

Lombroso, Cesare. (1968). *Crime: Its Causes and Remedies.* Montclair, NJ: Patterson Smith.

Lombroso-Ferrero, Gina. (1972). *Criminal Man According to the Classification of Cesare Lombroso.* Montclair, NJ: Patterson Smith.

Lozoff, Bo and Michael Braswell. (1989). *Inner Corrections: Finding Peace and Peace Making.* Cincinnati, OH: Anderson.

Lunden, Walter A. (1958). Pioneers in Criminology: XVI—Émile Durkheim (1858-1917). *Journal of Criminal Law, Criminology, and Police Science, 49*(1), 2-9.

Mankoff, Milton. (1971). Societal Reaction and Career Deviance: A Critical Analysis. *Sociological Quarterly, 12,* 204-218.

Mann, Coramae Richey. (1984). *Female Crime and Delinquency.* Tuscaloosa: University of Alabama Press.

Mann, Coramae Richey. (1987). Racism in the Criminal Justice System: Two Sides of a Controversy—The Reality of a Racist Criminal Justice System. *Criminal Justice Research Bulletin, 3,* 1-5.

Mann, Coramae Richey. (1988). Getting Even? Women Who Kill in Domestic Encounters. *Justice Quarterly, 5,* 33-51.

Mann, Coramae Richey. (1989). Minority and Female: A Criminal Justice Double Bind. *Social Justice, 16,* 95-114.

Mann, Coramae Richey. (1990a). Black Female Homicide in the United States. *Journal of Interpersonal Violence, 5,* 176-201.

Mann, Coramae Richey. (1990b). Female Homicide and Substance Use: Is There a Connection? *Women and Criminal Justice, 1,* 87-109.

Mann, Coramae Richey. (1993a). Maternal Filicide of Preschoolers. In Anna Victoria Wilson (Ed.), *Homicide: The Victim/Offender Connection* (pp. 227-246). Cincinnati, OH: Anderson.

Mann, Coramae Richey. (1993b). Sister Against Sister: Female Intrasexual Homicide. In Concetta C. Culliver (Ed.), *Female Criminality: The State of the Art* (pp. 195-223). New York: Garland.

Mann, Coramae Richey. (1993c). *Unequal Justice: A Question of Color.* Bloomington: Indiana University Press.

Mann, Coramae Richey. (1995). Women of Color and the Criminal Justice System. In Barbara Raffel Price and Natalie J. Sokoloff (Eds.), *The Criminal Justice System and Women: Offenders, Victims, and Workers* (pp. 118-135). New York: McGraw-Hill.

Mann, Coramae Richey. (1996). *When Women Kill.* Albany: State University of New York Press.

Mann, Coramae Richey and Marjorie S. Zatz. (1998a). Before and Beyond the Millennium: Possible Solutions. In Coramae Richey Mann and Marjorie S. Zatz (Eds.), *Images of Color, Images of Crime* (pp. 258-270). Los Angeles: Roxbury Publishing.

Mann, Coramae Richey and Marjorie S. Zatz (Eds.). (1998b). *Images of Color, Images of Crime.* Los Angeles: Roxbury Publishing.

Manning, Philip. (1992). *Erving Goffman and Modern Sociology.* Stanford, CA: Stanford University Press.

Martin, Randy, Robert J. Mutchnick, and W. Timothy Austin. (1990). *Criminological Thought: Pioneers Past and Present.* New York: Macmillan.

Martindale, Don. (1960). *The Nature of Sociological Theory.* Boston: Houghton Mifflin.

Marx, Karl. (1959). *Capital: The Communist Manifesto and Other Writings* (Max Eastman, Ed., with an introduction by Max Eastman). New York: Modern Library.

Marx, Karl. (1964). *Theories of Surplus Value.* London: Lawrence and Wishart.

Marx, Karl and Frederick Engels. (1965). *The Germon Ideology.* London: Lawrence and Wishart.

Matza, David. (1964). *Delinquency and Drift.* New York: John Wiley.

Matza, David. (1969). *Becoming Deviant.* Englewood Cliffs, NJ: Prentice Hall.

McDermott, M. Joan. (1994). Criminology as Peacemaking: Feminist Ethics and the Victimization of Women. *Women & Criminal Justice, 5,* 21-44.

Mead, George H. (1934). *Mind, Self, and Society.* Chicago: University of Chicago Press.

Mead, George H. (1955). *Mind, Self, and Society.* Chicago: University of Chicago Press.

Mehring, Franz. (1951). *Karl Marx: The Story of His Life.* London: Allen and Unwin.

Merton, Robert K. (1938). Social Structure and Anomie. *American Journal of Sociology, 3,* 672-682.

Merton, Robert K. (1968a). On Sociological Theories of the Middle Range. In Robert K. Merton (Ed.), *Social Theory and Social Structure* (pp. 39-72). New York: Free Press.

Merton, Robert K. (1968b). *Social Theory and Social Structure.* New York: Free Press.

Merton, Robert K. (1997). On the Evolving Synthesis of Differential Association and Anomie Theory: A Perspective From the Sociology of Science. *Criminology, 35,* 517-525.

Messerschmidt, James W. (1986). *Capitalism, Patriarchy, and Crime.* Totowa, NJ: Rowman & Littlefield.

Messerschmidt, James W. (1993). *Masculinities and Crime: Critique and Reconceptualization of Theory.* Lanham, MD: Rowman & Littlefield.

Messner, Steven F. and Richard Rosenfeld. (1997). *Crime and the American Dream*. Belmont, CA: Wadsworth.

Metzger, Linda. (Ed.). (1984). *Contemporary Authors* (Vol. 13). Detroit, MI: Gale Research.

Miller, Susan L. and Cynthia Burack. (1993). A Critique of Gottfredson and Hirschi's General Theory of Crime: Selective (In)Attention to Gender and Power Positions. *Women and Criminal Justice*, 4(2), 115-134.

Miller, Susan L. and Sally S. Simpson. (1991). Courtship Violence and Social Control: Does Gender Matter? *Law and Society Review*, 25, 335-365.

Mills, C. Wright. (1959). *The Sociological Imagination*. New York: Oxford University Press.

Milovanovic, Dragan. (1991). Images of Unity and Disunity in the Juridic Subject and Movement Toward the Peacemaking Community. In Harold E. Pepinsky and Richard Quinney (Eds.), *Criminology as Peacemaking* (pp. 209-227). Bloomington: Indiana University Press.

Milovanovic, Dragan. (1996). Postmodern Criminology: Mapping the Terrain. *Justice Quarterly*, 13, 567-610.

Minor, W. W. (1980). The Neutralization of Criminal Offense. *Criminology*, 18, 103-120.

Minor, W. W. (1981). Techniques of Neutralization: A Reconceptualization and Empirical Examination. *Journal of Research in Crime and Delinquency*, 18, 295-318.

Monachesi, Elio. (1972). Cesare Beccaria (1738-1794). In Hermann Mannheim (Ed.), *Pioneers in Criminology* (pp. 37-50). Montclair, NJ: Patterson Smith.

Morselli, Henry. (1897). *Suicide: An Essay on Comparative Moral Statistics*. New York.

Moulds, Elizabeth. (1978). Chivalry and Paternalism: Disparities of Treatment in the Criminal Justice System. *Western Political Quarterly*, 31, 416-430.

Mouzelis, Nicos. (1971). On Total Institutions. *Sociology*, 5, 113-120.

Moyer, Imogene L. (1980). Leadership in a Women's Prison. *Journal of Criminal Justice*, 8, 233-241.

Moyer, Imogene L. (1985a). Academic Criminology: A Need for Change. *American Journal of Criminal Justice*, 9, 195-210.

Moyer, Imogene L. (Ed.). (1985b). *The Changing Roles of Women in the Criminal Justice System: Offenders, Victims, and Professionals*. Prospect Heights, IL: Waveland.

Moyer, Imogene L. (1986). Gatekeepers for Academic Criminology: An Exploratory Study of the Status of Women. In *Proceedings of the Twelfth International Improving University Teaching Conference* (pp. 553-562). Heidelberg, Germany: University of Heidelberg.

Moyer, Imogene L. (1990). The Life and Works of Ruth Shonle Cavan: Pioneer Woman in Criminology. *Journal of Crime and Justice*, 13, 133-158.

Moyer, Imogene L. (1991). Ruth Shonle Cavan (1896-). In Mary Jo Deegan (Ed.), *Women in Sociology: A Bio-Bibliographical Sourcebook* (pp. 90-99). Westport, CT: Greenwood.

Moyer, Imogene L. (Ed.). (1992). *The Changing Roles of Women in the Criminal Justice System: Offenders, Victims, and Professionals* (2nd ed.). Prospect Heights, IL: Waveland.

Moyer, Imogene L. (1993). [Review of *Criminology as Peacemaking*, by Harold Pepinsky and Richard Quinney]. *Justice Quarterly*, 10, 165-168.

Moyer, Imogene L. (1996). Cavan's Continuum of Behavior: A Proposed Conceptual Model for the Expansion of Narrowly Focused Criminological Theory. *Journal of Crime and Justice*, 19, 181-194.

Naffine, Ngaire. (1987). *Female Crime: The Construction of Women in Criminology*. London: Allen and Unwin.

Naffine, Ngaire. (1996). *Feminism and Criminology*. Philadelphia: Temple University Press.

Nanda, B. R. (1981). *Mahatma Gandhi: A Biography*. Oxford, UK: Oxford University Press. Available: web.mahatma.org.in/books

National Victims Center and Crime Victims Research and Treatment Center. (1992). *Rape in America: A Report to the Nation*. Arlington, VA: National Victims Center.

O'Connell, Lucille. (1980). Frances Kellor. In Barbara Sicherman and Carol Hurd Green (Eds.), *Notable American Women: The Modern Period* (pp. 393-397). Cambridge, MA: Harvard University Press.

Park, Robert E. and Ernest W. Burgess. (1921). *Introduction to the Science of Sociology*. Chicago: University of Chicago Press.

Park, Robert E., Ernest W. Burgess, and Roderick D. McKenzie. (Eds.). (1967). *The City*. Chicago: University of Chicago Press.

Paternoster, Raymond. (1987). The Deterrent Effect of the Perceived Certainty and Severity of Punishment: A Review of the Evidence and Issues. *Justice Quarterly, 4,* 173-217.

Pepinsky, Hal. (1993). What Is Crime? What Is Peace? A Commentary. *Journal of Criminal Justice Education, 4,* 391-394.

Pepinsky, Hal. (1998). Empathy Works, Obedience Doesn't. *Criminal Justice Policy Review, 9,* 141-167.

Pepinsky, Harold E. (1980). *Crime Control Strategies: An Introduction to the Study of Crime*. Oxford, UK: Oxford University Press.

Pepinsky, Harold E. (1988). Violence as Unresponsiveness: Toward a New Conception of Crime. *Justice Quarterly, 5,* 539-563.

Pepinsky, Harold E. (1991a). *The Geometry of Violence and Democracy*. Bloomington: Indiana University Press.

Pepinsky, Harold E. (1991b). Peacemaking in Criminology and Criminal Justice. In Harold E. Pepinsky and Richard Quinney (Eds.), *Criminology as Peacemaking* (pp. 299-327). Bloomington: Indiana University Press.

Pepinsky, Harold E. and Paul Jesilow. (1984). *Myths That Cause Crime*. Cabin John, MD: Seven Locks Press.

Pepinsky, Harold E. and Richard Quinney. (Eds.). (1991). *Criminology as Peacemaking*. Bloomington: Indiana University Press.

Perry, Nick. (1974). The Two Cultures and the Total Institution. *British Journal of Sociology, 25,* 245-255.

Persons, Stowe. (1987). *Ethnic Studies in Chicago (1905-1945)*. Urbana: University of Illinois Press.

Piaget, Jean. (1969). *The Moral Judgment of the Child*. New York: Free Press.

Piaget, Jean and B. Inhelder. (1969). *The Psychology of the Child*. New York: Basic Books.

Platt, Anthony P. (1991). *E. Franklin Frazier Reconsidered*. New Brunswick, NJ: Rutgers University Press.

Plessy v. Ferguson. (1896). 163 U.S. 537.

Pollak, Otto. (1950). *The Criminality of Women*. Philadelphia: University of Pennsylvania Press.

Pollock, Joy. (1978). Early Theories of Female Criminality. In Lee H. Bowker (Ed.), *Women, Crime, and the Criminal Justice System* (pp. 25-55). Lexington, MA: Lexington Books.

Quinney, Richard. (1963). Occupational Structure and Criminal Behavior: Prescription Violation by Retail Pharmacists. *Social Problems, 11,* 179-185.

Quinney, Richard. (1964a). Adjustments to Occupational Role Strains: The Case of Retail Pharmacy. *Southwestern Social Science Quarterly, 44,* 367-376.

Quinney, Richard. (1964b). The Study of White Collar Crime: Toward a Reorientation in Theory and Research. *Journal of Criminal Law, Criminology, and Police Science, 55,* 208-214.

Quinney, Richard. (1970a). *The Problem of Crime.* New York: Dodd, Mead.

Quinney, Richard. (1970b). *The Social Reality of Crime.* Boston: Little, Brown.

Quinney, Richard. (1973). There's a Lot of Folks Grateful to the Lone Ranger: With Some Notes on the Rise and Fall of American Criminology. *The Insurgent Sociologist, 4,* 56-64.

Quinney, Richard. (1974). *Critique of the Legal Order: Crime Control in Capitalist Society.* Boston: Little, Brown.

Quinney, Richard. (1977). *Class, State, and Crime: On the Theory and Practice of Criminal Justice.* New York: Longman.

Quinney, Richard. (1980a). *Class, State, and Crime: On the Theory and Practice of Criminal Justice* (2nd ed.). New York: Longman.

Quinney, Richard. (1980b). *Providence: The Reconstruction of Social and Moral Order.* New York: Longman.

Quinney, Richard. (1985). Myth and Art of Criminology. *Legal Studies Forum, 9,* 291-299.

Quinney, Richard. (1991). The Way of Peace: On Crime, Suffering, Service. In Harold E. Pepinsky and Richard Quinney (Eds.), *Criminology as Peacemaking* (pp. 3-13). Bloomington: Indiana University Press.

Quinney, Richard. (1993). A Life of Crime: Criminology and Public Policy as Peacemaking. *Journal of Crime and Justice, 16,* 3-9.

Quinney, Richard. (1998). *For the Time Being: Ethnography of Everyday Life.* Albany: State University of New York Press.

Quinney, Richard and John Wildeman. (1991). *The Problem of Crime: A Peace and Social Justice Perspective.* Mountain View, CA: Mayfield.

Rafter, Nicole and Elena Natalizia. (1981). Marxist Feminism: Implications for Criminal Justice. *Crime and Delinquency, 27,* 81-98.

Rasche, Christine E. (1974). The Female Offender as an Object of Criminological Research. *Criminal Justice Behavior, 1,* 301-321.

Reckless, Walter C. (1933). *Vice in Chicago.* Montclair, NJ: Patterson Smith.

Reckless, Walter C. (1961). *The Crime Problem* (3rd ed.). New York: Appleton-Century-Crofts.

Reckless, Walter C. and S. Dinitz. (1967). Pioneering With Self-Concept as a Vulnerability Factor in Delinquency. *Journal of Criminal Law, Criminology, and Police Science, 58,* 515-523.

Reckless, Walter C., S. Dinitz, and B. Kay. (1957). The Self Component in Potential Delinquency and Non-Delinquency. *American Sociological Review, 22,* 566-570.

Reckless, Walter C., S. Dinitz, and E. Murray. (1956). Self Concept as Insulator Against Delinquency. *American Sociological Review, 21,* 744-764.

Reiman, Jeffrey. (1990). *The Rich Get Richer and the Poor Get Prison* (3rd ed.). New York: Macmillan.

Reiman, Jeffrey. (1993). A Radical Perspective of Crime. In H. Kelly Delos (Ed.), *Deviant Behavior: A Text-Reader in the Sociology of Deviance* (pp. 141-150). New York: St. Martin's.

Reiman, Jeffrey. (1995). *The Rich Get Richer and the Poor Get Prison* (4th ed.). Boston: Allyn & Bacon.

Reiman, Jeffrey H. and Sue Headlee. (1981). Marxism and Criminal Justice Policy. *Crime and Delinquency, 27,* 24-47.

Residents of Hull House. (Eds.). (1895). *Hull House Maps and Papers.* New York: Crowell.

Rice, Marcia. (1990). Challenging Orthodoxies in Feminist Theory: A Black Feminist Critique. In Loraine Gelsthorpe and Allison Morris (Eds.), *Feminist Perspectives in Criminology* (pp. 57-69). Philadelphia: Open University Press.

Rogers, Joseph W. and G. Larry Mays. (1987). *Juvenile Delinquency and Juvenile Justice.* New York: John Wiley.

Rosen, F. and J. H. Burns. (Eds.). (1983). *The Collected Works of Jeremy Bentham,* Vol. 1: *Constitutional Code.* Oxford, UK: Clarendon.

Ross, Edward A. (1901). *Social Control.* New York: Macmillan.

Ross, Edward A. (1939). *Social Control.* New York: Macmillan.

Rossi, Alice S. (Ed.). (1988). *The Feminist Papers: From Adams to de Beauvoir.* Boston: Northeastern University Press.

Rucker, Lila. (1991). Peacemaking in Prisons: A Process. In Harold E. Pepinsky and Richard Quinney (Eds.), *Criminology as Peacemaking* (pp. 172-180). Bloomington: Indiana University Press.

Sanzen, Peter L. (1991). The Role of Education in Peacemaking. In Harold E. Pepinsky and Richard Quinney (Eds.), *Criminology as Peacemaking* (pp. 239-244). Bloomington: Indiana University Press.

Scarpitti, Frank R., E. Murray, S. Dinitz, and W. C. Reckless. (1960). The Good Boys in a High Delinquency Area: Four Years Later. *American Sociological Review, 25,* 922-926.

Schrag, C. (1971). *Crime and Justice American Style.* Washington, DC: Government Printing Office.

Schreck, Christopher. (1999). Criminal Victimization and Low Self-Control: An Extension and Test of a General Theory of Crime. *Justice Quarterly, 16,* 633-651.

Schuessler, Karl. (Ed.). (1973). *Edward H. Sutherland: On Analyzing Crime.* Chicago: University of Chicago Press.

Schur, Edwin M. (1965). *Crimes Without Victims.* Englewood Cliffs, NJ: Prentice Hall.

Schur, Edwin M. (1968). *Law and Society.* New York: Random House.

Schur, Edwin M. (1969). *Our Criminal Society: The Social and Legal Sources of Crime in America.* Englewood Cliffs, NJ: Prentice Hall.

Schur, Edwin M. (1971). *Labeling Deviant Behavior.* New York: Harper & Row.

Schur, Edwin M. (1973). *Radical Nonintervention: Rethinking the Delinquency Problem.* Englewood Cliffs, NJ: Prentice Hall.

Schur, Edwin M. (1979). *Interpreting Deviance.* New York: Harper & Row.

Schur, Edwin M. (1980). *The Politics of Deviance.* Englewood Cliffs, NJ: Prentice Hall.

Schur, Edwin M. (1984). *Labeling Women Deviant: Gender, Stigma, and Social Control.* New York: Random House.

Schwartz, Martin D. and David O. Friedrichs. (1994). Postmodern Thought and Criminological Discontent: New Metaphors for Understanding Violence. *Criminology, 32,* 221-246.

Scimecca, Joseph A. (1991). Conflict Resolution and a Critique of "Alternative Dispute Resolution." In Harold E. Pepinsky and Richard Quinney (Eds.), *Criminology as Peacemaking* (pp. 263-279). Bloomington: Indiana University Press.

Sealock, Miriam D., and Sally S. Simpson. (1998). Unraveling Bias in Arrest Decisions: The Role of Juvenile Offender Type-Scripts. *Justice Quarterly, 15,* 427-457.

Seddon, Ayn Rand. (1995, March). *Frederick Milton Thrasher.* Paper presented at the meeting of the Academy of Criminal Justice Sciences, Boston.

Sedgwick, Peter. (1982). *Psycho Politics.* London: Pluto.

Seeman, Melvin. (1959). On the Meaning of Alienation. *American Sociological Review, 24,* 783-791.

Shaw, Clifford R. (1931). *The Natural History of a Delinquent Career.* Chicago: University of Chicago Press.

Shaw, Clifford R. (1966). *The Jackroller: A Delinquent Boy's Own Story.* Chicago: University of Chicago Press.

Shaw, Clifford R. and Henry D. McKay. (1929). *Delinquency Areas.* Chicago: University of Chicago Press.

Shaw, Clifford R. and Henry D. McKay. (1931). *Social Factors in Juvenile Delinquency.* Washington, DC: National Commission on Law Observance and Enforcement.

Shaw, Clifford R. and Henry D. McKay. (1972). *Juvenile Delinquency and Urban Areas.* Chicago: University of Chicago Press.

Shaw, Clifford R., Henry D. McKay, James F. McDonald, and Harold B. Hanson. (1938). *Brothers in Crime.* Chicago: University of Chicago Press.

Sheldon, William H. (1949). *Varieties of Delinquent Youth: An Introduction to Constitutional Psychiatry.* New York: Harper & Row.

Sheley, Joseph F. (1991). *Criminology: A Contemporary Handbook.* Belmont CA: Wadsworth.

Shoemaker, Donald J. (1996). *Theories of Delinquency: An Examination of Explanations of Delinquent Behavior* (3rd ed.). New York: Oxford University Press.

Simon, Rita James. (1975). *The Contemporary Woman and Crime.* Rockville, MD: National Institute of Mental Health.

Simpson, Sally S. (1989). Feminist Theory, Crime, and Justice. *Criminology, 27,* 605-631.

Simpson, Sally S. (1991). Caste, Class, and Violent Crime: Explaining Difference in Female Offending. *Criminology, 29,* 115-135.

Simpson, Sally S. and Lori Elis. (1995). Doing Gender: Sorting Out the Caste and Crime Conundrum. *Criminology, 33,* 47-81.

Simpson, Sally S. and Lori Elis. (1996). Theoretical Perspectives on Corporate Victimization of Women. In Elizabeth Szockyi and James Fox (Eds.), *Corporate Victimization of Women* (pp. 32-58). Boston: Northeastern University Press.

Simpson, Sally and Mervin F. White. (1985). The Female Guard in the All-Male Prison. In Imogene L. Moyer (Ed.), *The Changing Roles of Women in the Criminal Justice System: Offenders, Victims, and Professionals* (pp. 276-300). Prospect Heights, IL: Waveland.

Smart, Carol. (1995). *Law, Crime, and Sexuality: Essays in Feminism.* Thousand Oaks, CA: Sage.

Smith, Adam. (1937). *An Inquiry Into the Nature and Cause of the Wealth of Nations* (Edwin Cannon, Ed.). New York: Modern Library.

Snodgrass, Jon. (1976). Clifford R. Shaw and Henry D. McKay: Chicago Criminologists. *British Journal of Criminology, 16,* 1-17.

Spender, Dale. (1983). *Women of Ideas (and what men have done to them).* New York: Routledge and Kegan Paul.

Srole, Leo. (1956). Social Integration and Certain Corollaries: An Exploratory Study. *American Sociological Review, 21,* 709-716.

Stanko, Elizabeth A. (1985). *Intimate Intrusions: Women's Experience of Male Violence.* London: Routledge and Kegan Paul.

Stanko, Elizabeth. (1987). Typical Violence, Normal Precaution: Men, Women, and Interpersonal Violence in England, Wales, Scotland, and U.S.A. In Jalna Hanmer and Mary

Maynard (Eds.), *Women, Violence, and Social Control* (pp. 122-134). Atlantic Highlands, NJ: Humanities Press International.

Stanko, Elizabeth. (1990). *Everyday Violence: How Women and Men Experience Sexual and Physical Danger.* London: Pandora Press.

Stanko, Elizabeth A. (1992). The Case of Fearful Women: Gender, Personal Safety, and Fear of Crime. *Women and Criminal Justice, 4,* 117-135.

Stark, R. (1987). *Sociology.* Belmont, CA: Wadsworth.

Stark, W. (Ed.). (1952). *Jeremy Bentham's Economic Writings.* London: Allen and Unwin.

Steffensmeier, Darrell J. (1978). Crime and the Contemporary Woman: An Analysis of Changing Levels of Female Property Crime, 1960-75. *Social Forces, 57,* 566-584.

Sutherland, Edwin. (1924). *Criminology.* Philadelphia: J. B. Lippincott.

Sutherland, Edwin. (1934). *Principles of Criminology.* Philadelphia: J. B. Lippincott.

Sutherland, Edwin. (1937). *The Professional Thief.* Chicago: University of Chicago Press.

Sutherland, Edwin H. (1940). White Collar Criminality. *American Sociological Review, 5,* 1-12.

Sutherland, Edwin H. (1945). Is "White Collar Crime" Crime? *American Sociological Review, 10,* 132-139.

Sutherland, Edwin. (1947). *Principles of Criminology* (4th ed.). Philadelphia: J. B. Lippincott.

Sutherland, Edwin H. (1949). *White Collar Crime.* New York: Dryden.

Sutherland, Edwin H. (1973). *On Analyzing Crime* (K. Schuessler, Ed.). Chicago: University of Chicago Press.

Sutherland, Edwin H. and Harvey J. Locke. (1936). *Twenty Thousand Homeless Men.* Philadelphia: J. B. Lippincott.

Sykes, Gresham M. (1958). *The Society of Captives: A Study of a Maximum Security Prison.* Princeton, NJ: Princeton University Press.

Sykes, Gresham. (1978). *Criminology.* New York: Harcourt Brace Jovanovich.

Sykes, Gresham and David Matza. (1957). Techniques of Neutralization: A Theory of Delinquency. *American Sociological Review, 22,* 664-673.

Tannenbaum, Frank. (1922). *Wall Shadows: A Study in American Prisons.* New York: Putnam.

Tannenbaum, Frank. (1938). *Crime and the Community.* New York: Columbia University Press.

Tannenbaum, Frank. (1964). *Ten Keys to Latin America.* New York: Knopf.

Tannenbaum, Frank. (1975). *Wall Shadows: A Study in American Prisons.* New York: AMS Press.

Tappan, Paul W. (1947). Who Is the Criminal? *American Sociological Review, 12,* 96-102.

Tarnowsky, Pauline. (1908). *Les Femmes Homicides.* Paris: Felix Alcan.

Taylor, Ian, Paul Walton, and Jock Young. (1973). *The New Criminology: For a Social Theory of Deviance.* New York: Harper & Row.

Thomas, William I. (1923). *The Unadjusted Girl: With Cases and Standpoint for Behavior Analysis.* Boston: Little, Brown.

Thomas, William I. and Florian Znaniecki. (1918). *The Polish Peasant in Europe and America* (5 vols.). Boston: Richard G. Badger.

Thrasher, Frederick M. (1927). *The Gang.* Chicago: University of Chicago Press.

Thrasher, Frederick M. (1936). The Boys' Club and Juvenile Delinquency. *American Journal of Sociology, 12,* 66-80.

Tifft, Larry L. and Lyn Markham. (1991). Battering Women and Battering Central Americans: A Peacemaking Synthesis. In Harold E. Pepinsky and Richard Quinney (Eds.), *Criminology as Peacemaking* (pp. 114-153). Bloomington: Indiana University Press.

Toby, Jackson. (1979). The New Criminology Is the Old Sentimentality. *Criminology, 16,* 516-526.

Tonnies, Ferdinand. (1957). *Gemeinschaft and Gesellschaft* (C. P. Loomis, Trans.). East Lansing: Michigan State University Press.

Turner, Jonathan H. (1978). *The Structure of Sociological Theory.* Homewood, IL: Dorsey.

Turner, Jonathan H. (1991). *The Structure of Sociological Theory* (5th ed.). Belmont, CA: Wadsworth.

Vold, George B. (1979). *Theoretical Criminology.* New York: Oxford University Press.

Vold, George B., Thomas J. Bernard, and Jeffrey B. Snipes. (1998). *Theoretical Criminology.* New York: Oxford University Press.

Walby, Sylvia. (1990). *Theorizing Patriarchy.* Cambridge, MA: Basil Blackwell.

Wallace, Walter L. (1969). *Sociological Theory.* Chicago: Aldine.

Ward, David A. and Gene G. Kassebaum. (1965). *Women's Prisons: Sex and Social Structure.* Chicago: Aldine.

Warren, Karen J. and Duane L. Cady. (Eds.). (1996). *Bringing Peace Home: Feminism, Violence, and Nature.* Bloomington: Indiana University Press.

Weber, Max. (1958). *The Protestant Ethic and the Spirit of Capitalism* (Talcott Parsons, Trans.). New York: Scribner.

Wellford, Charles. (1975). Labeling Theory and Criminology: An Assessment. *Social Problems, 22,* 335-347.

Wilbanks, William. (1987). *The Myth of a Racist Criminal Justice System.* Pacific Grove, CA: Brooks/Cole.

Wilbanks, William. (1993). Color Blind [review of *Unequal Justice: A Question of Color,* by Coramae Richey Mann]. *National Review, 45,* 52-54.

Williams, Frank P., III. (1984). The Demise of the Criminological Imagination: A Critique of Recent Criminology. *Justice Quarterly, 1,* 91-106.

Williams, Frank P., III and Marilyn D. McShane. (1988). *Criminological Theory.* Englewood Cliffs, NJ: Prentice Hall.

Williams, Frank P., III and Marilyn D. McShane. (1994). *Criminological Theory* (2nd ed.). Englewood Cliffs, NJ: Prentice Hall.

Williams, Frank P., III and Marilyn D. McShane. (1999). *Criminological Theory* (3rd ed.). Upper Saddle River, NJ: Prentice Hall.

Williams, John A. (1970). *The King God Didn't Save.* New York: Coward-McCann.

Wilson, James Q. and Richard J. Herrnstein. (1985). *Crime and Human Nature.* New York: Simon & Schuster.

Wilson, Nanci Koser. (1985, November). *Witches, Hookers, and Others: Societal Response to Women Criminals and Victims.* Paper presented at the meeting of the American Society of Criminology, San Diego.

Wilson, Nanci Koser. (1991). Feminist Pedagogy in Criminology. *Journal of Criminal Justice Education, 2,* 81-93.

Wilson, Nanci Koser. (1993). Taming Women and Nature: The Criminal Justice System and the Creation of Crime in Salem Village. In Roslyn Muraskin and Ted Alleman (Eds.), *It's a Crime: Women and Justice* (pp. 52-73). Englewood Cliffs, NJ: Regents/Prentice Hall.

Wilson, Nanci Koser and Imogene L. Moyer. (1992). Affirmative Action, Multiculturalism, and Politically Correct Criminology. *Journal of Criminal Justice Education, 3,* 277-291.

Wilson, Nanci Koser and Constance M. Rigsby. (1975). Is Crime a Man's World? Issues in the Exploration of Criminality. *Journal of Criminal Justice, 3,* 131-140.

Wolfgang, Marvin E. (1958). *Patterns in Criminal Homicide.* Philadelphia: University of Pennsylvania Press.

Wolfgang, Marvin E. (1972). Cesare Lombroso (1835-1909). In Hermann Mannheim (Ed.), *Pioneers in Criminology* (pp. 232-291). Montclair, NJ: Patterson Smith.

Wolfgang, Marvin, Robert Figlio, and Thorston Sellin. (1972). *Delinquency in a Birth Cohort.* Chicago: University of Chicago Press.

Wonders, Nancy A. (1996). Determinate Sentencing: A Feminist and Postmodern Story. *Justice Quarterly, 13,* 611-648.

Wright, Richard A. (1987). Are "Sisters in Crime" Finally Being Booked? The Coverage of Women and Crime in Journals and Textbooks. *Teaching Sociology, 15,* 418-422.

Young, Jock. (1981). Thinking Seriously About Crime: Some Models of Criminology. In Mike Fitzgerald, Gregor McLennan, and Jennie Pawson (Eds.), *Crime and Society: Readings in History and Society.* London: Routledge and Kegan Paul.

Young, Vernetta D. (1980). Women, Race, and Crime. *Criminology, 18,* 26-34.

Young, Vernetta D. (1986). Gender Expectations and Their Impact on Black Female Offenders and Victims. *Justice Quarterly, 3,* 305-327.

Young, Vernetta D. (1989). *Criminal Justice in the Twenty-First Century: The Removal of the Mantle of Silence Surrounding Race.* Paper presented at the Twentieth Anniversary Conference, School of Criminal Justice, Albany, NY.

Young, Vernetta D. and Helen Taylor Greene. (1995). Pedagogical Reconstruction: Incorporating African American Perspectives Into the Curriculum. *Journal of Criminal Justice Education, 6,* 85-104.

Zatz, Marjorie S. and Coramae Richey Mann. (1998). The Power of Images. In Coramae Richey Mann and Marjorie S. Zatz (Eds.), *Images of Color, Images of Crime* (pp. 1-12). Los Angeles: Roxbury Publishing.

Zemans, Eugene and Ruth Shonle Cavan. (1958). Marital Relationships of Prisoners. *Journal of Criminal Law, Criminology, and Police Science, 49,* 50-57.

Zingraff, R. (1993). [Review of *Unequal Justice: A Question of Color,* by Coramae Richey Mann]. *Choice, 51,* 227.

Index

About the Authors

Imogene L. Moyer is Professor Emerita of Criminology and Women's Studies at Indiana University of Pennsylvania (IUP), where she retired in 1998. Before joining the faculty at IUP in 1984, she taught at universities in Kansas, Virginia, and Illinois and also taught on American military bases in Germany (University of Maryland) and in Spain (Troy State University). She also was a visiting professor of sociology at the University of Hawaii at Manoa during the spring of 1991. She received her M.A. in sociology from Kansas State University in 1968 and received her Ph.D. in sociology (with a specialization in crime and deviance) from the University of Missouri–Columbia in 1975. For more than 20 years, she has been an active participant in professional associations; in serving on and/or chairing committees; and in presenting papers at the state, national, and international levels. Her publications include articles in professional journals and book chapters on women's prisons, sex and race in police processing of offenders, child sexual abuse, status of women and minorities in academia, Ruth Shonle Cavan, and feminist criminology. Her edited book, *The Changing Roles of Women in the Criminal Justice System* (1992), is in its second edition. She has had a sustained interest in criminological theory since graduate school and has taught theory classes at the undergraduate and graduate levels. In addition to theory, her current research and writing interests include feminist criminology and peacemaking.

Contributing Authors:

Cavit S. Cooley is Assistant Professor of Justice Systems at Truman State University in Kirksville, Missouri. He currently is a candidate for a Ph.D. in criminology at Indiana University of Pennsylvania. He holds a B.S. and an M.A. in law enforcement administration from Western Illinois University and an A.S. in law enforcement from Lake Land College. In addition to his interest in criminological theory, he currently is examining the history of recidivist targeted sentencing in law in the United States.

Ayn Embar-Seddon chairs the Department of Criminal Justice and Paralegal Studies at Florida Metropolitan University in Orlando. She was born and raised in Pittsburgh, Pennsylvania. She received her bachelor degrees in philosophy and psychology from the University of Pittsburgh, her master's degree in clinical psychology from Edinboro University of Pennsylvania, and her Ph.D. in criminology from Indiana University of Pennsylvania. She teaches courses in philosophy, psychology, and criminology. Her research interests include workplace violence, vice, and sexual offending.

Shaun L. Gabbidon is Assistant Professor of Criminal Justice in the School of Public Affairs at Pennsylvania State University, Capital College. He is a graduate of the Ph.D. program in criminology at Indiana University of Pennsylvania and is the author of numerous journal articles, book chapters, and scholarly essays. He is the coauthor (with Helen Taylor Green) of *African American Criminological Thought* (2000).